FUNDAMENTALS OF
English
Grammar

FOURTH EDITION
TEACHER'S GUIDE

PEARSON
Longman

Martha Hall
Betty S. Azar

**Fundamentals of English Grammar, Fourth Edition
Teacher's Guide**

Pearson Education, 10 Bank Street, White Plains, NY 10606

Staff credits: The people who made up the *Fundamentals of
English Grammar, Fourth Edition, Teacher's Guide* team,
representing editorial, production, design, and manufacturing,
are Diane Cipollone, Dave Dickey, Christine Edmonds,
Ann France, Amy McCormick, and Ruth Voetmann.

Text composition: S4Carlisle Publishing Services
Text font: Helvetica

ISBN 10: 0-13-138334-5
ISBN 13: 978-0-13-138334-0

Printed in the United States of America
1 2 3 4 5 6 7 8 9 10—V001—17 16 15 14 13 12 11

Contents

Preface

This *Teachers' Guide* is intended as a practical aid to teachers. You can turn to it for notes on the content of a unit and how to approach the exercises, for suggestions for classroom activities, and for answers to the exercises in the text.

General teaching information can be found in the introduction. It includes:

- the rationale and general aims of *Fundamentals of English Grammar*
- classroom techniques for presenting charts and using exercises
- suggestions on using the *Workbook* in connection with the student book
- supplementary resource texts
- comments on differences between American and British English
- a key to the pronunciation symbols used in this *Guide*

The rest of the *Guide* contains detailed notes and instructions for teaching every chapter. Each chapter contains three main parts: the chapter summary, the background notes on charts and exercises (found in the gray shaded boxes), and the bulleted step-by-step instructions for the charts and most of the exercises.

- The Chapter Summary explains the objective and approach of the chapter. It also explains any terminology critical to the chapter.
- The gray background notes boxes contain additional explanations of the grammar point, common problem areas, and points to emphasize. These notes are intended to help the instructor plan the lessons before class.
- The bulleted step-by-step instructions contain detailed plans for conducting the lesson in class.

The back of the *Guide* contains the answer key for the student book and an index.

Acknowledgments

The author is very thankful for the ongoing support of Joe and Megan, Mimi and Babu, Anna, Mary, Lisa, Emily, Ali and Seab. She is equally grateful to her colleagues at The New England School of English, and to Pearson editors Amy McCormick and Ruth Voetmann.

Introduction

General Aims of *Fundamentals of English Grammar*

Fundamentals of English Grammar is a high-intermediate to advanced level ESL/EFL developmental skills text. In the experience of many classroom teachers, language learners like to spend at least some time on grammar with a teacher to help them. The process of looking at and practicing grammar becomes a springboard for expanding the learners' abilities in speaking, writing, listening, and reading.

Most students find it helpful to have special time set aside in their English curriculum to focus on grammar. Students generally have many questions about English grammar and appreciate the opportunity to work with a text and teacher to make sense out of the sometimes confusing array of forms and usages in this strange language. These understandings provide the basis for advances in usage ability as students experiment, both in speaking and writing, with ways to communicate their ideas in a new language.

Teaching grammar does not mean lecturing on grammatical patterns and terminology. It does not mean bestowing knowledge and being an arbiter of correctness. Teaching grammar is the art of helping students make sense, little by little, of a huge, puzzling construct, and engaging them in various activities that enhance usage abilities in all skill areas and promote easy, confident communication.

The text depends upon a partnership with a teacher; it is the teacher who animates and directs the students' language learning experiences. In practical terms, the aim of the text is to support you, the teacher, by providing a wealth and variety of material for you to adapt to your individual teaching situation. Using grammar as a base to promote overall English usage ability, teacher and text can engage students in interesting discourse, challenge their minds and skills, and intrigue them with the power of language as well as the need for accuracy to create understanding among people.

Suggestions for the Classroom

THE GRAMMAR CHARTS

Warm-up exercises precede the charts. They have been designed to help you present the information in the charts. (Please see Exercise Types for further explanation of warm-ups.) Here are some additional suggestions for using the charts.

The Here-and-Now Classroom Context

For every chart, try to relate the target structure to an immediate classroom or "real-life" context. Make up or elicit examples that use the students' names, activities, and interests. For example, when introducing possessive adjectives, use yourself and your students to present all the sentences in the chart. Then have students refer to the chart. The here-and-now classroom context is, of course, one of the grammar teacher's best aids.

Demonstration Techniques

Demonstration can be very helpful to explain the meaning of structures. You and your students can act out situations that demonstrate the target structure. For example, the present progressive can easily be demonstrated (e.g., "I *am writing* on the board right now"). Of course, not all grammar lends itself to this technique.

Using the Board

In discussing the target structure of a chart, use the classroom board whenever possible. Not all students have adequate listening skills for "teacher talk," and not all students can visualize and understand the various relationships within, between, and among structures. Draw boxes, circles, and arrows to illustrate connections between the elements of a structure.

Explanations

The explanations on the right side of the chart are most effective when recast by the teacher, not read word for word. Keep the discussion focus on the examples. Students by and large learn from examples and lots of practice, not from explanations. In the charts, the explanations focus attention on what students should be noticing in the examples and the exercises.

The Role of Terminology

Students need to understand the terminology, but you shouldn't require or expect detailed definitions of terms, either in class discussion or on tests. Terminology is just a tool, a useful label for the moment, so that you and your students can talk to each other about English grammar.

BALANCING TEACHER AND STUDENT TALK

The goal of all language learning is to understand and communicate. The teacher's main task is to direct and facilitate that process. The learner is an active participant, not merely a passive receiver of rules to be memorized. Therefore, many of the exercises in the text are designed to promote interaction between learners as a bridge to real communication.

The teacher has a crucial leadership role, with "teacher talk" a valuable and necessary part of a grammar classroom. Sometimes you will need to spend time clarifying the information in a chart, leading an exercise, answering questions about exercise items, or explaining an assignment. These periods of "teacher talk" should, however, be balanced by longer periods of productive learning activity when the students are doing most of the talking. It is important for the teacher to know when to step back and let students lead. Interactive group and pairwork play an important role in the language classroom.

EXERCISE TYPES

Warm-up Exercises

Newly created for the 4th edition, the Warm-up exercises precede all of the grammar charts that introduce new material. They serve a dual purpose. First, they have been carefully crafted to help students discover the target grammar as they progress through each Warm-up exercise. Second, they are an informal diagnostic tool for you, the teacher, to assess how familiar the class is with the target structure. While the Warm-ups are intended to be completed quickly, you may wish to write students' responses on the board to provide visual reinforcement as you work through the exercise.

What Do I Already Know Exercises

The purpose of these exercises is to let students discover what they do and do not know about the target structure in order to engage them in a chart. Essentially, these exercises illustrate a possible teaching technique: assess students first as a springboard for presenting the grammar in a chart.

In truth, almost any exercise can be used in this manner. You do not need to follow the order of material in the text. Adapt the material to your own needs and techniques.

First Exercise after a Chart

In most cases, this exercise includes an example of each item shown in the chart. Students can do the exercise together as a class, and the teacher can refer to chart examples where necessary. More advanced classes can complete it as homework. The teacher can use this exercise as a guide to see how well students understand the basics of the target structure(s).

General Techniques for Fill-in (written) Exercises

The fill-in or written exercises in the text require some sort of completion, transformation, discussion of meaning, listening, or a combination of such activities. They range from those that are tightly controlled and manipulative to those that encourage free responses and require creative, independent language use. Following are some general techniques for the written exercises:

Technique A: A student can be asked to read an item aloud. You can say whether the student's answer is correct or not, or you can open up discussion by asking the rest of the class if the answer is correct. For example:

TEACHER: Juan, would you please read number 3?
STUDENT: Ali *speaks* Arabic.
TEACHER (to the class): Do the rest of you agree with Juan's answer?

The slow-moving pace of this method is beneficial for discussion not only of grammar items, but also of vocabulary and content. Students have time to digest information and ask questions. You have the opportunity to judge how well they understand the grammar.

However, this time-consuming technique doesn't always, or even usually, need to be used, especially with more advanced classes.

Technique B: You read the first part of the item and pause for students to call out the answer in unison. For example:

TEXT entry: "Ali *(speak)* _____ Arabic."
TEACHER (with the students looking at their texts): Ali . . . .
STUDENTS (in unison): speaks (with possibly a few incorrect responses scattered about)
TEACHER: speaks Arabic. *Speaks.* Do you have any questions?

This technique saves a lot of time in class, but is also slow-paced enough to allow for questions and discussion of grammar, vocabulary, and content. It is essential that students have prepared the exercise by writing in their books, so it must be assigned ahead of time as homework.

Technique C: Students complete the exercise for homework, and you go over the answers with them. Students can take turns giving the answers, or you can supply them. Depending on the importance and length of the sentence, you may want to include the entire sentence, or just the answer. Answers can be given one at a time while you take questions, or you can supply the answers to the whole exercise before opening it up for questions. When a student gives an answer, the other students can ask him/her questions if they disagree.

Technique D: Divide the class into groups (or pairs) and have each group prepare one set of answers that they all agree is correct prior to class discussion. The leader of each group can present its answers.

Another option is to have the groups (or pairs) hand in their set of answers for correction and possibly a grade.

It's also possible to turn these exercises into games wherein the group with the best set of answers gets some sort of reward (perhaps applause from the rest of the class).

One option for correction of group work is to circle or mark the errors on the one paper the group turns in, make photocopies of that paper for each member of the group, and then hand back the papers for students to correct individually. At that point, you can assign a grade if desired.

Of course, you can always mix Techniques A, B, C, and D — with students reading some aloud, with you prompting unison response for some, with you simply giving the answers for others, or with students collaborating on the answers for others. Much depends on the level of the class, their familiarity and skill with the grammar at hand, their oral-aural skills in general, and the flexibility or limitations of class time.

Technique E: When an exercise item has a dialogue between two speakers, A and B, ask one student to be A and another B, and have them read the entry aloud. Then, occasionally say to A and B: "Without looking at your text, what did you just say to each other?" (If necessary, let them glance briefly at their texts before they repeat what they've just said in the exercise item.) Students may be pleasantly surprised by their own fluency.

Technique F: Some exercises ask students to change the form but not the substance (e.g., to change the active to the passive, a clause to a phrase, and question to a noun clause, etc.), or to combine two sentences or ideas into one sentence that contains a particular structure (e.g., an adjective clause, a parallel structure, a gerund phrase, etc.). Generally, these exercises are intended for class discussion of the form and meaning of a structure. The initial stages of such exercises are a good opportunity to use the board to draw circles and / or arrows to illustrate the characteristics and relationships of a structure. Students can read their answers aloud to initiate class discussion, and you can write on the board as problems arise. Or students can write their sentences on the board themselves. Another option is to have them work in small groups to agree upon their answers prior to class discussion.

Open–ended Exercises

The term "open–ended" refers to those exercises in which students use their own words to complete or respond to sentences, either orally or in writing.

Technique A: Exercises where students must supply their own words to complete a sentence should usually be assigned for out-of-class preparation. Then, in class students can read their sentences aloud and the class can discuss the correctness and appropriateness of the completions. Perhaps you can suggest possible ways of rephrasing to make a sentence more idiomatic. Students who don't read their sentences aloud can revise their own completions based on what is being discussed in class. At the end of the exercise discussion, you can tell students to hand in their sentences for you to look at or simply ask if anybody has questions about the exercise and not have them submit anything to you.

Technique B: If you wish to use a completion exercise in class without having previously assigned it, you can turn the exercise into a brainstorming session in which students try out several completions to see if they work. As another possibility, you may wish to divide the class into small groups and have each group come up with completions that they all agree are correct and appropriate. Then use only those completions for class discussion or as written work to be handed in.

Technique C: Some completion exercises are done on another piece of paper because not enough space has been left in the textbook. It is often beneficial to use the following progression: (1) assign the exercise for out-of-class preparation; (2) discuss it in class the next day, having students make corrections on their own papers based on what they are learning from discussing other students' completions; (3) then ask students to submit their papers to you, either as a requirement or on a volunteer basis.

Paragraph Practice

Some writing exercises are designed to produce short, informal paragraphs. Generally, the topics concern aspects of the students' lives to encourage free and relatively effortless communication as they practice their writing skills. While a course in English rhetoric is beyond the scope of this text, many of the basic elements are included and may be developed and emphasized according to your students' needs.

For best results, whenever you give a writing assignment, let your students know what you expect: "This is what I suggest as content. This is how you might organize it. This is how long I expect it to be." If at all possible, give your students composition models, perhaps taken from good compositions written by previous classes, perhaps written by you, perhaps composed as a group activity by the class as a whole (e.g., you write on the board what students tell you to write, and then you and your students revise it together).

In general, writing exercises should be done outside of class. All of us need time to consider and revise when we write. And if we get a little help here and there, that's not unusual. The topics in the exercises are structured so that plagiarism should not be a problem. Use in-class writing if you want to evaluate your students' unaided, spontaneous writing skills. Tell them that these writing exercises are simply for practice and that — even though they should always try to do their best — mistakes that occur should be viewed simply as tools for learning.

Encourage students to use a basic dictionary whenever they write. Point out that you yourself never write seriously without a dictionary at hand. Discuss the use of margins, indentation of paragraphs, and other aspects of the format of a well-written paper.

Error-Analysis Exercises

For the most part, the sentences in this type of exercise have been adapted from actual student writing and contain typical errors. Error-analysis exercises focus on the target structures of a chapter but may also contain miscellaneous errors that are common in student writing at this level (e.g., final -s on plural nouns or capitalization of proper nouns). The purpose of including them is to sharpen the students' self-monitoring skills.

Error-analysis exercises are challenging, fun, and a good way to summarize the grammar in a unit. If you wish, tell students they are either newspaper editors or English teachers; their task is to locate all the mistakes and then write corrections. Point out that even native speakers have to scrutinize, correct, and revise their own writing. This is a natural part of the writing process.

The recommended technique is to assign an error-analysis exercise for in-class discussion the next day. Students benefit most from having the opportunity to find the errors themselves prior to class discussion. These exercises can, of course, be handled in other ways: seatwork, written homework, group work, or pairwork.

Let's Talk Exercises

The fourth edition of *Fundamentals of English Grammar* has even more exercises explicitly set up for interactive work than the last edition had. In these exercises, students can work in pairs, in groups, or as a class. Interactive exercises may take more class time than they would if teacher-led, but it is time well spent, for there are many advantages to student-student practice.

When students are working in pairs or groups, their opportunities to use what they are learning are many times greater than in a teacher-centered activity. Obviously, students working in groups or pairs are often much more active and involved than in teacher-led exercises.

Pairwork and group work also expand student opportunities to practice many communication skills at the same time in that they are practicing target structures. In peer interaction in the classroom, students have to agree, disagree, continue a conversation, make suggestions, promote cooperation, make requests, and be sensitive to each other's needs and personalities — the kinds of exchanges that are characteristic of any group communication, whether in the classroom or elsewhere.

Students will often help and explain things to each other during pairwork, in which case both students benefit greatly. Ideally, students in interactive activities are "partners in exploration." Together they go into new areas and discover things about English usage, supporting each other as they proceed.

Pairwork and group work help to produce a comfortable learning environment. In teacher-centered activities, students may sometimes feel shy and inhibited or may experience stress. They may feel that they have to respond quickly and accurately and that *what* they say is not as important as *how* they say it — even though you strive to convince them to the contrary. When you set up groups or pairs that are noncompetitive and cooperative, students usually tend to help, encourage, and even joke with one another. This encourages them to experiment with the language and to speak more often.

- Pairwork Exercises: Tell the student whose book is open (usually Partner A) that she / he is the teacher and needs to listen carefully to his / her partner's responses. Vary the ways in which students are paired up, including having them choose their own partners, counting off, or drawing names / numbers from a hat. Walk around the room and answer questions as needed.

- Small Group Exercises: The role of group leader can be rotated for long exercises, or one student can lead the entire exercise if it is short. The group can answer individually or chorally, depending on the type of exercise. Vary the ways in which you divide the class into groups and choose leaders. If possible, groups of 3-5 students work best.

- Class Activity (teacher-led) Exercises:

  a. You, the teacher, conduct the oral exercise. (You can always choose to lead an oral exercise, even when the directions specifically call for pairwork; exercise directions calling for group or pairwork work are suggestions, not ironclad instructions.)

  b. You don't have to read the items aloud as though reading a script word for word. Modify or add items spontaneously as they occur to you. Change the items in any way you can to make them more relevant to your students. (For example, if you know that some students plan to watch the World Cup soccer match on TV soon, include a sentence about that.) Omit irrelevant items.

c. Sometimes an item will start a spontaneous discussion of, for example, local restaurants or current movies or certain experiences your students have had. These spur-of-the-moment dialogues are very beneficial to your class. Being able to create and encourage such interactions is one of the chief advantages of a teacher leading an oral exercise.

Discussion of Meaning Exercises

Some exercises consist primarily of you and your students discussing the meaning of given sentences. Most of these exercises ask students to compare the meaning of two or more sentences (e.g., *You should take an English course* vs. *You must take an English course).* One of the main purposes of discussion-of-meaning exercises is to provide an opportunity for summary comparison of the structures in a particular unit.

Basically, the technique in these exercises is for you to pose questions about the given sentences, and then let students explain what a structure means to them (which allows you to find out what they do and do not understand). You can summarize the salient points as necessary. Students have their own inventive, creative way of explaining differences in meaning. They shouldn't be expected to sound like grammar teachers. Often, all you need to do is listen carefully and patiently to a student's explanation, and then clarify and reinforce it by rephrasing it somewhat.

Listening Exercises

Depending on your students' listening proficiency, some of the exercises may prove to be easy and some more challenging. You will need to gauge how many times to replay a particular item. In general, unless the exercise consists of single sentences, you will want to play the dialogue or passage in its entirety to give your students some context. Then you can replay the audio to have your students complete the task.

It is very important that grammar students be exposed to listening practice early on. Native speech can be daunting to new learners; many say that all they hear is a blur of words. Students need to understand that what they see in writing is not exactly what they should expect to hear in normal, rapidly spoken English. If students can't hear a structure, there is little chance it will be reinforced through interactions with other speakers. The sooner your students practice grammar from a listening perspective, the more confidence they will develop and the better equipped they will be to interact in English.

The two audio CDs can be found at the back of *Fundamentals of English Grammar.* There are 97 listening exercises in the text, all marked with a headphone icon. They reinforce the grammar being taught — some focusing on form, some on meaning, most on both.

You will find an audio tracking list at the back of the student book to help you locate a particular exercise on the CD. The listening scripts for all the exercises are also in the back of the student book, beginning on page 405.

Pronunciation Exercises

A few exercises focus on pronunciation of grammatical features, such as endings of nouns or verbs and contracted or reduced forms.

Some phonetic symbols are used in these exercises to point out sounds which should not be pronounced identically; for example, /s/, /Pz/, and /z/ represent the three predictable pronunciations of the grammatical suffix which is spelled *-s* or *-es.* It is not necessary for students to learn the complete phonetic alphabet; they should merely associate each symbol in an exercise with a sound that is different from all others. The purpose is to help students become more aware of these final sounds in the English they hear to encourage proficiency in their own speaking and writing.

In the exercises on spoken contractions, the primary emphasis should be on students' hearing and becoming familiar with spoken forms rather than on their accurate pronunciation of these forms. The most important part of most of these exercises is for students to listen to the oral production and become familiar with the reduced forms. Initially, it can sound strange for students to try to pronounce reduced forms; because of their lack of experience with English, they may be even less understandable when they try to produce these forms.

Language learners know that their pronunciation is not like that of native speakers; therefore, some of them are embarrassed or shy about speaking. In a pronunciation exercise, they may be more comfortable if you ask groups or the whole class to say a sentence in unison. After that, individuals may volunteer to speak the same sentence. Students' production does not need to be perfect, just understandable. You can encourage students to be less inhibited by having them teach you how to pronounce words in their languages (unless, of course, you're a native speaker of the students' language in a monolingual class). It's fun — and instructive — for the students to teach the teacher.

Expansions and Games

Expansions and games are important parts of the grammar classroom. The study of grammar is (and should be) fun and engaging. Some exercises in the text are designated as Games. In this *Teacher's Guide*, other exercises have Expansions that follow the step-by-step instruction. Both of these activity types are meant to promote independent, active use of target structures.

The atmosphere for the activities should be relaxed, and not necessarily competitive. The goal is clearly related to the chapter's content, and the reward is the students' satisfaction in using English to achieve that goal. (For additional games and activities, see *Fun with Grammar: Communicative Activities for the Azar Grammar Series,* by Suzanne W. Woodward.)

MONITORING ERRORS

In Written Work

When marking papers, focus mainly on the target grammar structure. Praise correct usage of the structure. Depending on the level of your class, you may want to simply mark but not correct errors in the target structure, and correct all other errors yourself. However, if development of writing skills is one the principal goals in your class, you will probably want the students to correct most of their errors themselves. Regardless of how you mark errors, tell your students that these writing exercises are simply for practice and that – even though they should always try to do their best — mistakes that occur should be viewed simply as tools for learning.

You may notice that some errors in usage seem to be the result of the students' study of the most recent grammar structure. For example, after teaching perfect tenses you may notice students using past perfect more than they had previously, but not always using it correctly. This is natural and does not seem to be of any lasting harm. View the students as experimenting with new tools. Praise them for reaching out toward what is new usage for them, even as you correct their errors. Grammar usage takes time to gel. Don't expect sudden mastery, and make sure your students don't expect that either. Encourage risk-taking and experimentation; students should never be afraid of making mistakes. In language acquisition, a mistake is nothing more than a learning opportunity.

In Oral Work

Students should be encouraged to monitor each other to some extent in interactive work, especially when monitoring activities are specifically assigned. (You should remind them to give some *positive* as well as corrective comments to each other.) You shouldn't worry about "losing control" of students' language production; not every mistake needs to be corrected. Mistakes are a natural part of learning a new language. As students gain experience and familiarity with a structure, their mistakes will begin to diminish.

Similarly, students shouldn't worry that they will learn one another's mistakes. Being exposed to imperfect English in an interactive classroom is not going to impede their progress in the slightest. In today's world, with so many people using English as a second language, students will likely be exposed to all levels of English proficiency in people they meet — from airline reservation agents to new neighbors from a different country to a co-worker whose native language is not English. Encountering imperfect English is not going to diminish their own English language abilities, either now in the classroom or later in different English-speaking situations.

Make yourself available to answer questions about correct answers during group work and pairwork. If you wish, you can take some time at the end of an exercise to call attention to mistakes that you heard as you monitored the groups. Another possible way of correcting errors is to have students use the answer key in the back of the book to look up their own answers when they need to. If your edition of the student book comes without the answer key, you can make student copies of the answers from the separate *Answer Key* booklet.

OPTIONAL VOCABULARY

Students benefit from your drawing attention to optional vocabulary for many reasons. English is a vocabulary-rich language, and students actively want to expand both their passive and active vocabulary in English. By asking students to discuss words, even words you can safely assume they recognize, you are asking students to use language to describe language and to speak in a completely spontaneous way (they don't know which words you will ask them about). Also, asking students to define words that they may actually know or may be familiar with allows students a change of pace from focusing on grammar, which may be particularly challenging at any given time. This gives students a chance to show off what they do know and take a quick mini-break from what may occasionally feel like a "heavy" focus on grammar.

One way to review vocabulary, particularly vocabulary that you assume students are familiar with, is to ask them to give you the closest synonym for a word. For example, if you ask students about the word *optimistic,* as a class you can discuss whether *positive, hopeful,* or *happy* is the closest synonym. This is, of course, somewhat subjective, but it is a discussion that will likely engage students. Similarly, for a more advanced group, you can ask them for the closest antonym of a given word, and thus for *optimistic* students could judge among, *sad, negative,* and *pessimistic,* for example. However you choose to review optional vocabulary, most students will greatly appreciate and profit from your doing so.

HOMEWORK

The textbook assumes that students will have the opportunity to prepare most of the written exercises by writing in their books prior to class discussion. Students should be assigned this homework as a matter of course.

Whether you have students write their answers on paper for you to collect is up to you. This generally depends upon such variables as class size, class level, available class time, your available paper-correcting time, not to mention your preferences in teaching techniques. Most of the exercises in the text can be handled through class discussion without the students needing to hand in written homework. Most of the written homework that is suggested in the text and in the chapter notes in this *Teacher's Guide* consists of activities that will produce original, independent writing.

POWERPOINTS

PowerPoint lessons are included in this *Teacher's Guide* as an additional, optional resource. There are two types of PowerPoint lessons:

- Chart-by-chart instruction and practice for each chapter, designed to be used as you work through a chapter.

- Beyond-the-book activities based on real-world readings, intended for use at the end of a chapter as a whole class review.

The PowerPoints are also available for download at *AzarGrammar.com.*

Additional Resources

USING THE *WORKBOOK*

The *Workbook* contains self-study exercises for independent study, with a perforated answer key located at the end of the book. If you prefer that students not have the answers to the exercises, ask them to hand in the answer key at the beginning of the term (to be returned at the end of the term). Some teachers may prefer to use the *Workbook* for in-class teaching rather than independent study.

The *Workbook* mirrors the *Student Book*. Exercises are called "exercises" in the *Student Book* and "practices" in the *Workbook* to minimize confusion when you make assignments. Each practice in the *Workbook* has a content title and refers students to appropriate charts in the *Student Book* and in the *Workbook* itself.

Workbook practices can be assigned by you or, depending upon the level of maturity or sense of purpose of the class, simply left for students to use as they wish. They may be assigned to the entire class or only to those students who need further practice with a particular structure. They may be used as reinforcement after you have covered a chart and exercises in class or as introductory material prior to discussing a chart in class.

In addition, students can use the *Workbook* to acquaint themselves with the grammar of any units not covered in class. Earnest students can use the *Workbook* to teach themselves.

TEST BANK

The *Test Bank for Fundamentals of English Grammar* is a comprehensive bank of quizzes and tests that are keyed to charts or chapters in the student book. Each chapter contains a variety of short quizzes which can be used as quick informal comprehension checks or as formal quizzes to be handed in and graded. Each chapter also contains two comprehensive tests. Both the quizzes and the tests can be reproduced as is, or items can be excerpted for tests that you prepare yourself.

Azar Interactive

Students learn in many ways and benefit from being exposed to grammar in a variety of contexts. This computer-based program is keyed to the text and provides all-new exercises, readings, listening and speaking activities, and comprehensive tests. You can use this program concurrently with the text or as an independent study tool. You can assign the whole chapter to the entire class, or you can customize the exercises to particular students. For example, for those students who are proficient in written work, but need practice with oral production, you can assign the speaking, listening, and pronunciation exercises. Another way to assign exercises would be based on the target structure. If you notice that a student is struggling with a particular grammar point or section, you can assign the corresponding exercises for further out of class study. In addition, the chapter tests can be used as effective reviews prior to an in-class test.

Fun with Grammar

Fun with Grammar: Communicative Activities for the Azar Grammar Series, is a teacher resource text by Suzanne W. Woodward with communicative activities correlated to the Azar-Hagen Grammar Series. It is available as a text or as a download on *AzarGrammar.com*.

AzarGrammar.com

Another resource is *AzarGrammar.com*. This website is designed as a tool for teachers. It includes a variety of additional activities keyed to each chapter of the student book including additional exercise worksheets, vocabulary worksheets, and song-based activities tied to specific grammar points. This website is also a place to ask questions you might have about grammar (sometimes our students ask real stumpers), as well as also being a place to communicate with the authors about the text and to offer teaching/exercise suggestions.

Notes on American vs. British English

Students are often curious about differences between American and British English. They should know that the differences are minor. Any students who have studied British English (BrE) should have no trouble adapting to American English (AmE), and vice versa.

Teachers need to be careful not to inadvertently mark differences between AmE and BrE as errors; rather, they should simply point out to students that a difference in usage exists.

Differences in Grammar

Differences in article and preposition usage in certain common expressions follow. These differences are not noted in the text; they are given here for the teacher's information.

AmE	BrE
be in **the** hospital	be in **Ø** hospital
be at **the** university (be in college)	be at **Ø** university
go to **a** university (go to college)	go to **Ø** university
go to **Ø** class/be in **Ø** class	go to **a** class/be in **a** class
in **the** future	in **Ø** future (OR in **the** future)
did it **the next** day	did it **Ø** next day (OR **the next** day)
haven't done something **for/in** weeks	haven't done something **for** weeks
ten minutes **past/after** six o'clock	ten minutes **past** six o'clock
five minutes **to/of/till** seven o'clock	five minutes **to** seven o'clock

Differences in Spelling

Variant spellings can be noted but should not be marked as incorrect in student writing. Spelling differences in some common words follow.

AmE	BrE
jewelry, traveler, woolen	jewellry, traveller, woollen
skillful, fulfill, installment	skilful, fulfil, instalment
color, honor, labor, odor	colour, honour, labour, odour
-ize (realize, apologize)	-ise/ize (realise/realize, apologise/apologize)
analyze	analyse
defense, offense, license	defence, offence, licence (n.)

theater, center, liter	theatre, centre, litre
check	cheque (bank note)
curb	kerb
forever	for ever/forever
focused	focused/focussed
fueled	fuelled/fueled
practice (n. and v.)	practise (v.); practice (n. only)
program	programme
specialty	speciality
story	storey (of a building)
tire	tyre

DIFFERENCES IN VOCABULARY

Differences in vocabulary usage between AmE and BrE usually do not significantly interfere with communication, but some misunderstandings may develop. For example, a BrE speaker is referring to underpants or panties when using the word "pants," whereas an AmE speaker is referring to slacks or trousers. Students should know that when American and British speakers read each other's literature, they encounter very few differences in vocabulary usage. Similarly, in the United States Southerners and New Englanders use different vocabulary, but not so much as to interfere with communication. Some differences between AmE and BrE follow.

AmE	BrE
attorney, lawyer	barrister, solicitor
bathrobe	dressing gown
can (of beans)	tin (of beans)
cookie, cracker	biscuit
corn	maize
diaper	nappy
driver's license	driving licence
drug store	chemist's
elevator	lift
eraser	rubber
flashlight	torch
jail	gaol
gas, gasoline	petrol
hood of a car	bonnet of a car
living room	sitting room, drawing room
math	maths (e.g., a maths teacher)
raise in salary	rise in salary
rest room	public toilet, WC (water closet)
schedule	timetable
sidewalk	pavement, footpath
sink	basin
soccer	football
stove	cooker
truck	lorry, van
trunk (of a car)	boot (of a car)
be on vacation	be on holiday

Key to Pronunciation Symbols

THE PHONETIC ALPHABET (SYMBOLS FOR AMERICAN ENGLISH)

Consonants

Phonetic symbols for most consonants use the same letters as in conventional English spelling: /b, d, f, g, h, k, l, m, n, o, p, r, s, t, v, w, y, z/.*

*Slanted lines indicate phonetic symbols.

Spelling consonants that are <u>not</u> used phonetically in English: c, q, x.

A few additional symbols are needed for other consonant sounds.

/ θ / (Greek theta) = voiceless *th* as in **thin, thank**
/ δ / (Greek delta) = voiced *th* as in **then, those**
/ ŋ / = *ng* as in *sing, think* (but not in *danger*)
/ š / = *sh* as in *shirt, mission, nation*
/ ž / = *s* or *z* in a few words like *pleasure, azure*
/ č / = *ch* or *tch* as in *watch, church*
/ ǰ / = *j* or *dge* as in *jump, ledge*

Vowels

The five vowels in the spelling alphabet are inadequate to represent the 12-15 vowel sounds of American speech. Therefore, new symbols and new sound associations for familiar letters must be adopted.

Front	**Central**	**Back** (lips rounded)
/i/ or /iy/ as in *beat*		/u/, /u:/, or /uw/ as in *boot*
/ɪ/ as in *bit*		/ʊ/ as in *book*
/e/ or /ey/ as in *bait*		/o/ or /ow/ as in *boat*
		/ɔ/ as in *bought*
/ɛ/ as in *bet*	/ə/ as in *but*	
/æ/ as in *bat*	/a/ as in *bother*	

Glides: /ai/ or /ay/ as in *bite*
/ɔi/ or /ɔy/ as in *boy*
/æ/ or /aw/ as in *about*

British English has a somewhat different set of vowel sounds and symbols. You might want to consult a standard pronunciation text or BrE dictionary for that system.

Chapter 1
Present Time

CHAPTER SUMMARY

OBJECTIVE: This chapter includes some of the most fundamental and useful structures in everyday English. Students learn to ask and answer questions that are useful in getting and giving information, describing current circumstances, and keeping a conversation moving along. In learning to do so, students distinguish between situations requiring use of either simple present or present progressive and also learn when either form is acceptable.

APPROACH: The book, in general, emphasizes everyday English, a style and register acceptable and even preferred in most situations. The first exercise models a simple dialogue for an interview to help classmates get better acquainted. The charts and exercises then focus on the structure and uses of basic present tenses. The text emphasizes the accurate use of frequency adverbs to help students understand present tense as used for usual activities and/or general statement of facts. Finally, the chapter introduces short answers to yes/no questions and gives students ample opportunities to practice using them.

TERMINOLOGY: The text does not differentiate between "tenses" and "aspects." The assumed understanding of the term "tense" is a verb form that expresses time relationships; most students are comfortable with the term, and the idea of tense as related to time has meaning in many other languages. The text seeks to present and explain structures with a minimum of technical terminology and a maximum of practical usage. The hope is that students will leave their formal study of English one day with good control of its structures; terminology can and probably will soon be forgotten.

The present progressive is also called the present continuous in some texts and students are likely to have met both tenses at some stage. The text refers to stative verbs as "non-action" and to the auxiliary verb forms required to form reduced answers to yes/no questions simply as "short answers."

❑ **EXERCISE 1.** Listening and reading.
Page 1
Time: 10–15 minutes

Part I
- Tell the class that they are going to hear a conversation between two people meeting one another for the first time.
- Ask students what kinds of questions they may hear and write their responses on the board. For example:

   Where are you from?
   How old are you?
   What do you like to do?

- If appropriate, you can discuss what kinds of introductory questions are typical to ask when you first meet someone, as these may vary from country to country or depending on gender.
- Have a student read the directions to Part I aloud. Write and define the term *resident assistant* on the board.
- Have students close their books. Play the audio through once without stopping.
- Tell students to open their books and follow along as you play the audio again.

Part II
- Give students time to read through conversation on their own and answer any questions they may have.
- Now ask students to turn to Part II on Page 2. Explain that Part II is Sam's introduction of Lisa to the class.
- Ask students to complete Sam's introduction, using information from Part I.
- Review this introduction on the board, calling on students to help you fill in the answers.

Part III
- Now ask students to imagine Lisa's introduction of Sam and to tell you what Lisa would say about Sam. Let students know they can turn back to look at the conversation between Sam and Lisa on page 1.
- Write the imagined introduction of Sam on the board. For example:

   Sam is from Quebec.
   He is studying Italian.
   His last name is S-A-N-C-H-E-Z.

Optional Vocabulary
jet lag	hike
hobby	surf the Internet
free time	time is up

❑ **EXERCISE 2.** Let's talk: interview. Page 2
Time: 20–25 minutes

- First, explain to students that they will interview and introduce one another in the same way they heard in Exercise 1. Explain that they will first get information from their classmates and then use that information to introduce their partners to the class.
- If students are not too shy or reluctant to do so, have them pick their own partner. If this process takes too long or students seem hesitant, pick a partner for them. It is always fine to have one or two groups of three if needed.

- Instruct students to write their partner's name on their paper and to write their partner's answers in note form.
- Circulate while students are interviewing one another. Answer any questions and make sure that they can understand each other.
- Conclude the exercise by having students introduce their partner to the class. If helpful, use yourself or a student as a model.

Expansion: Take notes as students introduce each other. Then review information at the end of the class. Once students have shared their partner's information, ask one "repeat" question for each student and allow anyone but the interviewee or his/her partner to answer. While completing this quick review, you can write one short sentence for each student. You can also easily turn this review into a quick competition that you score on the board.

If students do know each other well, you could give them new "identities" such as those of famous people, and students could use commonly known information to describe "themselves" to their partners. For example:

Teacher: So, who is this person?

Class: David Beckham.

Teacher: Right, and what is David Beckham's favorite sport?

Class: Soccer.

❏ EXERCISE 4. Warm-up. Page 3
Time: 10 minutes

> This Warm-up is intended to show the difference between the two present tenses. The book assumes that students have some familiarity with both.

- Have students read through each question and circle *yes* or *no*.
- Ask individual students to read each sentence aloud by first introducing the sentence with *Yes* or *No* and making any necessary changes in structure (negatives, contractions, etc.).
- Ask related questions in order to emphasize the difference between *usual activities* and *actions in progress*. For example:

Student: 1. Yes, Min uses a computer every day.

Teacher: What else does Min do every day?

Student: She does homework every day.

Student: 2. No, Paco is not sitting in front of a computer right now.

Teacher: Okay. What is Paco doing right now?

Student: He is studying English right now.

- Give students time to work with a partner, and then report their information to the class.

CHART 1-1. Simple Present and Present Progressive. Page 3
Time: 10–15 minutes

> It is assumed that students are already familiar with these two present tenses, their negative and question forms, and contractions with *our, are, is,* and *not.* It is not assumed that students have full control of these forms and their uses, however.
>
> The time line diagrams in the chart are used to illustrate verb tenses throughout the text, with the vertical crossbar representing "now" or "the moment of speaking." Students will see this basic time line again and again throughout the text, and teachers should become adept at replicating it on the board.
>
> ```
>                              now
>    past_____|_____future
> ```

- Write the chart heading (*Simple Present and Present Progressive*) on the board.
- Underneath the main heading write *Simple Present* on the left-hand side of the board and draw the time line from the book.
- Read and write the simple present sentences (a)–(e) beneath the time line or create sentences of your own. For example:

Class begins at 9 A.M. each morning.

Megan and Lily play board games every weekend.

The temperature rises each July.

The sun doesn't shine at 9 P.M.

Does the weather get cold in January?

- Ask students what the verb in each sentence is. Underline it. Do the same for the time words.
- Explain (and write) that simple present is used for situations that are true all the time, for habits, or usual activities. For example:

Simple Present—Usual activities
      Habits
      Situations that are always true

- Write how to form the simple present on the board.

Form:

Statement: Subject + base form of verb

(Remember final -s for third person singular.)

Negative: Subject + doesn't + base form

Question: Does + subject + base form

- Now write *Present Progressive* on the right-hand side of the board and draw the time line from the book.
- Explain that present progressive is used to express that an action is happening <u>right now</u>, at this very moment. Repeat that this is different than an action that is true in general or is a usual action or habit. For example:

Present Progressive—Actions that are happening right
      now
      At this moment

- Ask students what they are doing right now and write their responses on the board. For example:

  Teacher: What are you doing right now?

  Student: I am listening to you.

  Teacher: Yukiko is listening to her teacher right now.

- Go through the example sentences in the chart (f) – (j) with students and write the sentences on the board, underlining the verb form and the time cues.
- Explain (and write) that present progressive is used for actions that are happening right now, at this very moment.
- Write how to form present progressive on the board.

  Form:

  Statement: Subject + verb to be in present + -ing form of verb

  Negative: Subject + verb to be in negative + -ing form of verb

  Question: Verb to be + subject + -ing form of verb

CHART 1-2. Forms of the Simple Present and the Present Progressive. Page 4
Time: 10–15 minutes

This chart should be used to emphasize and practice the forms presented in Chart 1-1. The chart provides a chance for both you and students to reiterate the uses and formation of both tenses. Students will benefit from reading sentences from the chart aloud and having you ask pointed questions and provide reminders. Thus, even though it can be time-consuming, replicating the chart with students' input can prove very useful. It can give students confidence in accessing the newly learned grammar, and it can also pinpoint areas where students will need additional practice.

- Ask students to give you examples of their daily habits (in simple present) and be prepared to contrast these with actions that are happening right now (in present progressive).
- On the board, write the sentences generated as well as your questions to show contrast with present progressive. For example:

  Pilar brushes her teeth every day.

  Is she brushing her teeth right now?

  Bertrand talks on the phone with his girlfriend every evening.

  Is he talking on the phone with his girlfriend right now?

- Look at the *Simple Present* chart on the left-hand side of Chart 1-2 and ask students to give you an alternative to the verb **to work**.
- Tell students that because they are practicing with simple present, they should provide you with a verb that is an everyday action.
- Using the verb selected, have students conjugate the verb in the same way the simple present of *work* is shown in the chart.
- Write the conjugation on the board under the heading *Simple Present* and have students give you all the

subjects and verb forms required to complete the conjugation. For example:

Simple Present: Study

Statement	Negative	Question
I study.	I don't study.	Do I study?
You study.	You don't study.	Do you study?
He / She / It studies.	He / She / It doesn't study.	Does he / she / it study?
We study.	We don't study.	Do we study?
You study.	You don't study.	Do you study?
They study.	They don't study.	Do they study?

- Using the same verb, conjugate the verb in present progressive by having students provide you with the correct subjects and verb forms.
- Write these forms on the board below the heading *Present Progressive*. For example:

Present Progressive: Study

Statement	Negative	Question
I am studying.	I am not studying.	Am I studying?
You are studying.	You are not studying.	Are you studying?
He / She / It is studying.	He / She / It is not studying.	Is he / she / it studying?
We are studying.	We are not studying.	Are we studying?
You are studying.	You are not studying.	Are you studying?
They are studying.	They are not studying.	Are they studying?

- Discuss and review how to form contractions with students.
- Then have students provide you with the correct contracted forms for:

  *pronoun + **be**, **do** + not*, and ***be** + **not***.
- Write these contraction forms on the board.

❏ EXERCISE 5. Listening and grammar.
Page 4
Time: 5–10 minutes

- Ask students to study the picture while you play the audio through once without stopping.
- Then have students look at the reading and follow along as you play the audio again.
- Line by line, have the class look at each verb in italics and ask students why each tense is used. They should answer either because the action is happening right now or because it is a usual activity.

Optional Vocabulary

lunch break	spicy
fire station	skips
co-worker	

❏ EXERCISE 8. Let's talk. Page 6
Time: 10–15 minutes

- Explain the directions to students and make sure they understand why you are asking them to "perform."

- Model the example with one student.
- Next, go through the entire exercise calling on different students to do/perform each request.
- Ask what each student is doing and encourage the rest of the class to call out descriptive answers in present progressive, as in the example.
- Write the sentences generated on the board and correct pronunciation, grammar, vocabulary, and usage as needed.

Optional Vocabulary
whistle
erase
scratch

Expansion 1: Bring in a set of blank index cards. After you have completed Exercise 8, ask students to write new actions to be performed on their cards. Tell students to write just the verb. Tell students not to copy any of the verbs used in Exercise 8. Collect the cards, shuffle them, and redistribute them so that no student gets his/her original card. Have the first student come to the front of the room, give you his/her card, and perform the verb or verb phrase listed on it. Other students then have to guess what the student is doing, using present progressive appropriately.

Suggested actions (if students can't come up with enough on their own):

hum a popular song
skip around the room
hop on one foot
walk backwards
wave at an imaginary friend
rub palms together
wink at a classmate
clear your throat
leave the classroom
stomp your feet
kneel on the floor

Expansion 2: Encourage students to bring this expansion activity into their everyday life by silently narrating what they and others are doing, using present progressive. For example, if a student is entering his/her apartment, the student can say, *I'm turning the doorknob. I'm opening the door. I'm walking into the apartment. I'm closing the door.* Tell students that they can gain a lot of valuable practice by speaking to themselves in English as they go through their day. You can ask them if they ever talk to themselves in their own language and assure them that most people do. By choosing to talk to themselves in English, they will gain valuable practice.

Expansion 3: Ask a student to pretend to be a television news reporter covering a live event: a dynamic ESL or EFL class at (*name of your school*). Because the television audience doesn't know much about this kind of class, the reporter needs to describe the action as it is happening. After one student has had the chance to describe the class minute-by-minute, give another student a chance to do so. In order to make sure students understand this task, it is best to demonstrate it before asking them to play the role of reporter.

Expansion 4: Show a DVD or video of a scene in a movie but mute the sound. As the action unfolds, have students describe it in writing using the present progressive tense. They can also be asked to discuss what is going on in the movie in terms of plot as well as moment-by-moment physical action.

❏ **EXERCISE 10.** Game: trivia. Page 7
Time: 5–10 minutes

Optional Vocabulary

Eiffel Tower	spoil
honey	common

Expansion: Ask students to come up with one true/false question based on a fact or statistic about their country, city, or language background. They can write their questions on a piece of paper or index card, and then either you or each student can read it aloud.

❏ **EXERCISE 11.** Let's talk. Page 7
Time: 10–15 minutes

- Model the activity with one student. Make sure students understand that each partner needs to keep his/her partner's version of the pictures covered.
- Remind students that they are looking at a still illustration of a moment caught in time (right now). Because of this, they need present progressive to accurately describe their picture to their partner.
- You may want to have students sit back-to-back in pairs while you circulate, assisting students with vocabulary and tense use.
- Take mental or actual notes on mistakes that you hear in use or pronunciation for later correction on the board.
- Review by having both partners look at both sets of pictures and have the class come up with comparison statements using both pictures and the appropriate tense.
- Write the comparison statements on the board if time. For example:

  In Partner A's picture the baby is crying, but in Partner B's picture the baby is smiling and playing.

Optional Vocabulary
Though students will be creating their own descriptions, you may want to introduce the following terms:

approaching	curling
landing gear	handing
crib/playpen	purchasing
blocks	recliner/reclining
doorstep	footstool
overhead	relaxing

❏ EXERCISE 12. Let's read and write.

Page 9
Time: 15–20 minutes

> This reading gives students a chance to experience the use of simple present to describe general facts. By asking students to research and report on another part of the body, students will gain practice in this particular use of simple present.

Part I
- Give students ample time to read the paragraph and complete the questions that follow.
- Have students take turns reading the paragraph aloud. Pay special attention to how students pronounce the final -s of verbs and provide encouraging but immediate correction.
- Correct the follow-up questions as a class.

Part II
- Assign Part II for homework and encourage students to use every resource at their disposal, including the Internet.
- Collect and discuss these brief reports when students hand them in.
- Correct verb forms, if necessary.

Optional Vocabulary
scalp	organize
strands	topic
rests	

Expansion: After the class has learned other interesting facts about other parts of the body (by sharing these reports), make a brief true/false quiz based on the facts presented by each student. Include at least one fact per student report or body part and be sure to use the actual verbs students used, in simple present.

CHART 1-3. Frequency Adverbs. Page 10
Time: 10–15 minutes

> The charts are more meaningful to students when you present and even replicate them on the board. In order to activate students' knowledge and engage them in this presentation, ask them for as much information as they can give. You will end up with a close copy of the chart as it is presented in the book, but because you will have explained each step and called on students to contribute to and expand upon your explanation, they will learn more from your active explanation of the material than from simply reading it on their own.

It may work best to present the frequency of some activity and ask students which adverbs work best. For example:

I drink coffee every morning of the week. = always
I drink coffee six mornings a week. = usually
I drink coffee four mornings a week. = often
I drink coffee two or three mornings a week. = sometimes
I drink coffee once every two or three weeks. = seldom
I drink coffee once or twice a year. = rarely

Other points to consider and discuss, depending on the needs of your class:

1) *Usually* and *often* are close in meaning. If any students want to pursue a distinction, you might say that *usually* = 95% of the time and *often* = 90% of the time. Or, you might say that *usually* means "most of the time, regularly" while *often* means "many times, repeated times, frequently." At this level these subtle differences are not very important, and unless a student brings this up, you may not want to raise such nuances.

2) *Often* can be pronounced *offen* or *of-ten*.

3) In discussing the difference between *seldom* and *rarely*, you might describe *seldom* as 5% of the time and *rarely* as only 1% of the time.

- Write the heading *Frequency Adverbs* on the board.
- Elicit from students which frequency adverb can best be described as 100% of the time and which one can best be described as 0% of the time.
- Students should be able to answer *always* and *never* in response.
- Draw a vertical line and at the top write *100% - always*.
- At the bottom of the vertical line, write *0% - never*. For example:

| 100% - always

| 0%- never

- With students, discuss the meanings of the other frequency adverbs included in Chart 1-3, and assign each one a percentage and place on the chart.
- One way to engage students is to ask each student to tell you something he/she does *always, almost always, usually, often, frequently, generally, sometimes, occasionally, seldom, rarely, hardly ever, almost never, not ever,* and *never*.
- As students describe the frequency of their habits, write the frequency adverb and percentage in the appropriate place on the vertical line.
- Make sure students tell you the frequency of their habits using simple present.
- Explain the placement of frequency adverbs and go over question forms and negatives with students.
- Have students take turns reading points (a)–(h) aloud. Discuss each one with them. You can also generate a new example for each point with the students in your class and write this on the board.

❏ EXERCISE 14. Grammar and speaking.
Page 10
Time: 10–15 minutes

Part I
Expansion: Ask students to write a sentence describing an activity that they think they may do much more or less often than other people do. For example:
I seldom check my email.

Part II
Expansion: After students have shared their information with one another, ask the class who does a certain activity most frequently and who does a certain activity least frequently. Encourage students to simply shout out their answers, which will be the names of their classmates, and then ask students to give you complete sentences to write on the board. For example:

Teacher: *Who never cooks their own dinner?*

Student(s): *Mario.*

Teacher *(while preparing to write on board): Okay, give me a complete sentence about Mario.*

Student(s): *Mario never cooks his own dinner.*

❏ EXERCISE 15. Let's talk. Page 11
Time: 10–20 minutes

- Have students answer the questions independently.
- Ask students to walk around and compare their answers with other students while you circulate and facilitate meaningful discussion.
- As a class, review the questions one by one, discussing the meaning of each frequency adverb as well as individual students' responses.

Expansion: If you have a class of many nationalities, your students may well have a wide range of responses to questions 2 and 3, about what a polite person does or does not do. If students seem comfortable, spend extra time on 2 and 3, asking students to compare their cultures in terms of politeness. The topic of politeness should give students many opportunities to form simple present sentences while describing polite norms.

❏ EXERCISE 18. Let's talk: pairwork.
Page 12
Time: 10–20 minutes

The "Let's Talk: pairwork" exercises included in this series are a great way for you to facilitate free production of the structures students are acquiring. However, in order to ensure their success, you, the facilitator, need to participate actively. Help students make the most of what could be a stilted question-answer exchange by circulating and participating in as many conversations as you can. Asking leading questions or those that require the student to elaborate. You can also provide vocabulary that students may be reaching for. Whenever natural and possible, encourage student interactions to go beyond

what has been scripted in the book so that each "Let's Talk" exercise becomes an opportunity not only for practicing English, but also for getting to know one's classmates better. This is also an ideal opportunity for you to make a list of common errors that you overhear, which you can explicitly bring to everyone's attention when you summarize the content of the exercise.

- If students can find partners quickly, have them do so. Otherwise, assign partners by having students count off a-b or 1-2. Be prepared to have a group of three.
- Model the example with one student so that students completely understand the task at hand before beginning.
- Circulate and help students as needed.
- When students have had time to take turns at both roles, regroup and go over mistakes you have heard with the class. Write the mistakes on the board and encourage students to correct them.
- Choose a couple of the questions to discuss as a class by way of summary and follow-up. Questions 5, 7, and 9 are most likely to spur general discussion.

CHART 1-4. Singular/Plural. Page 13
Time: 10–15 minutes

You might mention to students that final -s causes ESL/EFL students a lot of trouble. Students most often omit it erroneously, but sometimes they add a final -s when it is not needed. Students need to pay special attention to their usage of final -s from beginning to advanced levels of study because it often becomes a fossilized error early on.

It is important for students to understand that when added to a noun, final -s indicates plural number. Added to a verb, it indicates singular. (You may want to review the terms *noun* and *verb* with students.) Draw students' attention to this contrasting use of final -s, with verbs and nouns respectively, and correct their usage frequently and encouragingly.

- Write the heading *Singular / Plural* on the board.
- Using either the noun presented in the chart or a countable noun of a student's choosing, write the following:

  Singular: one bird (fish, skier, student, etc.)

- Ask students to give you the plural form of whatever noun was chosen. Replicate point (b) on the board. For example:

  Plural: two, three, four, four thousand birds, books, skiers, students

- Ask students to give you a simple present sentence for a third person singular noun as in (c). Write the sentence on the board.
- Ask students to come up with a simple present sentence for a third person plural subject noun as in (d). Write this sentence beneath (c).
- Discuss the rest of the chart and highlight the many forms a third person singular subject noun can take, as in (e).

❏ EXERCISE 21. Listening. Page 14
Time: 5–10 minutes

Optional Vocabulary

natural disaster	damage
create	financial
flood	

❏ EXERCISE 22. Warm-up. Page 14
Time: 5 minutes

> The endings of third person verbs will be review for most students. Enlist students in discussing this, and encourage them to show you and their classmates what they already know.

- Give students time to complete the exercise individually.
- While students are working, write the three headings on the board.
- Assign each word to a different student, and have students write their answers on the board in the correct column.
- As a class, try to figure what the spelling rules are.

CHART 1-5. Spelling of Final -s/-es. Page 14
Time: 15 minutes

> You may want to review what vowels and consonants are before starting this chart.
>
> A common error is adding -es when only -s is needed (INCORRECT: visites; growes). Emphasize when -es is not added.
>
> You may want to explain that adding -s to pay does not change the pronunciation of the vowel sound. However, adding -s to say does; i.e., says rhymes with sez but not with pays. You can also take this opportunity to explain that the pronunciations of goes and does are different and that many common short words in English have similarly odd pronunciation (their, says, was, has).
>
> In conjunction with discussing spelling, you may want to present the pronunciation of final -s and -es, which is also presented later in this text. A summary of the pronunciation of final -s/-es follows:
>
> It is pronounced /s/ after voiceless sounds: meets.
>
> It is pronounced /z/ after voiced sounds: needs.
>
> It is pronounced /ez/ after -sh, -ch, -s, -x, -z and -ge/-dge sounds: wishes, watches, passes, mixes, sizes, judges.

- Write the heading of the chart on the board.
- Write student-generated examples of (a)–(f) on the board. If students are not able to give you ready examples, you can simply rewrite the verbs you find in the chart and add more of your own. Ask students to supply the endings.

- Suggestions of additional verbs to use: (a) begin-begins (b) come-comes (c) watch-watches; push-pushes; guess-guesses; mix-mixes; fizz-fizzes (d) worry-worries (e) play-plays.
- Using the rules that students wrote in the Warm-up, write rules for adding -s and -es on the right-hand side of the board, to correspond with the verbs on the left.
- Tell students that they will meet other irregular verbs such as those presented in (f) and let them know that they will need to learn these irregular verbs by rote as there is no way of predicting their endings.

❏ EXERCISE 23. Looking at grammar.
Page 15
Time: 10 minutes

> Make sure students understand the roles of subjects and verbs. If necessary refer to the related chart in Chapter 6 of this text first.

- Give students time to complete this exercise on their own.
- Encourage students to refer back to Chart 1-5 when spelling the verb endings.
- Review as a group either by writing the sentences on the board or calling on students to read their answers aloud.

Optional Vocabulary

float	freeze
flow	boil
term	block
game shows	

❏ EXERCISE 24. Grammar and listening.
Page 15
Time: 5–10 minutes

Expansion 1: Have students use each third-person singular verb in a sentence as they give the correct form and pronunciation.

Expansion 2: Give a spelling test. Give the simple form of the verb and ask students to give the third-person singular -s/-es form and write it on their quiz. Students can then grade each other's papers or correct each other's boardwork. Possible verbs to use (some of which students will be unfamiliar with but should still be able to spell the final -s/-es form of): stay, supply, hiss, flash, taste, disappear, break, match, cry, enter, explain, finish, exist, marry, occur, rely, relay.

Expansion 3: Prepare index cards with the names of animals, professions or world-famous people on them, one for each student. The object of this expansion is to have students describe the name on their index card by using only third person verb sentences. Students take a few minutes to prepare such sentences to describe the word on their card and then circulate around the room, explaining the sentences to other students until the name is correctly guessed. At this level, it is very important to describe how to carry out the expansion activity, model it, and reiterate why students are doing it (to gain practice using third person -s/-es).

Example: Students have cards with names of animals on them.

One student's card says monkey.

He/She prepares the following sentences and says them to classmates until someone guesses "monkey."

This animal swings *from trees in the jungle.*

This animal acts *like a human being.*

This animal eats *bananas.*

This animal holds *things the way people do.*

❏ EXERCISE 26. Game. Page 16
Time: 10–20 minutes

The principle purpose of this exercise is to get students up, moving, and talking to each other while they are focusing on the correct use of the target structures.

The vocabulary in this practice may prove difficult for many of the students, and you can reassure students that vocabulary development is one of the goals of the exercise. You can ask for and answer questions about the meaning of words before students begin. You can also encourage students to work on the meanings of words together. In any case, a list of optional vocabulary is included.

- Explain to the students that they will each copy down half of a sentence and find the student with the other half (the correct match).
- Tell students that they should say the words on their slip of paper to others in the class rather than allow others to read them.
- Remind students that the two halves must make complete sense as one sentence.
- Tell the students to decide with their newly found "partner" who will write the completed sentence on the board.
- Review the sentences on the board as a class by asking students to identify the subject and verb in each sentence.
- Then ask a volunteer to read the sentence aloud.

Optional Vocabulary

air pollution	improves
stretch	hurricane
support	produce
variety	trunk
marine life	supply
destruction	

CHART 1-6. Non-Action Verbs. Page 17
Time: 15 minutes

The key point to emphasize with students is the difference between "states of being" (or condition) and actual, observable "activities." No verb is inherently non-progressive. The intention of this chart and its terminology is to inform students that certain common verbs are usually not used in the progressive form.

The list of non-action (i.e., stative or non-progressive) verbs is by no means complete. It presents only a few common verbs.

Remind students about negative verb forms:

Progressive: *I'm studying English now.*
*I'm **not** studying French.*

Non-progressive: *I like tea.*
*I **don't** like coffee.*

- Write the chart heading *Non-Action Verbs* on one side of the board <u>and</u> write *Action Verbs* on the other so that you have two columns.
- Explain that in order to understand when to use progressive or non-progressive, students need to be able to picture the verbs in their minds.
- Explain that if they can picture or "see" the verb happening (using their imagination), it can be considered an activity. If they can't clearly see a physical expression of the verb, it could be non-progressive.
- Pick a non-progressive verb such as *know* and contrast it with an action verb such as *hit* and write both verbs on the board.
- Ask a student to demonstrate the meaning of *hit*. The student will likely pretend to hit someone or thing.
- Now ask the same student to demonstrate *know*. As there is no easy way to "show" this verb (as it has no action per se), the difference should be obvious.
- Have students give you a sample sentence for each verb and write these on the board, under each column heading. For example:

Progressive   *Non-progressive*
Marc is hitting his brother.   *John knows Sam.*

- Review the chart point-by-point, (a)–(c), and write additional sentence examples on the board, showing the correct form clearly.
- Review the list of verbs included in the chart.
- Draw special attention to the comparison points (d)–(g) and have students help you generate more examples for the board.

❏ EXERCISE 28. Looking at grammar.
Page 17
Time: 5–10 minutes

This exercise emphasizes non-action (i.e., non-progressive, stative) verbs, which describe a state that exists now (rather than an activity that is happening now).

- Have students spend a few minutes completing the exercise individually.
- Look at the example sentence. Ask students what information can help them.
- Prompt students to consider whether the verb in the first sentence, *like*, describes a state of being or an observable activity in progress.
- Write the example on the board in such a way that the non-action nature of the verb in sentence (A) is noted. For example:

    1. A: What do you *like* better: coffee or tea? like = condition or state; not action

       B: I *prefer* tea. prefer = condition or state; not action

- Review each sentence, asking students to take the time to justify their answers as above.
- Write examples on the board to clarify and emphasize the meaning of the verbs used.

Optional Vocabulary

prefer	report
set the table	several

❏ EXERCISE 31. Warm-up. Page 19
Time: 5 minutes

- Call on students to complete the Warm-up by sight reading each question and choosing the correct short answer.
- Write the term *Short Answer* on the board and ask students what is true of each short answer.
- Ask questions that lead students to arrive at the elements of a short answer: **yes / no** + verb **to be** in either affirmative or negative.

Optional Vocabulary
vegetarian

CHART 1-7. Present Verbs: Short Answers to Yes / No Questions. Page 20
Time: 15 minutes

Students will need to understand that auxiliary verbs can take the place of complete verb phrases in these sentences. They have probably heard this use of auxiliary verbs many times but may not know the grammar practices controlling it.

- On the board, write *Short Answers*.
- Under the *Short Answers* heading, write *Do / Does* on the left-hand side of the board and *Be* on the right.
- Now, with the involvement of students, write a simple present question featuring a regular verb under *Do / Does*.
- Then do the same with *Be*.
- Next, just as presented in the text, write first the short answer(s) for *yes* and *no*, and then long answers for each verb. For example:

Short Answers
Do / Does

Question: Does Bob play tennis?

Short Answers: Yes, he does.
No, he doesn't.

Long Answers: Yes, he plays tennis.
No, he doesn't play tennis.

Be

Question: Is Jill angry?

Short Answers: Yes, she is.
No, she isn't.

Long Answers: Yes, she is angry.
No, she isn't angry.

- Replicate the above on the board with student-generated verbs.
- Draw students' attention to the note on contractions below the chart.
- Explain that in many cases, using only a short answer can seem somewhat abrupt in a conversation. What is more typical is for a short answer to then be followed by more detailed information.

❏ EXERCISE 32. Looking at grammar.
Page 20
Time: 10 minutes

You may want to have students work in pairs, with one student taking the part of A and one of B.

Encourage students to try to not only read the answer (as a cloze) in the book, but also, if possible, to listen to the question and respond based on the initial *Yes* or *No*.

Optional Vocabulary
mood
grumpy
table tennis

❏ EXERCISE 33. Listening. Page 21
Time: 10–15 minutes

- Explain that the way we write **do/does** + subject *pronouns* often differs from the way we say these combinations.
- Explain that the way we usually say such combinations in real, everyday speech is called "reduced pronunciation."
- Write this term on the board.

Part I
- Read the examples for the students so that they can hear and identify the corresponding sentences.
- Answer any questions that may come up.

Part II
- Play the audio through once without stopping.
- Then play again and stop after each item.
- Model correct reduced pronunciation while correcting each question.
- Write particularly challenging items on the board.

Optional Vocabulary

pain	appointment
cough	waiting room
sore throat	

Expansion: Students may enjoy reenacting the questions above but perhaps using a different setting or ailment. With your class, rewrite the questions using a dentist's office or a different problem brought to the attention of a doctor. You can begin this by changing the first sentence to *Do you have pain in your mouth?* From there, have students brainstorm all related questions and act them out if inclined.

❏ EXERCISE 34. Let's talk: interview.
Page 22
Time: 10–15 minutes

> Make sure you have read through this exercise and are knowledgeable of content beforehand. You may want to review/pre-teach the Optional Vocabulary first.

- You can assign one question to each student or a number of students depending on the size and dynamics of your class.
- Tell students to prepare their question and then ask it rather than read it.
- Instruct students to collect information in response to the question for later reporting to the class.
- Circulate and assist students, taking notes on errors that you overhear for later review.
- Ask students what all these verbs have in common.
- Review the exercise by choosing one student to ask and respond to each question.

Optional Vocabulary

revolve	the wild
planets	mosquitoes
whales	carry
lay	malaria
gorillas	

❏ EXERCISE 37. Reading, grammar, and listening. Page 24
Time: 15 minutes

Optional Vocabulary

aerobic exercise	oxygen
increases	lively
heart rate	type
beats	

❏ EXERCISE 38. Check your knowledge.
Page 25
Time: 10–15 minutes

- Have students complete this as seatwork first while you walk around the classroom, making yourself available to students and encouraging them.
- Have students read corrected sentences aloud in turn so students can all correct their own.
- Ask students to also explain what is wrong and how, mechanically, they "fixed" the sentence. Doing so gives students a chance to speak spontaneously and firm up their own understanding of the target grammar.

Optional Vocabulary

brand new	considerate
aunt	nephew
favorite	head back
elderly	

Expansion: For homework, have students write a simple story or description that incorporates both simple present and present progressive. Direct them to include mistakes in verbs so that their classmates can correct them. Students can exchange work at the next class meeting and correct one another's intentional errors as well as unintentional ones. Use these descriptions to complete the above steps and the creative error correction as a summary of the entire chapter.

Chapter 2
Past Time

CHAPTER SUMMARY

OBJECTIVE: In this chapter students learn to use the simple past and past progressive. They learn to associate the simple past with actions that were completed at a specific time before the present, and the past progressive with actions that co-occurred with other actions at some time before the present.

APPROACH: It is helpful to highlight the fact that most of the talking students do in English is in the past tense. Most of the time, people are describing actions that others were not there to witness. By considering why past tenses are necessary and learning how to think about and use "time clauses," students reinforce their understanding of past time and become more adept at using past tenses. The chapter also focuses on irregular verb forms and spellings that arise in the simple and past progressive tenses. This approach greatly expands the learner's ability to express and understand fairly complex ideas in English.

TERMINOLOGY: The term "verb tense" is used more broadly here than in some other grammar books. Whereas some grammar books identify the progressive form as an "aspect," here this distinction is not made in order to keep terminology to a minimum. A "time clause" is a subordinate or adverbial clause that shows when an action took place. An irregular form of a verb is one that does not follow the common pattern of adding -ed to the simple form to signal the past form or past participle.

❑ **EXERCISE 1.** Warm-up. Page 26
Time: 3–5 minutes

- Write the three sentences on the board exactly as written in the book.
- Tell students that if none of the statements are true for them, they can make up their own.
- Write students' sentences on the board and/or write additional sentences that are true for you. For example:

    _____ I cooked dinner last night.
    _____ I watched television last night.

CHART 2-1. Expressing Past Time: The Simple Past. Page 26
Time: 15–20 minutes

> It is assumed that most students at this level are already familiar with the basic use and forms of the simple past (but still need a lot of practice and clarification). Learners often have trouble using *did* to form questions with regular simple past verbs, and, therefore, this part of the chart may require extra attention.

- Write the chart title on the board.
- Draw the verb tense time line on the board. For example:

<pre>
                       present
past_____|_____future
</pre>

- Using the examples presented and generated in the Warm-up, write simple past sentences on the board and mark them with an X on the time line. For example:

<pre>
                       present
past_____X_____|_____future
        I stayed up late last night.
        I slept well last night.
        I was tired this morning.
        I cooked dinner last night.
        I watched television yesterday.
</pre>

- Explain that these actions are in the simple past because they took place in the past and were completed in the past.
- Emphasize that the time for these actions is finished and, with students' help, underline the verb endings that show simple past and the past time words. For example:

<pre>
                       present
past_____X_____|_____future
</pre>
I stay<u>ed</u> up late <u>last night</u>.
I sle<u>pt</u> well <u>last night</u>.
I <u>was</u> tired <u>this morning</u>.
I coo<u>ked</u> dinner <u>last night</u>.
I watc<u>hed</u> television <u>yesterday</u>.

- Read through (a)–(h) in Chart 2-1 with students. Ask different students to read sample sentences aloud.
- Ask students how to make a yes/no question from a simple present verb. If this isn't immediately available to someone in the class, begin to write a simple present sentence on the board. For example:

    I stay up late.

- Remind students that they looked at this in the previous chapter and lead them through the question form of the example above.

    <u>Do</u> you stay up late? Yes, I <u>do</u>.

- Explain that just as they use the auxiliary *do / does* to make a question with a simple present verb, they use the past of *do / does* to make a question for the past tense.
- Write the following sentence on the board:

    I stayed up late.

- Write the *Did* to begin the question form and have students give you the remainder of the sentence:

  Did you stay up late?

- Ask students for possible short answers to this question and write those on the board:

  Yes, I did.

  No, I didn't.

- Read through the related section of the chart (Forms of the Simple Past: Regular Verbs) with students.
- Tell students you will focus on the simple past of *be* and refer to the third sentence in the group above: *I was tired this morning.*
- Ask students to contribute other sentences using *be* to describe their condition in the past few days.
- Write their sentences on the board. For example:

  I was hungry last night.

  You were worried about your mother yesterday.

  Juan was surprised by the snowstorm.

  Martha and Xiao-Ming were excited about the party last weekend.

- Refer students to the final part of Chart 2-1: Forms of the Simple Past: *Be.*
- Ask students to make questions and short answers for the above simple past sentences. Write their questions and answers on the board beneath the original statements. For example:

  I was hungry last night.

  > *Were you hungry last night?*

  > *Yes, I was. / No, I wasn't.*

  You were worried about your mother yesterday.

  > *Were you worried about your mother yesterday?*

  > *Yes, I was./ No, I wasn't.*

❏ **EXERCISE 2.** Looking at grammar.
Page 27
Time: 5–10 minutes

> This exercise helps students gain the habit of learning a tense first in the affirmative and then immediately learning the negative and question forms as well. This methodical presentation and reinforcement will give students a strong base as they learn more complex tenses.

- Give students time to complete the activity individually.
- Ask for volunteers to write each verb, its negative form, and question form on the board.
- As a class, correct the answers on the board.

❏ **EXERCISE 3.** Let's talk. Page 27
Time: 5–10 minutes

- Ask one student to read the example sentence aloud.
- Read the two sample answers aloud. Exaggerate the correct intonation for *didn't* as this contraction is sometimes hard for students to both pronounce and distinguish.

- Continue by asking individual students to read initial sentences aloud and make the two statements.
- To give more students a chance to practice, write the following sentences on the board, and work as a class.

  7. *Most students traveled here on submarines.*

  8. *All doctors studied law.*

  9. *Albert Einstein lived in the 1600s.*

  10. *Michael Jackson was a famous scientist.*

  11. *Rome was built in a day.*

  12. *Dinosaurs existed in the 1950s.*

Optional Vocabulary

accurate (from directions)	popular
invented	submarines
hot-air balloon	existed
movie director	

❏ **EXERCISE 4.** Listening. Page 27
Time: 5–10 minutes

> It is important to prepare students for listening exercises by reading the directions aloud and reviewing the completed example with them. Because students receive less input with an audio recording (an audio does not have facial expressions, and students can't lip-read it), students can become lost even if the exercise at hand is very simple.

❏ **EXERCISE 5.** Listening. Page 28
Time: 5–10 minutes

- After reading the notes on distinguishing *was/wasn't* and *were/weren't* aloud, have students pronounce both correctly so that the final *"t"* is audible.
- Now pronounce *wasn't/weren't* in a reduced fashion, without saying the *"t"* clearly.
- Have students repeat the reduced pronunciation of both contractions. Write on the board *wasn/weren*, pointing to them when they are said.

Part I
- For extra practice, pause the audio after each example and have students repeat these aloud.

Part II
- Ask a student to read the directions aloud, correcting his/her pronunciation.
- Confirm that students understand the task by asking them what words they will circle.
- Preview *wedding, nervous, excited ceremony,* and *reception.*

Even though students may not be able to explain the spelling rules, many will be able to apply them in this Warm-up. Encourage students to try different spellings to see if they look familiar or appear to make sense. Take this (and every opportunity) to remind students of what has previously been studied. Encourage students to tell you as much about what they know of English grammar (and, in this case Chapter 1) as possible.

Part I
• Ask students when they use the *-ing* form. They should be able to give you examples or key words (i.e., *right now*) even if they can't come up with the term *present progressive*.
• Write *Present Progressive* on the board and then write the four possibilities for adding *-ing* beneath it.

Part II
• Ask students the name of the tense that is formed with *-ed* and write *Simple Past* above the four possibilities for adding *-ed*.
• Review the answers to both parts as a class.

CHART 2-2. Spelling of *-ing* and *-ed* Forms.
Page 29
Time: 10–15 minutes

Students will need assistance understanding this chart. You should ensure students understand what consonants, vowels, and syllables are before referring to these terms.

Be prepared to demonstrate the rules on the board and relate them to the examples in the text. Suggestions for additional examples include

(a) *use, phone* (b) *count, turn* (c) *join, shout, need* (d) *drop, grab* (e) *open, order* (f) *refer, permit* (g) *stay, annoy* (h) *marry, pity* (i) *lie.*

Two-syllable verbs that end in *-l* (*control, cancel, travel*) are not included in this chart. However, *control* follows rule (f): The second syllable is stressed, the consonant is doubled: *controlled, controlling. Cancel* and *travel* follow rule (e) in American English: The first syllable is stressed, so the consonant is not doubled: *canceled, canceling, traveled, traveling.* Note that the *-l* is doubled in British spelling: *cancelled, cancelling, travelled, travelling.* Another similar spelling variation is *worshiped, worshiping* in American English and *worshipped, worshipping* in British English. You can tell students that they are correct whether they double the consonant or not in these particular words. Students can always consult a dictionary when in doubt.

• Write the chart heading on the board.
• With students' books closed, continue from the Warm-up by drawing Chart 2-2 on the board and labeling each column accordingly.
• Elicit a verb ending in *-e* from students and use this to complete the chart below.

End of Verb	Double the Consonant	Simple	-ing	-ed
-e	NO	smile	smiling	smiled

• Continue through the chart by eliciting more verbs of the various ending types until you have completed it and covered each verb ending presented on the left.
• After the entire Chart 2-2 has been replicated on the board with verbs given by students, erase the simple, *-ing* and *-ed* forms and complete the chart again using new verbs.
• As you review the chart with a second set of verbs, have students read the notes included to the right of the chart aloud and discuss them as a class.

CHART 2-3. The Principal Parts of a Verb.
Page 31
Time: 10–15 minutes

The "simple form" is also frequently called the "base form" or "infinitive form."

Point out that the present participle is always regular, even when the verb in question is irregular. This form is always the simple form + *-ing.* Refer to Chart 2-2 for spelling rules.

Highlight the variations in patterns of irregular verbs in the simple form, simple past, and past participle. Students should know that the following patterns all exist:

All three parts of the verb may be different (see, saw, seen).
Two parts may be the same (make, made, made).
All three parts may be the same (put, put, put).

Students may question why *see*, which is presented as a non-action verb in Chapter 1, also has a present participle *-ing* form. Explain that *see* has more than one meaning. When it means *visit* or *consult*, it can be used in the progressive, i.e., *Bob is seeing his doctor this afternoon.* You can also mention that the *-ing* form has another use, as a gerund, but there is no need to go into a lengthy explanation of gerunds at this point.

• Write the heading *Regular Verbs* on the board and write the four columns beneath this:

Simple Form   Simple Past   Past Participle   Present Participle

• Complete the chart with the help of students using first the verbs listed in the book. Write each form in the appropriate column.
• Using other regular verbs, expand on the chart and give students an opportunity to add to the chart.
• Suggestions for other regular verbs to use include: *need, look, cook, kiss,* and *want.*

CHART 2-4. Common Irregular Verbs.
Page 32
Time: 10–15 minutes

Students can feel overwhelmed when they look through Chart 2-4 and see the number of irregular verbs. There are over 250 irregular verbs in English, and many of these are high frequency. Chart 2-4 contains 100 common irregular verbs. (For a longer list that also includes less frequently used irregular verbs, consult *Understanding and Using English Grammar*.)

Students and teachers often wonder whether memorizing this list is helpful. The text provides ample practice opportunities, but it does seem beneficial to most EFL/ESL students to simply know these forms by memory. Most educated speakers of English can recite the principal parts of most irregular verbs (though many may stumble on some of the more troublesome or easily confused ones).

Students at this level will already know many of the more common irregular verbs. It could be profitable for students to memorize a few of the new ones every day. And of course, practice is essential. Verbs used less often than others naturally come less readily to mind. (For example, most native speakers would not readily recall all verb parts for irregular verbs such as *slay*, *forebear*, and *stride* because these verbs are relatively uncommon.)

You might want to take a few minutes in each class to conduct a quick drill; say the simple form and have the class say the other forms from memory, developing a kind of quick, rhythmic chant. Choose new verbs each day and include a few that were difficult in earlier days. Answer questions about meaning as necessary, and give students sample sentences to solidify their memories of these verbs.

The irregular verb emphasis in this chapter is on the simple past form. In memory work, the students should start learning the past participles, too, even though they won't need to use them until Chapter 4, where particular exercises help students learn and practice them.

Burnt and *dreamt* are principally British English but also occur in American English and are included in the chart. Some other verbs (not included in the chart) that are regular in American English but have variant spellings with *-t* in British English are *leant*, *leapt*, *learnt*, *spelt*, *spilt*, and *spoilt*.

• Write the heading *Irregular Verbs* and write the four columns (one for each verb part) beneath it. These headings are: Simple Form, Simple Past, Past Participle and Present Participle.
• Present some of the irregular verbs included in the chart by writing each verb part in its appropriate column.
• Draw students' attention to the fact that among irregular verbs, there are irregular verb patterns. Tell students that these patterns will become more familiar to them as they use them.
• Use any unfamiliar irregular verbs in sentences and write these on the board to illustrate meaning to students.

Optional Vocabulary
Students will be familiar with most irregular verbs' meanings, but you may want to go over the meanings of some, including the following:

beat   shave
blow   spread
prove

❑ EXERCISE 12. Let's talk: pairwork.
Page 35
Time: 10–15 minutes

• Put students into pairs and have them close their books.
• Explain that they both will be asking and answering questions.
• Read the situation aloud to the class and then have one person in each pair open their book.
• Circulate and assist those pairs who seem reluctant.
• After each partner has had a turn, you can ask two students to reenact the questions and the rest of the class can help supply alternative and more imaginative answers.

Optional Vocabulary
imagine   emergency room
slipped   exhausted
cast   waiting room

Expansion: Create a pack of index cards with additional scenarios on each card. Each should have a title and then two sets of questions, one on either side. Use the cards for additional practice with alternative scenarios. For example:

A Black Eye
Did you get in a fight?
Did you run into a door?
Did your eye swell?
Did you put ice on it?
Did you have a headache?
Did you try to cover it up?

A Winning Lottery Ticket
Did you buy a ticket?
Did you choose the right number?
Did you realize you won?
Did you believe you won?
Did you call your friends?
Did you buy yourself a treat?
Did you celebrate?
Did you feel lucky?

A Broken Heart
Did you fall in love?
Did you tell all your friends?
Did you imagine the future?
Did you have a favorite song?
Did you cry?
Did you become angry?
Did you feel sad for a few weeks?
Did you feel better?

❏ EXERCISE 14. Looking at grammar.
Page 35
Time: 10–15 minutes

Optional Vocabulary

whirlwind	sluggish
energetic	lazy
typical	elderly

❏ EXERCISE 15. Let's talk: pairwork.
Page 36
Time: 10–15 minutes

The goal is for the performance of the action to prompt immediate and spontaneous production of the target structure. Encourage students to respond in a relaxed, fluent manner, taking risks and not worrying about making mistakes. Mistakes in language learning are natural and normal, and should be viewed only as opportunities for learning.

In terms of keeping the pace lively, this exercise works best if teacher-led. Pair or group work, however, allows students more opportunity for interactive speaking and listening practice.

Expansion: Write the term *Nonverbal Communication* on the board and ask students what it means. With students' input, write a working definition of the phrase on the board: For example:

Nonverbal Communication is behavior that does not include spoken or written words that communicates meaning. Gestures are a type of nonverbal communication.

Write the following gesture phrases on the board and demonstrate them:

Tap your toes
Shrug your shoulders
Drum your fingers
Raise your right hand
Hold your nose
Point to your chest
Raise your eyebrows
Wink
Put your thumb up
Put your thumb down
Tap your watch
Nod
Shake your head
Clear your throat
Twiddle your thumbs
Ask someone to come closer (with index finger or hand)
Shoo someone or something away

Ask students how they indicate *yes/no, come here, go away* with their heads, hands, and bodies in their culture. Specifically, ask students to show the class the way they would express the meanings of the gestures nonverbally. Ask students if any of the above gestures would be considered rude in their countries (If you have a class with Asians and non-Asians, the non-Asians may be surprised that when indicating that someone should come closer, the hand is turned down toward the floor rather then upwards.)

❏ EXERCISE 18. Looking at grammar.
Page 38
Time: 10–15 minutes

This exercise can be done individually, in pairs, small groups, or as a class. Regardless, be sure to have various students write the revised version of the paragraph on the board so that you can review and correct as a class.

❏ EXERCISE 19. Listening. Page 38
Time: 10–15 minutes

Part I
- Ask various students the preview questions.
- Write the heading *Symptoms* on the board and make a list of the symptoms students describe in their answers.
- Help students generate a list of unrelated symptoms as a way of engaging them in the listening and expanding their active vocabulary. Some possible symptoms might include:

headache	stomachache
ear ache	fever
nausea	upset stomach
cough	sore throat
runny nose	congestion
swollen glands	tiredness
itchy eyes	sneezing

- Tell students to close their books.
- Play the audio through once without stopping.

Part II
- Tell students to open their books and answer the three True/False questions. Let them know you will review these answers after Part III.

Part III
- Play the audio again and have students write the words they hear. Replay again if necessary.
- Now that students have heard the audio multiple times, correct the answers for Parts II and III as a class.

Optional Vocabulary
worldwide
victims

CHART 2-5. Regular Verbs: Pronunciation of -ed Endings. Page 39
Time: 10–15 minutes

> Learning the pronunciation of -ed endings for regular verbs in simple past tense will give students confidence and can help them chip away at their own fossilized errors.
>
> Emphasize the logic of these simple past pronunciation practices and encourage students to test incorrect pronunciations for themselves. Encourage students to try to omit the pronunciation of -ed after a verb ending in t or d. They will find it impossible to do so. The goal is to get students feeling confident in their ability to pronounce simple past verbs accurately in every day speech.
>
> To that end, the chart includes the phonetic spellings of the verb endings. Students should not worry that they don't know the phonetic alphabet endings but rather, should know that these symbols are included as extra support. What matters is that students can put the pronunciation of regular past verbs into practice.

• Draw three columns and write the type of verb at the top of each column. For example:

End in Voiceless	*End in Voiced*	*End in /d/ or /t/*
-ed pronounced /t/	-ed pronounced /d/	-ed pronounced /əd/; add syllable

• Using the verbs included in the chart, carefully model the correct pronunciation of voiceless and voiced endings.
• Explain to students that they need to be able to hear and distinguish voiceless and voiced endings.
• Instruct students to repeat after you and then write the verb under the appropriate heading. For example:

End in Voiceless	*End in Voiced*	*End in /d/ or /t/*
-ed pronounced /t/	-ed pronounced /d/	-ed pronounced /əd/; add syllable
talked	called	waited
stopped	rained	needed
hissed	lived	skated
watched	robbed	greeted
washed	stayed	added

• Note that additional verbs ending in /d/ and /t/ have been included.

Expansion: Put students in pairs or small groups. Now that the chart on the board is complete, challenge teams to come up with sentences containing one verb from each column (in simple past, of course). Tell students they can put the verbs in any order they like. The sentence that seems most realistic will "win".

Ask teams to write their sentences on the board. As a class, make sure the sentences are correct. Then vote on the best one. For example:

Andre called his mother, waited for her to come to the phone and then talked for several hours.

It rained and then stopped, but the flowers needed it.

❏ **EXERCISE 22.** Listening. Page 40
Time: 5 minutes

• Introduce the exercise by reviewing time words.
• Write three columns on the board (*Simple Present, Present Progressive, Simple Past*).
• Ask students what time words they are likely to hear with each tense.
• As students give you time words, write these words beneath the appropriate heading. For example:

Simple Present	*Present Progressive*	*Simple Past*
every day	right now	yesterday

❏ **EXERCISE 23.** Listening and pronunciation. Page 40
Time: 5 minutes

• Write the three -ed endings on the board and assign them numbers:

  1. /t/ 2. /d/ 3. /əd/

• Play the audio through once without stopping.
• Play it again and pause after each item.
• Check answers by asking individual students to pronounce the word and then identify the ending. For example:

  Tania: "Cooked. That's #1, /t/."

CHART 2-6. Simple Past and Past Progressive. Page 42
Time: 15–20 minutes

> It is critical that students understand that the action of past progressive, like present progressive, was in progress at a particular moment in time. One way to emphasize this is by relating the past progressive to the present progressive, which students are already familiar with. If your class meets at the same time every day, you can provide examples that make this similarity very clear. For example, you can say and write:
>
> *It is 10:45 A.M. I am teaching grammar class right now.*
>
> *Yesterday at 10:45 A.M. I _____ teaching grammar class.*
>
> The distinction between *when* and *while* is not always as clear as the chart indicates. In fact, sometimes *when* can be used in place of *while,* and this occurs frequently in every day speech. For example, both of the following sentences are acceptable:
>
> *While I was living in Nepal, I ate rice every day.*
>
> *When I was living in Nepal, I ate rice every day.*
>
> However, making a sharp distinction between *when* and *while* can help students learn the differences in meaning between simple past and past progressive. At this level, students often find concrete practices and rules more helpful than being exposed to all possible meanings. The text uses *when* as a cue for the simple past in an adverb clause and *while* is a cue for the past progressive in an adverb clause.

- On the left hand side of the board, write *Simple Past* and draw the simple past time line.
- As you begin to draw it, ask students where to put the past tense and engage them in the review of simple past as much as possible.
- Ask students for a simple past sentence and write it on the board under the X. For example:

                              present
past_____X_____|_____future
*Evie wash*ed *her hair last night.*

- On the right hand side of the board, write *Past Progressive*.
- Explain to students that we use past progressive to show an action that was in progress at a particular point in the past.
- Draw another time line. Write a ? on the time line and label it *9:30 last night.*

                          present
past_____?_____|_____future
      9:30 last night

- Ask students what they were doing at 9:30 P.M. last night.
- Write just the *-ing* phrases of their answers on the board, For example:

  sleeping

  doing homework

  talking to my boyfriend

- Explain that just like with present progressive, they will use a part of the verb *be* + *-ing* to form past progressive.
- Remind students that also just like present progressive, the activity lasted longer than one precise moment during its duration.
- Now illustrate past duration by drawing an arrow on the time line. For example:

                          present
past——————→?_____|_____future
      9:30 last night

- Write complete past progressive sentences beneath the time line.
- Underline the past form of the verb *be*, the *-ing* ending, and the specific time.

  Luis was *sleep*ing *at 9:30 last night.*

  Mei-Wei and Rolf were *do*ing *their homework at 9:30 last night.*

  Lara was *talk*ing *to her boyfriend at 9:30 last night.*

- Write *Forms of the Past Progressive* on the board.
- Ask the class to pick one of the sentences on the board.

- Together, transform the past progressive into a negative statement, question, and short answer exchange. For example:

	Forms of the Past Progressive
Statement	*Luis was sleeping at 9:30 last night.*
Negative	*Luis wasn't sleeping at 9:30 last night.*
Question	*Was Luis sleeping at 9:30 last night?*
Short Answer	*Yes, he was. (Yes, he was sleeping at 9:30 last night.)*

- Review the chart and ask students to read various parts of the chart aloud.
- Explain that *when* is used with simple past and shows that an action happened at one specific time in the past.
- Give students an example of *when* + simple past and write this on the board. For example:

  I hurt my shoulder **when** *I fell.*

- Tell students that falling takes very little time and that therefore, this particular action did not have significant duration.
- Explain that *while* is used to show duration over time in the past and is used with past progressive.
- Tell students that because *while* shows duration, it should be used with verbs that do not take place instantaneously, but rather with verbs that take time. For example:

  The movie started while I was speaking on the phone.

- Summarize the above by writing clear and simple notes that remain on the board throughout the next exercise. For example:

  When: with simple past, meaning "at that time", short

  While: with past progressive, meaning "during that time", over time

❑ **EXERCISE 26.** Looking at grammar.
Page 43
Time: 10–15 minutes

❏ EXERCISE 27. Looking at grammar.
Page 44
Time: 10–15 minutes

- Tell students that it is extremely helpful for them to think about how long certain activities last in real life.
- On the board write the three verb phrases found under *Activity in Progress* in the exercise.
- Ask students how long each of those activities typically takes. Tell them that of course there will be a range of times but that you just want to see what they think.
- Ask questions and make appropriate comments ("*If it takes 15 minutes in the elevator, it must be a tall building.*")
- Write the durations for each underneath the appropriate heading. For example:

    Sitting in a café
    30 minutes–2 hours

    Standing in an elevator
    1–10 minutes

    Swimming in the ocean
    10 minutes–1 hour

- The point of the above is to get students to picture the actual activities and imagine their duration in terms of real time, so emphasize this. Students should realize and appreciate that the Activities in Progress naturally take more time than do the corresponding actions of Beth, David and Lily, which happened at one moment in the past, while the activity was in progress.
- Have a student or students read the actions taken by Beth, David and Lily and ask them how long these actions usually take.
- Lead students toward the realization that the actions taken by each can be very, very brief in duration. For example, it takes a split second to drop coffee on your lap. Act out the brevity of these actions for emphasis.
- Ask students to complete the exercise and review as a class.

❏ EXERCISE 28. Let's talk. Page 45
Time: 10 minutes

This exercise requires modeling and explanation. You need to get two students doing two things at the same time. One has to begin an activity and continue it as the other begins and ends an activity. When both finish, other students describe these activities using the simple past and the past progressive.

Spend ample time modeling the task with the first pair (Students A, B) so that students know exactly what to expect. Remind the other students (C, D) to describe the actions using the appropriate tenses.

❏ EXERCISE 29. Looking at grammar.
Page 45
Time: 10 minutes

The focus here should be on students' ability to distinguish which action was in progress (past progressive) and which action interrupted that progress (simple past). Students benefit from using all the resources available to them when making this distinction. Therefore, encourage students to think critically about which action usually takes more time.

Be prepared to draw time lines for both past progressive and simple past. You can emphasize the duration of the activity in progress by highlighting the continuous time in the past on the time line. You can emphasize the brevity of the interruption (and need for it to be in simple past) by marking the X dramatically at just one point in the past on the time line. Take the time to illustrate any examples that were troublesome in this way.

❏ EXERCISE 30. Reading. Page 46
Time: 10–15 minutes

This reading can be an appropriate whole-group exercise. You can give each student a sentence or question to read aloud. As they read, you can correct pronunciation and intonation, and discuss vocabulary. You can then correct as a class.

See the Teaching Suggestions at the front of this book for additional suggestions for Reading Activities.

Optional Vocabulary

made the call	stared
communications company	wondered
placed the call	behavior

❏ EXERCISE 32. Looking at grammar.
Page 47
Time: 5–10 minutes

- Have students read the exercise independently then underline verbs as instructed.
- Ask students to tell you what they know about the present progressive tense and write this on the board, under a heading.
- Now ask students what they now know about past progressive and include their comments in a second column. For example:

Present Progressive	*Past Progressive*
formed with be *and* -ing	*formed with past of* be *and* -ing
describes something happening at one time (right now)	*describes something that was happening at one time in the past*
shows action that is in progress	*shows action that was in progress*

- Discuss the exercise by drawing attention to verb tenses and time words.

Optional Vocabulary

traveling	Web site
interrupted	announcer
describing	damage

❏ EXERCISE 33. Looking at grammar.
Page 47
Time: 10–15 minutes

> The principal purpose of this practice is for students to see the relationships between present and past verbs. Part I is told from a present-time perspective; the students are given a present-time setting and a dialogue. Part II reports the same events from a past perspective. See the Teaching Suggestions at the front of this book for various ways of handling fill-in-the-blank exercises.

Optional Vocabulary

stare	offer
skateboarder	basics
amazing	

CHART 2-7. Expressing Past Time: Using Time Clauses. Page 48
Time: 10–20 minutes

> Most students at this level have already been understanding and producing time clauses successfully without knowing what these structures are called. Point this out to students and let them know that much of what is presented in this chart they <u>already</u> know (but may not realize they know).
>
> Point out that a time clause is not a complete sentence. It cannot stand alone. It must be connected to a main clause. *I made dinner* is a complete sentence but *Before you arrived* is not. Show students that time clauses such as *Before you arrived* even seem like incomplete ideas. If students hear only *Before you arrived,* they will automatically be waiting for the main clause.
>
> Make sure to emphasize that there is no difference in meaning between examples (a) and (b). Discuss punctuation and tell students that if you begin a sentence with a time clause, you put a comma before the main clause.
>
> In speaking, the voice drops low at the end of a sentence, but it tends to drop a little and then rise a little at the end of a time clause, before a main clause. This intonation also signals that the time clause is not a complete sentence. You might want to demonstrate this for students and help them reproduce this throughout the next few exercises.
>
> *When, after, before, until, as soon as,* and *while* are subordinating conjunctions, but the text does not use

that terminology. They can simply be called "words that introduce time clauses" or "time clause words."

After, before, and *until* are also used as prepositions, so they do not always introduce a time clause; they may be followed by a (pro)noun object rather than a subject and verb:

> I walked home **after class**.
> I will call you **before dinner**.
> We stayed there **until six o'clock**.

The other conjunctions in this chart (*as soon as, while,* and *when*) are not used as prepositions.

Most students could benefit from your discussing additional examples with *as soon as* and *until*. Develop examples from the classroom context if possible or take them from students' lives. For example (after students perform these actions):

> Maria raised her hand as soon as Po raised his.
> Maria didn't raise her hand until Po raised his.
> Maria didn't sit down until Anna sat down.
> Maria sat down as soon as Anna sat down.

- Ask students if they can define the term *clause.* Inform them that even if they cannot, you are sure they can recognize clauses in practice.
- Write the term *Clause* on the board. Explain that there are many types of clauses in English, but today they'll be studying two types.
- Beneath the term *Clause,* write:
  > Must have subject and verb
- Write:
  > Main Clause: "I made dinner."
- Write:
  > Time Clause: "Before you came home . . .
- Have students identify the subject and verb in each of the above clauses.
- Write under *Main Clause:*
  > - Can stand alone
  > - A complete sentence
  > - Not waiting for other information
- Explain that when they hear *I made dinner,* they are not automatically waiting for more information.
- Write under *Time Clause:*
  > - Can NOT stand alone
  > - NOT a complete sentence
  > - Waiting for more information
- Explain that when they hear *Before you came home,* they should be waiting for more information.
- Read through the chart with students and have them take turns reading sentences (a)–(j) aloud.
- Discuss the notes next to each example sentence (a)–(l) and provide additional examples as necessary.
- Be prepared to spend extra time on (e) and (f): *as soon as* and *until.*
- Write additional example sentences on the board for *as soon as* and *until* that you develop from the classroom context.

- Demonstrate that *until* is a negative version of *as soon as*.
- Write the following example sentence or an original one on the board.

    Xiao-ling answered the question <u>as soon as</u> Viola asked it.

- Ask students when Xiao-ling answered the question, eliciting the response that it was immediately after Viola asked it.
- Write the following example sentence on the board or come up with one of your own.

    Xiao-ling <u>didn't</u> answer the question <u>until</u> Viola asked it.

- Ask students when Xiao-ling answered and elicit the response that she had been quiet before Viola asked the question. Emphasize that Xiao-ling only chose to answer after Viola asked her question.

❏ EXERCISE 35. Looking at grammar.
Page 49
Time: 5–10 minutes

- Write the word *Clause* on the board and ask students to remind you again what elements every clause must have.
- Write these elements under *Clause*.
- Tell students that in this exercise, they should put a checkmark (✓) next to each clause they see.
- Tell them that what is not a clause can be considered a phrase.
- Correct the exercise as a class, having students read aloud and explain their answers whenever possible.
- Since many or even all of your students may have had to apply for a visa, use this topic as a discussion starter.

Optional Vocabulary
applying for a visa
passport photos
application

❏ EXERCISE 37. Looking at grammar.
Page 49
Time: 5–10 minutes

This is an exercise on complex structure and punctuation. It is intended to provide further examples for discussion of the grammar in Chart 2-10. It can be done as seatwork leading to boardwork.

❏ EXERCISE 38. Looking at grammar.
Page 50
Time: 10–15 minutes

This exercise can be completed orally or in writing. If you lead it orally, you may want to ask students to take turns reading aloud. If students complete this in writing, ask them to identify the time clauses when correcting as a group.

Optional Vocabulary
gift	change the oil
yard	hammer
plant	hurricane

❏ EXERCISE 40. Warm-up. Page 51
Time: 5–10 minutes

Part I
- Have students complete Part I independently and then ask them to think of other past habits related to when they first learned English.
- Explain that you want to also know other actions, thoughts, or even feelings they had as new students of English.
- Write any additional, student-generated statements on the board. For example:

    I blushed when I tried to start a conversation.
    I sometimes answered questions in my own language.
    I became frustrated.

- Include these statements as you work through Part I.

Optional Vocabulary
remained
frequently
translated

CHART 2-8. Expressing Past Habit: *Used To.*
Page 52
Time: 10–15 minutes

Explain to students that they can use simple past to describe past actions, but that *used to* has a special meaning. It expresses more than simply an action that happened in the past. In fact, you will need to point out that it is not used to replace simple past in general, but only when the simple past verb describes a past habit, state of mind, or condition of being.

The question and negative forms of *used to* (*did you used to* vs. *did you use to,* and *didn't used to* vs. *didn't use to*) appear to be an area of English grammar that is still being debated. Some references say one is correct but not the other (and they don't agree on which of the two forms is the correct one); other texts (especially dictionaries) say that both are correct. Given the lack of agreement, this text presents both forms as possible and correct.

Because of the idiomatic expression *be used to*, take care to explain *used to* as a special way of expressing the past and that it is different from the phrases *get used to* and *be used to*.

- Ask students to tell you something they used to do when they were children and write their sentences on the board in simple past.
- Explain that *used to* describes past habits, feelings, and conditions. Write this information on the board:

    Used To: past habits, feelings, conditions

- Write on the board how *used to* is formed:

    used to + base form

- As a class, transform the simple past sentences into ones using *used to*. For example:

  Abdul played soccer on a team. ⇒ Abdul <u>used to</u> play soccer on a team.

  Astrid hid from her parents. ⇒ Astrid <u>used to</u> hide from her parents.

  Kenji was afraid of teachers. ⇒ Kenji <u>used to</u> be afraid of teachers.

- Write the question and negative forms of the above sentences on the board. For example:

  Question: <u>Did</u> Abdul <u>used to</u> play soccer?
  Negative: Abdul <u>didn't used to</u> play soccer.

- Explain that *didn't use to* is rarely used as people usually use *never* to express this idea.

❏ EXERCISE 42. Interview: find someone who.... Page 53
Time: 10–15 minutes

Optional Vocabulary
roller skate
swing on a rope swing
catch frogs or snakes

❏ EXERCISE 45. Let's read and write.
Page 54
Time: 10–20 minutes

> This exercise is a cumulative review of all the charts in this chapter and requires students to recognize and produce the forms studied in Chapter 2. Explain to students that a variety of tenses will be used, and in some cases, more than one is appropriate. The second part of this exercise can be assigned for homework or completed in class. In either case, discuss who students will select and the ways in which tenses can be used to establish how past actions can be put in chronological order when narrating a personal history.

- See the Teaching Suggestions at the front of this book for additional ideas in dealing with written work.

Optional Vocabulary

naps	accepted
rejection letters	shortly
publishing company	publication

Chapter 3
Future Time

CHAPTER SUMMARY

OBJECTIVE: In this chapter students learn common spoken and written structures for future time. These future structures allow students to express plans, make predictions, and show willingness to do an action. The differences between future forms used for planning and those used to express spontaneous willingness are examined in detail. Students also practice expressing the future through adverb clauses of time and condition, while also reviewing present and past tense verb forms.

APPROACH: Becoming comfortable with expressing future time, explaining plans, and making predictions is important for meaningful communication in English. The tenses presented in this chapter are used often in the course of normal conversations about daily life.

English has no verb endings that signal future time. Future structures are formed by modal auxiliaries and periphrastic modals, and / or time expressions located elsewhere in the sentence.

The goal, as always, is to present and explain structures with a minimum of terminology and a focus on active recognition and production of the targeted structures. The hope is that students will leave their formal study of English one day with good control of its structures; most terminology can and probably will be soon forgotten.

TERMINOLOGY: Since there are various ways of expressing future time, this textbook generally just uses the phrase "expressing future time" instead of referring specifically to **will** + *simple form of the verb* as "future tense." For pedagogical ease and convenience, however, the traditional term "future tense" can be used in the classroom for verb phrases that include either *will* or *be going to*. The students' understanding of the term "tense" is generally a form of a verb that expresses the verb's relationship to time. Most students are comfortable with the term.

❏ **EXERCISE 1.** Warm-up. Page 55
Time: 3–5 minutes

You may not get as much information about sentences 1 and 3 as suggested below, and students may not be able to detect a subtle difference between sentences 1 and 3. However, because some students may be familiar with the difference, you can begin to introduce it now. What is presented below gives you a format to

follow on the board and a direction to go in as you introduce the chart.

Because students may not be able to articulate a subtle difference, you may need to explain that both *be going to* and *will* can be used to express future time. Tell students that in this chapter they will discuss instances when only one or the other can be used correctly, but that in the Warm-up, they are interchangeable.

- Write the three sentences on the board exactly as they appear in the book.
- Have students first identify which sentences express future time.
- Ask students whether sentences 1 and 3 are exactly the same. Ask students to decide which one seems "better" to them.
- Write students' comments on the board next to the sentences they refer to. For example:

   1. The train is going to leave a few minutes late today.
   It seems okay.
   It doesn't sound wrong.
   It sounds like the train is planning to leave late, but trains can't plan.
   2. The train left a few minutes late today.
   Past time
   3. The train will leave a few minutes late today.
   It seems more correct than sentence 1.
   It sounds like the speaker is sure the train will leave a few minutes late.
   It does not seem like a plan.

CHART 3-1. Expressing Future Time: *Be Going To* and *Will*. Page 55
Time: 15–20 minutes

Both *be going to* and *will* are included in this chart. They are often, but not always, interchangeable. The differences in meaning are presented in Chart 3-5.

The text emphasizes *be going to* first and relates it to present and past verbs. Then the text deals with *will*.

The use of *will* is sometimes called "the simple future tense," but, as noted above, *will* is actually one of several modals and periphrastic modals used to express future time. What you could point out here is that *be going to* and *will* are used to express that an event is, in the speaker's mind, 100% certain to occur in the future. This can be seen in the chart, in examples (a), (b), and (e). We can't, of course, always feel certain about future events and, for this reason, other auxiliaries (see Chapter 5) are also used frequently to express future time.

- Draw the time line as shown in the chart.
- Ask a few students what they *are going to* or *will* do after class.
- Using their responses, write complete sentences beneath the chart.
- Use both **be going to** + *simple form* and **will** + *simple form* to show that both structures can be used.
- Underline the target structures.
- Make an *X* on the right-hand side of the time line to show that these events will occur in the future. For example:

    _____|_X_____

    Firoz *is going to eat* lunch with his uncle.
    Firoz *will eat* lunch with his uncle.
    Emi *is going to write* her essay.
    Emi *will write* her essay.

- Explain that *be going to* and *will* can often be used interchangeably, particularly when the time for the future is close at hand (in this case, just after class).

CHART 3-2. Forms with *Be Going To.*
Page 56
Time: 10 minutes

Going to is sometimes pronounced /gɔnə/ or /gənə/, which — though not an accepted written form — may be presented in writing as *gonna*. Model *gonna* for your students so that they will be aware of it, but don't insist on its use by learners at this level. When learners force *gonna*, it may sound as though they are speaking careless, nonstandard English. The appropriate use of *gonna* will develop as the students gain experience with the language.

One common error is the omission of *be*:

INCORRECT: *I going to go to the market tomorrow.* (Or *I going to the market tomorrow,* in which the present progressive is used to express future time. See Chart 3-7).

Note: The different uses of *be going to* and *will* will be explained in Chart 3-5. At this point, if individual students want to address this difference, you can do so briefly, but Charts 3-2 and 3-3 focus on the ways in which these two future forms can be used interchangeably and that should be your emphasis here.

- Write the following question on the board:

    What are you going to do this weekend?

- Underneath this question, write the "formula" for the *be going to* future so students can see it as they tell you their plans. For example, write:

    Be Going To Future
    Subject + Be + Going To + Simple Form of Verb

- Underneath, create a sentence that is true for you and write actual words directly below the "formula" parts of speech. For example:

    Be Going To Future
    Subject + Be + Going To + Simple Form of Verb
    I am going to clean my house.

- Ask students to provide you with sentences describing what they are going to do. Write student-generated sentences on the board.
- Write some exactly as stated by the student, in the first person; write some in the second person as you are repeating a plan back to the student who said it; and write some with the student's name, in the third person. For example:

Be Going To Future

Subject	Be	Going To	Simple Form of Verb
I	*am*	*going to*	*clean my house.*
I	*am*	*going to*	*study all day Saturday.*
You	*are*	*going to*	*sleep late Saturday morning.*
But you	*are*	*going to*	*wake up early.*
Michel	*is*	*going to*	*call his girlfriend on Sunday.*
Pei-Ling and Jose	*are*	*going to*	*travel to Washington, D.C.*

- Remind students that as always, a new "formula" is needed for a question.
- Ask students how they make questions from statements and write the correct word order for the required parts of speech. For example:

    Questions:
    Be + Subject + Going To + Simple Form of Verb
    Are you   going to make a cake?

- With your students, make additional questions using *be going to* and include those on the board, following the pattern established above. For example:

Questions:

Be	Subject	Going To	Simple Form of Verb
Are	*you*	*going to*	*make a cake?*
Is	*Juan*	*going to*	*have a party?*
Are	*we*	*going to*	*watch a movie?*

- Now, ask students how to make negative statements. They should be able to tell you where to insert the *not*.
- Write this new formula on the board.

    Negatives:
    Subject + Be + Not + Going To + Simple Form of Verb

- Challenge students to transform the questions on the board into negative statements.
- Write these negative statements on the board.

- Again, write the appropriate word underneath the part of speech it matches. For example:

  Negatives:

Subject	+ Be	+ Not	+ Going To	+ Simple Form of Verb
You	are	not	going to	make a cake.
Juan	is	not	going to	have a party.
We	are	not	going to	watch a movie.

- Now, have students take turns reading through the examples (a)–(e) in the chart aloud.

❑ EXERCISE 4. Looking at grammar.
Page 57
Time: 10 minutes

This exercise is a quick check on the written forms of *be going to:* statement, negative, question, and short answer.

Optional Vocabulary

prescription	lecture
pharmacy	reduce
project	text

❑ EXERCISE 5. Let's talk: pairwork. Page 57
Time: 10 minutes

The purpose of this exercise is oral practice with typical conversational questions and answers about the future. Speaker B should be encouraged to answer truthfully, but some students enjoy using their imaginations and making up funny answers. This approach is also acceptable.

Students don't always immediately know how to do this task or how to manipulate these words, so take the time to make sure they understand the task. Modeling the examples with a student or students can help.

❑ EXERCISE 6. Listening. Page 58
Time: 10–15 minutes

You may want to introduce the context of the listening by asking students some general questions about apartment hunting. Since almost everyone has rented an apartment at some point in their lives, this should be an easy conversation to facilitate. Some possible questions include:

Do you live in an apartment or house?

Do you rent or own your place?

Did you go "apartment hunting" alone or with a friend?

What is it like to look for an apartment in your country?

Is it common for students to rent temporary housing together?

Do you have to pay a deposit when renting?

- Write key vocabulary on the board and keep it there during the listening. For example, write:

rent	search
area	cheaper
deposit	first and last month's rent
landlord	fees
application	credit check

- Complete Parts I and II and review as a class.

❑ EXERCISE 7. Let's talk: interview. Page 58
Time: 10–15 minutes

This is a straightforward review of the forms of the past, present, and future verbs: affirmative, negative, questions, and short answer. The sentences the students create can be silly and imaginative. This is an exercise on form; the emphasis is not on realistic dialogue. (It is helpful for students to concentrate principally on forms of structures at times; not everything they say needs to be "real communication.") After finishing the exercise, be sure to point out to students all the different forms they have mastered in this exercise.

For ease of use, you can enlarge the sample conversation and put it on an overhead projector so that students can have a ready visual. Or you can simply ask a student to write the sample on the board.

❑ EXERCISE 9. Warm-up. Page 59
Time: 5 minutes

- Write *will* and *won't* on the board.
- Have students complete the Warm-up.
- Ask individual students to take turns reading the completions.
- Ask individual students how they chose *will* or *won't* for each, focusing especially on sentences 1 and 2.
- Write their responses on the board. For example:

  Today the weather is good.

  I saw the weather report on TV.

- Ask students specific questions leading to the conclusion that they can't know 100% whether their answers for 1 are correct.
- Explain that based on the evidence they have (today's weather), their completions are reasonable.

CHART 3-3. Forms with *Will.* Page 60
Time: 10 minutes

You may want to model contractions with *will.* Include some examples of nouns and question words contracted with *will* in speech: *Tom'll be here soon. Where'll you be around eight o'clock tonight?* Mention that contractions are natural in conversations both formal and informal. In fact, fluent speakers of English find it impossible not to use them: speech without contractions sounds stilted or bookish.

After a consonant, the contraction *'ll* is pronounced as an additional syllable: /əl/. For example, *Bob'll* is pronounced like the word "bobble" or "bauble": /bab əl/.

The negative contraction *shan't* (*shall not*) occurs in British English but rarely in American English.

- Elicit from students the general formula for a sentence (S + V + O), and write it on the board.
- Explain that the modal auxiliary *will / won't* goes directly in front of the simple form of the verb.
- Explain that *will / won't* remains the same for every person / subject pronoun. For example:

  Will Future
  Statements:
  Subject + Will + Simple Form of Verb

- Using student information, write sample sentences on the board. For example:

  Statements:
  Subject + Will + Simple Form of Verb
  Bin-Su   will   finish his homework later.
  Maya and I   will   exercise at the gym tonight.

- Explain how to use the negative *won't* and write sentences made from student information on the board. For example:

  Negatives:
  Subject + Will Not / Won't + Simple Form of Verb
  Faisal   won't   attend class tomorrow.
  They   won't   come with us to the party.

- Ask students what changes in word order need to be made for the question form, eliciting the response that the subject and verb need to change places.
- Write the formula for questions on the board as well as examples using student information.

  Questions:
  Will + Subject + Simple Form of Verb
  Will   Megan   take swimming lessons?
  Will   Angela and Dong Su   watch a movie?

- Ask students to take turns reading through the chart.

❏ **EXERCISE 10.** Listening. Page 60
Time: 5–10 minutes

The sentences in this exercise are intended as models for everyday spoken English. In Part 1, ask the students to repeat after you. Point out to them that the *'ll* is not emphasized, and its sound is low and fast. It is hard to discern this sound unless you know it is supposed to be there by knowing the form, meaning, and use of *will*. One of the reasons learners study grammar is to enable them to understand normal, reduced, and contracted speech. If students know the form and use of *will*, they can understand that *dinner'll* is actually two verbs spoken as one rather than a new vocabulary word. They will also understand that *Dinner'll be ready soon* expresses future time. You

might point out that a common mistake in student production is a statement such as *Bye. I see you tomorrow.* Errors such as this arise because learners don't hear *'ll*, and they don't hear *'ll* because they haven't learned to expect it.

❏ **EXERCISE 11.** Listening. Page 61
Time: 5–10 minutes

Optional Vocabulary
prescription   generic
pharmacist   side effects
cough syrup

❏ **EXERCISE 12.** Warm-up. Page 61
Time: 5 minutes

Students may or may not have familiarity with the concept of certainty. Before discussing how to show gradations of certainty, emphasize that *will* and *be going to* are <u>only</u> for 100% certain future events.

CHART 3-4. Certainty About the Future.
Page 62
Time: 15–20 minutes

Will and *be going to* express that the speaker feels 100% certain about a future event and is completely confident that it will occur in the future. Even though we can never be absolutely sure about the future, *will* and *be going to* are used to express confidence in future events.

Because we don't always feel 100% certain about future events, it is important to be able to express degrees of certainty about the future activities and events. There are many ways to qualify statements about the future. Adding *probably* to *will* is one common way. Using *may* or *maybe* are other common ways. In Chapter 5, the students will learn other ways of qualifying their statements about the future by using other auxiliaries (*might, should, can,* etc.)

The figures of 100%, 90%, and 50% to indicate degrees of certainty are approximate and figurative; they are not intended to be nor should be interpreted as statistically exact (as some students will invariably want to do). However, using percentages does help students better understand certainty.

You may want to discuss with students how they can make reasonable, educated guesses about the future. Mention the fact that knowledge of previous behavior and actions can inform our ability to predict the future with some degree of accuracy.

- Ask students what they will do this weekend, and then ask them how certain they are that they will, in fact, do the action.
- Write the percentages next to the action, and then with students' help, look at the chart and choose an appropriate way (using *probably, may* or *maybe*) to modify the degree of certainty.
- With the students, create sentences for each action and write these on the board. For example:

  Sayeed eat dinner / with family / Saturday: 100%
  Sayeed will eat dinner with his family on Saturday.
  Tassos / go swimming: 90%
  Tassos will probably go swimming this weekend.
  Jin / finish all his homework / early: 50%
  Jin may finish all his homework early.
  Maybe Jin will finish all his homework early.

- Ask students to take turns reading sentences (a)–(e) from the chart aloud.
- Review the notes in the chart as you discuss its contents.

❏ EXERCISE 16. Let's talk: interview.
Page 63
Time: 10–15 minutes

Interviews can be carried out in many ways, most of which are also discussed in the introduction to this book. One way to keep students moving and interacting with many of their classmates is to arrange the students into rotating pairs. To do this, line students up facing one another. After students have spent three to five minutes speaking to the classmate directly across from them, instruct a student on one of the ends of the two lines to leave his / her spot and go to the beginning of the line, forcing everyone else to move down one spot, thus getting a new partner. You can also play background music while students are talking to one another. This creates a social atmosphere and allows students to know that their mistakes are only being heard by the person they are talking to, rather than by the whole class.

- Write the following cues on the board:

  will - 100%
  be going to - 100%
  probably - 90%
  may - 50%
  maybe - 50%

- Walk around the room as your students interact with one another.
- Ask questions that require students to produce brand new structures, and correct both target and non-target issues.

❏ EXERCISE 18. Reading, grammar, and speaking. Page 64
Time: 15–20 minutes

Students at this level benefit a great deal from sight reading aloud. Doing so gives them a chance to hear themselves tackle new words. Because you can correct them when they mispronounce words, students receive immediate feedback for their particular needs. If you ask just one or two students to take turns reading a passage such as "An Old Apartment" aloud, take frequent breaks and ask other students what various words mean. Even though your students may recognize all the vocabulary in the passage, they won't anticipate which words you will ask clarification of. In doing so, you can give them a chance to use their English spontaneously.

This exercise also provides a chance for a discussion of content and a comparison of cross-cultural norms. As you explore the reading with students, ask them whether people from their country prefer old buildings or modern ones. You can also discuss at what age young people from their countries move from their parents' homes to their own. Using the actual reading, find ways to engage students in a lively discussion of any related topics the passage lends itself to.

Part I
- Because Part III of this exercise asks students to discuss the most important things they want to have in their home, introduce the topic by asking them what their home is like: whether it is new or old, what they like about it, and what they don't like about it.
- Have students take turns reading parts of the passage aloud until it has been read through aloud completely.
- Gently interrupt the readers to ask the class as a whole to try to define certain vocabulary words (included in Optional Vocabulary below.)

Part II
- Ask a couple of students who didn't read aloud how they would describe Ted and Amy's current apartment.
- Work through the items as a class by asking different students to complete the items aloud.

Part III
- This part can be completed in small groups or individually for homework.
- If students complete this in class, put them in small groups.

Optional Vocabulary
run-down	drip
ceiling	flush
leaks	laundry facilities
faucets	laundromat

CHART 3-5. *Be Going To* vs. *Will*. Page 65
Time: 10–15 minutes

> The chart's purpose is to point out specifically and as simply as possible when *be going to* and *will* have clearly recognizable differences in their use. Remind students that there is often no difference in meaning between *will* and *be going to*.
>
> There are other differences between *will* and *be going to* and, in particular, other uses of *will* that the text does not address. As is true of most other modal auxiliaries, *will* is a complicated word with a variety of meaning and uses. The text does not view explanations of all the nuances in meaning and usage of *will* and *be going to* to be productive for ESL / EFL students, especially at this proficiency level. What the text intends is to build a basic understanding and usage ability of the two, laying groundwork for more sophisticated use of these structures as students gain experience with the language. It is helpful to remember that teaching grammar at this level is largely a matter of laying the groundwork for growth in the students' linguistic skills.

- Ask students about their future plans, what they plan to do tomorrow, this weekend, during their next vacation, etc. The question should generate examples of "prior plans."
- Write *Be Going To* on the left-hand side of the board. Beneath the heading write *used for prior plans* and then write examples of *be going to* sentences formed from students' responses. For example:

  Be Going To

  Used for prior plans

  Sergei is going to drive to Boston next week.

  My husband and I are going to travel to Paris in May.

  Kinako is going to study law in Tokyo.

- Now, on the right-hand side of the board, write *Will*.
- With a bit of flourish, and making sure you have your students' attention, drop the marker, an eraser, or this textbook, etc., on the floor.
- Ask a student to pick it up for you: *Samira, will you pick that book up for me?*
- She will say, *Yes.*
- Ask the class, *Should Samira say, "Yes, I am going to" or "Yes, I will"?*
- Most students will know that *will* is the correct form here, even if they are not sure why.
- Turn back to the board and write beneath *Will*:

  Will

  Shows spontaneous willingness—<u>not</u> a prior plan

  Speaker decides to do something at the moment of speaking

  Samira will pick up the book.

- Explain that the correct way for Samira to express her willingness to pick up your marker, eraser, textbook, etc., is to use *will*.
- Have students take turns reading the sentences (a)–(d) aloud.
- Elaborate on the notes to the right of the chart after each example sentence is read.

❏ EXERCISE 20. Looking at grammar.
Page 66
Time: 10–15 minutes

- Give students time to work through this exercise individually.
- Discuss each situation as a class. Ask students for any details from each situation that indicate a plan.
- Put any situations that prove particularly challenging on the board and look at those elements in detail. If it is a prior plan, point to actual evidence of this.
- Reiterate that the speaker decided to take an action at the moment of speaking in the *will* sentences.

❏ EXERCISE 24. Warm-up. Page 67
Time: 5 minutes

> Though this may be new grammar for some, most students at this level have been using subordinate clauses in some fashion. After completing the Warm-up, you may want to prepare students for the chart by having them look at the clauses.

- Give students time to complete the sentences individually.
- Go around the room asking various students to read their sentences aloud. Restate each response. For example:

  Reisa: *After I leave school, I'm going to visit my aunt.*

  You: *After Reisa leaves school, she's going to visit her aunt.*

- Ask students about the verb tenses, eliciting that the first verb they see is in simple present and the second verb is a future form.

Expansion: To remind students what a clause is, have students cover the main clause of each sentence and try reading the subordinate (time or *if*) clause aloud. You may need to identify this clause by its first word or instruct students to cover the part of the sentence after the comma. Ask students if the clause they have just read aloud sounds complete. Each subordinate clause should feel incomplete to them, and students should be able to imagine what the main clause would be. When students invariably say "no" that the clause does not feel complete, congratulate them on their understanding that some clauses cannot stand alone.

CHART 3-6. Expressing the Future in Time Clauses and *If*-Clauses. Page 68
Time: 15–20 minutes

> Students studied time clauses in Chapter 2. Asking them to form a few time clauses will remind them of this and will increase their confidence.
>
> Explain that the form of a verb in a time clause is simple present, but the meaning is future. Emphasize that *will* and *be going to* are not (generally) used in time clauses. Mistakes such as *before I will go to class*

tomorrow and *after I'm going to eat dinner* are very common.

There is a situation in which *will* is used in an *if*-clause. The text doesn't teach this use, but the question may arise. Sometimes when a person is making a deal or trying to reach an agreement, *will* is used in the *if*-clause. *If you'll make the sandwiches, I'll pour the drinks*. *Will* in an *if*-clause is close to the meaning of a polite question with *will*: *Will you make the sandwiches? If you do, I will pour the drinks. Is that agreeable to you?*

- Turn back to Chart 2-7 in the previous chapter. Remind students that they have studied time clauses with past tenses.
- Explain that when the main clause shows future tense, the time clause remains in the present but that the meaning is also future.
- Ask students to tell you actions they will take *before* they leave your class.
- Write their responses on the board. For example:

    Write down the homework for tomorrow

    Close my book

    Check my cell phone

    Say good-bye to our friends

    Say good-bye to my teacher

    Put my books in my backpack

    Pick up my jacket

- Write on the board: *Before I leave this class, _____.*
- Explicitly remind students that the time clause should be in simple present, but that the *will* or *be going to* future should be used in the main clause.
- Ask students to make sentences on their own. Write these on the board. For example:

    Before I leave this class, I will write down the homework for tomorrow.

    Before Felipe leaves this class, he will check his cell phone.

    Before Maria and I leave this class, we will say good-bye to our friends.

- Have students open their books and ask some to read (a)–(h) aloud.
- Provide additional examples and expand on the notes included in the right-hand side of the chart.
- Next, introduce *if*-clauses and explain that *if*-clauses follow the same grammar as time clauses above.
- Tell students that when the meaning is future, the simple present (not *will* or *be going to*) is used after *if*.
- Write on the board: *If I win $10 million, I _____.*
- Ask students to tell you what they will do if they win $10 million. For example:

    If I win $10 million, I will travel to Australia.

    If Po wins $10 million, he will buy his parents a house.

    If Jean and Annette win $10 million, they will pay for their children to go to an expensive university.

- Have a student read (i). Provide additional examples on the board if necessary.

❏ **EXERCISE 27.** Let's talk: pairwork.
Page 69
Time: 10 minutes

Expansion: Bring in index cards. Distribute to students. Have students write their partner's responses on each card. For example:

If he has some free time tomorrow, he'll play soccer with his roommate.

If it rains tomorrow, he won't go to the beach.

If it doesn't rain tomorrow, he will be in class on time and then he will go to the beach.

If the teacher is absent tomorrow, he will try to teach the class himself.

Collect the cards and read the sentences aloud. Ask students to guess who the person is based on the contents of the cards.

❏ **EXERCISE 28.** Looking at grammar.
Page 70
Time: 5–10 minutes

Expansion: Prepare sample day planners for people in well-known professions by writing notes on index cards. Students will use these to make and present sentences using *be going to*. The remainder of the class should guess what profession the student's day planner refers to. For example:

Movie Star

May 1, 2010

10:00 A.M. wake up

10:30 call agent

11:00 meet with personal assistant to go through schedule

11:30 pick up by chauffeur

12:00–1:00 meet make up artist and stylist

1:00–4:00 be on set

4:30 meet with personal trainer

6:00 return to mansion for swim in pool

7:00–9:00 nap

9:30 dress

10:00 eat light dinner

11:00–4:00 A.M. go to clubs

❏ **EXERCISE 29.** Reading, grammar, and writing. Page 70
Time: 10–20 minutes

Part I
- Introduce the topic of the passage by asking students what homes were like 50 years ago.
- Ask students if they can think of typical items in a home today that were not in a home 50 years ago. Write their responses on the board. Possible answers could include:

microwaves	*CDs*
computers	*CD players*
remote controls	*iPods*
DVDs	*cordless phones*
DVD players	

- Now ask students to think about what homes will be like 50 years in the future.
- Have students take turns reading the passage aloud.
- Ask comprehension questions every few sentences to ensure that students have understood and can paraphrase from the passage in response.

Optional Vocabulary

plasma screens	preheat
scenery	racks
electronic features	energy efficient
remote control	solar heat

CHART 3-7. Using the Present Progressive to Express Future Time. Page 72
Time: 10–15 minutes

> The use of present progressive to express future time is common, especially with the verbs presented in the chart and other verbs that express planned activities. Some common ones are *bring, build, eat, call, finish, get, give, make, meet, move, start,* and *visit.*
>
> The present progressive and *be going to* are used to talk about future events that the speaker has present knowledge of: *Do you have plans for this evening? Yes, I'm watching a baseball game on TV this evening.* (The speaker knows at the moment of speaking what his / her plans are for the future.) OR: *We're going to Thailand for our vacation.* (The speaker's vacation plans are a present reality.) OR: *Sarah's having a baby in October.* (The speaker is discussing a future event based on present knowledge.)
>
> When the present progressive is used to express future time, usually *be going to* is equally possible (but not vice versa: not all situations in which *be going to* is used can the present progressive also be expressed). *I'm watching TV this evening* and *I'm going to watch TV this evening* have no difference in meaning.

- Explain to students that especially in speaking, native speakers use present progressive with a future meaning.
- Ask students to remind you of how to form present progressive. Write the formula for this tense on the board. For example:

  Present Progressive: Subject + Verb Be + -ing Verb

- Ask students what time they normally use the present progressive to express. They should remember that it is for an action that is happening *right now*.
- Explain that present progressive can also be used for plans for the future that were already made at the moment of speaking.
- Write a few sentences on the board about your plans for the weekend. For example:

  I am going to plant a garden this weekend.
  I am going to have a barbecue in the evening.
  My parents are going to come to the barbecue.

- Underline *be going to* + verb in the first sentence. Then write the same sentence with present progressive underneath it.

  I am going to plant a garden this weekend.
  ⇒ *I am planting a garden this weekend.*

- Explain that these have the same meaning.
- Distribute markers or chalk to two students and ask them to change the tense. For example:

  I am going to plant a garden this weekend.
  ⇒ *I am planting a garden this weekend.*
  I am going to have a barbecue in the evening.
  ⇒ *I am having a barbecue in the evening.*
  My parents are going to come to the barbecue.
  ⇒ *My parents are coming to the barbecue.*

- Have those students who didn't write on the board correct the sentences. If you wish, you can ask them to label the parts *subject* and *verb.*
- Ask students to take turns reading sentences (a)–(h) from the chart aloud.
- Erase the board and write sentences (i) and (j) on the board.
- Explain that (j) is not possible and cross it out in an exaggerated fashion so that students understand that (j) is never okay.
- Underneath (i) and (j), write:

  NOT possible to use present progressive for predictions

❑ EXERCISE 32. Looking at grammar.
Page 72
Time: 5–10 minutes

- Give students time to work through the exercise independently.
- Ask students to write their versions of the completed answers on the board.
- Have other students write *Future* or *Present* next to the completions.
- Correct as a class and ask students which particular words informed them of whether the present progressive indicated future or present.

Optional Vocabulary

engineering
semester
physics

❑ EXERCISE 35. Let's write. Page 73
Time: 10–20 minutes

Expansion: Put students into groups and, using the questions included for the exercise, have students write an advertisement for a group trip to an exotic or exciting locale. Using the present progressive, students should advertise their trip as attractively as possible. When students have completed their advertisement, one student from each group should read their ad aloud to the class. Write the names of the trips on the board. Explain that groups can only vote for other trips, and have students vote for the most appealing itinerary.

CHART 3-8. Using The Simple Present to Express Future Time. Page 74
Time: 10 minutes

> The use of simple present to express future time in an independent clause is limited to relatively few verbs, ones that deal with schedules and timetables.
>
> To help students understand this special use of the simple present, tell them that, as a general rule, it is used only when the activity is considered scheduled and will occur at a definite time.

- Pick one of the verbs from the chart (*arrive, leave, start, begin, end, finish, open, close, be*) and conjugate it on the board.
- Ask students to take turns reading sentences (a)–(d) aloud. Explain that only verbs that can be used to describe scheduled events can be used in simple present tense with a future meaning.
- Write a sentence similar to (e) on the board. Reiterate the explanation of why it is impossible and have a student come to the board to cross out the simple present and put in a correct tense.

❏ EXERCISE 37. Looking at grammar.
Page 74
Time: 5–10 minutes.

> Point out that the simple present can carry the same meaning as the present progressive or *be going to* in expressing future time, as in item 1. Also point out that its use in expressing future time is limited to special situations. It is not always interchangeable with the present progressive or *be going to* to express future time, as illustrated in item 2, where the situation does not deal with a schedule or a timetable but is simply a statement of intention about the future.

- Lead this exercise by having students read the sentence and possible completions on sight.
- After identifying which completions are *not* possible, ask students to go back and change the sentence as necessary so that the remaining completions could be used correctly.

CHART 3-9. Immediate Future: Using *Be About To*. Page 75
Time: 10 minutes

> The text treats *be about to* as an idiom; that is, its meaning is not predictable by simply looking at the meaning of words themselves or the usual rules of grammar. In Chapter 13, students are taught that gerunds, not infinitives, immediately follow prepositions. This is a special case (i.e., an "idiom"). In other words, *about* followed by an idiom has a special meaning.

> *Be about to* is very common in spoken English and most students are familiar with it at some level.

- Write the subject pronouns on the board.
- Ask students to supply the *be* verbs.
- Add *about to* after each. For example:

  I am <u>about to</u>   *we are <u>about to</u>*
  you are <u>about to</u>   *you are <u>about to</u>*
  he / she / it is <u>about to</u>   *they are <u>about to</u>*

- Write on the board: *What am I <u>about to</u> do?*
- Choose from the following actions suggested below and perform them, one by one.

  open your cell phone and begin dialing: about to make a call

  wad up a piece of paper and aim for wastebasket: about to throw that away

  pick up an eraser and stand ready to erase the board: about to erase the board

  pull out a chair and begin to sit down: about to sit down

  open the door of the classroom and put one foot over the threshold: about to leave

  sniffle and make an exaggerated "aaaahhh" noise while closing your eyes: about to sneeze

  frown and sniffle: about to cry

  clear your throat and say, "Ladies and gentlemen": about to give a speech

- Once students have decided what it is you are about to do, write complete sentences on the board using *be about to*.
- Have students read (a) and (b) aloud and reiterate the notes to the right-hand side of the chart.

❏ EXERCISE 39. Let's talk. Page 76
Time: 5 minutes

> This exercise is easily teacher-led. Students can work through this by reading aloud and figuring out each situation as they encounter it. In addition to asking students what is about to happen, ask them to tell you one thing that is not about to happen.

❏ EXERCISE 41. Warm-up. Page 77
Time: 5 minutes

- Before asking students to complete the Warm-up, write the following sentence on the board and ask students if it is correct:

  You are attending classes here and learned English.

- Students should be able to identify that the tenses don't match and that the sentence is incorrect.
- After students have completed the Warm-up alone, as a class discuss why students did or did not choose each answer.

CHART 3-10. Parallel Verbs. Page 77
Time: 10 minutes

This chart introduces parallelism, a concept that is fundamental to English grammar. Parallelism is revisited and expanded upon in Chapter 9, when students study connecting ideas with coordinating conjunctions. Students can often identify when parallelism hasn't been achieved because something sounds wrong to them. Reassure them that in this way, they are already familiar with the idea of parallelism.

Errors in parallelism are common, with a second of two verbs in the same sentence often found in the simple or -ing form.

INCORRECT: I opened the door and look around.

INCORRECT: A good teacher prepares interesting lessons and explaining everything clearly.

- Explain that we often use one subject for two verbs and that we do not need to repeat the subject a second time.
- Ask a student to tell you two things he/she did earlier that day. Create a parallel sentence using the information you receive.
- Write the sentence on the board and underline the simple past verb. Label the subject and both verbs by writing an "S" above the subject and a "V" above each verb. For example:

> S   V   V
>
> *Gabriela washed her hair and brushed her teeth.*

- Have students read (a) and (b) aloud. Explain the notes to the right.
- Tell students that we don't need to repeat the helping verb and can use the helping verb to apply to *both* verbs that follow, as long as the subject is the same.
- Ask one student to tell you two things he/she is doing at the moment.
- Create a parallel sentence with this information and write this on the board, labeling and underlining as for the simple past sentence above. For example:

> S   V   V
>
> *Jin Won is thinking and writing notes.*

- Point out that in the above example, we understand that the first *is* applies to both *thinking* and *writing.*
- Have students read (c)–(e) aloud. Elaborate on the notes to the right.

❏ EXERCISE 44. Listening. Page 79
Time: 10 minutes

Many students will know what fortune cookies are. Ask students if they are familiar with fortune cookies and if they know any stereotypical "fortune cookie" fortunes. You can write students' descriptions on the board and ask them what kind of future tense fortune cookies use, leading them into a discussion of fortune cookies as predictions. You can take this opportunity to ask your students whether they have fortune-tellers in their cultures and whether they believe that such people can really predict the future.

Part II
Expansion: Give each student another classmate's name by distributing names on slips of paper. Take care that no student receives his/her own name. Students can then write fortunes for that particular student. Have students read these fortunes aloud, and others can guess which student it is intended for.

Optional Vocabulary
fortune cookies
unexpected
communication

❏ EXERCISE 46. Let's write. Page 80
Time: 10–20 minutes

Following a discussion of the previous exercise, have students choose a subject (friend, family member, colleague) to focus their writing on. They can write in the third person, as shown in the example in the book, or they can address a second person and even write in the style of a letter. They could even begin their assignment by explaining how they came by their special abilities to predict the future. Though this practice is intended to be written, you could turn it into an oral exercise conducted in small groups. One student at a time could be fortune-teller and tell fortunes for all others in the group.

Chapter 4
Present Perfect and Past Perfect

CHAPTER SUMMARY

OBJECTIVE: In this chapter, students will learn to use the present perfect and past perfect, though there is much more focus on mastery of the present perfect. Students learn to associate the present perfect with actions that began in the past and are still continuing in the present. They will begin to understand the past perfect as useful to show that two events began and finished in the past. Using past perfect, the speaker can show that one action occurred before the more recent past action.

This perfective aspect of verb tenses is not unique to English, but it is not easy for learners to understand and control. It is a useful feature of the language because it gives us important information about the sequence of events, their completion or continuation, their duration, and their relationship to the present time or to another time in the past.

APPROACH: The primary emphasis in the chapter is on the present perfect, which is a frequently used verb tense. The text actively encourages its use in the students' creative language production, The section on the past perfect, which is an infrequently used verb form, comes at the end of the chapter and is intended only as a minimal introduction.

Because the grammar in this chapter can prove difficult for many students at this level, you may want to delay introduction of some of the more challenging details, or even delay until later in the term. It is here because many teachers and grammar curricula present Chapters 1–4 as a complete review of tenses, but the chapters do not need to be taught in the order they are presented in the book. Less advanced students may benefit from skipping to Chapter 5 and 6 at this point and then returning to Chapter 4 later. Chapter 5 (Asking Questions) does contain some exercise items with the present perfect and present perfect progressive; however, the fact that students have not studied those tenses prior to doing Chapter 5 does not present a pedagogical problem. It is beneficial for students to gain exposure to structures prior to concentrated study of them.

TERMINOLOGY: The terms "aspect" and "tense" are not used here. The text simply refers to "present perfect" and "past perfect."

CHART 4-1. Past Participle. Page 81
Time: 5–10 minutes

Chapter 4 is the first time in the text that students are asked to use the past participle. The principal purpose of this chart is to define the term "past participle."

Remind students frequently that they do know the grammar terms that come up in practice as they have used the simple form and the simple past extensively. It is useful for them to become familiar with terms they will later need access to, but the emphasis should always be on actual use as opposed to grammar terminology.

- Write the following terms the board:

  Simple Form   Simple Past   Past Participle

- Explain to students that they know the forms from everyday use, but that they will benefit by also learning the names for these forms as they move ahead.
- Ask a student to tell you what he/she did last night and instruct the student to give you an answer in a completed sentence.
- Write the student's answer on the board. For example:

  Ahmed watched TV last night.

- Ask another student to go to the board and underline the verb, and then, using the underlined verb, to write the simple form, simple past, and past participle forms beneath the appropriate headings. For example:

  Ahmed <u>watched</u> TV last night.

Simple Form	*Simple Past*	*Past Participle*
watch	*watched*	*watched*

- Ask several more students to write sentences on the board about what they did last night.
- Invite others students to underline the verb in the sentences and write the forms beneath each verb form heading.
- If a student gives you an irregular verb sentence, simply point out that the verb is irregular and provide help with writing the verb forms appropriately. For example:

  Anika <u>ate</u> dinner at home last night.

Simple Form	*Simple Past*	*Past Participle*
eat	*ate*	*eaten*

- Read through the chart as a class and respond to any questions.

□ **EXERCISE 4.** Warm-up. Page 82
Time: 5 minutes

> Students tend to have a better passive comprehension of grammar forms than they realize. Because of this, they should be able to understand that these sentences describe actions or states that have not yet ended, although they may not be able to explain how or why.

- Ask a student to read each sentence aloud before telling you which description is correct, a or b.
- Once the student has told you which is correct, ask how the grammar of the original sentence would need to change in order to make the other description equally accurate. For example:

  Correct, Ahn-Soo. How would you need to change the original sentence if the bus picked her up?

CHART 4-2. Present Perfect with *Since* and *For.* Page 83
Time: 20–30 minutes

> This is the first time in the text where students have been presented with a verb form that uses *have* as an auxiliary in a verb tense. Using *have / had* as an auxiliary in a verb form defines a perfect verb and you may want to explain this to students. Explain that the past participle is the main verb in present perfect.
>
> The chart introduces present perfect with *since* and *for* because students have probably seen present perfect used most often with these terms and are likely to recognize them. Understanding the meaning and use of *since* helps students understand the meaning and use of the present perfect. Illustrating with a time line will make it much easier for students to "see" that present perfect describes actions begun in the past and continuing now, in the present.
>
> Students will see *since* used as a preposition, which is placed before the name of a time or event in the past. Later in the chapter students will also see that *since* can also introduce a time clause with simple past. The corresponding main clause would be in present perfect. It is not necessary to teach the more sophisticated uses of *since* at this point, but be ready to discuss them superficially if they arise.
>
> *Since* has other uses. It can be used as an adverb indicating continuity since a time in the past. For example: *He got a job in a factory in 1993 and has worked there ever **since***.

> It can also be used with the meaning of *because* in an adverb clause. In this case, the verb does not need to be in a particular tense. For example: ***Since** Paulo had a bad experience his first time, he does not want to join us for skiing this coming weekend*. This use is not presented in this text, but it is covered in detail in *Understanding and Using English Grammar*. Since the question may arise, it is important to be able to explain this use.
>
> *For* is used to express duration and is used with countable periods of time. For example:
>
> *for ten minutes*
> *for six months*
> *for 18 years*

- Ask students if they play any instruments or sports.
- When you receive answers, ask a second question: *When did you start . . . ?*
- Using student-generated information, write a simple present sentence on the board and then write a simple past sentence on the board. For example:

  Misha plays soccer.
  Misha started soccer in 2004.

- Now explain that you can use present perfect to combine these two ideas.
- Tell students that the present perfect is formed with the auxiliary *has / have* and the main verb, which is the past participle.
- Draw a time line on the board and use Misha's information to create a meaningful sentence illustrated by the time line. For example:

  ```
  ____X_____
  2004                    present year
  ```
  Misha <u>has played</u> soccer <u>since 2004</u>.

- Ask students whether Misha still plays soccer now and emphasize that he started soccer in 2004 and continues soccer now.
- Now, ask students how many years have passed since 2004.
- Explain that we can also express present perfect with countable periods of time, such as seconds, days, minutes, hours, years, decades, centuries, etc.
- Ask students to form the same sentence but to use *for* + *countable periods of time*.
- Invite a student to write the correct sentence on the board:

  Misha <u>has played</u> soccer <u>for 7 years.</u>

- Ask other students to makes sentences about themselves with *since* and *for*.
- Read through the chart together, asking students to read the example sentences aloud.
- Go through the chart as slowly as needed and stop to write examples and notes on the board frequently to support student comprehension.

❏ EXERCISE 5. Looking at grammar.
Page 84
Time: 5–10 minutes

One purpose of this exercise is for students to arrive at their own conclusions about the forms and meanings of grammatical structures. A second purpose is for students to become aware of what information they will need to pay attention to when discerning *since* and *for*. This exercise also provides teachers with a variety of examples to use in introducing grammar points.

- Before beginning the exercise, ask a student to explain what *since* precedes (dates, events, and specific times in the past).
- Ask another student to explain what *for* precedes (countable periods of time).
- Write both reminders on the board. For example:

  since + date / event / specific time in past
  for + countable periods of time

- Give students turns completing the sentences with *since* and *for* on sight.

  Optional Vocabulary
  term
  substitute
  engagement

❏ EXERCISE 6. Looking at grammar.
Page 84
Time: 5–10 minutes

Students should complete the sentences with accurate information about themselves. Ask students to give accurate answers for item 1 as well. Remember that students may need a few extra minutes to formulate real answers using information from their own lives.

❏ EXERCISE 8. Let's talk. Page 85
Time: 10–15 minutes

Make it clear that Speaker A is to use *since* and that Speaker B is to use *for* to paraphrase Speaker A's response. If this is teacher-led, it can progress very quickly. Group work could take longer, but of course would involve more students in oral practice.

CHART 4-3. Negative, Question, and Short-Answer Forms. Page 87
Time: 10–15 minutes

The negative, question, and short answer forms of the present perfect can pose some problems for students in terms of word order. There are simply a greater

number of words for students to rearrange and this can cause confusion. Remind students that the word order for making negatives and questions is the same as it is with other tenses. Illustrate these forms clearly and slowly on the board.

Students sometimes struggle with *ever* and *never*. Explain that both of these adverbs are used to indicate and emphasize that a person's entire history is being reviewed. For example:

Have you ever eaten eel?

This question asks if this action has happened at any time in the person's life.

I have never eaten eel.

This response explains that the person has not done this even once, again during the whole course of the speaker's life.

Explain to students that *ever / never* are placed between the auxiliary and the past participle.

Provide immediate and definitive correction as students first begin to use the forms. By doing so, you can help students gain control and confidence.

- Explain the formula for present perfect negative and write it on the board. For example:

  subject + has / have + not + past participle

- Ask a student if he/she has ever visited Botswana, Tibet, Lichtenstein, Utah, the Galapagos, or any other somewhat uncommon world destination.
- Using this information, ask students to create a sentence according to the formula on the board. Write the sentence beneath it. For example:

  subject + has / have + not + past participle
  Manuela has not visited Botswana.

- Ask students to restate the sentence with a contraction of *has + not*. Write the resulting sentence on the board.

  Manuela hasn't visited Botswana.

- Now, ask students what two parts of speech need to change places in order to create a question. They should respond *subject* and *verb*.
- Tell students that when working with sentences whose verbs contain an auxiliary (i.e., *has / have* with present perfect), the parts of speech that are inverted are the subject and the auxiliary. The main verb (in this case, the past participle) does not change its position.
- Write the formula for present perfect questions on the board:

  has / have + subject + past participle

- Now, ask students to make a question based on the negative sentence above. Tell them not to include the negative.
- Write the newly formulated question on the board. For example:

  Has Manuela visited Botswana?

- Now, using this question, write the formula for present perfect short answers on the board. For example:

  Yes / No + subject + has(n't) / have(n't)

- Ask students to make a short answer to the above question, according to the formula. Write this on the board.

   No, she hasn't.

- Ask students a few more questions to give them practice with *ever* and *never*.

- Write some questions and responses on the board. For example:

   Have you ever slept through an important exam or event?

   No, I have never slept through an important exam. But, I did once sleep through an important meeting at work!

   Have you ever gone skiing?

   No, I have never gone skiing.

- With students taking turns reading the example sentences (a)–(h), go through the chart.

- Explain to students that the grammar itself is not difficult and follows patterns they are already familiar with.

- Remind students that the main challenge is mastering word order when there are several auxiliaries. Remind students to refer back to this chart as often as is helpful for them as they gain control of the forms.

❏ EXERCISE 11. Looking at grammar.
Page 87
Time: 10 minutes

This is a straightforward exercise on form but also intended for teacher presentation of the meaning of the present perfect. Keep emphasizing that the tense conveys the idea of "before now" or "at an unspecified time in the past." The items in this exercise all convey the idea of "in one's entire lifetime up to now."

In item 1, *Have you ever eaten an insect?* = *In your entire lifetime, at any unspecified point, have you ever eaten an insect?* The questioner is not interested in exactly when such a thing might have happened. The present perfect does not concern itself with exact points of time in the past; that is the job of the simple past.

Because these forms can challenge students, allow sufficient time to slowly review the answers. You might want to put students in pairs so that they complete the conversations aloud with a partner.

❏ EXERCISES 12–14. Pages 88 and 89

These exercises are designed to provide students practice with the present perfect, using real information from students' lives. The grammar emphasis here is on adverbial expressions frequently used with the present perfect in both questions and statements.

❏ EXERCISE 12. Listening. Page 88
Time: 5–10 minutes

- Play the audio through once without stopping. Then play it again, stopping after each item.
- Give students ample time to answer the questions.
- Discuss the answers as a class.
- Reiterate that the above use of present perfect is only concerned with whether the action ever occurred at any time before the present.

Optional Vocabulary

limousine	scary
volunteer work	embarrassed

❏ EXERCISE 13. Let's talk: interview.
Page 88
Time: 10 minutes

This exercise provides further practice with information from students' lives. The present perfect is often used to make small talk and learn more about others' experiences. Make sure that students know that they are trying to find out whether the other person has ever (at any time before the present) had a certain experience. Explain that once they have received a *yes / no + short answer* to their questions, it is common to ask for details about the event. These detail questions are in simple past. This exercise can be done in pairs or small groups.

- Give students ample time to form the questions from the cues in the text on their own.
- If they wish, they can write the complete questions out on a card or piece of paper to refer to as they interview their classmates.
- Encourage students to get up and walk around the room while interviewing each other.
- Join pairs and groups of students to model both asking the original present perfect questions and then asking natural, follow-up questions (which will be in simple past as they now refer to one definite event in time).
- When students have had a chance to ask all the questions, have them return to their seats.
- Direct students to read the correct question aloud and respond with an answer in present perfect. You can also write the questions and answers on the board.
- Encourage students to elaborate on the answers they received and share additional information they heard from their partners. For example:

   Have you ever cut your own hair?

   Yes, Guillermo has cut his own hair. He did this when he was in the army. He used clippers to trim his hair.

❏ EXERCISE 14. Let's talk and write:
interview. Page 89
Time: 15–25 minutes

This can be a quick review or written homework. Items 8 and 9 have stative passive verbs, so there are two past participles: *I have never **been married***. Some students may wonder about this. In the passive, the auxiliary *be* carries the tense form (for example: *have been* for the present perfect) and is followed by a past participle (for example: *married*). You can also refer students to the related chart in Chapter 10.

Expansion: Collect the paragraphs. Make the subject of the paragraph anonymous. Explain that students are going to guess who the paragraph is about. You can replace students' actual first sentences by saying, *I'd like to tell you a little bit about your classmate, Mister / Miss X.* Then, read the paragraph aloud, replacing any student names with *he / she.* When you have finished reading the paragraph aloud, students guess which one of them it describes.

CHART 4-4. Present Perfect with
Unspecified Time. Page 90
Time: 10–15 minutes

This chart emphasizes present perfect as it is used to discuss experiences that have or have not happened at any time in the past. Explain that this use does not focus on whether an action that began in the past continues now, but whether it occurred at any time before now. *Already, yet, just, recently, ever,* and *never* are adverbs that can emphasize the relative recentness of the completed action.

- Ask students if any of them have looked at all the chapters in their grammar text. (Hopefully, one will have. If this question does not work for your group, come up with one that can employ *already* to show that the action took place in the past, and sooner than anticipated.)
- Write the answer to your question on the board, using *already,* if possible. For example:

  Vaclev has looked at all the chapters in our grammar book already.

- Now, draw the time line as presented in the book to further illustrate this use of present perfect.

                    present
  past _____X_____X_____future
  Vaclev has looked at all the chapters in our grammar book already.

- Explain that *already* is used in affirmative sentences to show that the action has happened before this time.
- Tell them that *already* should come at the end of the sentence.
- Ask students again if they have looked at the chapters in their grammar book. It is likely that at least one won't have.

- Write the answer to this question on the board, using *yet,* to emphasize that up to this time, the action has not happened. For example:

  Pilar hasn't looked at all the chapters in our grammar book yet.

- Explain that *yet* used to show a negative emphasis and that it comes at the end of the sentence.
- Ask your original question again, hoping to find someone else who has looked at all the chapters in the grammar book several times in the past.
- Write the desired response on the board. If no one has looked at the book several or many times in the past, you can certainly use yourself as the new subject. For example:

  I have looked at all the chapters in our grammar book many times.

- Draw the time line again, but this time show that the action has taken place repeatedly in the past by drawing a number of Xs. For example:

                    present
  past _____X_X X X_____X_____future
  I have looked at all the chapters in our grammar book many times.

- Return to the chart in the book.
- Ask students to take turns reading the example sentences and questions (a)–(e) and to refer to the first time line you drew on the board.
- Move on to examples (f) and (g) and refer to the second time line, which shows repeated actions in the past.

❏ EXERCISE 16. Looking at grammar.
Page 91
Time: 10 minutes

- Put students in small groups.
- Draw the time line for Situation 1 on the board so that students can clearly see when Sara was on the phone (from 12:00–12:59) in relation to now (1:00). For example:

  _____X_____X_____

                    now–1:00 P.M.
  phone rang   *Sara hung up*
  12:00 P.M.   *12:59 P.M.*

- Ask students to now consider which statements, (a)–(e), are true.
- Tell students to draw their own time lines as a way of seeing what the situation would look like.
- Give students time to work through all three situations and review as a class.
- If other situations prove challenging for students, illustrate them on the board with a chart.

❏ EXERCISE 19. Listening. Page 92
Time: 5–10 minutes

- Model contracted forms of *is* and *has* for your students by switching back and forth between careful pronunciation and natural, reduced speech.

- Give example sentences similar to those in the book and exaggerate the pronunciation of the participle following the contraction (present or past). Additional example sentence pairs:

  My sister's going to North Carolina.

  My sister's gone to North Carolina.

  He's eating all the ice cream.

  He's eaten all the ice cream.

- Instruct students to listen for an *-ing* on the end of a participle. Explain that *has* + _____*-ing* is not a possible combination.

- Remind students that by listening carefully to the form that follows the contraction of either *is* or *has,* they can best understand which contraction preceded it.

❏ EXERCISE 20. Listening. Page 93
Time: 10–15 minutes

> Before listening to the audio, you may want to spend some time building on the context of this exercise. Some additional questions to discuss before listening include:
>
> *What is a job interview?*
>
> *How do you prepare for one?*
>
> *What kind of questions are you asked?*
>
> *Do you know anyone who is a nurse?*
>
> *If so, what does he or she like about the job?*
>
> *Is being a nurse considered a high-paid position in your country?*
>
> *What do you think the pros and cons of such a job would be?*

Optional Vocabulary

manager	challenges
résumé	provides
general	training
community	staff

CHART 4-5. Simple Past vs. Present Perfect.
Page 94
Time: 15–20 minutes

> Because there are times (particularly in spoken English) when both simple past and present perfect can be used interchangeably, it can be challenging to teach this difference. For example:
>
> *I already finished my work.*
>
> *I've already finished my work.*
>
> Both these sentences are common and acceptable, especially in informal, spoken American English. However, the intent of the chart is to draw clear distinctions between the two tenses so that students

> can learn when present perfect can or cannot be used. Students can blur and blend the two tenses later, as they gain experience with the language. Trying to explain the ways in which the two tenses can express the same meaning can create more confusion than enlightenment at this point. Note that the simple past and present perfect are not interchangeable in examples (a), (c), and (d).
>
> It often helps students to learn clear and simple rules at this stage. Thus, you can explain that if they see *ago* or a specific date or time in the past (without *since*), they need to use simple past. If they see no mention of time whatsoever, they should use present perfect.

- Ask students a question (*ever / never*) using present perfect about their experiences in life to date. Write this question on the board. For example:

  Have you ever tried skiing / waterskiing / bungee jumping, etc.,?

- Remind students that by using present perfect, you are asking about any time before now, but no specific time.

- The goal is to have students naturally move from present perfect (*I have tried skiing*) to simple past. To do so, you will change from asking a general question to a specific one.

- With the help of the whole class, create a present perfect sentence that gives a student or students' answer to your question, and write this on the board. For example:

  Have you ever flown in a small plane?

  (at some unspecific time in the past)

  Mika has. Mika has flown in a small plane.

- Illustrate the shift from present perfect in the original questions to simple past questions when asking for specifics by asking follow-up questions in the simple past. For example.

  Did you enjoy it? *(at one specific time in the past)*

  Were you very scared?

- Explain that these questions are in present perfect and in contrast to questions we can ask Mika about this specific event, which are in simple past.

- Explain that you switched from present perfect to simple past in your question because you knew you were now asking about a **specific** time in the past.

- Using this pattern, you can ask more students:

  - whether they have ever had certain experiences, at any time in the past (present perfect)

  - what the details of a specific event were (simple past)

- Write as many examples as needed on the board until you sense students understand the pattern.

- Turn to the chart and ask students to take turns reading examples (a)–(f).

- Spend ample time on the explanatory notes.

So far, you the teacher, have been providing repeated explications of the meanings of the present perfect. Now the text assumes that the students have sufficient understandings of differences in meanings between the simple past and the present perfect that they can explain these themselves.

In discussion-of-meaning exercises, students find their own inventive ways of expressing meanings. Their explanations won't necessarily sound like yours or the text's, but once you discern the meaning, you can restate it slightly if necessary.

This exercise is an ideal opportunity for you to see how much of Chart 4-5 students have already absorbed, and what they still need to work on.

- Instruct one student to read the question aloud and other students to read the sentences that follow aloud.
- Work through each set of sentences, comparing and discussing the differences.
- Help students by framing specific questions that will lead them to discover and articulate the differences. For example, with the second set of sentences (e) and (f), it will help students if you ask, *In e, does the speaker still have the bicycle? How do you know?*

□ **EXERCISE 23.** Looking at grammar.
Page 95
Time: 5 minutes

This exercise should now be easy for students, who should be able to offer explanations while discussing this exercise. The text repeatedly emphasizes that the present perfect and simple past both express past occurrences, with the difference being unspecified vs. specified times.

□ **EXERCISE 25.** Let's talk: pairwork.
Page 96
Time: 10 minutes

The purpose of this exercise is to practice the present perfect while using real information taken from students' lives.

You can ask a question that elicits present perfect, and then follow up with a related question that elicits the simple past. Pursue interesting responses, but connect to as many student ideas as possible. Lead and encourage spontaneous conversation among as many participants as you can engage.

Students' books should be closed. There is no need for them to read the question, and relying on their ears for understanding is good practice for them. Remind students of this point.

□ **EXERCISE 28.** Warm-up. Page 97
Time: 5 minutes

Before students complete the Warm-up sentences, ask for volunteers to reiterate what kind of time markers follow *since* and what kind follow *for.*

CHART 4-6. Present Perfect Progressive.
Page 98
Time: 10–15 minutes

You can use the step-by-step demonstration described below to introduce the exact need for present perfect progressive. If you choose not to use the drawing presentation idea, you can perform or have a student perform any action and have another student time it.

Because students already know how to describe what is happening with the present progressive, you can make a clear transition to include addressing duration of the continuous action. Focus students' attention on the fact that because duration of the action is now being considered, the following changes are needed:

- the past needs to be considered because only through the past can the beginning of the action be represented grammatically
- the tense needs to be changed to present perfect progressive to reflect the reference to the past and duration

Try to avoid getting into differences between the present perfect and the present perfect progressive at this stage. Remind students that some verbs (stative or non-action verbs) are not used in any progressive tenses, as is pointed out in examples (g)–(j).

- As a way of introducing this chart, ask a student with a watch to time you when you begin to draw something on the board (something like a tree or some flowers).
- As you are drawing, ask the students what you are doing. (They should respond, *You are drawing on the board.*)
- Continue drawing for 30 seconds or a minute and then, without stopping, ask the student with the watch how long you have been drawing.
- Explain that, *You are drawing on the board for 30 seconds* is not possible. The tense has to shift to the present perfect progressive when duration is added to the description of the activity.
- Keep drawing and ask, *Now how long have I been drawing?* and *What am I drawing?* as you switch from a tree to a bird, perhaps.
- If you prefer, ask a student to be the artist so that you can concentrate on leading the discussion.
- Ask students to tell you what form they can expect to see in a progressive verb, of any tense. They should be able to tell you that the participle ends in *-ing.*
- Ask students to help you write the formula for the present perfect progressive on the board. For example:

Present Perfect Progressive:

subject + has / have + been + _____ -ing

- Now draw the time lines for present progressive and present perfect progressive on the board and label them.
- Explain the fact that because the action is still in progress at the moment of speaking, we use present progressive <u>if</u> no past / continued duration is referred to.
- Write a sentence that illustrates this clearly on the board. For example:

  I am teaching grammar.

- Explain that, as demonstrated above, once duration is included, present perfect progressive must be used.
- Write a sentence that illustrates the action and its past / continued duration. For example:

  I have been teaching grammar for 15 minutes.

- Have students read through the example sentences (a)–(j) included in the chart.
- Repeat the idea of past / continued duration as central to the use of present perfect progressive often.

❑ **EXERCISE 29.** Looking at grammar.
Page 99
Time: 5–10 minutes

This exercise reinforces Chart 4-6 by emphasizing the relationship between the two tenses in order to demonstrate when and how the present perfect progressive is used.

- Give students time to complete the sentences before reviewing as a group.
- Ask students to justify answers by referring to time cues that refer to the present only or that refer to past / continued duration.

Optional Vocabulary
cafeteria
physics
experiment

❑ **EXERCISE 30.** Let's talk. Page 99
Time: 10–20 minutes

The questions are intended to help you come up with ways to elicit the present perfect progressive in teacher-student conversation. The questions do not need to be read verbatim. For example, in item 1, set up the situation verbally to lead up to the present perfect progressive questions *What time is it now? What time did you get to class this morning? Does it seem like you've been here for a long time? How long* **have** *you* **been sitting** *here?*

Ask questions 2, 6, 7, and 8 to more than one student and compare responses in order to model the target tense.

Be ready to ask additional questions in order to promote an engaging discussion. Additional questions can be tailored to your class and your knowledge of them and could include:

When did you first begin using a computer?
How long have you been using a computer?
When did you first begin: *practicing yoga ?*
How long have you been: *playing the piano?*
                                 playing basketball?
                                   painting in watercolor?
                                   studying law?

❑ **EXERCISE 31.** Listening. Page 100
Time: 10 minutes

Students often have difficulties discerning *has* and *have* contractions. Tell students to listen carefully for the subject noun that precedes the auxiliary *has or have.* The subject noun provides clues about singular and plural.

Part I
- After students listen for the contractions, repeat the contracted form of each of the six sentences.
- Exaggerate the contraction in each sentence.
- Ask students to repeat the contractions and whole sentences after you.

❑ **EXERCISE 32.** Warm-up. Page 100
Time: 5–10 minutes

As you lead the Warm-up, elicit observations and questions from your students about the three different tenses in bold. Put student-generated notes on the board regarding tense usage.

- Ask three students to take turns reading the situations aloud.
- Call on four more students to answer questions (a)–(c).

CHART 4-7. Present Perfect Progressive vs. Present Perfect. Page 101
Time: 15–20 minutes

The text seeks to make the distinction between these two tenses by comparing repeated action to duration.

In examples (f)–(i), the text points out that in certain situations, there is little or no difference in meaning between the present perfect and the present perfect progressive. (Any subtle difference can be attributed to the idea that the progressive emphasizes the continuous nature of the activity, while the present perfect is concerned more with a simple factual statement of duration. However, the nuances of difference don't seem significant and are very difficult to pinpoint—even for native speakers.)

A challenge for students is often that the present perfect and the present perfect progressive have exactly the same meaning when they express the duration of an occurrence from the past to the present time. The difference is that the present perfect progressive expresses the duration of "activities" and uses a fairly wide range of verbs. On the other hand, the present perfect uses only stative verbs with *since* and *for.* The present perfect expresses the duration of "states of being" (or conditions of existence) rather than "activities." This information can prove very confusing to many students. The chart presentation is fairly complicated for this proficiency level; it anticipates questions students might have, but the point doesn't need to be belabored.

When presenting the chart, explain the difference as one between activity/action verbs and state/condition verbs. This may be an oversimplification, but it gives students a more concrete way to look at the two tenses. Thus, you can tell students:

If the speaker is actively doing something, present perfect progressive is preferable.

If the speaker is passively being, living, remaining, etc., present perfect is preferable.

One use that is not presented here is that present perfect progressive can express an activity in progress recently, with no mention of duration. For example:

A: *Hi John. How's it going?*

B: *Okay. **I've been studying** a lot, but finals are almost over.*

For further explanation, see the related chart in Chapter 3 of *Understanding and Using English Grammar.*

- Ask students what they have been doing since they arrived in class.
- You will receive a variety of answers. Pick the most "active" verbs, and then ask students to remind you how the present perfect progressive is formed.
- Put the formula on the board and then, with help from students, write an appropriate present perfect sentence beneath it, lining the parts of speech up with the formula.

Present Perfect Progressive

subject +	has / have +	been +	_____ -ing
Thalia	has	been	writing notes since she arrived in class.

- Explain that because "writing notes" is an "activity" and involves action, present perfect progressive is used.
- Now ask students where they have been since class started. They will say, invariably, *in class.*

- Emphasize that the verb *be* is not used to describe an "activity" but shows a state of being, or condition.
- Explain that in this case, present perfect is used.
- Ask a student to remind you of the formula for present perfect and write this on the board. For example:

Present Perfect

Subject +	has / have +	past participle
The students	have	been in class since 9:00 A.M.

- Read through the chart with your students and ask students to take turns reading the example sentences (a)–(i) aloud.

❏ **EXERCISE 33.** Looking at grammar.
Page 102
Time: 10–15 minutes

Optional Vocabulary

hike	kindergarten
chemistry	serve
dozen	unemployed
elementary school	accounting firms

❏ **EXERCISE 35.** Looking at grammar.
Page 103
Time: 10 minutes

Encourage students to explain the meaning in their own words. See the Teaching Suggestions at the front of this book for ways of handling discussion-of-meaning exercises.

Expansion: You can distribute index cards and in pairs, have students create three sentences involving more than one past tense. These sets of sentences should be modeled on the sets in items 1–5. Encourage students to be as creative as possible and to take time to create grammatically correct and interesting sentences. Walk around and assist students while they are creating their sentences. Finally, collect all the index cards and redistribute one to each pair, ensuring that no pair gets the set they have just developed. Ask each pair to read their sentences aloud, provide an explanation for each tense used, and then guess which pair authored the set of sentences.

❏ **EXERCISE 37.** Listening and speaking.
Page 104
Time: 10–20 minutes

Expansion: You can use the topic to engage students in natural discussion that practices present perfect forms. Using the following questions, lead a discussion on symptoms, treatments, over-the-counter medicine, and going to the doctor.

The following questions are only suggestions to engage students in a lively discussion. Ask only those questions you feel comfortable asking.

– What are "symptoms" and what are "treatments"? Are over-the-counter medicines widely used in your country?

– Do most people use Western drugs in your country, or do they use Eastern methods and alternative therapies? **Have you ever** used any alternative therapies yourself?

– What kind of alternative therapies are popular in your country? Do people use acupuncture? chiropractic? herbal remedies? homeopathy?

– How serious does a sickness or illness have to be before you would go see a doctor? **Have you ever** neglected to go to a doctor and become even sicker because of this decision?

– **Have you ever** missed work or school because you were sick?

– What do you know about the U.S. health-care system, and how does the U.S. system compare to that in your country?

– Can you describe some traditional remedies for common ailments in your country?

– What kind of childhood illnesses **have you had**? **Have you had**:

mumps	colds
measles	scarlet fever
chickenpox	stomach bugs
flu	

– What does "infection" mean? Do you know the difference between a bacterial and a viral infection?

Optional Vocabulary for Expansion

illness	alternative therapy
sickness	acupuncture
treatment	herbs
cure	chiropractic
remedy	ailments
bugs	infection
bacterial	viral
disease	

❏ EXERCISE 39. Reading. Page 106
Time: 10–15 minutes

See the Teaching Suggestions at the front of this book for additional Ideas for working with Reading exercises.

Optional Vocabulary

disappearing	colony
crops	collapse
losses	hives
produce	growing conditions
depends	research

❏ EXERCISE 40. Grammar and writing.
Page 107
Time: 15–25 minutes

The three paragraphs asked for in Part II should elicit a variety of verb tenses—including, it is hoped, correct and appropriate use of the present perfect.

Discuss paragraphing: form and purpose.

- A paragraph is indented in from the left text margin.

- It contains one principal idea, and the questions asked for each paragraph share one principal idea.

- When the writer moves on to a new idea, a new paragraph is started.

If your students are more advanced in their understanding of English rhetoric you could use Part II as an opportunity to assign a traditional five-paragraph essay with introduction, three body paragraphs, and conclusion.

See the Teaching Suggestions in the front of this book for additional idea for working with Writing exercises.

❏ EXERCISE 41. Warm-up. Page 108
Time: 5 minutes

The past perfect is not an especially common and useful tense for language students at this level. The text's intention is to quickly introduce the form and meaning. A thorough understanding, and usage mastery, are neither sought nor expected. The students will come across the past perfect again in Chapter 14, where it is used in verb changes made when moving from quoted to reported speech.

CHART 4-8. Past Perfect. Page 108
Time: 15–20 minutes

Both the present perfect and the past perfect relate two points of time to one another. The present perfect relates an event in the past to the present. The past perfect relates an event in the past to another event in the past that occurred at a different time.

Tell students that many native speakers either neglect to use the past perfect when they should or use it incorrectly. It is not easy to hear the past perfect used correctly in native speech, but it will be helpful for students to have a basic understanding of it.

Because students at this level may have little or no experience with past perfect, you may want to diagram on the board which event happened first. It may also help students to hear the following questions:

Jane passed her driver's test. ⇒ *Jane was happy.* ⇒ *Jane met me for lunch.*

Why was Jane happy?

She passed her test.

When did Karen learn that Jane was happy?

At lunch.

Did the test take place before or after lunch?

Before. Otherwise how would Karen know that Jane was happy about it?

- Begin by asking various students for an action that they started and completed before arriving in class. Write students' answers on the board. Some answers might be:

    Jose called his family in Spain.

    Michelle completed her homework.

- Then, draw a time line on the board, mark an *X* on the far left, and write down one of the student's answers. For example:

    ```
    ____X_____|_____
    called his family                      NOW
    ```

- Now ask the same students to tell you an action they performed and completed <u>after</u> the action they described above. Some answers might be:

    Jose arrived in class.

    Michelle greeted her friends and teacher.

- Write these answers on the board and add to the time line. For example:

    ```
    ____X_____X_____|_____
    called his family  arrived in class   NOW
    ```

- Explain that past perfect is used when there are two events that began and finished in the past. Past perfect is used for the earlier of the two actions, and simple past is used for the more recent past event.

- Underline the earlier action on the time line. For example:

    ```
    ____X_____X_____|_____
    called his family  arrived in class   NOW
    ```

- Explain how the past perfect is formed and write the formula on the board.

    Past Perfect = subject + had + past participle

- Then write a past perfect sentence under the first action on the time line. For example:

    ```
    ____X_____X_____|_____
    Called his family       arrived in class   NOW
    Jose had called his family
    ```

- Ask the class, *Did Jose call his family before or after he arrived in class?* They should respond, *Before.* Write *before* on the time line and complete the sentence.

    ```
                before
    ____X_____X_____|_____
    Called his family       arrived in class   NOW
    Jose had called his family before he arrived in class.
    ```

- Next, ask students how *after* could be used with the same sentence. Help them create a sentence such as:

    Jose arrived in class after he had called his family.

- Read through the chart with your students. Ask students to take turns reading the example sentences (a)–(h).

- Review the notes on the right-hand side of the chart as you proceed through the examples with your students.

❏ **EXERCISE 42.** Looking at grammar.
Page 109
Time: 10 minutes

This exercise can be done in pairs to encourage students to explain to each other the sequence of events in each item.

To help students visualize which event ended before the more recent event began, refer frequently to the diagram of the past perfect drawn on the board.

Optional Vocabulary

jump for joy	poured
match	noodles

Chapter 5
Asking Questions

CHAPTER SUMMARY

OBJECTIVE: Although general question word order is introduced in earlier chapters, this chapter presents and summarizes those patterns, adds other types, and provides ample practice to help students gain control of and comfortable fluency with question words and forms.

APPROACH: Because questions occur primarily in conversational English, exercises on form are followed by ones that encourage a lot of speaking practice. Even though students can easily make themselves understood by simply raising their voices to indicate a question (rather than using correct question word order), they often don't receive enough correction of word forms. In our experience as teachers, many ESL students don't attempt question word order, and it quickly becomes a fossilized error. By providing immediate and specific correction, you can help students become aware of this habit and alert them to the need for self-correction.

TERMINOLOGY: Information questions are also called *wh*-questions because they use the words *who, which, when, where,* and *how.* The chapter generally uses the term "helping verb" for an auxiliary, to distinguish it from the "main verb" in a sentence or clause.

CHART 5-1. Yes / No Questions and Short Answers. Page 111
Time: 10–15 minutes

Students studied the forms of yes / no questions in conjunction with each verb tense presented in Chapters 1 through 4. Refer to Chart 5-2 if students need a reminder of basic question word order: *helping verb + subject + main verb.*

Remind students of the names of the tenses used in the examples, and review how questions are formed for each tense. For example: (a) simple present (discuss the use of *does*), (b) simple past, (c) present perfect, (d) present perfect progressive, and (e) the future with *will.*

If you skipped all or parts of Chapter 4 (Present Perfect and Past Perfect), you'll need to give a quick overview of the form of the present perfect at this juncture, explaining that *have* and *has* are used as auxiliary verbs. The present perfect occurs relatively infrequently in the exercise items in this chapter, so it should not prove to be a problematic distraction. Use the examples and exercise items with the present

perfect as a means of making a quick introduction to it, and tell your students they will concentrate on it more fully later in the term, when you return to Chapter 4.

Model the spoken form of the short answers. The emphasis is on the auxiliary verb (*Yes, I do. No, I don't.*) Additional information not given in the chart: If a negative contraction is not used in a short answer, the emphasis is placed on *not* rather than on the verb (*No, I'm not. No, I do not.*)

The presentation pattern in this chart of *question + short answer + (long answer)* is used in the exercises on form in this chapter.

Include an example with *can* in your discussion of this chart, relating it to *will* in question forms (both are modal auxiliaries). *Can* occurs in the exercises and in succeeding charts.

- Write a simple statement on the board and transform it into a yes / no question.
- Label the parts of speech in both the sentence and the question. For example:

Subject	Verb	Object
I	like	chocolate ice cream.

Helping Verb	Subject	Verb	Object
Do	you	like	chocolate ice cream?

- Explain that short answers include **Yes / No** + subject + *helping verb.*
- Write student responses on the board and label the parts of speech.
- Then ask students to expand each short answer to a long answer. For example:

	Subject	Helping Verb
Yes,	Maiko	does.

(Maiko likes chocolate ice cream.)

	Subject	Helping Verb
No,	Diego and Zara	don't.

(Diego and Zara don't like chocolate ice cream.)

- Read through Chart 5-1 with your students.
- Remind students that they must correctly identify the appropriate helping verb in order to use it in a yes / no question and short answer.

❏ EXERCISE 2. Looking at grammar.
Page 111
Time: 5–10 minutes

Emphasize that the tense determines whether a main or helping verb is needed in the formation of the yes/no question and short answer.

❏ EXERCISE 3. Looking at grammar.
Page 112
Time: 5–10 minutes

This is an exercise on the form of yes/no questions and short answers. It can be done as seatwork or in pairs. The directions tell the students not to use a negative verb in the question. It is better that negative yes/no questions not be discussed with students at this level, as negative questions have complicated meanings and uses. (See *Understanding and Using English Grammar.*) The only negative questions practiced in this text are those preceded by *why*.

Optional Vocabulary
acupuncture
relieves

Expansion: Take the opportunity to improvise additional oral questions to engage students and allow them to use their new skills spontaneously.

Additional questions could include the following:

1. *Do you know my cousin?*
2. *Do salamanders have legs?*
3. *Is Portugal in North America?*
4. *Will you be at work later today?*
5. *Do you have a motorcycle or moped?*
6. *Has Simon returned?*
7. *Has Simon returned with Kate?*
8. *Does chiropractic relieve pain?*

❏ EXERCISE 5. Let's talk: interview.
Page 113
Time: 5–10 minutes

- First, ask students to create the correct questions from the given words.
- Instruct students to stand up and move around the classroom, asking their questions to as many other students as possible.
- Ask students to write notes so that they can share their answers as a class.
- Review by asking students to read a question and the answer they received.

Expansion: You might want to have students <u>not</u> include the name in their answer, such as, *He has had a pet snake.* Then the class can guess who the person is.

❏ EXERCISE 6. Listening. Page 113
Time: 10–15 minutes

Understanding contractions and reduced pronunciation is very important for students of English. Stress the importance of listening to the beginning of yes/no questions in order to understand the tense used.

Part I
- Play the audio through at least once.
- Go back over each item and exaggerate the pronunciation of the reductions.

Part II
- Play the audio through once without stopping. Then, play it again, stopping and replaying as necessary.
- Review completed questions with students and compare the reduced vs. the non-reduced forms by writing what students hear and the proper form on the board, side by side. For example:

    1. *Ih-ze available?* ⇒ *Is he available?*

❏ EXERCISE 7. Warm-up. Page 114
Time: 5 minutes

Most students at this level have some experience with *wh*-questions. Before students answer the questions in the Warm-up, ask them what piece of information the question seeks.

CHART 5-2. Yes/No and Information
Questions. Page 114
Time: 10–15 minutes

One purpose of this chart is to relate the form of yes/no questions to the form of information questions so that the students can see the overall pattern in English. Make sure students understand that the inverted subject-verb form is the same in both types (yes/no and information) questions. However, there is an exception in examples (k) and (l). In those sentences, the question word itself is the subject of the question.

On the board, write the basic question pattern so that students will have it as a reference and reminder throughout the discussion of this chapter:

question word + helping verb + subject + main verb

Model and discuss rising intonation at the end of each question.

- Before looking at the chart, elicit from students the basic question pattern and write the pattern on the board:

    question word + helping verb + subject + main verb

- Ask students a variety of *wh*-questions.

- Instruct students to answer you with both the information and the category of information the *wh*-question elicits.
- Put students' responses on the board. For example:

  Where are you from, Sasha?

  I am from Kiev. "Where" asks for a location or place.

- Read through the examples (a)–(j) with students and highlight the notes on the right-hand side of the chart.
- Draw students' attention to the fact that (k) and (l) are different because in those examples the question words are also the subject of the sentences.

❑ EXERCISE 9. Listening. Page 116
Time: 5–10 minutes

- Ask students to put their pencils or pens down. Play the audio through once.
- Ask students to paraphrase the situation or story.
- Play the audio again and instruct students to complete the statements and questions, accordingly.
- Review as a class.

Optional Vocabulary
around the corner
lately

CHART 5-3. *Where, Why, When, What Time, How Come, What . . . For.* Page 117
Time: 10–15 minutes

> Because many students have developed fossilized errors with question forms, it is important to bring students' attention to these and help them self-correct. Typical errors include: *Where you went? Where did you went? Why you stayed home? When your children do they go to school? Where your children go to school?*
>
> Because the structure and word order of *How come _____?* and *What _____ for?* are not easy to explain, emphasize that these are idiomatic phrases that are used in speaking more than in writing. You may want to point out to students that these are very common questions, particularly in spoken English.
>
> *How come* is another way of asking *why*, and it is used often when discussing a past event. It essentially means, *Why did this happen?* However, the tone is much more conversational.
>
> *What _____ for?* also asks why something happened or will happen, and it refers to purpose of action. You can explain it to students by modeling the example, *What did you do that for?*

- Ask students to close their books. Write the *wh*-words presented across the top of the board. For example:

  where   why   what time / when   why / what for / how come

- Ask students to explain what each *wh*-word or phrase asks about. Write these categories underneath the *wh*-word or phrase presented. For example:

  where   what time / when   why / what for / how come
  place   time expression   reason

- Present the chart by having students take turns reading through each question, (a)–(f).
- Spend extra time introducing and giving practice of (e) and (f).
- Explain that both *How come _____?* and *What _____ for?* are used to ask why something happened or will happen.
- Point out that both phrases are especially useful in everyday speaking, especially when asking others about their intentions or purposes.
- Give students an opportunity to practice using these phrases by asking students what they did the previous weekend and *How come* they did these actions or *What they did them for.* For example:

  Paulo, what did you do last weekend?

  I stayed in my room all day.

  <u>*How come you stayed*</u> *in your room all day?*

  I was waiting for a call from my girlfriend.

  Anya, what did you do last weekend?

  I spent too much money!

  <u>*What did you do that for?*</u>

  I needed a haircut, so I went to a very expensive salon, but I didn't realize it would cost so much!

- Discuss the variety of answers for each question and review the notes in the chart.

❑ EXERCISE 11. Looking at grammar.
Page 117
Time: 10–15 minutes

Optional Vocabulary
catch that   transferring
downtown

Expansion: Prepare index cards with the name of a famous international landmark or site on each one. Possible landmarks are included below. It should be pointed out that some are man-made and some are natural. Put students into pairs. Tell the pairs that they will try to determine which famous site or landmark other pairs of students have on their cards by asking a series of *wh*-questions. Distribute the index cards and make sure that each pair is familiar with their own landmark. Have pairs get up and move around the classroom, asking *wh*-questions to determine each targeted landmark. After students have succeeded in learning all the landmarks, put the names of the landmarks on the board and ask students which question / answer combinations allowed them to successfully guess the landmark in question.

> *Possible famous landmarks include:*
> *the Great Wall of China*
> *the Eiffel Tower*
> *Big Ben*
> *the Great Barrier Reef*
> *Ayers Rock*
> *the Great Pyramid*
> *the Coliseum*
> *Stonehenge*
> *Machu Picchu*
> *the Taj Mahal*
> *the Grand Canyon*
> *Mount Everest*
> *Angkor Wat*
> *the Panama Canal*
> *the Acropolis*
> *Disney World*

❏ EXERCISE 13. Reading and grammar.
Page 118
Time: 10–15 minutes

- Ask different students to read parts of the passage aloud.
- Ask students to create correct questions from the given words in items 1–5 and to ask them aloud.
- Instruct other students to respond to the questions. Review as a class.
- Ask the following additional questions and have students who haven't yet participated answer them orally.

> *What was Nina doing when Tom arrived home?*
> *Why was Nina worried?*
> *When is Nina's birthday?*
> *What did Tom think?*
> *How come Tom landed in a ditch?*
> *Why wasn't Nina upset about her birthday present?*

❏ EXERCISE 15. Warm-up. Page 118
Time: 5 minutes

> In this Warm-up, students are exposed to the fact that a question word can refer to a subject, an object, or an indirect object. Students need to read the questions very carefully in order to know which piece of information is sought.

CHART 5-4. Questions with *Who, Who(m),* and *What.* Page 119
Time: 10 minutes

> This grammar will be difficult unless students clearly understand the roles of subjects and objects in sentences. It is helpful to review subjects and objects before delving into this topic. Refer to Chart 6-3 (Subjects, Verbs, and Objects) in Chapter 6 if necessary.
>
> *Whom* is rarely used in everyday conversation. Native speakers prefer *who: Who did you see at the party? Who did you talk to? Who does Bob remind you of?*

- First, revisit the difference between subjects and objects by referring to pronouns that students are already familiar with.
- Give students a simple sentence that has a subject and a object.
- Write the sentence on the board and label the parts of speech. For example:

Subject	Verb	Object
I	called	Bob.

- Show students how to change the above sentence into a question in which *Who* is the subject.
- Illustrate these changes on the board by crossing out the original subject and replacing it with *Who.* Point out that *Who* replaces the subject *I* and write the answer to the question on the board as well.

Subject	Verb	Object	
~~I~~	called	Bob	
Who	called	Bob?	I did.

- Using the same question, demonstrate how *whom* changes the focus of a question.
- First, write the question on the board using *whom.*

> *Whom   did   I   call?*

- Ask students what the answer to the question is, and write it on the board.

> *Whom   did   I   call?   Bob.   I   called   Bob.*

- Then, ask students to label the parts of the speech in the question and the answer.

	Helping		Main				
O	Verb	S	Verb	O	S	V	O
Whom	did	I	call?	Bob.	I	called	Bob.

- Now, have students look at the two sets of questions and answers, and ask them to try to explain the differences between *who*-questions and *whom*-questions.
- Next, ask students to create a sentence with a subject and object that could be replaced by *what.* Write the sentence on the board. For example:

Subject	Verb	Object
A tornado	hit	the high school.

- With the help of students, transform the sentence into a *wh*-question by crossing out the original subject and replacing it with *what.*

Subject	Verb	Object	
~~A tornado~~	hit	the high school.	
What	hit	the high school?	A tornado.

- Using the original sentence again, replace the object with *what,* and change the sentence accordingly.

~~A tornado~~	hit	~~the high school.~~	
Object	Helping Verb	Subject	Main Verb
What	did	a tornado	hit?
The high school.			

- Read through the chart with your students and provide additional examples on the board as needed.

❏ EXERCISE 16. Looking at grammar.
Page 119
Time: 5–10 minutes

> The purpose of this practice is to help students figure out if the word order is or is not inverted when the question word is *who* or *what.*
>
> Help students make the connection between subjects and objects in statements and in questions by showing that the answer (*someone / something*) parallels the grammatical function of the question word. The question word can be substituted for *someone / something.* If it is a subject, no change is made in word order. If it is an object, the word order is inverted.

❏ EXERCISE 18. Let's talk: interview.
Page 120
Time: 10 minutes

> The purpose of this exercise is to help students readily produce the question and answer forms in free practice with one another. Encourage responses longer than one sentence. Encourage the questioner to ask follow-up questions.

- Ask students to get into pairs.
- Model the example.
- Show students how to make further conversation by asking follow-up questions.
- Tell students that these follow-up questions don't have to use the target grammar but will help them practice "making small talk." For example:

  Speaker A: What are you currently reading?
  Speaker B: A book about a cowboy.
  Speaker A: <u>What</u> is its title? <u>Who</u> is the main character?

- Walk around the classroom and interact with pairs of students. Help students expand on each exchange.

Optional Vocabulary
currently
memorable event
stresses you out

❏ EXERCISE 19. Listening. Page 120
Time: 5–10 minutes

- After students complete the exercise, discuss the final sentence.

- Ask students if they really think Speaker B feels better and have them explain why or why not.

Optional Vocabulary
confidential

❏ EXERCISE 20. Let's read and talk.
Page 121
Time: 10–15 minutes

> It is helpful for students to refer to their dictionaries as needed throughout this exercise. However, it is also very useful for students to discuss the italicized words with one another and you, as you go around the room engaging pairs. Reminding students to ask you for vocabulary help provides them with additional opportunities for active practice of the target material.

Expansion: If it seems an appropriate task for the class, ask students to give examples of each type of book. In addition, you can ask students to discuss similar categories for films. Additional vocabulary could include:

feature film	*animated film*
documentary	*musical*
blockbuster	*short film*
independent film	*Academy Award winner*
foreign film	

best picture / director / actor / actress / supporting actor / supporting actress

CHART 5-5. Using *What* + a Form of *Do.*
Page 121
Time: 10–15 minutes

> Use your students' lives and activities to demonstrate *What* + *do* questions. For example, *What is Miguel doing? What was Yoko doing before she sat down? What are you and your friends going to do during vacation? What did Kazu do yesterday afternoon?*
>
> Show the relationship between the verb form in the answer and the form of *do* in the question.

- Ask students questions about their lives that elicit the full range of tenses as shown in the chart.
- Write these questions on the board in order of the tenses in the chart.
- Write students' responses on the board and underline the tense to illustrate the connection between the verb tense in the response and the verb tense used in the *What* + a form of *do* question. For example:

  <u>What does Seiko</u> drink every morning?
  <u>She drinks</u> coffee.

- Have students open their books to Chart 5-5, and take turns reading the questions and answers in the chart.

❑ EXERCISE 23. Let's talk: interview.
Page 122
Time: 15–20 minutes

- Ask students to get up and move around the room while interviewing classmates.
- Interact with pairs and groups of students, writing down the most common question errors (usually with *verb + subject* inversion) for later review.
- Provide the vocabulary that students are seeking and assist in maintaining a conversational style among the groups.
- Review the exercise by asking students to tell you one piece of information learned about each member.
- Finish by writing on the board any errors you overheard, and correcting them together as a class.

❑ EXERCISE 24. Warm-up. Page 122
Time: 5 minutes

Expansion: Seemingly mundane topics often provide rich points of comparison. Exploit this Warm-up as a chance to learn more about your students' personal tastes as well as a bit about their culture. Though some version of ice cream is popular in most countries, its form can vary widely from country to country.

Because American English is being taught, ask your students to compare their ice cream to its American counterpart and describe how it is similar or different.

Additional questions to warm students up include:

– Is ice cream from your country similar to that in the United States?

– Are any of these cold and / or frozen desserts popular in your country?

frozen yogurt	sherbet
frozen custard	ice milk
gelato	popsicles
sorbet	

– How often do people from your country eat ice cream? Once or twice a week? Once a month? On special occasions?

– Are specific ice cream-only restaurants common in your country?

– In the U.S., many ice cream shops offer 20–40 flavors. How many flavors are generally offered at similar establishments in your country?

– Is "gourmet" ice cream a specialty where you live?

– What other kind of desserts or sweets are popular where you come from?

– Do people eat dessert every evening?

CHART 5-6. Using *Which* and *What Kind Of*.
Page 123
Time: 10–15 minutes

You might want to introduce the expressions *What sort of* and *What type of* as well. They have the same meaning as *What kind of*.

Use objects in the classroom to demonstrate what information can be elicited when *What kind of* is used. You can ask students what kind of shoes they are wearing, what kind of watches they have, etc., but it may be wise to avoid a discussion of brands and labels among a socioeconomically mixed group of students. You can always steer exchanges headed in that direction toward functionality / features as opposed to maker (For example: *What kind of watch do you have? Is it digital?*)

Which can also be used as a relative pronoun in adjective clauses, but unless a student asks a question about adjective clauses, it is best not to discuss this dual usage at this point. (See Chapter 12 if needed.)

One way to demonstrate the general difference between *which* and *what* is to put two different books on a student's desk. Focus the attention of the class on the two books and make sure students can see that they are different books (preferably different colors). Pick one of the books up and ask, *Which book did I just pick up? The red one or the blue one?* (*The grammar book or the dictionary?*) For contrast, walk to another student's desk and pick up any object from it. Hold it up so the class can see what you have in your hand and ask, *What did I just pick up?*

- Introduce *which* by giving students a choice among different class activity options. For example:

  Do you want to listen to an explanation of the grammar in Chart 5-6, or do you want to have a surprise test?

  Which class activity do you want to do?

- Highlight *or* in the first question and *which* in the second to illustrate the fact that *which* is used for known options and alternatives. Write a note about this on the board, such as:

  Which: used for known alternatives

- Contrast *which* with *what* by asking students a new question and writing it on the board. For example:

  What kind of class activity do you want to do next?

- If students don't immediately respond with original ideas, ask questions that will elicit these, such as:

  Do you want to play a game?

  Do you want to have a class party?

  Do you want to have a class nap?

  Do you want to have a break from grammar and questions?

  What kind of class activity do you want to do?

- Emphasize that *which* is for known or established alternatives and choices, but *what kind of* asks for information about a specific kind. Write this explanation on the board:

  What kind of: used for information about a specific kind

  What kind of class activity do you want to do next?

- Explain to students that they can answer the *which* question with <u>any</u> category of class activity they can think of. Remind them they are not limited to known options.
- Ask students to take turns reading through sentences (a)–(f). Review the explanatory notes.

❑ EXERCISE 26. Let's talk: interview.
Page 124
Time: 10–15 minutes

> This exercise is intended to demonstrate how the target structure can elicit real information and is used in everyday conversation. Emphasize that *what kind of* refers to a variety of specific types within a category, The questions ask about a category, and the answers supply specific kinds.

- Ask students to first complete each question by looking at the specific answer given by Speaker B and generalizing to a whole category.
- Instruct students to move around the room as they interview one another and to ask further questions as they naturally arise.
- Join the conversations and engage reluctant speakers before asking the students to return to their seats.
- If time permits, ask students to report back something about the tastes and preferences of each member of the class.

CHART 5-7. Using *Whose*. Page 125
Time: 10 minutes

> The two principal ways of asking questions about possession are to use *whose* and the verb phrase *belong to*. *Whose (book) is this?* vs. *Who(m) does this (book) belong to?*
>
> *Whose* is more common and conversational than *belong to.*
>
> Because most Americans do not use *whom* when speaking, it may be best to avoid teaching the object form of *who* at this stage. It can be introduced at a later stage, as needed.
>
> *Whose* is also used in adjective clauses such as, *That's the man whose house burned down.* See Chapter 12 for more information on this usage.
>
> In comparing the pronunciation of *whose* and *who's,* the text explains that *who's = who + is.* However, it is useful for students to know that *who's* can also be a contraction for *who + has* when *has* is used as the auxiliary of the present perfect. (Example: *Who's been to Disneyland?*) You can mention this meaning of *who's* if your students seem ready.

- Go to a student's desk and pick up his/her book, showing it to the class.
- Ask students, *Whose book is this?* and write the question on the board.

- Now ask students, *Who does this book belong to?* and write this related question underneath.
- Explain that *whose* is used to demonstrate a relationship of ownership or belonging between a person and another person or a person and an object.
- Add a note on this explanation to the boardwork. For example:

  Whose: shows ownership or relationship
  Whose book is this? = Who does this book belong to?

- Explain that *whose* can easily be confused with the contraction of *who + is.*
- Write an example of a question using *who's.* For example:

  Who's = who + is
  Who's going to come to our party?

- Tell students they need to pay attention to a question's subject and verb to distinguish the uses when relying on listening.
- Also, explain that only *whose* will be followed immediately by a noun.
- Ask students to take turns reading the example sentences from the chart. Elaborate on the notes included in the chart as needed.

❑ EXERCISE 28. Let's talk: pairwork.
Page 125
Time: 10–15 minutes

Expansion: Tell students they are going to practice using *whose* while also exploring how observant they are about each other and each other's possessions. Ask three to four students to leave the room for 5 minutes and make sure they are not able to see what is going on during their absence. During their absence, ask the remaining students to bring one personal item up to the front of the room to be temporarily displayed on a table/desk. Not every student need do this, but a collection of 5–10 items works well. Students should bring up possessions that differ from one another's. (For example, because everyone will have the same book, the text itself is not an option, but dictionaries could be.) However, students should be encouraged to contribute easily removed personal items such as watches, cell phones, notebooks, earrings, necklaces, scarves, dictionaries, handbags, and backpacks. The items should not have names or monograms on them.

Now invite the students who had left the room back in. They should be instructed to show an item to the rest of the class, ask an appropriate *whose* question, and guess who the owner of the item is. Their classmates can give hints as needed. Finally, the students should continue asking questions until they have been answered and the objects returned to the correct people.

❏ EXERCISE 30. Listening. Page 126
Time: 5–10 minutes

> Emphasize that the task is to distinguish between *whose* and *who's* when listening.
>
> Remind students to listen for the subject and the verb and that only *whose* can be immediately followed by a noun.

CHART 5-8. Using *How*. Page 127
Time: 10–15 minutes

> In general, *how* asks about manner, means, condition, degree, and extent. Because these terms themselves are not easy for students at this level, it is not always useful to use them when explaining *how*. In fact, because *how* doesn't lend itself to an easy definition, it is better for students that you don't attempt one. It is enough to say that *how* is used to get more information about some part of a sentence.
>
> Starting with this chart, the text introduces common uses of *how* in four separate charts so that students may slowly build their understanding of its meanings and uses.

• Ask your students *how* they got to class and write the question on the board. For example:

  How did you get to class today?

• Write students' responses on the board, in full sentences. For example:

  How did you get to class today?
  Mika took the bus.
  Chang and Layla walked.
  You drove to class.

• Explain that one distinct use of *how* is to discuss means of transportation. Explain that *means* also answers the question of *in what way?*

• Introduce the second use of *how,* as presented in the chart.

• Explain that *how* can also be used with adjectives or adverbs.

• Ask students some simple *how + adjective* questions and put both their questions and answers on the board. For example:

  How old is your mother?
  My mother is sixty-three years old.

  How tall are you?
  I am 5' 4", if I stretch myself.

• Ask students to read the example sentences. Put them on the board, as is useful.

• Review the notes included on the right-hand side of the chart.

❏ EXERCISE 32. Reading and grammar.
Page 127
Time: 10 minutes

• Give students ample time to read independently and complete the questions.

• Then ask students to take turns reading sentences from the passage aloud.

• Answer the questions as a class.

• Ask students in what way the question in item 5 is different from those in questions 1–4.

CHART 5-9. Using *How Often*. Page 129
Time: 10 minutes

> Compare: *How often* is the common way to ask for general information about frequency, as in (a). The listener can respond in many different ways, as indicated by the sample answers given in the chart. *How many times* is used to elicit more specific information about a given length of time. *How many times* also limits the ways in which the listener can respond to it, as in (b).
>
> Discuss the frequency expression included in the chart, and write notes to show how they are used with *how often*. Even though some of the frequency expressions are hard to define precisely, your attempt to do so will support students' understanding of these terms.

• Remind students that they have already met *How often* when using simple present tense.

• Ask students a question in this form and write both the question and the answers it generates on the board, for further exploration. For example:

  How often do you speak to your parents in your country?
  I speak to my parents at least once a week.
  How often do you go to the doctor?
  Jose goes to the doctor once a year, for a checkup.

• Underline students' use of the simple present in their responses and ask them why they need to use this tense. You should be able to elicit an answer linking simple present tense to regularly scheduled or occurring events. For example:

  How often do you speak to your parents in your country?
  I speak to my parents at least once a week.
  How often do you go to the doctor?
  Jose goes to the doctor once a year, for a checkup.

• Introduce *How many times* by asking students a newly generated question and writing both the question and response on the board. For example:

  How many times a week do you eat dessert?
  I eat dessert two times a week.

• Explain that when using *How many times* questions, the response has to include a number of times.

• Have students take turns reading sentences under sections (a) and (b) while also reviewing the notes on the right-hand side of the chart.

- Contrast the two forms with a direct comparison on the board:

  How often do you go grocery shopping?

  I go grocery shopping frequently, whenever I need something.

  How many times a week do you go grocery shopping?

  I go grocery shopping three or four times a week.

- Remind students that the answers to *How many times* questions must include a number of times. *How many times* questions cannot be answered with a frequency adverb such as *often*.

❑ EXERCISE 36. Let's talk: pairwork.
Page 130
Time: 10–15 minutes

> This exercise focuses not only on questions with *How often* but, just as importantly, on common ways to answer such questions. Even though these frequency expressions are not presented in a separate chart, some of your teaching should focus on them.

Optional Vocabulary
podcasts
attend
download

CHART 5-10. Using *How Far.* Page 131
Time: 10–15 minutes

> This chart teaches expletive *it* for expressing distances as well as for asking questions about distance. Elicit further examples of the grammar patterns in (b) by using local destinations that your class is familiar with.
>
> One way to introduce the topic is to gradually give pieces of information about a well-known distance until students know what the distance is and what its significance is. As students participate in contributing what they know about this universally recognizable distance, write notes on the board. Possible distances include: marathon distance, distance from earth to moon, length of Great Wall of China, the circumference of the world.

- Write *26.2 miles / 42.195 kilometers* on the board.
- Write the phrase *Olympic Event* nearby.
- Because a marathon is an internationally recognized distance, ask questions about the distance and put any information generated by students on the board.
- It is likely that at least one student will know about the legend of the marathon, and that a marathon represents the distance from Marathon to Athens.

- Write as many notes as possible about this on the board. Students may be able to contribute the following:

  Greek warrior Pheidippides

  Battle of Marathon

  Ran to announce Athens victory

  Died on arrival

- Explain that *How far* is used to find out more about distance.
- Once you have enough facts to pose a question regarding the distance of a marathon, form a related *How far* question and write it on the board. For example: *How far is a marathon? How far is it from Marathon to Athens?*
- With your students taking turns, read sentences / questions (a)–(g) aloud and further explain the notes on the right-hand side of the chart.
- Remind students that just like when using *How many times*, *How many miles* requires a very specific response that provides an actual number of miles.

❑ EXERCISE 40. Looking at grammar.
Page 132
Time: 10 minutes

> This exercise is intended for discussion of known distances, and it lends itself to a competition. Before you begin, find the information required to complete the questions so that you will immediately have a sense of whose guess is close and whose is not. In order to engage students maximally, ask them to both come up with the correct form of the question and take a guess at the answer. Part of the fun will become seeing who comes close to these famous distances and who is not even close to the answer.

Expansion: Prior to class, make a list of local distances that students would have some idea of. Using an Internet mapping tool, learn how far each local distance is. Write only the names of two locations on each card and distribute one to each student. Each student must come up with the correct form of the question and then should poll classmates to see who can come closest to the actual distances. Points can be awarded to the student who comes closest to the actual distance without exceeding it.

Though most start points and destinations will be known proper names, some common distances to have students guess are:

this school ⟷ the nearest bank
my desk ⟷ the closest bathroom
this classroom ⟷ the closest ice cream shop
the school ⟷ the X dormitory
the school ⟷ the nearest international airport
the school ⟷ the nearest movie theater

Students may or may not be familiar with the idiomatic use of *take* featured here. You can help students engage with this topic by talking about the huge variation in the amount of time different people spend on different everyday tasks.

Expansion: Prepare additional conversation questions to use with this Warm-up. Ask random questions (such as the ones listed below) modeling the correct word order and being careful to pronounce the third person -*s* in *takes*. Offer information about yourself, your commute, and your daily habits to further heighten students' interest.

Possible Questions:

Who takes longer to get ready to go out at night: men or women?

How long does it take you to fully wake up in the morning? Do you jump out of bed or press the snooze button?

How long does it take you to shower?

How long does it take you to get to class here?

When you are at home, how long does it take you to go to work? Do you have a long commute?

Which takes longer to prepare, a breakfast of hot cereal and fruit or one of eggs and bacon?

How long does it take you to fall asleep at night? Do you fall asleep as soon as your head hits the pillow, or do you need to count sheep?

CHART 5-11. Length of Time: *It + Take* and *How Long.* Page 132
Time: 10 minutes

In this section, the text is teaching expletive *it + take* for expressing length of time as well as *how long* to ask questions about length of time.

The text deals with infinitives following expletive *it* in Chapter 13.

Using two examples of activities whose duration can easily and definitively be compared is a useful way to start the chart presentation.

- Ask your students which takes longer: making a cup of tea or baking and decorating a cake.
- Write the two related questions on the board, using the new target grammar and underlining the important parts. For example:

  How long does it take to make a cup of tea?
  How long does it take to bake a cake?

- Explain that this question, *How long does **it** take,* asks for an informed estimate of time spent.
- Explain that the above form can be modified to include one particular person's or subject's experience by adding a person between *take* and *to.*

- Write new examples, using the same questions. For example:

  How long does it take you / one / a person / your mother to make a cup of tea?

  How long does it take you / one / a person / your mother to bake a cake?

- Ask students to take turns reading through questions (a)–(g) from the chart and to review the notes carefully.

CHART 5-12. Spoken and Written Contractions with Question Words. Page 134
Time: 10–15 minutes

It is critical for students to understand that the contractions in (a)–(i) are regularly used in spoken English but are not used in written English.

Tell students that in their everyday interactions with native speakers they are likely to hear a great deal of contracted English. Explain that at this stage in their learning, it is more important for them to understand spoken contractions than to speak them. By learning the correct and non-contracted form, they will be prepared to comprehend the spoken form. It is important for them to have a strong grasp of *what*-questions and verbs in their standard form before they attempt using contractions.

- Begin by writing in capital letters across the top of the board:

  SPOKEN ONLY; NOT IN WRITING

- Explain that the question word contractions in (a)–(i) are not used in written English, but that you will be writing the questions just so students can see how to pronounce the contractions.
- Ask students why they are studying English and write this question on the board. For example:

  Why are you studying English?

- Write a few student responses on the board. For example:

  I'm studying English because my boyfriend is from California.

  I'm studying English because I want to get a job in an American trading company.

- Now, contract *why* and *are* and ask the question again. For example: *Why're you studying English?*
- Expand on this by asking, *What's your purpose in studying English?*
- Have students repeat after you and correct their pronunciation.
- Ask students more contracted *wh*-questions and have students repeat after you. For example:

  What's your favorite part of studying English?
  How've you enjoyed studying prepositions?
  When're you going to return to your country?
  How're you going to maintain your English there?

- Now that students have had practice using *wh*-contractions, ask them to take turns reading each question in examples (a)–(i) aloud.
- Stress that the contractions shown in (j) are found in writing but that they are not used in formal writing.

❑ EXERCISE 47. Listening. Page 135
Time: 5–10 minutes

Expansion: Prepare discussion questions (preferably on a handout) to engage students in a discussion of this topic. Students can use contracted *wh*-forms when providing the typical questions their parents asked them at this age. In addition, this discussion topic gives students practice with many of the question forms they have studied in Chapter 5.

Possible Discussion Questions:

How old were you when you began going out with your friends at night?

In general, how old are teenagers in your country when they begin doing so?

What sort of questions do / did your parents ask you before you go / went out with friends?

How often do / did you go out with your friends?

What sort of questions do / have you ask(ed) your teenage children when they go / have gone out with friends?

How late do / did your parents allow you to stay out at night?

How often do / did you stay out later than your parents allowed?

In the United States, many parents would agree that teenagers want to spend a lot of time with their peers and friends and relatively little time with their families. Is this situation also true in your country?

If so, why do you think this is true?

What do teenagers learn from spending time with their friends?

How much time do teenagers in your country spend socializing via computer on Facebook, Twitter, MySpace, or similar social networking sites?

What are some concerns that parents have about social networking sites?

CHART 5-13. More Questions With *How*.
Page 137
Time: 10–15 minutes

This chart consists of some miscellaneous but common questions with *how*. Explicitly teaching these questions, especially (d)–(f), is extremely beneficial for students and will help them become more confident users of English.

Most students have been using questions (a)–(c) already to refine their language skills. Being able to form the expected question (*How do you _____?*)

enhances their English language learning experience. With these forms, students can autonomously seek new information, correction, and refinement from native speakers who are not teachers.

When explaining (d)–(f), emphasize that these questions are often used as greetings themselves and in conjunction with *Hi there / Hey*. Though most students are familiar with similar linguistic exchanges in their languages ("Ça va?" " ¿ Qué pasa?"), this type of greeting may be less common in other languages. By teaching the use of these questions and the most common responses explicitly, students are much better prepared to use their English with native speakers and in a variety of social settings.

In (f), *How's it going?* is another way of asking *How's everything going?*

Example (h) needs a little discussion and perhaps role-playing. Ask Speaker A to introduce B to Speaker C. Ask B and C to use *How do you do?* Have them shake hands at the same time. You should take time to discuss forms of introduction and compare the much more formal (and now quite old-fashioned) *How do you do?* with the more common *Hello. Nice to meet you.*

Because students desperately want to use the language that will make them fit in best, discussing register and what phrases are most common is beneficial for non-native speakers. You may find that many students have been taught a more formal register than suits their purposes. While it is far better for students to learn standard, written grammatical forms first before they begin breaking rules and reducing their English, register is a somewhat different matter. Students appreciate when you correct them if they begin to use a formal phrase that is no longer common in spoken English.

- Ask students to pick a word in English that they find difficult to spell or say / pronounce.
- Write on the board *How do you _____?*
- Have students go to the board and write questions using their "difficult" word choices. For example:

    How do you say "knowledge"?

- Ask other students to respond with correct spelling and pronunciation.
- Ask students to turn to the chart. Review (a)–(c).
- Begin presenting (d)–(f) by asking students to think about what sort of a greeting is commonly exchanged between people in their country meeting in an informal setting.
- If practical, ask them to share with the class what the greeting translates to (roughly) in English.
- Ask students to take turns reading (g).
- Review the notes and discuss responses as well as context.
- Finish by presenting (h) and stress that this greeting is not commonly used.

❏ EXERCISE 50. Game. Page 137
Time: 10–15 minutes

This exercise is a spelling game and works best in small groups. Many of the words on this list are frequently misspelled by second-language students and native speakers as well.

Item 1: A mnemonic device is to remember that it consists of three individual words *to + get + her*.

Items 4, 5, and 9: Remind students of the spelling rules they learned in Chart 2-5.

Item 6: The old spelling rule is "i" before "e" except after "c" or when pronounced /ey/ as in *neighbor* and *weigh*. That rule accounts for the spelling of *receive* and *neighbor;* it does not, however, account for the spelling of the word *foreign* in item 5. Tell your students that you sympathize with them as they face challenges in English spelling. Remind them that they can always look up words in their dictionaries.

❏ EXERCISE 51. Let's talk. Page 138
Time: 10–15 minutes

Students generally enjoy this discussion, but obviously it works best in a multilingual classroom. You can expand this exercise to include other words and phrases that students may want to know in one another's languages.

In some languages, there is no direct translation for *thank you.* Survey the language groups in the class and discuss various ways of expressing thanks and gratitude.

Some classes like to list all the way to say "I love you" in as many languages as they can. Some students assiduously copy down each one.

Expansion: Additional expressions include:
I love you.
I'm sorry.
I don't want to go out with you anymore.
That's great! (or any other way to show enthusiasm)
Congratulations.

CHART 5-14. Using *How About* and *What About.* Page 138
Time: 10 minutes

How about and *What about* invite the listener to respond with how he / she feels about the idea the questioner suggests. The questioner is saying, *I think this is a possible idea for you / us to consider. What do you think about it?*

The *-ing* form in examples (c) and (d) is a gerund. Gerunds are introduced in Chapter 13.

In examples (e) and (f) *How about* and *What about* are "conversation continuers." They are used to promote the sharing of information in polite conversation. In some situations, if someone asks you if you are hungry, it is polite to ask if he / she is hungry, as in (f).

- Write on the board *How about . . . ?* and *What about . . . ?*
- Explain that:
  - *both questions can be used to make a suggestion and to invite others to make suggestions*
  - *both questions are most commonly used when more than one person is involved in a plan*
- Introduce a hypothetical situation to students such as a class vacation structured to improve students' speaking.
- Provide an example and write it on the board. For example:

  How about traveling to a small town in the middle of the United States where there are very few people who speak other languages?

- Ask students for other ideas for a class vacation structured to enhance their English. Have them use *How about . . . ?* and *What about . . . ?*
- Write some of the most imaginative or interesting suggestions using the target grammar on the board.
- If it makes sense to do so, ask students to vote on the best suggestion.
- Ask students to take turns reading (a)–(d) aloud.
- Discuss and expand on the notes included in the chart.
- Next, explain that another use of *How about* and *What about* is to check in with others' feelings and physical condition at the moment.
- Explain that when using *How about* and *What about*, the speaker first states his / her feelings, and condition, then asks about yours.

❏ EXERCISE 53. Grammar and listening. Page 138
Time: 5–10 minutes

This listening exercise allows students to become familiar with *How about* and *What about* as they are used in everyday conversations.

- Make sure that students realize the task: choosing the best response to either a *How about* or *What about* question.
- While reviewing the answers, ask students if they can also give you a question that would call forth the incorrect responses.

CHART 5-15. Tag Questions. Page 140
Time: 15–20 minutes

It is important for students to understand that a question with a tag indicates the speaker's belief about the validity of the idea being expressed. The speaker believes to be true what is expressed in the statement before the tag.

Students are already familiar with the idea of a rising intonation at the end of a question. In the examples and exercises on tags, a rising intonation should be used throughout. By explicitly pointing out intonation to students now, as they master tags, you will help them become more confident when having actual conversations with native speakers.

You may want to stress that falling intonation is used when speakers are quite sure of the intention or response of the person they are speaking to. This makes the question "rhetorical." The questioner, in this case, is not genuinely seeking information. In these cases, the speaker is really confirming information but using a question form to do so. The best way to teach your students this is to model and exaggerate the falling intonation that is used. For example:

Max, English grammar is easy, isn't it?
You assume Max agrees that English grammar is easy.
Lin-Fang, you don't want to take a test today, do you?
You assume that Lin-Fang doesn't want to take a test today.

Other possible informal tags that turn statements into questions follow:

It's really cold today, eh?
We take Route 66, right?
The thunder is deafening, huh?
You borrowed my dictionary, no?

Point out the polarity or opposition of tags, explaining what the plus and minus symbols indicate. The plus is for affirmative verbs, and the minus is for negative verbs. Be prepared to spend ample time on this aspect of tags. Though they are very commonly used, and non-native speakers have probably heard them before this, they can be challenging to form and master use of.

- Explain that tag questions are often ways of confirming what you think is true.

- Tell students that in order to form tag questions, the speaker states his/her supposition and immediately follows it with a question.

- This question is the tag, and it is formed with the original statement's auxiliary verb and the subject, inverted to make a question.

- Explain that if the statement is positive, the tag is negative, and the expected response is affirmative. Write the formula on the board:

  Affirmative Statement + Negative Tag ⇒
  Affirmative Expected Answer

- Explain that if the statement is negative, the tag is positive, and the expected response is negative. Write the formula on the board:

  Negative Statement + Affirmative Tag ⇒
  Negative Expected Answer

- Ask a student to observe something about the class and state it.
- Write his/her statement immediately beneath the formula and add a comma to indicate a tag question is coming. For example:

  Affirmative Statement + Negative Tag ⇒
  Affirmative Expected Answer
  It's a bit stuffy in here,

- Now with the help of the class, identify the verb and subject and create a negative tag. Write this after the original statement.

  Affirmative Statement + Negative Tag ⇒
  Affirmative Expected Answer
  It's a bit stuffy in here, isn't it?

- Now complete the whole exchange by adding the expected response.

  Affirmative Statement + Negative Tag ⇒
  Affirmative Expected Answer
  It's a bit stuffy in here, isn't it?   Yes. (Yes, it is.)

- Take time to draw students' attention to the falling intonation used with these tag questions.
- Explain to students that these tag questions and the falling intonation used are ways to confirm the listener's agreement with the speaker and are not part of a genuine question.
- Tell students that falling intonation (rather than rising intonation, as used with a real, information-seeking question) further indicates that the speaker assumes the listener agrees with the "question."
- Model the following "questions" with tags and falling intonation with students.
- Ask students what the speaker/you expect the listener's response will be. For example:

  You: *It is warm out today, isn't it?*
  You: *Do I think my listener agrees with my opinion of the weather?*
  Students: *Yes.*
  You: *How do you know what I think when I ask this question?*
  Students: *You are using a tag and falling intonation.*

- Follow the same step-by-step boardwork using a student-generated negative statement.
- Ask students to take turns reading (a)–(e) aloud.
- Review the notes on the right-hand side of the chart.
- Present intonation and demonstrate the difference between seeking information and inviting conversation.

❏ EXERCISE 56. Listening and grammar.
Page 140
Time: 5 minutes

- Play the audio through once without stopping. Play it again with pauses as many times as necessary.
- Discuss the responses as a class. Make sure to model the falling or rising intonation.

This exercise reviews Chapters 1–5. Because it has several distinct parts, and students often need different lengths of time to absorb the same material, it can be helpful to break this exercise up into seatwork, group work, and homework.

Optional Vocabulary

futures	lonely
village	drowning
jewels: emerald, ruby, diamond	miserable
announced	affection
claim	castle
grand	poorly

Chapter 6
Nouns and Pronouns

CHAPTER SUMMARY

OBJECTIVE: Nouns are the basic tools for giving names to and talking about things and concepts. Learners need usage ability of not only nouns, but also of associated words, such as pronouns, adjectives, and prepositions.

APPROACH: This chapter seeks to provide an acquaintance with basic noun structures and related terms in English grammar. It explains how these structures fit into the fundamental patterns of the simple sentence in English. It also provides students with ample practice recognizing and producing the various structures. This practice will allow students to gain confidence when using nouns and associated parts of speech so that they can self-correct as needed.

TERMINOLOGY: Some books use the term "noun adjunct" for the word *vegetable* in *vegetable garden*. This text, however, simply calls this type of noun "a noun used as an adjective." A distinction is made between "possessive pronouns" (for example: *my*) and "possessive adjectives" (for example: *mine*).

❏ **EXERCISE 1.** What do I already know?
Page 146
Time: 5–10 minutes

> For this exercise, you will need to supply an elementary understanding of the concepts these grammar terms present. Some students will be quite familiar with these terms, and some students will not be, in which case this exercise should highlight what they need to learn in this chapter.
>
> When discussing this exercise, you can use the following explanations after first seeing if students can provide you with working definitions of their own.
>
> *Noun: person, place, or thing*
>
> *Pronoun: a word that takes the place of a noun*
>
> *Preposition: a word that goes in front of a noun and gives information about place, time, direction, and other relationships*
>
> *Adjective: a word that both precedes a noun and describes it*

- Have the students take turns reading the first four sentences and the related parts of speech aloud.

- Put each part of speech on the board as it comes up and ask students what they can tell you about it.
- Write any thoughts or notes students provide you with on the board.
- Have students complete the remainder of the exercise as a class. Add to the working definitions on the board as new information comes up.

❏ **EXERCISE 2.** Warm-up. Page 146
Time: 5–10 minutes

- Write the terms *singular* and *plural* on the board.
- Ask students to define both. Write their definitions underneath the terms. For example:

SINGULAR	PLURAL
one	more than one, many

CHART 6-1. Plural Forms of Nouns. Page 147
Time: 10–15 minutes

> You may wish to model the nouns in (a) to illustrate the three different pronunciations of final /s/ and /es/: *birds* = bird + /z/; *streets* = street + /s/; and *roses* = rose + /əz/.
>
> In section (f), you may point out that *-s*, not *-es*, is added to nouns that end in *-o* when the noun is a shortened form (for example: *auto* instead of *automobile*), when the noun is related to a musical term, and when the noun ends in two vowels. Or, you can simply say that sometimes one adds *-s*, and sometimes one adds *-es*; when in doubt, look it up.
>
> Section (i) is included simply to inform the students that some oddities in the formation of plural nouns do exist. Words with foreign plurals are not emphasized in this text; they are dealt with more fully in *Understanding and Using English Grammar*. The two words in section (i) are difficult vocabulary for most students at this level. You might want to add that these rather unusual noncount nouns are in the process of being Anglicanized; that is, they are often spoken with more regular forms, for example: *one bacteria*. In formal writing, however, the forms in this chart are still preferred.

- Remind students to add -s to third person verbs and that certain spelling rules apply for doing so.
- Explain that special spelling rules apply when making singular nouns plural and that the nouns presented in (b), (c), and (f) are similar to verbs that also end in the same consonants, vowels, or blends.
- Ask students to take turns reading each section of the chart aloud. After they have read the examples provided in the text, give your own example of a noun for students to make plural and write this on the board.
- After you have read through the chart with students, ask them to help you create an abbreviated chart of (a)–(f) on the board for immediate review.
- Instruct students to keep their books closed while doing so, and be ready to give them prompts. For example:

  (a) most nouns + -s
  book ⇒ books
  (b) nouns ending in -sh, -ch, -ss, -x: + -es
  guess ⇒ guesses
  Etc.

- Explain to students that (g)–(i) simply need to be memorized because there is no obvious pattern.
- Tell students that their first job is to simply recognize that these nouns do not follow the patterns above. Then they can practice the patterns in exercises.

❑ EXERCISE 4. Looking at grammar.
Page 148
Time: 10 minutes

- Redraw this chart on the board, just as it is in the book.
- Give students an opportunity to look through the list of nouns. Then hand out chalk or markers.
- Assign each student one word from the list of singular nouns.
- Tell them to transform the singular nouns to plural forms and add them to the correct column on the board.
- When the board version of the chart is complete, review it as a class.

Expansion: Create index cards with categories on them. Each phrase on the card should describe an entire category. For example:

  things people eat at breakfast
  places people can swim
  good birthday gifts
  cute animals

Prepare enough different index cards to allow every two students to work with two unique cards with sets of descriptive phrases. Divide students into pairs and give each pair two category cards. Carefully explain directions for the activity. You can also write directions on the board.

Tell students that this activity will give them opportunities to practice using and comprehending plural nouns. Then, explain to students that each student will look at his / her card and begin giving his / her partner clues to the category simply by giving

examples (in plural nouns) of the category described. Each student needs to be prepared to give enough plural noun examples so that their partner can guess the category. For example, for the categories given a student might say (possible examples in italics):

things people eat at breakfast
  toast, eggs, bacon, pancakes, waffles, cereal

places people can swim
  lakes, ponds, public swimming pools, private swimming pools, beaches, rivers

birthday gifts
  gift cards, money, dinners out, clothes, books

cute animals
  puppies, kittens, bunnies, guinea pigs

❑ EXERCISE 6. Warm-up: listening.
Page 149.
Time: 5 minutes

- Before students listen, ask them to pay attention to the different pronunciations of final -s / -es.
- When reviewing with students, ask them to share their observations about the differences they have noticed.

CHART 6-2. Pronunciation of Final -s / -es.
Page 149
Time: 10 minutes

Final -s / -es is challenging for most ESL and EFL students. Paying special attention to its pronunciations can be helpful. In a way, students need to train themselves to be aware of hearing -s / -es as an aid to using it correctly in their own production, both spoken and written.

Explain and model the pronunciation of the examples.

To explain voiceless vs. voiced, tell the students to put their hand to their voice box to feel vibrations. A voiceless sound such as / t / or / s / comes from air being pushed over the tongue and through the teeth; a voiced sound such as / d / or / z / emanates from the voice box.

Point out that in voiceless-voiced pairs such as / s / and / z /, the tongue and teeth are in the same position. The only difference is the addition of the voice box to the / z / sound.

Some other voiceless vs. voiced pairs are / t / and / d /, / p / and / b /, / f / and / v /.

Define buzz (the sound a bee makes).

The upside down "e" in the symbol sounds like / əz / and is called a "schwa."

- Write three separate columns on the board and label them as follows:

  1. / s /   2. / z /   3. / əz /

- Go through each set of words (a)–(c) with students.
- Explain voiceless and voiced sounds, and ask your students to put their hand on their voice box (larynx) in their neck.

- Make sure that your students can really feel the vibrations or the lack thereof, depending on which sounds students are making.
- Explain to students that though they may often have trouble with these three endings and how to pronounce them, it is easy to recognize why certain words are pronounced in certain ways.
- To demonstrate this, ask students to attempt to pronounce one of the plural examples in this chart with the wrong ending.
- As students try to use the wrong pronunciation for different endings, they will quickly realize that the existing pronunciation has developed because it is hard work to pronounce certain combinations. For example, if a student were to try to pronounce a word ending in /t/, a voiceless sound with the /z/ version of -s, they would find it nearly impossible to do so.
- Ask students to suggest different words to try out with each of the three endings. As they do so, write these new examples under the appropriate column headings. For example:

1. /s/	2. /z/	3. /əz/
slots	eggs	watches
ships	kids	ages

❑ **EXERCISE 7.** Listening. Page 150
Time: 5–10 minutes

- Play the audio and ask students to circle the sound they hear.
- After reviewing the exercise, read through nouns again and ask students to repeat the correct pronunciation of each item after you.
- Look at each item again and ask students to come up with other nouns that have the same ending sounds.

❑ **EXERCISE 9.** Listening and pronunciation. Page 150
Time: 5–10 minutes

Reinforce the information in Chart 6-2 by asking students to define voiced and voiceless sounds. For example, point out that the final -s is pronounced /z/ in item 1 because /m/ is a voiced sound, and pronounced /s/ in item 2 because /k/ is a voiceless sound.

❑ **EXERCISE 11.** Warm-up. Page 150
Time: 5 minutes

You may want to make lists of your own and model the task by writing an abbreviated list for each item on the board.

Part III
- Lead the discussion by asking students the questions in items 1–4.
- Ask students to define *subjects* and *objects,* and write on the board any examples or definitions given.

CHART 6-3. Subjects, Verbs, and Objects.
Page 151
Time: 5–10 minutes

This chart contains a simplified explanation of the simple sentence. Students only need a basic understanding of subjects, verbs, and objects. Many students will already have some understanding of the basic patterns.

You may want to delay a discussion of intransitive vs. transitive until Chapter 10, where the distinction is dealt with in connection with the passive form. If you decide to introduce the terminology here, you could point out that dictionaries might label intransitive verbs as *v.i.*, *V*, *I*, and transitive verbs as *v.t.*, *V + O*, or *T.*

- Create a sentence or two using students' names and/or real lives to show the subject of a sentence. For example:

    Bo Young wrote a letter.
    Manuel rode his bicycle to class today.

- Explain that the subject of a sentence does not simply come before the verb, but in fact is the "doer" of the verb's action.
- After you have written these sentences on the board, ask your students to help you label the subject and verbs of these sentences. For example:

    S   V
    Bo Young wrote a letter.
    S   V
    Manuel rode his bicycle to class today.

- When reviewing the above sentences, emphasize that it is the subject that does the action of the verb.
- Next, illustrate the role of the object by asking questions. For example:

    Ask: *What did Bo Young write?*
    Answer: *a letter*

    Ask: *What did Manuel ride to class?*
    Answer: *his bicycle*

- Explain that the subject of the verb does the action, but the object of the verb receives or feels the effect of the action.

❏ EXERCISE 12. Looking at grammar.
Page 151
Time: 5–10 minutes

> This is a simple exercise, but the grammar it demonstrates is essential for students of this text to understand.

- Explain to students that this exercise allows them to analyze a sentence and separate out each of its parts.
- Explain that some verbs cannot be followed by an object at all, and that later in this book these intransitive verbs (as they are called) will be discussed at length.
- Tell students that some verbs can be followed by an object, but this is not necessary. To illustrate this, write the following examples on the board.

    Our teacher is eating.

    Our teacher is eating a sandwich.

- Ask students to label each part of the sentences on the board.
- Give students time to complete the exercise as seatwork and then review as a class.

❏ EXERCISE 13. Looking at grammar.
Page 152
Time: 5–10 minutes

> You might want to discuss the sentence structure of some of these items. Ask students how they know that the italicized word is a noun or a verb, and ensure that they look beyond where the word is placed in the sentence.

Optional Vocabulary

name . . . after	vacant
relatives	express
runways	hobby

CHART 6-4. Objects of Prepositions.
Page 153
Time: 10–15 minutes

> What is a preposition? A simplified definition: A preposition is a word that occurs most often in front of nouns (or pronouns) to give information about place, time, and other relationships.
>
> Prepositions can also be humorously defined as "little words that cause second language learners a lot of trouble!"
>
> A definition may not be necessary or desirable. The text approaches recognition of prepositions (1) by supplying a list and simply telling the students that these words are prepositions, and (2) by demonstrating their grammatical structures and function in the examples and exercises.

> Unit C in the Appendix contains preposition combinations with verbs and adjectives, with a reference list and exercises. The combinations are broken into small groups as an aid to learning. You may want to incorporate lessons from the Appendix into your class syllabus following the study of this unit. Students might use the Appendix to study one group of prepositions a week for the rest of the term.

- Explain that prepositions are used in combination with nouns. When used in this way, they give more information about where, when, how often, and in what way the action of the sentence takes place.
- Ask students to tell you any prepositions that they know, and write these on the board.
- Then ask for very basic questions that will call forth a response including a preposition, and write these on the board. For example:

    Where do you keep your cell phone?

    Where did you put your book?

- Write the answers on the board, and label the parts of speech in the sentences. For example:

    S V   O   P   Obj. of P

    I keep my cell phone in my backpack.

    S V   O   P Obj. of P

    I put my book on my desk.

- Look through the chart with your students and ask them which, if any, of the prepositions included, are not familiar to them.
- Have students "try out" prepositions by generating new sentences with a few of them.

❏ EXERCISE 17. Let's talk. Page 154
Time: 5–10 minutes

> Have the students physically demonstrate the spatial relationships described by prepositions of place. This exercise can be very effective, but it is necessary that students understand what is expected of them so be sure to model a few sentences.

❏ EXERCISE 18. Game: trivia. Page 154
Time: 10–15 minutes

> Make copies of maps beforehand so that students can correct their answers independently.

❏ EXERCISE 19. Reading. Page 155
Time: 10–15 minutes

- Ask students to first read the passage and answer the questions independently.
- Ask students what the passage is about and write their answers on the board.
- Read the passage aloud, having different students take turns every few sentences.

- Make sure to correct students' pronunciation of the endings of nouns.
- Review the questions in items 1–5 as a class and ask students to locate key words in the passage that helped them respond directly.
- Please see the Teaching Suggestions at the front of this book for additional ideas for working with Reading passages.

Optional Vocabulary

rainforest	vines
habitats	surface
layers	common

❏ EXERCISE 20. Warm-up. Page 156
Time: 5–10 minutes

Expansion: Ask students to line up according to their calendar birthdays. The students whose birthday falls closest to January 1st should be first in line and other students should place themselves accordingly. The student whose birthday falls as close to December 31st should be last in line. This expansion can be fun and requires that students exchange the information they have completed about themselves in the Warm-up.

CHART 6-5. Prepositions of Time. Page 156
Time: 10–15 minutes

Your students might remember these prepositions of time with the help of a triangle written on the board.

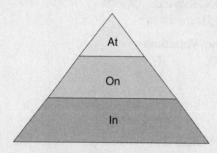

The triangle above shows that the preposition *at* is related to the smallest, most specific point in time (*at 9:30, at noon,* etc.); *on* is related to a single day; and *in* is related to the longest, most general and least specific period of time (*in the evening, in 1997, in the 21st century*). Some phrases, however, do not fit as well into this scheme (for example: *at the present, in a few minutes, in the afternoon* vs. *on Monday afternoon*). Special attention should be paid to these cases.

- Draw the above triangle.
- Explain that *at* generally refers to the most specific point of time—the actual clock hour (*at 1:50* P.M.)—and put the *at* example at the point of the triangle.

- Explain that *on* refers to a slightly less specific time—the day or date (*on November 22nd, 2000*)—and label this example to the side of the triangle, where it is less narrow than the point.
- Tell students that *in* refers to more general periods of time—years, months, centuries, etc. (*in 2000, in November, in the 21st century*) and write this example at the widest point of the triangle, its base.
- Remind students that preposition usage is not necessarily logical or predictable, and that while the triangle explanation above can be helpful, it is not a "rule."
- Review the examples in the chart by having students read the phrases aloud, and draw students' attention to the notes on the right-hand side of the chart.
- Respond to any questions that students may have and remind them to refer to this chart as often as needed.

❏ EXERCISE 23. Warm-up. Page 157
Time: 5 minutes

- After students have checked all the grammatically correct sentences, have them take turns reading <u>all</u> the sentences aloud, as they are written.
- Ask students how they know that b in item 1 and c in item 2 are incorrect. Point out their skill in recognizing that these sentences sounded wrong.

CHART 6-6. Word Order: Place and Time.
Page 157
Time: 10–15 minutes

"Place before time" is a helpful phrase for students to know.

For the most part, time expressions are placed at the beginning of a sentence if the writer wants to emphasize the time element, to vary his / her structure for stylistic reasons, or to clarify a long and complicated sentence.

Students should learn that, in general, prepositional phrases are either at the beginning or the end of a sentence. Stress that *subject + verb + object* is the basic word order and that prepositional phrases can come before or after this basic pattern.

Stress that the reason *subject + verb + object* is not interrupted is because the *subject* does the action of the *verb*; the *verb* then impacts the *object*.

- Explain to students that the action should not be interrupted by place or time expressions.
- Draw the following on the board:

  S ⇒ V ⇒ O

- Then, ask students to create a sentence and put the required parts of speech in the correct places. For example:

  S ⇒   V ⇒   O
  Hasan sold his CD collection.

- Now, ask students to add to this with a prepositional phrase explaining place.

    S ⇒   V ⇒   O   P

    Hasan sold his CD collection at the yard sale.

- Finally, ask students to provide even more information by giving a time phrase. Add it to the sentence on the board, with appropriate grammatical labels.

    S ⇒   V ⇒   O   P   T

    Hasan sold his CD collection at the yard sale on Saturday.

- Explain to students that place phrases generally go in front of time phrases, and that both come either at the beginning or the end of the sentence.
- Read through the chart with your students and answer any questions that come up.

CHART 6-7. Subject-Verb Agreement.
Page 158
Time: 10–15 minutes

> Singular-plural agreement can be a troublesome area for students. This chart presents only a few basics of subject-verb agreement.
>
> In (h): With *there + be*, nowadays a singular verb is common (informally) even when the subject is plural. (For example: *There's some books on the desk.*) It certainly wouldn't hurt to mention this peculiarity as well as the fact that students should acquire the correct form before departing from it. This usage is dealt with in the more advanced text in this series, *Understanding and Using English Grammar.*

- Begin by having students help you come up with a simple sentence and write it on the board. For example:

        S   V   O

    The book describes the author's life.

- Expand on the sentence above and add in a long prepositional phrase with additional nouns. Write this on the board. For example:

    The book on the table between the two couches describes the author's life.

- Explain to students that in order to identify the real subject of any sentence, they should look for the first preposition in the sentence, and then locate the noun to its left.
- Ask a student to go to the board and locate the first preposition and then find the noun that precedes it. For example:

        S

    The book <u>on the table between the two couches</u> describes the author's life.

- Ask the student at the board or another student to locate the verb of the sentence.
- Explain that the prepositional phrase between the subject and its verb describes the subject but does not constitute essential information.
- Ask a student to cover up the prepositional phrase with paper or erase it and see what remains. In doing

so, students will see that the original sentence exists and the basic meaning is unchanged.

        S

    The book (<u>on the table between the two couches</u>)

        V   O

    describes the author's life.

- Explain to students that the most important step in achieving agreement between subject and verb is simply to locate the subject among other nouns in the sentence.
- Ask students to take turns reading the example sentences (a)–(j).
- Explain the notes included on the right-hand side of the chart.
- Pay special attention to (g), (h), (i), and (j). Students often find it hard to make these phrases agree with verbs. Remind them that *each* and *every* are always singular.

❏ EXERCISE 27. Looking at grammar.
Page 159
Time: 5–10 minutes

> The grammar dealt with in this exercise can be troublesome for students and represents frequent sources of errors. It Is helpful to spend ample time encouraging students to explain why the errors they see are incorrect and how to fix them.

❏ EXERCISE 28. Listening. Page 159
Time: 5–10 minutes

Optional Vocabulary

sweat	chest
fur	flap
panting	mud
paw	roll

❏ EXERCISE 29. Warm-up. Page 160
Time: 5–10 minutes

- Begin by asking a number of questions about when students first went to school and met their first teacher. For example:

    How old were you when you first went to school?

    How did you like your first day of school? Were you frightened or excited?

    Was your first teacher a man or a woman?

    Was he or she young or old?

    How did your first teacher treat you?

- As students share their memories of their first teachers with you, write student-generated sentences on the board. For example:

    Juan's first teacher was a young woman. She was very friendly.

    Kwon Jung's first teacher was a middle-aged man. He was serious but patient.

CHART 6-8. Using Adjectives to Describe Nouns. Page 160
Time: 10–15 minutes

The emphasis of this chart is on the terminology "adjective" and its function and form.

Some languages inflect adjectives by changing their form for number, gender, or some other category. However, adjectives never change their form in English, and there are no singular or plural versions, and therefore no inflected endings.

- Explain that adjectives are words used to describe or modify nouns.
- Tell students that adjectives usually come immediately before nouns, and that subjects and objects can both be modified by adjectives.
- Think of a familiar noun, such as *vacation*, and write it on the board.
- Now ask students to think of adjectives that can describe or even define the noun above.
- Write a sentence on the board using the adjectives students have given you. For example:

    Maya went on a <u>long, relaxing, fun</u> vacation.

- Read through the chart with students and ask students to read examples (a)–(h) aloud.
- Stress that adjectives usually precede (rather than follow) the noun they modify.
- Next, explain that adjectives can also follow the verb *to be*.
- Write the word *ice cream* on the board and ask students to call out adjectives that describe ice cream.
- Create a sentence using the adjectives students have given you. For example:

    Ice cream is a <u>cold, sweet, delicious</u> dessert.

- Point out that adjectives do not change depending on the form of the nouns that follow them, and remind students that adjectives have no plural form.

❏ EXERCISE 30. Looking at grammar.
Page 160
Time: 3–5 minutes

This exercise can be done quickly as a class or in groups. The goal is to make sure that everyone in the class understands what an adjective is. The concept of adjectives will be revisited in the chapters on adjective clauses and comparisons.

Before beginning the exercise, ask students where they can find adjectives in a sentence and remind them that adjectives come before nouns or after the verb *to be*.

❏ EXERCISE 31. Looking at grammar.
Page 160
Time: 5–10 minutes

The emphasis here is on the placement and function of adjectives. In addition, the sentences created should be meaningful.

- After students have had a chance to read through the exercise, ask them to take turns writing their sentences on the board.
- Instruct the students who have not gone to the board to evaluate the sentences on the board to see if all are correct.
- If students have made unexpected sentences, discuss whether the sentences and adjectives used also make sense.

❏ EXERCISE 32. Looking at grammar.
Page 161
Time: 15–20 minutes

With any luck your students will create very funny passages to read aloud.

This type of activity is usually called a Mad Lib. Mad Libs were invented in 1953 by Leonard Stern and Roger Price, who published the first *Mad Libs* book themselves in 1958. Mad Libs books are still published by Price Stern Sloan, an imprint of Penguin Group, cofounded by Price and Stern.

Part I
- Put students into small groups.
- Instruct students to cover Part II below with a sheet of paper while completing Part I.
- Encourage students to be creative when thinking of answers.

Part II
- Explain to students that they will be completing Part II with the word chosen for the blank with the same number in Part I.
- Have students take turns reading the completed sentences aloud. Discuss which responses make the most sense and which are the silliest.

CHART 6-9. Using Nouns as Adjectives.
Page 162
Time: 10–15 minutes

> Nouns in this structure can be called "noun adjuncts" or simply "nouns that are used as adjectives."
>
> Common problems that arise with this structure are:
>
> 1) making the noun adjunct possessive, for example:
>
>   INCORRECT: flower's garden
>
> 2) making the noun adjunct plural, for example:
>
>   INCORRECT: the shoes store
>
> Sometimes a noun describing another noun becomes a single compound noun: firefighter, doorbell, earphone, etc. Tell the students to use their dictionaries when in doubt about spelling a noun-noun combination as one word or two. (There is no definitive rule to predict the form.)

- It is likely that students have already come across a number of nouns used as adjectives, and, therefore, you can introduce the topic by asking students if they know any.
- Write any appropriate nouns that students come up with, and if they cannot produce any, help them get started by writing a few of your own on the board, such as:

bus stop	yoga mat
school bus	textbook
wine glass	yearbook
water bottle	toothpaste

- Explain that these kinds of nouns are common and that students should realize that the first noun acts as an adjective and does not become plural when modifying another noun.
- Explain to students that they cannot always predict when such nouns will be formed from two separate words and when these words will be combined; occasionally both forms are expected.

Expansion: Prepare index cards that each have one noun on them. Choose these nouns by taking a list of noun-noun combinations and writing one noun on each card. Distribute one card per student and instruct students to "combine" their words with as many other nouns as make sense. Review all the possibilities as a group.

❏ EXERCISE 37. Warm-up. Page 163
Time: 5 minutes

- Before beginning this Warm-up, ask students to give you very basic definitions of the parts of speech they have recently been studying.
- Write the following notes (hopefully generated by students) on the board:

  subject = doer of action; verb = action
  object = receiver of action

CHART 6-10. Personal Pronouns: Subjects and Objects. Page 164
Time: 15–20 minutes

> This chart contains a lot of information, but it is assumed students are already familiar with personal pronouns (subject vs. object, singular vs. plural). You may wish to proceed directly to Exercise 38, using it as an additional preview for the chart.
>
> In examples (e) and (f), teachers should be aware that the use of I as an object pronoun rather than me (as in Eric and me) seems to be gaining in popularity in spoken English. One can hear a lot of sentences like Ann met Eric and I at the museum, even from educated speakers of English. You might mention to your students that they might hear native speakers misusing subject pronouns in this way in spoken English. However, students should know that this usage, no matter how often they hear it, is still incorrect and not accepted in formal English.
>
> Along the same lines, everyone being followed by the possessive adjective pronoun their has become accepted in recent years. Unlike the use of a subject pronoun where an object is needed, using their as a possessive adjective to agree with everyone does reduce cumbersomeness. This combination now occurs in spoken English more commonly than does everyone . . . his / her and for good reason. This change allows people to avoid using the awkward his / her that gained popularity in the 1980s in an attempt to be more inclusive.

- Because students are likely to be familiar with both subject and object pronouns, begin by simply having students take turns reading the sample sentences (a)–(i).
- Using either a sample sentence from the chart or one that students create, write a sentence on the board and have other students identify and label the parts of speech by coming to the board. For example:

  >   **S**   **V**   **O**
  >
  > Nadia greeted Aiko and me at the train station.

- Have students transform every proper name they can into personal pronouns and write the resulting sentence.

  > **S**   **V** **O**
  >
  > She greeted us at the train station.

- Remind students that pronouns must agree in person and number with the subjects or objects they replace.
- Review all the notes for singular / plural pronouns as well as subject / object.

❏ EXERCISE 39. Looking at grammar.
Page 165
Time: 5–10 minutes

- Tell students that if compound objects are challenging for them, they can cover both the and and the noun preceding it to see if an object pronoun is still required.

- Demonstrate this on the board with a sentence based on students' lives. For example:

  S   **V**   **O**

  Ali congratulated <u>Ben and me</u> on our engagement.

❏ **EXERCISE 40.** Looking at grammar.
Page 165
Time: 5–10 minutes

> This gives practice in identifying an antecedent and supplying the correct pronoun. To do so, the students must consider function, meaning, and form (subject vs. object, singular vs. plural, and gender).
>
> During class discussion, ask students why they chose their answers.

Optional Vocabulary

borrowed	injure
returned	grain
intensity	invention

CHART 6-11. Possessive Nouns. Page 166
Time: 15–20 minutes

> Proper placement of apostrophes in possessive nouns can be confusing, for native speakers as well as for second language learners. (Because the placement of apostrophes cannot be distinguished in spoken English, this is only a problem in written language and not in speech.)
>
> Use plenty of examples to explain this chart, writing each on the board. For example, demonstrate *boys'* vs. *men's* and *girls'* vs. *women's*. Ask three male students to place their pens on one desk and three female students to place their pens on another. Then use the pens to demonstrate the meaning and placement of the apostrophe: *This is a man's pen. These are the men's pens. These are the boy's pens.* Etc.
>
> You may wish to point out that the apostrophe has more than one meaning and use. In this chart, it expresses possession (and its placement indicates number). In contractions, it indicates the omission of letters (for example: *isn't = is not,* with the "o" omitted).

- Read through examples (a)–(c) with your students.
- Write the following new examples on the board:

  The girl's brother lives in Denmark.

  The girls' brother lives in Denmark.

  The woman's brother lives in Denmark.

  The women's brother lives in Denmark.

- Ask a student or students to go to the board and write *Singular* or *Plural* over the possessive noun. For example:

  SINGULAR
  The girl's brother lives in Denmark.

  PLURAL
  The girls' brother lives in Denmark.
  SINGULAR
  The woman's brother lives in Denmark.
  PLURAL
  The women's brother lives in Denmark.

- Read through examples (d)–(g) with your students and respond to any questions.
- Write examples of contractions of the verb *to be* or *to have* with nouns and pronouns and point out that students need to attend to the entire sentence to ensure they know whether a possessive or a contraction is used.

❏ **EXERCISE 43.** Looking at grammar.
Page 167
Time: 5–10 minutes

> Students may not be familiar with the workings of a family tree. If so, take the time to talk through the family relationships in the image. You may want to even label it.

❏ **EXERCISE 45.** Warm-up. Page 167
Time: 5 minutes

> In this exercise, as in others, some students will be able to identify which forms are grammatically correct without being able to explain why they know this. Point out to students that their ability to recognize what does and does not sound correct shows how much their English skills are progressing.

CHART 6-12. Possessive Pronouns and Adjectives. Page 168.
Time: 10–15 minutes

> The term "possessive adjective" can be confusing. *My, your, our,* etc., are pronouns in that they are noun substitutes. However, they function as adjectives because they modify and precede nouns (for example: *my textbook, our textbooks*). In this way, they are different from *mine, yours, ours,* etc., which the text labels "possessive pronouns."
>
> The misuses of *it's* vs. *its* are common among native speakers as well as second language learners. Even educated native speakers often have to pause and figure out whether to use the apostrophe when they write **it** + **s**. Students might welcome the knowledge that even teachers have to be careful when using *its* and *it's.*
>
> *It's* can also be a contraction for *it* + **has** in the present perfect form: *It's been a long time since I last talked to him.*

- Write the example sentences (or an original version of them) on the board. For example:

    This textbook is <u>mine</u>. = *possessive pronoun*
    It's <u>my</u> textbook. = *possessive adjective*

- Explain to students that the meanings of the above sentences are essentially the same.
- Ask students what differences they notice between the two forms. Write their observations underneath the forms, respectively. For example:

    This textbook is <u>mine</u>. = *possessive pronoun*
    Can follow verb to be
    Does not come in front of a noun
    It's <u>my</u> textbook. = *possessive adjective*
    Goes in front of a noun the way adjectives do

- Ask students to take turns reading through (c)–(j). Elaborate on explanatory notes.
- Apart from *mine*, students should notice that all other possessive pronouns end in -*s*.
- Make sure students notice that there is no possessive pronoun for *it*.
- Spend ample time on (k)–(l) and (m)–(o) as these represent common errors for second language learners as well as native speakers.

CHART 6-13. Reflexive Pronouns. Page 169
Time: 10–15 minutes

Explain the form and meaning by using a mirror (a small pocket mirror will do). Incorporate the Warm-up above into the presentation of this chart. Explain to your students that *reflexive* actually means "to bounce back or reflect," as light or images are reflected by a mirror.

Briefly answer questions about the vocabulary listed at the bottom of the chart. Some notes:

-*feel sorry for yourself* = *engage in self-pity*

-*help yourself* = *serve yourself (as in a cafeteria)*

-*pinch yourself* = *(jokingly and figuratively pinch yourself to make sure that what you are experiencing is real) I couldn't believe my good fortune. I had to pinch myself to make sure it was real.*

-*work for yourself* = *be self-employed*

Remind students that talking to themselves is a good way to practice their English.

- Using a mirror, demonstrate looking at yourself.
- With your students' input, write subject pronouns on the board as you would to conjugate a verb.
- Next to these, write the reflexive pronouns. Your students will soon catch on to the fact that they simply need to add -*self* / -*selves*. For example:

I	*myself*	*we*	*ourselves*
you	*yourself*	*you*	*yourselves*
he / she / it	*himself / herself / itself*	*they*	*themselves*

- Have students read the example sentences (i)–(k) aloud.
- Explain to your students that reflexive pronouns are also used for emphasis when expressing surprise or

pride that someone did not require help to complete a task.

- Write the following example (or one like it) on the board:

    I can't believe that Leila cut her hair <u>herself</u>! It looks beautiful and is very trendy!

- You may want to explain that normally, people pay hairdressers to cut and style their hair.

❏ EXERCISE 50. Let's talk: interview.
Page 170
Time: 10–20 minutes

The purpose of this exercise is to further familiarize students with common expressions in which reflexive pronouns are used and to get students using reflexive pronouns in a relaxed, natural way.

- Ask students to get up and move around the classroom, taking notes as they interview their peers.
- Move around the room and help students engage one another and ask follow-up questions.
- After students have gained information and anecdotes about their peers, discuss the questions as a whole and encourage students to compare their responses.

CHART 6-14. Singular Forms of *Other: Another* vs. *The Other.* Page 171
Time: 10–15 minutes

The sole focus of this chart is to distinguish between *another* and *the other*. Additional forms of *other* are discussed in the next chart.

Many English language learners erroneously put *the* in front of *another*. Point out that *another* is simply two words combined: *an* (meaning *one*) and *other*. *An* is an article. *The* is an article. You only use one article in front of a noun and never two articles together. You can't say *This is the an apple.* Similarly, you can't put two articles together with *the* and *another*.

- Explain that both *another* and *the other* are singular forms and thus, both have singular grammar when combined with a verb.
- Put the following notes on the board:

    Another = one more, one in addition
    The other = a remaining, or not yet chosen, one

- Ask your students to take turns reading the notes for (a) and (b) aloud.
- Underline or highlight the *an* in *another* and the *the* in *the other*.

    <u>An</u>other = *one more, one in addition*
    <u>The</u> other = *a remaining, or not yet chosen, one*

- Create your own example sentences using your students' names and lives. If possible, have students create these sentences and discuss the difference between them. For example:

Marta asked for <u>another</u> piece of pizza. (There are many pieces left.)

Marta asked for <u>the other</u> piece of pizza. (There is only one piece left.)

- Remind students that *an* is an indefinite article and when you want *another,* you just want one more of whatever is already being offered.
- Remind students that *the* is a definite article and, therefore, when you want *the other*, you have a specific object in mind.
- Explain the notes from the chart in detail, and write additional examples on the board.
- Ask students to read (c) and (d) aloud. Stress that both *another* and *the other* can be used as pronouns.

CHART 6-15. Plural Forms of *Other: Other(s)* vs. *The Other(s).* Page 173
Time: 10 minutes

The key here is to distinguish between the use of *other(s)* as a pronoun and *other* as an adjective. Remind students that adjectives are not inflected; they have no added endings such as *-s / -es.*

- Explain to students that *other* is an adjective and they will recognize it as such when it precedes a noun. When *other* does not precede a noun, it is a pronoun and an *-s* can be added to make it plural.
- With the help of your students, create and write sample sentences on the board. For example:

    Julio is carrying three books in his backpack. One book is this text and <u>the other</u> books are novels.

    Hye Jin put one of her four notebooks on the desk. She put <u>the others</u> beneath the desk.

- Ask students to read the example sentence (a)–(f) in the chart aloud. Review the explanatory notes with students.

❏ EXERCISE 56. Let's read and write.
Page 175
Time: 15–25 minutes

Part I
- Give students an opportunity to read through the passage on their own.
- Then if time permits, have students take turns reading this passage aloud.
- As a class, respond to the comprehension questions and locate where these answers can be found.

Part II
- Provide time for your students to read and consider this passage, and answer any questions they might have.

Part III
- Give students a chance to use the model to start their own paragraph.
- Tell students to complete their writing assignment for homework. (Collect and then respond to students' passages at the next class meeting.)

Optional Vocabulary

nervous	peaceful
anxious	inhaling
variety	exhaling
techniques	methods

CHART 6-16. Summary of Forms of *Other.*
Page 176
Time: 10 minutes

The main point of this chart is to show when *other* has a final *-s* (i.e., only when it is a plural pronoun). A common problem is that learners add final *-s* to *other* when it is used as an adjective. For example:

INCORRECT: *I bought some others books.*

This unit on *other* does not deal with all the uses of *other.* See *Understanding and Using English Grammar* for more information.

- Explain to students that there are two basic ways to use the forms of *other.* Tell students that one of these ways is as an adjective.
- Ask students what kind of word follows all adjectives, and anticipate the response "noun."
- Write the following examples on the board and remind students that the uses immediately below are also as adjective.

    another student
    another movie
    another English class

- Remind students that *another* is the same as *an + other.*
- Next, explain to students that *other* precedes a plural noun.

    other students
    other movies
    other English classes

- Remind students that when they use *the other* as an adjective, *the other* is in contrast to a noun previously named.
- Write examples on the board to show the contrast between one item and the other. For example:

    I have two books here. One is <u>War and Peace</u>. <u>The other book</u> is <u>Harry Potter</u>.

    We have a number of delicious dishes. Some were brought from a restaurant. <u>The other dishes</u> were made here.

- Now explain to students that when using a pronoun version, no noun is used at all. As in all cases, the pronoun form takes the place of the noun itself.
- Using the examples from above, show how the pronoun is different from the *adjective + noun* form by changing the board examples accordingly. For example:

    I have two books here. One is <u>War and Peace</u>. <u>The other</u> is <u>Harry Potter.</u>

    We have a number of delicious dishes. Some were brought from a restaurant. <u>The others</u> were made here.

Chapter 7
Modal Auxiliaries

CHAPTER SUMMARY

OBJECTIVE: The goal of this chapter is to help students gain mastery of modal auxiliaries. Familiarity with the meanings of modal auxiliaries is extremely important to a student's autonomy in English because these words communicate small but important differences in the user's attitudes and feelings. Misuse of modal auxiliaries can result in confusion and even anger among people who are trying to communicate in either speech or writing.

APPROACH: This chapter is organized on the basis of lexical meanings. The format progresses from presentation to controlled practice to more open practice. Most exercises are interactive and emphasize conversational forms.

TERMINOLOGY: To keep terminology simplified for student purposes, the text uses the term "modal auxiliary" for both single-word (for example, *must*) and periphrastic or multiple-word (for example, *have to*) modals. The term "helping verb" is mentioned in the first chart as synonymous with "auxiliary."

❏ **EXERCISE 1.** Warm-up. Page 178
Time: 5 minutes

> Students will naturally identify at least some of the incorrect sentences. Point out how skilled they are becoming at recognizing and hearing sentences that don't quite seem right. Remind them that this is a sign of just how much their English skills are improving.

CHART 7-1. The Form of Modal Auxiliaries.
Page 178
Time: 10–15 minutes

> This chart is simply an introduction to terminology and form. Subsequent charts in this chapter explain the expressions and their use in detail.
>
> Be sure to discuss the meanings of the example sentences. Modals have a variety of meanings, as any glance at their definitions in a dictionary tells us. Mention that modals can have different meanings that may illustrate different tenses, moods, or intentions.

For example, in the sentence, *I could meet you for coffee after class, could* indicates future possibility, whereas in example (b) in the chart, *could* expresses past ability. In example (c), *It may rain tomorrow, may* expresses possibility, but in the sentence *You may pay by credit card but not by personal check, may* expresses permission.

Point out for (j) and (k) that *study* is the main verb. The word *have* in *have to* and *have got to* is inflected or changed for number and tense (**has to, had** to, etc.). The main verb is never inflected after a modal. This can be especially confusing for learners when the main verb is also *have*. Examples: *He **ought to have** more patience. She **has to have** a new dress for graduation. Mr. Smith **had to have** his car repaired yesterday.*

- Explain that modal auxiliaries are used to express a number of meanings, which, in the most general terms, have to do with <u>possible</u> actions.
- Write *possible* on the board and ask students to give you a loose definition of it. Write their ideas around it in a word web (see example). It doesn't matter what words students come up with, but it is likely they will give you back a modal auxiliary in response to this prompt. For example:

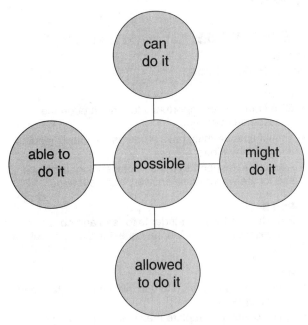

- Write *modal auxiliaries* on the board and explain that modal auxiliaries are followed by the simple form of the verb:

  Modal Auxiliaries
  can, could, may, might, should, had better, must, will, would

- Underline any modals in the student responses.
- Point out that students already know some modals, and that now they are going to study modals in depth.
- Explain some of the rules of modals.

  Not followed by to.
  Don't put -s after main verbs.
  Don't put -ed after main verb.
  Don't put -ing after main verb.

- Have students read through the example sentences (a)–(i). Explain the meaning of each one. When feasible, have students try the modals out in sentences they create on the spot.
- Tell students that there are also some auxiliaries that have *to* as their last part, but that they are <u>complete phrases</u> and <u>all parts must be included</u>.
- Write the following on the board:

  Modal Auxiliaries—Complete Phrases
  have to, have got to, be able to, ought to

- Emphasize that the modal auxiliaries included in (j)–(m) are different. They are complete phrases and must be kept together.

❏ EXERCISE 3. Listening. Page 179
Time: 10 minutes

This is an exercise in form, but you should discuss meaning as you go along. Paraphrase the sentences for the students as a way of introducing them to the content of this chapter.

❏ EXERCISE 4. Warm-up. Page 179
Time: 5–10 minutes

- Instruct students to circle the best completion. Review as a class.
- Encourage students to talk about themselves and the topic, in general.
- Write students' sentences on the board and underline the modal auxiliaries. For example:

  Taka <u>could</u> walk when he was only nine months old.
  Maria's son <u>could</u> crawl when he was seven months old, but her daughter <u>couldn't</u> crawl at that age.

CHART 7-2. Expressing Ability: *Can* and *Could.* Page 180
Time: 10–15 minutes

Can is presented as expressing ability, but it is richer than that. Usually it expresses a subtle combination of ability and possibility. In this text, however, the term "possibility" is reserved for *may / might / could* (see Charts 7-3 and 7-4).

It is not easy to define modals. The text seeks principally to give the students a general notion of their meaning and then provide, through the exercises, numerous situations in which they are used so that students may become familiar with the range of meanings and nuances they can express.

Explain that the "l" in *could, would,* and *should* is not pronounced.

- Ask students to tell you some of their abilities. Write these on the board, in complete sentences.
- If students are reluctant, ask them if they can do certain things. The more outlandish or specialized these "skills," the more they stress "ability" as opposed to mere "possibility." For example, ask:

  Junko, can you juggle?
  Faisal, can you ride a unicycle?
  Lily, can you snowboard?
  Viktor, can you cook gourmet food?

  Then write complete related sentences on the board, expanding on them with extra information as it arises.

  Junko can't juggle, but she can wiggle her ears.
  Faisal can't ride a unicycle, but he can surf.
  Lily can snowboard.

- Have students read example sentences (a)–(d) aloud.
- Explain to students that it can be extremely hard for non-native speakers to both produce and comprehend *can* as distinct from *can't*.
- Model the pronunciation of both *can* and *can't* and ask students to repeat after you.
- Explain to students that if *can't* continues to give them problems, they can choose to use the uncontracted *cannot*.
- Review the stresses in (e) and (f) and again, model these distinctions for your students, and ask them to repeat after you.
- Explain that the past of *can* to express ability is *could*.
- Look at the student-related sentences above and, with help from students, transform them into the past.
- Ask students to first highlight the use of *can* and then create new sentences using *could* or *couldn't*, referring to when the students were young. Make sure that the new sentences truly make sense. For example:

  Junko can't juggle, but she can wiggle her ears.
  Junko <u>couldn't</u> juggle when she was younger, and she still can't now. She <u>could</u> wiggle her ears, though.

Faisal can't ride a unicycle, but he can surf.

Faisal <u>couldn't</u> ride a unicycle when he was young, and he also <u>couldn't</u> surf.

Lily can snowboard.

Lily <u>could</u> snowboard as a child.

- Explain that *can / could* can be replaced by *is able to / was / were able to*.

- Together, change one of the past sentences on the board by using *able to*:

  Junko <u>isn't able to</u> juggle, but she <u>is able to</u> wiggle her ears.

- Read (i)–(l) with students and answer any questions students have.

❏ **EXERCISE 6.** Let's talk: interview.
Page 180
Time: 10–15 minutes

One of the purposes of this practice is to provide relaxed time for directed conversation. The end result should be eight written sentences containing the target structure, which students will then share with the class. Of course, you don't need to follow the directions in the book. You can simply lead a discussion with your class based on the given items.

Model the pronunciation of *can* and *can't*. *Can* is reduced to /kn/, spoken with a low tone and no stress. *Can't* is produced with a full vowel but not a strong final "t": /kæn/. However, in short answers they both receive full pronunciation and stress: *Yes, I can. No, I can't.*

Try to give the students a feel for the idea that *can* expresses a combination of ability and possibility.

Expansion: Distribute index cards, one to each student. Ask students to write a special skill or ability they have, that they think no one else in the class has. Tell them not to include their names. Collect the cards and shuffle them. Either read the skills aloud (using the target structures) or redistribute the index cards, making sure that no student receives his / her original one. If you are reading the skills aloud, students should guess who has the special skill discussed. If students have others' cards, they should walk around and ask questions using the target structure until they discover whose skill they have. If appropriate, students can model some of their skills in class.

❏ **EXERCISE 7.** Listening. Page 181
Time: 10 minutes

Students often struggle with comprehending *can* and *can't*. Be prepared to spend additional time ensuring students can both produce and understand these reductions.

❏ **EXERCISE 8.** Let's talk. Page 181
Time: 10 minutes

Expansion: Ask students to think about their own past abilities and create sentences about things they used to be able to do but can no longer manage. Write some of their sentences on the board. For example:

When Diego was a child, he could sleep in the car, but now he can't.

Five years ago, Sunny could still speak Thai with a perfect accent, but now she can't.

❏ **EXERCISE 9.** Warm-up. Page 182
Time: 5 minutes

Encourage students to think of other predictable conditions (for example: the relative toughness of an exam, quality of a sequel movie, mood of a friend or family member). After students have looked at the first three items, ask them to make other predictions.

CHART 7-3. Expressing Possibility: *May, Might, and Maybe;* Expressing Permission: *May* and *Can*. Page 182
Time: 10–15 minutes

Review Chapter 3 by comparing *may / might* to *will: It will rain tomorrow* = The speaker is as close as possible to being 100% certain that it will rain. *It may / might rain* = The speaker gives it a 50% chance.

The difference between the adverb *maybe* and the verb *may* should be clarified for the class through several additional examples. Emphasize that the adverb *maybe* usually comes at the beginning of a sentence, while the verb *may be* comes in the main verb position following a subject.

Make it clear that <u>two</u> meanings of *may* are being presented in this chart: possibility and permission. Listeners can ascertain the meaning from the speaking context.

Can is regularly and correctly used to ask for and permission, and it has been used that way for centuries. Using *may* for permission, however, communicates a certain tone of propriety and formality that may be absent from *can*.

The negative contractions for *may* and *might* are *mayn't* and *mightn't*. They are rarely used.

- Ask students what the top headline in international news will be in the coming days, and write this question on the board.

  What will the top headline news be tomorrow?

- Because students cannot know for sure, they should be encouraged to tell you their opinions. Some may automatically use *may* or *might*, though some may use the qualifying introduction, *I think . . .*

- Write students' ideas on the board. For example:

  Lena thinks the top news will be the election in Europe.
  Ming-Hsieh thinks it will be the economy.

- Tell students that *may* and *might* are used to express possibility for both present and future. Ask students to restate the example sentence on the board with *may* and *might*. For example:

  It <u>might</u> be the election in Europe.
  It <u>may be</u> the economy.

- Ask students to take turns reading sentences (a)–(e). Discuss the notes.

- Expand on the idea of *may be* by asking students what kind of weather there will be one week from the current date.

- Write the following question on the board, along with the words *may be*.

  What will the weather be one week from today?
  Use "may be."

- Tell students that because the weather prediction for one week's time is of course far less than certain, this question provides a natural opportunity for additional practice with *may be*.

- Write student-generated possibilities on the board:

  The weather <u>may be</u> windy because it is often windy at this time of year.
  The weather <u>may be</u> rainy, or it <u>may be</u> sunny. It is too early to predict.

- Now explain to students that *maybe* is an adverb, and it can also be used to make sentences less certain.

- Explain that *maybe* is an adverb in the same way that *possibly* is.

- Warn students not to confuse *may be* (a modal + verb *be*) with *maybe,* an adverb.

- Tell students that they can place *maybe* in front of a sentence and that by doing so they will make a sentence less certain.

- Tell students you are going to give them an opportunity to practice using *maybe* and that the first step in this practice is to tell you what they *will* do right after class.

- Write a few student-generated sentences on the board, for example:

  Jeong will check her phone for messages.
  Eyad will do his homework.

- Instruct students to add *maybe* at the beginning of each sentence, in order to make the plan less certain.

  Maybe Jeong <u>will check</u> her phone for messages.
  Maybe Eyad <u>will do</u> his homework.

- Ask students how the new sentences with *maybe* are different than the original versions with *will,* above.

- Tell students to consider that the use of *will* made the sentences 100% certain.

- Explain that by using the adverb *maybe,* the above sentences are only 50–60% certain, which is not very certain at all.

- Ask students to take turns reading sentences (f)–(h). Review the notes.

- Make sure that students have a strong grasp on *may / might* for possibility before moving onto the more limited use of *may* for permission.

- Read through sample sentences (i)–(k) with students and review the grammar notes.

❏ EXERCISE 10. Looking at grammar.
Page 183
Time: 5–10 minutes

Expansion: Discuss the topic with students and have them compare traffic fines and legal procedures in their countries with those described here.

❏ EXERCISE 12. Let's talk. Page 184
Time: 10–15 minutes

> You may want to include *will* and *be going to* in the discussion to distinguish between degrees of certainty. For example, compare *I will / am going to go downtown* to *I may / might go downtown.*

CHART 7-4. Using *Could* to Express Possibility.
Page 184
Time: 10–15 minutes

> *Could* is a complex modal, with several meanings and many nuances. Questions that students may ask about *could* are not as easy to answer as the charts may make it seem. Sometimes *could* is interchangeable with *may / might* for possibility, and sometimes it is not. The text seeks to minimize confusion by presenting *could* separately from *may / might.*
>
> When *could* is used in the negative to express possibility, it takes on the meaning of "99% impossible." For example:
>
> *That could be true.* = Maybe it is true and maybe it isn't.
>
> *That couldn't be true!* = I think it is impossible for that to be true. (COMPARE: The speaker would say, *That isn't true* to express 100% certainty about impossibility.)
>
> The use of *couldn't* to express impossibility is not presented in this text but is covered in *Understanding and Using English Grammar.*
>
> Let students know that, as with much of English grammar, their ability to sense correct usage is every bit as helpful to them as being able to explain it. As they grow in confidence, they will become more comfortable with those distinctions that are hard to articulate.

- Ask students, *Is there anything you can't do now, because you are too big, that you could do when you were a child?*
- You can also ask them, *What can you do now that you couldn't do when you were younger?*
- Start by using your own experiences and write a sample sentence on the board:

  When I was a child, I <u>could</u> hide inside my toy chest. I was much smaller than now, so my whole body could fit.

  When I was a child I <u>could</u> understand French well because my family lived in Quebec. Now, I can only understand a few simple words.

- Write students' answers to this question on the board and compare students' responses. For example:

  Mario <u>could</u> speak both Italian and Portuguese when he was a child. Now he can only speak Italian fluently.

  Oleg <u>couldn't</u> ride a bicycle when he was a boy. Now, he rides competitively!

  Junko <u>could</u> do a triple backflip off the diving board when she was ten.

- Explain that another use of *could* is for possibility, both in the present and in the future.
- Tell students that *could* is often used when discussing future plans, especially when people are thinking aloud about possibilities.
- Tell students that this use of *could* comes in handy when making social plans, and so you would like them to think about activities that the class <u>could</u> do instead of studying grammar.
- Put one of your own ideas on the board, and ask students to add theirs. For example:

  We <u>could</u> leave class and go to the beach.
  We <u>could</u> take a plane to Paris.
  We <u>could</u> go to lunch at a fancy restaurant.

- Ask students to take turns reading sentences (a)–(c).
- Discuss these examples as a class.

❏ **EXERCISE 15.** Looking at grammar.
Page 185
Time: 10–15 minutes

The purpose of this exercise is to distinguish between two meanings of *could* by relying on context. It should be noted that a context in which grammar is presented does not need to be long and involved. The dictum to teach "grammar in context" does not require long paragraphs of dialogues. Indeed, clear but brief contexts often enhance students' ability to understand and learn aspects of English by allowing them to focus on particular forms and meanings without distraction. Concentrating on smaller contexts is an efficient language-learning device that leads to increased understanding and usage ability in larger contexts.

Expansion: Ask each student to write his/her own sentence using *could* as a modal auxiliary on an index card. Instruct students to exchange index cards and ask them to take turns reading the sentence on their card aloud and deciding as a class what the function of *could* is and what time frame it reflects (past, present, future).

❏ **EXERCISE 16.** Let's talk. Page 185
Time: 10–15 minutes

- If you do this exercise as a class, instruct students to close their books.
- Read the situation and then invite students to give you answers, which you will then write on the board.
- Once all their answers are on the board, read the situation again.
- Ask students to decide which suggested solution is most useful.
- If you decide to have students work through this exercise in groups or pairs, make sure to circulate and discuss suggestions with each group.
- If students are working in groups, call everyone together at the end of the exercise to discuss the likely success or failure of given suggestions.

CHART 7-5. Polite Questions: *May I, Could I, Can I.* Page 187
Time: 10–15 minutes

Modal auxiliaries allow the speaker to show politeness. Discuss the difference between *Give me your pen* vs. *May I please borrow your pen?* The imperative *Give me your pen* can sound rude and aggressive. Because imperative commands are reserved for certain work / direction situations and imply that the speaker feels superior to or has authority over the listener, students should learn to use modals appropriately. The use of modals allows the speaker to show respect for the listener.

Compare the meanings of *could* that the text presents:
I could run fast when I was younger. = past ability (Chart 7-2)
Could I help you? = polite question (Charts 7-4 and 7-5)
It could start raining any minute. = possibility (Chart 7-4)

Contrary to what some of us were taught as children, the use of *can* to request permission is both common and acceptable, as any dictionary reveals. The use of *can* instead of *may* does, however, signal a subtle difference in the relationship between the speaker and the listener. *Can* may signal familiarity and equality while *may* keeps a polite distance. *Can* is less formal than *may*.

- In order to help get started, ask the following question:

  Do you use the exact same question form in your native language when you ask a favor of a boss as when you ask a favor of a friend or a sibling?

- Most students will say *no* and may describe the difference as indicated in person or some other inflection. Put students' responses on the board, along with the name of the language, as an informal survey. For example:

Language	How To Make Request More Polite
French	Use different form of verb
Egyptian Arabic	Add in additional words, "kindly," etc.
Chinese	Start question with "May I trouble you"
Spanish	Use different form of verb

- Have your students look at the chart and begin reading through the polite questions (a)–(e).
- Ask students to whom they imagine each question is addressed and write the question on the board, next to their responses. For example:

  May I please borrow your pen? boss, government official

  Could I please borrow your pen? teacher, someone giving you job application

  Can I please borrow your pen? classmate, coworker

  Can I borrow your pen? sibling, good friend

- Spend ample time reviewing the notes on the right-hand side of the chart and stress that appropriate modal use will make students' interactions with native speakers much more pleasant.

❏ **EXERCISE 19.** Looking at grammar.
Page 187
Time: 10–15 minutes

You may want to take the role of Speaker A, the person who answers the phone.

- Choose different students to play the role of Speaker B in each item.
- Ask students to respond to the cues given in the role-play on sight, and correct these as a class.
- Write requests on the board for additional clarification.

Optional Vocabulary
transfer
appointment desk

Expansion: After discussing the exercise in class, set up additional phone role-plays. For example: Assign Speaker A to place a call to Speaker B, but actually talk to Speaker C (Speaker B's roommate). Tell Speaker A to call a school office for certain information and have Speaker B play the role of the school's secretary, who must look up the information and call back later.

You can prepare such role-plays beforehand and write the scenario up on index cards, creating a separate set of instructions for each speaker. Walk around the room and assist students in creating the right register and tone through their modal choices.

CHART 7-6. Polite Questions: *Would You, Could You, Will You, Can You.* Page 189
Time: 10–15 minutes

The use of *may* is an occasional problem with this pattern, as noted at the bottom of the chart. Be prepared to remind students that *may* shows politeness when it refers to the first-person subject.

If you want to assign "degrees of politeness," *would* and *could* could be called the most polite. *Will* is a bit less polite, and *would* is a softer version of *will*. *Can* loses a slight degree of politeness by signaling familiarity rather than respectful distance. For the students' purposes, however, any of these modals will allow them to show appropriate politeness when making a request as compared to an imperative, such as *Open the door*.

Be sure to point out that even polite modals can be made threatening or angry by the speaker's tone of voice.

- Ask students to take turns reading through sentences (a)–(d).
- As with the last chart, ask students to suggest who the listener may be in each case.
- Emphasize that it is often wise to default to the politest forms, as the others can sound more abrupt than intended.
- Review the notes on the right-hand side of the chart and ensure that students don't use *may* when *you* is the verb's subject.

❏ **EXERCISE 23.** Let's talk: pairwork.
Page 189
Time: 10–15 minutes

Pairs can create short dialogues for each of the items. These can be very short role-plays. If time permits, students can use the situations and characters to create "dramas."

Expansion: If students don't easily come up with creative ideas on their own, expand the situations by giving more detailed directions. For example, in item 1, instruct Speaker A that he/she is an impatient clerk and that Speaker B is a customer who can't make up his/her mind. In item 2, tell "Mr. Jenkins" that he is an unreasonable and unsympathetic boss speaking to a persistent and ill employee.

Optional Vocabulary
catch server's eye   clerk
approaches   slight
on second thought

❏ **EXERCISE 24.** Warm-up. Page 190
Time: 5 minutes

- Discuss why certain pieces of advice included (items 3 and 4) may or may not be useful.

- Ask students if they feel that the tone of *should* differs from that of *ought to*.

CHART 7-7. Expressing Advice: *Should* and *Ought To.* Page 190
Time: 10 minutes

When advice is given with these modal expressions, they indicate that results usually implied rather than stated will occur if a certain course of action is taken. These results may be good or bad.

Ought to is often pronounced /ədə/ or /atə/.

Should can also be used to express expectations. (For example: *Mary left at 10:00. She should arrive by 10:30.*) This usage is not introduced in this text but is discussed in *Understanding and Using English Grammar*.

- Introduce modals for advice by asking students what advice they would give to a new student planning on studying English.
- Explain to students that they can use the modals *should* and *ought to* in their advice.
- Write students' pieces of advice on the board. For example:

    What advice would you give new students of English?
    They should read books in English every day.
    They should not live with people who also speak their language.
    They ought to have a language partner to help them practice outside of class.
    They ought to study in an English-speaking country.
    They should watch television in English every day.

- Ask students to read through example sentences (a)–(e) and review the explanatory notes with students.
- Explain how using *maybe* softens the advice given and can help the listener be more receptive of it. Call on different students and ask them to add *maybe* to the example sentences on the board.

❏ EXERCISE 25. Let's talk: pairwork.
Page 191
Time: 5–10 minutes

- Put students in pairs and instruct them to give their partners the best advice they can think of.
- Walk around the room, taking notes on the pieces of advice you hear and recording any mistakes with the target structure that students will need help with.
- Review by asking the class for advice for each item.
- Then put some of the samples you overheard on the board and correct them as a class.

Optional Vocabulary
throat   bent
hiccups   lounge
frames

❏ EXERCISE 26. Warm-up. Page 191
Time: 5 minutes

Point out to students that the more "urgent"-sounding pieces of advice also include the more extreme responses to the situation.

CHART 7-8. Expressing Advice: *Had Better.*
Page 191
Time: 5–10 minutes

Had better is a little stronger than either *should* or *ought to*. In the negative, *had better not* usually communicates a threat of bad results. The affirmative use of *had better* also implies a warning that is not implied with the use of *should* or *ought to*.

Had better is also commonly used simply to give friendly advice among peers. *Had better* is not used to give advice to a superior, but *should* and *ought to* maintain a polite enough distance and can be used when giving advice to bosses, teachers, professors, etc. For example, one might say to one's boss, *I think you should consider Mr. Loo for that project*. One would not say to one's boss, *I think you'd better consider Mr. Loo for that project*.

- Explain to students that *had better* implies some sort of warning or urgency, which is not included in *should* or *ought to*.
- Tell students that they will hear and use *had better* in situations where taking action quickly is important.
- As a class, think of some situations where *had better* would be used, and write these on the board. For example:

    Obey the speed limit
    Study for a test
    Apply for a job
    Get to the airport on time

- Then have students make complete sentences with *had better*. Remind them that these should sound stern.
- Ask students to take turns reading through sentences (a)–(d).
- Review the notes and use the board to discuss any more challenging examples.

❏ EXERCISE 27. Looking at grammar.
Page 192
Time: 5–10 minutes

Expansion: Write various pieces of advice using *should, ought to,* and *had better* on index cards. Distribute these cards to students so that each has one piece of advice. Looking at the piece of advice only, students must come up with a situation that could have reasonably prompted the advice. Remind students that *had better* is most appropriate when a situation appears more urgent and time is of the essence. Once students have written situations to match the advice they received, discuss their answers as a class. Possible pieces of advice (to call forth various scenarios or problems):

You should take a picture of it and ask everyone in the neighborhood if they know whose it is.

(A lost pet has arrived on your doorstep.)

You had better call a plumber before the entire bathroom floods.

(The bathtub faucet can't be turned off.)

You had better call the airline immediately to see if the flight is leaving on time and what other options there are.

(You are stuck in traffic and about to miss your flight.)

You ought to keep a food diary and track everything you eat.

(You want to lose five pounds.)

You ought to set aside an amount of money from your paycheck and put it into a savings account.

(You want to save money for a trip to Europe.)

❏ **EXERCISE 29.** Let's talk. Page 192
Time: 10–15 minutes

In this exercise, students do all the talking and the teacher is silent, unless giving directions or answering a question. You may want to walk around the room and join some groups, answering questions when they arise. You can write down any common mistakes and use them for later review as a class.

❏ **EXERCISE 30.** Warm-up. Page 193
Time: 5–10 minutes

Be sure to tell students what information is standard on a résumé in the United States, especially that personal information is not included. You can then start a mini-discussion of what is true in each country represented.

CHART 7-9. Expressing Necessity: *Have to, Have Got to, Must.* Page 193
Time: 10–15 minutes

Students may be inclined to use *must* more than is natural. However, *must* generally carries a forceful meaning, and is often too forceful to use in everyday conversation about everyday affairs. In these cases, *have to* and *have got to* are usually used to convey the notion of necessity. The text emphasizes the use of *have to* and *have got to* for necessity.

Model the usual pronunciation of *have to* and *have got to* and let students experiment producing it. Don't insist that students use contracted forms right away.

Contracted speech develops as students become aware of it and gain experience with English.

Emphasize that the past form of *must* is also *had to*.

- Ask students to read through example sentences (a)–(e).
- Review notes at the right and make sure that students know that native speakers reserve *must* for written rules or regulations, and that *must* is not common in every day speech.
- Write the question forms of (f) and (g) on the board and ask students to repeat the question forms aloud.
- Take time to write on the board that the past of *must* is also *had to*.
- Pronounce the contracted forms (i)–(k) for students and tell them that these will become more natural for them as they get used to the target forms in general.

❏ **EXERCISE 31.** Let's talk. Page 194
Time: 10–15 minutes

This exercise is meant to be a teaching springboard for questions, practice, and discussion. Elicit several responses for each item. Expand the items with leading questions of your own. Model spoken forms. Distinguish between *should* (advisability) and *must / have to / have got to* (necessity).

❏ **EXERCISE 33.** Let's read and talk.
Page 195
Time: 10–15 minutes

This exercise is intended for group discussion but works equally well as a writing assignment. If done as group work, the group could prepare written advice together. You might want to ask them to underline the modals they use.

Discuss how typical Mark Hill's behavior is of teens, in general.

- Ask various students to read the passage in turn, and ask them to paraphrase meaning as they go along.
- Ask students to identify the problems. Write students' collective advice on the board.
- Underline the modals used and discuss alternative ways to give advice.

CHART 7-10. Expressing Lack of Necessity: *Do Not Have To;* Expressing Prohibition: *Must Not.* Page 195
Time: 10 minutes

> Use gestures and tone of voice to reinforce the distinction between these two forms. For *do not have to*, shrug your shoulders and look nonchalant and unconcerned. For *must not*, use facial expressions and gestures to show sternness. For example, English speakers often shake their head from side to side or shake their index finger up and down (mostly to small children) to gesture *must not*.

- Ask students to suggest actions that new students don't have to take when learning English for the first time. Write students' suggestions on the board. For example:

  They don't have to buy an electronic dictionary.

  They don't have to worry about having a strong accent.

- Now have students advise international travelers about behavior that is prohibited on airplanes.
- Underline target structures in both sets of sentences. For example:

  They must not lose their passports.

  They must not bring illegal items on the plane.

  They must not use their cell phones during takeoff or landing.

- Ask students to read example sentences (a)–(d).
- Review all the notes on the right-hand side of the chart.
- Highlight the correct pronunciation of *mustn't* in (e) and point out that *mustn't* is most often used when speaking to children, and is not appropriate for use with adults.

CHART 7-11. Making Logical Conclusions: *Must.* Page 197
Time: 10 minutes

> Compare: *She must be sleepy* = The speaker is 95–99% sure.
>
> *She is sleepy* = The speaker is 100% sure.
>
> Point out that this chart has three different meanings of *must:* logical conclusion, necessity, and prohibition.

- Write the words *educated guess* on the board and ask students what they think it means.
- If they have difficulty, break the word down by asking what *educated* means (possible answers: smart, intelligent, knows a lot), and then ask them what *guess* means (think, idea, maybe).
- Explain that *educated guess* is another way to say *logical conclusion*, and add this to the board:

  Educated guess = logical conclusion

- Next, use the class as the topic for logical conclusion sentences. Some topics could be:

  If someone always does well on tests

  If someone is absent

  If someone is sleepy

  If someone sneezes, coughs, laughs, etc.

  Lee always gets 100% on tests.

  He must study a lot.

  Max is absent.

  He must be sick.

- Explain that *must* can also be used in the negative for logical conclusions, but that the reason (the conclusion) has to change. For example:

  Max must be sick. → *Max must not feel well.*

- Ask various students to change the *must* sentences above to *must not* sentences. Remind them that they will need to change the reason in order for the sentence to make sense.
- Next, write the following on the board:

Positive—*Must*	Negative—*Must not*
1. Logical Conclusion	1. Logical Conclusion
Lee always gets 100% on tests.	*Mari is sleepy.*
He must study a lot.	*She must not have slept very much last night.*

- Explain that *must* and *must not* each have another use. In the appropriate columns, write the following on the board:

2. Necessity	2. Prohibition
If you want to pass the class, you must study every day.	*Pilots must not fly when they are sleepy.*

- Ask students if they can explain the difference between the two new sentences above. Write their responses in the appropriate column.

2. Necessity	2. Prohibition
If you want to pass the class, you must study every day.	*Pilots must not fly when they are sleepy.*
good idea, need to, necessary, important, etc.	*bad idea, very important NOT to do it, dangerous, etc.*

- Review the chart as a class and answer any remaining questions.

❏ EXERCISE 41. Warm-up. Page 199
Time: 5–10 minutes

- Ask students what they already know about using tag questions.
- Write their responses on the board. For example:

  Tag Questions

  short questions

  end of sentence

  use negative if statement part is affirmative

  use affirmative if statement part is negative

- Complete the Warm-up exercise and discuss.

CHART 7-12. Tag Questions with Modal Auxiliaries. Page 199
Time: 10 minutes

> Tag questions are especially common with requests and thus, modals. Though it may take some time for your students to produce these tag questions on their own, they will certainly hear these in every day speech.
>
> Focus students' attention on the fact that these tag questions are formed in just the same way tag questions are formed with simpler verb structures.

- Ask students for two sentences, one using *can, would, will,* or *should,* and one using *have to, has to,* or *had to.* For example:

    Lena can sing well, can't she?

    Marcus has to go early, doesn't he?

- Ask students what the modals are in these sentences and underline them as they are called out.
- Now ask students how the two sentences are different. They should come up with answers such as:

    One has two modals and the other only has one.

    The first sentence uses the same modal.

    *The second sentence has **do** at the end.*

- Have students make the sentences on the board negative and write their answers on the board.

    Lena can sing well, can't she?

    Lena can't sing well, can she?

    Marcus has to go early, doesn't he?

    Marcus doesn't have to go early, does he?

- Then have students open their books. Review the chart together.

CHART 7-13. Giving Instructions: Imperative Sentences. Page 200
Time: 10-15 minutes

> Discuss the form of imperative sentences. Explain the concept of the "understood *you*" as the subject of an imperative verb, with *you* being the listener(s). For example, in (a): *Open the door!* = *You,* (the listener the speaker is addressing) *open the door.*
>
> The addition of *please* and a pleasant tone of voice can make an imperative sentence quite polite, as in *Please open the door.* When making a polite request, however, the students can be assured they are using a high level of politeness if they use *would* or *could* (for example: *Could you please open the door?*) *Please open the door* in the wrong tone of voice can seem inappropriate, unfriendly, or haughty.
>
> Demonstrate various tones of voice that can be used with imperative sentences, from barking out an order to making a polite request.

- Read through example sentences (a)–(c) aloud and exaggerate the tone of voice.
- Explain the difference between an order and a request.

- Ask students to give you examples of the kinds of situations where orders are expected and tolerated. Some ideas include:

    In the military

    On a team

    A parent to a child

    During an emergency

    Talking with the police

- Read through example sentences (d)–(i) and exaggerate using tones of voice to both soften and strengthen the orders and requests.

❏ EXERCISE 44. Let's talk. Page 201
Time: 10-15 minutes

Part I
- Explain that instructions (as in a recipe) are usually written in the imperative form.
- Put students in pairs or small groups and have them choose the correct order for each step.
- As a class, read the chronologically ordered recipe aloud.

Part II
- Encourage students to write the directions for cooking something simple but representative of their culture's cooking.
- You may want to have students work in pairs or small groups of the same nationality. This allows students to help each other with vocabulary and techniques unique to their cultural cooking.
- Exchange "recipes" and discuss whether the completed dishes are similar to those from other countries.

❏ EXERCISE 45. Listening. Page 201
Time: 10 minutes

> This number puzzle is intended for fun and variety. In Part II, have students work in groups to encourage as much discussion as possible.

Part I
- Instruct students that they will complete the directions as a listening cloze (fill-in-the-blank) exercise.
- Write the symbols for *add, subtract,* and *multiply* on the board and have students explain their functions.

Part II
- Students can perform the puzzle's directions in groups.
- If students don't get the predicted answer, have them re-read the imperative statements given in the listening and work through the math again.

❑ **EXERCISE 46.** Reading and writing.
Page 202
Time: 15–25 minutes

Part I
- It may be that there are no suggestions that don't apply in another country. If this is the case, simply have students add to the list of suggestions.
- Discuss all the suggestions given and share your own experiences with students.

Optional Vocabulary

impression	eye contact
flip-flops	confidence
punctual	research
references	

CHART 7-14. Making Suggestions: *Let's* and *Why Don't*. Page 203
Time: 10 minutes

Relate *let's* and *why don't* to *should*. In (a) and (b), the speaker is saying "We should go to the beach. Going to the beach is a good idea."

The speaker isn't using *why* to ask for a reason. The listener would not respond to any of these suggestions by giving a reason. *Why don't* is an idiomatic use of *why*.

Model intonation with *Why don't* sentences: The intonation usually falls instead of rises as is normal with questions. *Why don't* sentences are suggestions, not actual questions.

- Ask students to make suggestions for a class outing.
- Write their suggestions on the board, just as they are given. For example:

  We should go to New York City as a class.
  We should cancel class today and go white-water rafting instead.

- Ask students to rephrase the above suggestions using *Let's* and / or *Why don't*.
- Write the new suggestions on the board. For example:

  Let's go to New York City as a class.
  Why don't we cancel class and go white-water rafting instead?

CHART 7-15. Stating Preferences: *Prefer, Like . . . Better, Would Rather.* Page 204
Time: 10–15 minutes

The forms of these patterns need special attention when the chart is presented in class. Take time and ask pointed questions to make sure that students understand these target structures clearly. Elicit additional examples from the class and write them on the board, pointing out the characteristics of each pattern.

Would rather may be new to some students. Perhaps lead a chain exercise to introduce the pattern orally:

Teacher: *What would you rather do than study?*

Student: *I'd rather watch TV than study.*

Teacher: *What would you rather do than watch TV?*

Student: *I'd rather read a book than watch TV.*

The *-ing* verb referred to in the explanation in this chart is a gerund. It is also possible to use an infinitive after *like*; the text presents only the gerund pattern here. Using an infinitive with *like . . . better than* can lead to awkward sentences and confusion with placement of the *to*. Native speakers would be likely to avoid such structures and, therefore, they aren't presented here.

- Write the following notes on the board so that students can refer to them throughout the presentation of the chart.

  prefer X to Y
  like X better than Y
  would rather have X than Y

- Invite students to read sentences (a)–(b) aloud. Review the accompanying notes.
- Ask students to help you create new examples using *prefer + -ing* form.
- Write these student-generated preferences on the board. For example:

  Matteo prefers playing soccer to watching it.
  Jeong Sun and Ariana prefer cooking their own meals to dining out.

- Ask other students to read example sentences (c) and (d) aloud. Highlight the form notes to the right.
- Using the student-generated sentences on the board, ask students to attempt transformation to the *like . . . better* forms. Write these on the board. For example:

  Matteo likes playing soccer better than watching it.
  Jeong Sun and Ariana like cooking their own meals better than dining out.

- Ask other students to read (e)–(h) aloud and warn students about the incorrect forms presented in (h).
- Have students transform the sentences on the board to *would rather* forms. Write the resulting sentences on the board. For example:

  Matteo would rather play soccer than watch it.
  Jeong Sun and Ariana would rather cook their own meals than dine out.

❑ **EXERCISE 53.** Let's talk: pairwork.
Page 205
Time: 10–15 minutes

In this exercise, students use the target structures while speaking about their personal preferences.

- Pair students up with partners, preferably with students they don't always work with.

- Ask students to not only ask and answer the questions given, but also to expand on the questions with related small talk.
- Review all the questions as a class and compare students' responses.

❏ EXERCISE 54. Let's talk: interview.
Page 205
Time: 10 minutes

Expansion: Make up silly questions tailored to your class, its demographics, and what you know about them. Ask these additional questions and take a poll among your students. For example:

Would you rather be a jock or a nerd?

Would you rather be a zombie or a vampire?

Would you rather use a Mac or a PC?

Would you rather have no homework today or less homework each day for the rest of the week?

❏ EXERCISE 55. Looking at grammar.
Page 206
Time: 10–15 minutes

Multiple-choice tests are simply other kinds of exercises. If you want to give students practice in taking multiple-choice tests, make this a timed exercise and allow 30 seconds per item.

- Explain that this exercise allows students to review all the target structures in Chapter 7.
- Give students time to complete this exercise independently as seatwork.
- By way of review, have students read their completions aloud and correct pronunciation as well as grammar. Ask students to explain their choices. Offer alternatives not shown.

Optional Vocabulary

upset	denim
promotion	chores
wrestling	shift
conference	skateboard
supervisor	helmet

Chapter 8
Connecting Ideas

CHAPTER SUMMARY

OBJECTIVE: Because many students need to write English for academic purposes, this chapter focuses on the basic conventions of standard written English. These include parallelism, punctuation, coordination, and subordination. Students who are not interested in academic writing may still find this chapter useful because many of these concepts are common in speaking as well as writing.

APPROACH: This chapter presents **compound sentences** in which *and, but, or*, and *so* are **coordinating conjunctions**, and **complex sentences** in which *because, even though,* and *although* are **subordinating conjunctions**.

TERMINOLOGY: The above terminology is not used in the text, except for the term *conjunction*, which is only applied to *and, but, or,* and *so*. An independent clause is also called a **main clause**. A **dependent clause** may also be called a **subordinate clause**. An **adverb clause** may also be called a **subordinating adverbial clause**. The punctuation mark at the end of a sentence is called a **period** in American English but is called a **full stop** in British English.

❑ **EXERCISE 1.** Warm-up. Page 208
Time: 5 minutes

> Students may not be able to identify that item 4 is a comma splice. If it helps for the purposes of discussion, have students identify subjects, verbs, and objects in each item.

CHART 8-1. Connecting Ideas with *And.*
Page 208
Time: 10–15 minutes

> *And* is a coordinating conjunction. It connects parallel elements (elements that have the same structure). These elements may be compound subjects, verbs, or objects, or may be two independent clauses. (It is also possible to use *and* to connect three independent clauses: *I walked, he ran, and Mary drove.* This use is not taught in the text, but it is possible.) The text keeps students' focus on avoiding comma splices between two independent clauses: *I walked, he ran.* = a

comma splice. Example (e) in this chart is also a comma splice, which is a type of run-on sentence.

In Chapter 3, students are presented with the concept of parallel verbs. Chart 8-1 extends parallelism to nouns and adjectives. You may wish to use the term "parallel" and explain its meaning by drawing two parallel lines, then three, then four—showing that the form of each element is identical to the others. Then draw two parallel lines and another line that is not parallel to make an analogy to grammar. For example, if the first two elements are adjectives (represented by the parallel lines), the third in a series should not be a noun. All the elements of speech connected by *and* must be the same.

> INCORRECT: *She is a kind, affectionate, and a grandmother.*
>
> CORRECT: *She is a kind, affectionate grandmother.* OR *She is kind, affectionate, and wise.*

The use of a comma before *and* in a series, as in example (b), is a matter of style. Some style manuals say to omit it, as it is unnecessary punctuation. Others say to include it for clarity. This text takes the latter view, but either is correct. This use of a comma before the *and* in a series is called an Oxford comma. In the Answer Key to the exercises and practices in this unit, the comma is shown before *and* in a series.

For students unfamiliar with the punctuation of English, Chart 8-1 can be confusing. Write examples on the board and identify the parallel elements connected by *and*. Go over the structure elements and punctuation as many times as necessary. Once students truly understand this chart, the use of the comma and the period will seem much less mysterious; run-on sentences should start disappearing from students' writing as they become more comfortable with standard punctuation. You might mention to your class that many native-speaking students in high school and college make punctuation errors in their writing and thus, need to study this same grammar in their own English classes.

In normal, spoken English, *and* is often reduced to /ən/. Model normal contracted speech for your students and give them opportunities to practice.

- Review the definition of a clause with your students and ask students to give you basic definition for parts of a sentence: subject, verb, object.
- Ask a student to tell you two of his / her favorite foods. Create a sentence to put on the board. For example:

Miguel likes sushi <u>and</u> frozen yogurt.

- With your students, identify the parts of speech in the sentence and label these by writing "S," "V," and "O" above each word, respectively. For example:

  S   V   O   O
  Miguel likes sushi <u>and</u> frozen yogurt.

- Explain that the verb *like* in the above sentence has two objects connected by the conjunction *and*.

- Now ask another student what his / her favorite foods are and create a sentence similar to the one above. Write this new sentence on the board. For example:

  Xiao Wei likes empanadas and sorbet.

- Ask a student to go to the board and label the parts of speech with "S," "V," and "O," accordingly.

  S   V   O   O
  Xiao Wei likes empanadas and sorbet.

- Explain that because you have two independent clauses, you can also use *and* to link them. For example:

  S   V   O   O   S   V
  Miguel likes sushi and frozen yogurt, <u>and</u> Xiao Wei likes

  O   O
  empanadas and sorbet.

- Explain that *and* can be used to link two equal parts of speech, such as objects, in the first two sentences.

- Explain that *and* can also be used to link entire independent clauses, as in the board example. Tell students that when two independent clauses are linked, a comma is often used before the *and*.

- Emphasize that in both cases explained above the items linked are parallel.

- Review the chart by having students read example sentences (a)–(e) aloud.

❏ EXERCISE 2. Looking at grammar.
Page 209
Time: 5–10 minutes

This exercise deals only with parallel elements within a sentence, for example, within one independent clause. It does not deal with connecting independent clauses.

- Give students time to complete the exercise on their own first.
- Remind students that items in a series require commas after each element.
- Review this exercise as a class.
- Write sentences on the board as needed, taking time to ensure students recognize elements that are parallel.

Optional Vocabulary

ghost stories	mooed
celebrate	roared
entertain	barked

❏ EXERCISE 4. Looking at grammar.
Page 210
Time: 10 minutes

This exercise focuses on punctuation of independent clauses but also deals with parallel elements within a sentence. If your students will use English in academic writing or reading in their professional lives, they will need to be able to discern the structure of sentences like these and punctuate them correctly.

Punctuation marks are signals to the reader. In most cases, they mark boundaries of segments of speech, naturally marked by pauses or intonation changes. For example, a comma often indicates a pause in speech. A period usually signals an even longer pause as well as a dropping of the voice.

While most rules of punctuation are straightforward, some conventions are, as in the spoken language, flexible within limits. Learners should control the basic rules of use presented here before they experiment with any options. Students may ask if they can begin a sentence with *and*. The answer is yes, although not in very formal or academic writing. In other registers, from personal letters to magazine articles, beginning a sentence with a coordinating conjunction is common. In item 4, it is possible to write *I talked to Ryan about his school grades. And he listened to me carefully.*

CHART 8-2. Connecting Ideas with *But* and *Or*. Page 210
Time: 10–15 minutes

If the students understood Chart 8-1, they should have no problems with this chart. It expands on what they learned about using *and* to two other coordinating conjunctions, *but* and *or*.

In normal speech, *or* is unstressed: /ər/.

- Introduce the chart by explaining that the structure of the conjunctions *but* and *or* within a sentence is the same as that of *and,* but the function and meaning of each conjunction is different.

- Tell students that *but* is a conjunction that shows the opposite or an unexpected result in comparison with what has preceded it.

- Write a sample sentence on the board. For example:

  I wanted to go to the movies, <u>but</u> I didn't have time.

- Highlight the conjunction and discuss its meaning and function. Point out the fact that the first clause states an intention, and the second clause gives opposite information.

- Introduce *or* by explaining that it is used to give options.

- Ask a student to tell you two weekend activities that he / she might do this coming weekend.

- With the help of your students, write the two options as two separate clauses on the board. Connect the two with *or* to show that both are options. For example:

Annika might visit her sister in New York, or she might go skiing in Vermont.

- Ask students to take turns reading example sentences (a)–(c). Review the notes.
- Read through example sentences (d) and (e) and discuss their meanings.

❏ EXERCISE 6. Looking at grammar.
Page 211
Time: 5–10 minutes

> The focus of this exercise is on both meaning and structure. To select the correct conjunction, students need to decide on the relationship between the given ideas. Using punctuation appropriately depends on understanding the underlying structure.

- Have students take turns reading the sentences aloud and completing them with the appropriate coordinating conjunction on sight.
- Review each sentence as you go and have students cite particular words, phrases, or full clauses that show either connection, contrast, or choice.
- Write any challenging sentences on the board.

Optional Vocabulary
flight attendants
appetizing

CHART 8-3. Connecting Ideas with So.
Page 212
Time: 10 minutes

> Like other coordinating conjunctions, *so* connects two independent clauses. Unlike *and, but,* and *or,* the word *so* is not used to connect parallel elements within a clause.
>
> In addition to *and, but, or,* and *so,* there are other coordinating conjunctions: *for, nor,* and *yet.* They are not introduced in this text and are less commonly used than those discussed so far. Please see *Understanding and Using English Grammar* for a presentation of those conjunctions not included in this chapter.

- Write a clause on the board that students can add on to. This clause should show an intention, plan, or condition that could precede an expected result. For example:

  Amit and Anjali were extremely hot, _____ .

- Review what kind of clause would follow *and* and *but.*
- Ask students to give you possible clauses using each and write these on the board. For example:

  And   *Amit and Anjali were extremely hot, and they jumped into the swimming pool.*

- Emphasize that *and* connects two parallel elements or clauses.

  But   *Amit and Anjali were extremely hot, but they continued running.*

- Remind students that *but* indicates an opposite idea.
- Now go back to the original sentence and ask students to complete it with *so.*

  Amit and Anjali were extremely hot, so they jumped into the swimming pool.

- Explain that it is possible to use *and* above, but that *so* shows an expected result or cause-and-effect.
- Ask students for alternative completions for the original sentence using *so* and write these on the board.

  Amit and Anjali were extremely hot, so they drove to get some ice cream.
  Amit and Anjali were extremely hot, so they decided to take cold showers.
  Amit and Anjali were extremely hot, so they changed into lighter clothing.

- Ask a student to read example sentence (a) aloud and discuss the notes.
- Contrast example sentence (a) with example sentence (b) and discuss the notes.

❏ EXERCISE 9. Looking at grammar.
Page 212
Time: 5–10 minutes

> This exercise contrasts cause-and-effect and opposition. The students will encounter this contrast again in the unit on *because* vs. *even though.*

- Lead the class through this exercise, reminding students to choose either *so* or *but.*
- Provide immediate correction and make sure that students understand whether the second clause shows an expected result or an unexpected one.

❏ EXERCISE 10. Looking at grammar.
Page 212
Time: 10–15 minutes

Optional Vocabulary

grasshoppers	dolphins
beetles	conscious
approximately	drown

❏ EXERCISE 11. Listening and grammar.
Page 213
Time: 10–15 minutes

> This unpunctuated listening passage is difficult to read as it is, and highlights the need for punctuation. By listening to it first, students can make sense of the passage. After listening, students can add in the required punctuation and fully decipher the sentence structures. Again, stress how important proper punctuation and capitalization are in making written English easier to read.

delays   highway construction
ran into   toll booth

CHART 8-4. Using Auxiliary Verbs after *But*.
Page 214
Time: 10 minutes

> The focus in this chart is on which auxiliary to use to echo or match the main verb. The information in this chart is preparatory to the presentation of the patterns with *and* + *too*, *so*, *neither*, and *either* in the next chart, where the emphasis is on word order.

- Ask students a few simple yes / no questions in order to remind the class which auxiliaries are used with the simple present. Write the questions on the board. For example:

Yes/No Questions	Short Answers with Auxiliaries
Do you love grammar?	*No, I don't.*
Can you juggle?	*Yes, we can.*
Did they call earlier?	*Yes, they did.*
Will you come with me?	*No, I won't.*

- Explain that a similar construction can be used after *but*.
- Ask students to work with you to create a few example sentences of this use of *but*. Write them on the board.

  I like studying grammar, <u>but</u> my boyfriend <u>doesn't</u>.
  They never go to bed early, <u>but</u> their son <u>does</u>.
  I can't whistle, <u>but</u> my daughter <u>can</u>.

- Point out the pattern in the examples:

  negative + ***but*** + *affirmative*
  affirmative + ***but*** + *negative*

❏ EXERCISE 13. Looking at grammar.
Page 214
Time: 10 minutes

> For the first few items, ask the students to tell you the full meaning of the auxiliaries they supply. For example: In item 2, *don't* = *don't read a lot of books.*

❏ EXERCISE 14. Let's talk. Page 215
Time: 10 minutes

- Ask students to move about the room with books in hand, asking and answering questions in order to complete the exercise.
- When students have collected information and completed the exercise, ask one student to write any of the items on the board about another student. Proceed in this manner until each student is the "star" of one sentence on the board.
- Review the boardwork carefully and answer any questions that arise.

CHART 8-5. Using *And* + *Too, So, Either, Neither.* Page 216
Time: 10–15 minutes

> The patterns in this chart are principally used in conversation. They are ways of sharing experiences and opinions. First, the patterns are presented and practiced in connected clauses with *and*; then they are practiced in the more typical dialogue form shown in examples (e)–(h).
>
> To some arbiters of correct English usage, the responses in (g) and (h) are substandard and grammatically unacceptable. However, native speakers, including educated speakers, often use these expressions in normal conversation.
>
> Some strict traditionalists insist that a comma must precede *too*. Today one increasingly sees *too* used without the comma in both popular and academic settings. It's curious that traditional usage does not mandate a comma before *either,* which has exactly the same adverbial function as *too*. A comma is possible in the sentence, "Jack came to the meeting, too" but not in the sentence, "Mary didn't come to the meeting either."

- Ask students a question that more than one of them is likely to have the same response to. For example:

  Who wishes they could go back to bed this morning?

- Write two distinct sentences on the board:

  Esther wishes she could go back to bed.
  Marco wishes he could go back to bed.

- Explain that this common wish can be expressed using *and* + *too*.
- Write the combined clause sentence on the board following the pattern in (a) in the chart.

  Esther wishes she could go back to bed, <u>and Marco does too</u>.

- Explain that another way to express the same concept is to use *so* + *auxiliary* before the second subject.
- Tell students that this construction (*so* + *auxiliary*) can be challenging because the word order seems backwards: *so* + *auxiliary* + *subject*.
- Combine the original sentences using *so* + *auxiliary* + *subject* and write the new sentence on the board. For example:

  Esther wishes she could go back to bed,
  <u>and so does</u> Marco.
  <u>and Marco does too</u>.

- Introduce negatives by using the same original sentences.
- Explain that with a negative *either* and *neither* are used, and write the new combined sentences on the board.

  Esther <u>doesn't</u> wish she could go back to bed, <u>and Marco doesn't either</u>.
  Esther <u>doesn't</u> wish she could go back to bed, <u>and neither does Marco</u>.

- Have students take turns reading the sentences in the chart.

- Discuss example sentences (e)–(h) with sentences and explain the conversational frequency of (g) and (h).

❑ **EXERCISE 17.** Looking at grammar.
Page 217
Time: 5–10 minutes

Expansion: Direct students to look around the room and make observations about their classmates' style and color of dress, length of hair, presence of facial hair, and / or anything else that is equally observable to all in the class. Ask students to come up with five sentences comparing the appearances of their classmates. These sentences and comparisons should be modeled on the task in the exercise.

❑ **EXERCISE 19.** Let's talk and write.
Page 218
Time: 10 minutes

Optional Vocabulary
produces   equator
earthquakes   Nobel Prize winner

Expansion: Ask students to choose a country that is **not** mentioned in any of the items in the exercise. Tell them they may select their own country, if they wish. However, if there are many students from the same country in the class, encourage them to pick another country. Ask students to discuss simple and well-known facts about the country they have selected, and to find one point of comparison with another country in the room. Each student should create one sentence, using either of the following two auxiliary constructions:

_____ does / is / has _____, and so_____.

_____ doesn't / isn't / doesn't have, and _____ doesn't / isn't either.

Finally, ask students to each offer their sentence to the rest of the class, either by simply reading it aloud or by writing it on the board. As a class the students should then decide whether the sentence is correctly structured and whether they agree with its content.

❑ **EXERCISE 20.** Let's talk: pairwork.
Page 219
Time: 10–15 minutes

The directions ask only for *so* and *neither,* but the patterns with *too* and *either* could also be used if the students wish, as well as the informal rejoinders *me too* and *me neither.*

Mention to the students that this dialogue format is the usual way these patterns are used: one person makes a statement, and the other person uses these expressions to show interest in what the first speaker has said and to share information. Other ways of showing interest and continuing the conversation (but without sharing information) would be to respond by saying, *Oh?* or *Really?*

- Model the example and stress that in each item, Speaker B needs to find a way to mirror the initial statement either in the affirmative or negative.
- Instruct students that they should decide and discuss whether Speaker B's response is appropriate.
- Assign students to pairs and walk around as students work with one another.
- Review the exercise by having each pair complete one exchange in front of the whole class.

Optional Vocabulary
vampire   mushrooms
aerobic   volcanoes
activity   lay eggs

❑ **EXERCISE 21.** Let's listen and talk.
Page 219
Time: 10 minutes

You may want to put two lists on the board with the target structures. For example:

More Information	*To Disagree*
You are? Why?	I don't.
Really? Are you sure?	I did.
You can?	I'm not.
Etc.	Etc.

Students can refer to these as they complete Parts II and III.

CHART 8-6. Connecting Ideas with *Because.* Page 221
Time: 10–15 minutes

The students were introduced to adverb clauses of time in Chapter 2. This is the first chart, however, in which the term "adverb clause" is used. One of the purposes of this chart is to define an adverb clause. You might want to connect the term with the time clauses the students studied in Chapter 2 so that they get an overview of this important English structure.

The first part of this chapter dealt with compound sentences. Now the text turns to complex sentences. Both kinds of sentences allow the speaker / writer to connect and show relationships between ideas.

Because of is not presented in this text. See *Understanding and Using English Grammar* for a discussion of this prepositional phrase. In brief, *because* introduces an adverb clause, but *because of* is a two-word prepositional phrase followed by a (pro)noun object. A common error is the use of *because of* instead of *because* to introduce an adverb clause. For example:

INCORRECT: *He drank some water because of he was thirsty.*

- First, write an adverb clause of time on the board and leave the main clause as an extended blank. For example:

  When Hsin Xao entered the room, _____.

- Then ask your students to correctly complete this sentence with any main clause they can come up with, such as:

  the sun was shining

  the teacher was talking

  class had already started

- Ask students (again) what elements each clause must have, prompting the answer *subject + verb.*
- Ask students to label the subject and verb in the adverb clause on the board.
- Remind students that because the above adverb clause tells us <u>when</u> something happens (the way an adverb can also tell us when, how, why, etc., a verb happens), the clause is an <u>adverb clause</u>. Write this label on the board:

  ADVERB CLAUSE

       S   **V**

  When Hsin Xao entered the room, _____.

- Tell students that now you will look at another type of adverb clause, one that tells us why the verb happens.
- Write an adverb clause using *because* on the board. Use your students' real lives as springboards for this clause. For example:

  Because Ricardo is from Brazil, _____.

- Ask students to come up with a reasonable main clause and to label the elements of the adverb clause. For example:

           S   **V**

  Because Ricardo is from Brazil, <u>the first snowstorm of the winter surprised him</u>.

- Ask your students to create a few more adverb clauses that they can also label and provide the main clauses for.
- Put these additional examples on the board.
- Use one of these examples to show the different placements of the adverb clause. For example:

  Because Yuko likes to study, she always gets 100%.

  Yuko always gets 100% because she likes to study.

- Ask students to take turns reading through each of the examples presented in the chart aloud. Review the notes included in the chart.
- Emphasize that when the adverb clause precedes the main clause, students must use a comma before the main clause.
- Stress the grammatical differences between what is accepted in writing versus what is okay when speaking, in examples (f) and (g).

❏ **EXERCISE 24.** Looking at grammar.
Page 221
Time: 5–10 minutes

The items in this exercise are essentially additional examples to help explain the grammar presented in Chart 8-6. Ask the students to identify the main clause and the adverb clause in each item.

❏ **EXERCISE 27.** Looking at grammar.
Page 222
Time: 10 minutes

- Remind students that this exercise reviews all the charts they have met so far in Chapter 8.
- Lead students through this exercise by first giving students markers or chalk to write the corrected forms on the board and then discussing as a group.

❏ **EXERCISE 28.** Listening. Page 223
Time: 5–10 minutes

Remind students that correct punctuation makes comprehension easier. Sentences that are run together without correct punctuation are confusing. It is the writer's job to clarify the meaning by marking the structures appropriately, with commas and periods, and the speaker's job to reflect this punctuation by pausing correctly.

- To illustrate the importance of punctuation, in general, write the following two sentences on the board:

  Let's eat Grandma.

  Let's eat, Grandma.

- Invite students to try to explain the difference between the two sentences. (In the first sentence, it seems that we are going to eat Grandma).
- Ask students to listen carefully and change the passage according to what they hear.
- Review the correct pronunciation by having students read aloud the sentences that comprise the passage.

CHART 8-7. Connecting Ideas with *Even Though / Although.* Page 223
Time: 10 minutes

What students have just learned about adverb clauses with *because* in Chart 8-6 is extended here to the use of *even though* and *although.*

Understanding the relationship expressed by *even though / although* is difficult for some students.

A common mistake among learners is to use both *although* and *but* within the same sentence. This sends confusing signals to the reader because *although* indicates subordination and *but* indicates coordination. Because the concepts of subordination and coordination may not yet be very meaningful to students, simply emphasize that they only need one way to link the two clauses and using both provides two.

INCORRECT: *Although I was not hungry, but I did not eat.*

Though is not presented here in order to keep the focus on adverb clauses.

Though has various adverbial uses:

1) It can be used in the same ways as *even though* and *although*:
   Though I was hungry, I did not eat.
2) *I was hungry. I didn't eat, though.* (principally spoken English)
3) *I didn't eat anything, though my wife did.* (a use similar in form and meaning to *but*)
4) *Jack looked as though he were ill.*

The text seeks to simplify the students' (and teacher's) task by focusing only on *even though* and *although*. Some students, depending on their familiarity with English, may spontaneously use *though* instead of *although* or *even though*, which is fine.

- Present students with two sentences of your own invention, using *because* and *even though*, or *although*.
- Write these sentences on the board and make sure they draw from students' lives and information.
- Highlight both adverb clauses and show how the word order and syntax is the same, but the meaning is different. For example:

  Because Samira was exhausted, she went to bed early.
  Although Samira was exhausted, she stayed up late studying.

- Have students label the subjects and verbs in both sentences and point out that in both sentences, the comma is required after the adverb clause. For example:

        S   *V*
  Because Samira was exhausted, she went to bed early.

        S   *V*
  Although Samira was exhausted, she stayed up late studying.

- Explain that the difference between the two sentences is that *because* precedes an expected result, but *although / even though* introduce an unexpected result.
- Compare the above explanation to the use of *and / so* vs. *but*.
- Tell students that *but* is a conjunction, and *although / even though* precede adverb clauses. However, the function or meaning is similar.
- Ask students to take turns reading the examples (a)–(d). Review notes on the right-hand side of the chart.

❏ **EXERCISE 31.** Looking at grammar.
Page 224
Time: 5–10 minutes

The emphasis here is on meaning. You may need to rephrase some of the sentences to make sure the students understand the relationship expressed by *even though* compared to *because*.

Optional Vocabulary
training
carry a tune

❏ **EXERCISE 32.** Looking at grammar.
Page 224
Time: 5–10 minutes

To check on students' understanding, ask them to explain some of the items in their own words. It's a good way to discuss the meaning of these structures.

- Lead students through this exercise.
- With each item, ask students to state why the alternative choices wouldn't work.

Optional Vocabulary
fairly	downhill
failed	soil
robbery	muddy
occurred	melting
leading	

❏ **EXERCISE 35.** Reading and grammar.
Page 226
Time: 15–20 minutes

This is a cumulative review exercise of the compound (**coordination:** made with conjunctions) and complex (**subordination:** made with adverb clauses) sentences in this chapter.

Part I
- Give students time to read the passage individually.
- Circulate, providing help with any unknown vocabulary or sentences students have trouble comprehending.

Part II
- Tell students that by using *because, although / even though* or *so,* they will be restating the general ideas learned in the passage.
- Give students ample time to complete the items.
- Review and correct the completed items and ask students to justify their structural choices

Optional Vocabulary
substance
surface
available
essential
industry
poison
suffers
exist
natural resource

❑ **EXERCISE 37.** Let's write. Page 227
Time: 15–25 minutes
- Read through instructions with students and discuss note taking.
- Instruct students to use the conjunctions (*and, but, or, so,* and adverb clause structures *because* + clause; *although / even though* + clause) they have studied to link the facts about their animals to one another.
- Highlight the facts on giraffes and have students read aloud the sample sentences created from these facts.
- Assist students in choosing a topic and work with students individually during seatwork time.
- Have students complete the assignment for homework. Collect and respond to the assignment at the next class meeting.

Chapter 9
Comparisons

CHAPTER SUMMARY

OBJECTIVE: In order to both broaden students' knowledge of English grammar and increase their ability to engage in daily conversation, this chapter focuses on making grammatical comparisons. Students will learn how to form comparisons and order syntax within a comparative sentence. They will learn a wide variety of expressions to express comparison, contrast, and related ideas.

APPROACH: The chapter assumes that students have already been introduced to simple phrases of comparison. This chapter first reviews these basic functional phrases and expands on those forms, emphasizing idiomatic usage.

TERMINOLOGY: The terms "comparative" and "superlative" are used traditionally here and associated with *-er / more* and *-est / most,* respectively.

❏ **EXERCISE 1.** Warm-up. Page 229
Time: 5–10 minutes

This exercise provides an oral introduction to the function of comparisons, especially those using *as . . . as.* Because students will have some basic understanding of the structure targeted, encourage them to give additional information if they so choose. Write all of their sentences on the board, underlining the elements of *as . . . as* patterns.

CHART 9-1. Making Comparisons with *As . . . As.* Page 229
Time: 10–15 minutes

The use of the modifiers *quite, nearly, almost,* and *just* may be difficult for some learners and require special teaching attention. Return to Exercise 1 and elicit comparisons that use these modifiers or make up additional situations for oral work using objects / people in the classroom or pictures drawn on the board. A topic that easily lends itself to comparison is people's heights (for example: *Ali isn't quite as tall as Roberto,* etc.). If you use height as a springboard for comparison, be sure that you know your students well enough to trust that the shortest or tallest person in the group does not feel sensitive about his / her height. Other things that could be compared are hair length,

book size, or size of circles drawn on the board, to name a few. Practices in the *Worbook* also emphasize use of modifiers with *as . . . as.*

In the negative, *so* can be used instead of the first *as* with no change in meaning. *Not so . . . as* has the same meaning and use as *not as . . . as.* For example: *Line A is not so long as line B = Line A is not as long as line B.* The use of *so* in negative comparisons is no longer as common in everyday English as it once was. Many people use *not as . . . as.*

- Pick three students who you know do not mind being the focus of others' attention and ask them to stand up so that all the students can assess their height.
- Ask each student how tall he / she believes himself / herself to be and put their names and heights on the board. (Be aware that you may have to help students calculate their height in feet and inches from centimeters.) For example:

  Malaika = 5 feet, 6.5 inches

  Boris = 5 feet, 7 inches

  Leonardo = 5 feet, 9 inches

- Invite the standing students to sit down again.
- Remind students of the structure they have just met in the Warm-up, and write the basic grammar on the board. For example:

  As . . . As

- Ask students to give you modifiers or adjectives that can modify other adjectives or even adverbs of degree. Write these on the board:

  almost, quite, nearly, just

- Ask students which of the two students are closest in height.
- With the help of your students, make three new sentences about the heights of the three students who stood.
- Write these sentences on the board and highlight the elements (*as . . . as*) of the basic structure and highlight any modifiers as well. For example:

  Malaika is <u>almost as</u> tall <u>as</u> Boris.

  Boris is <u>not quite as</u> tall <u>as</u> Leonardo.

  Leonardo is <u>nearly as</u> tall <u>as</u> the board.

- Ask students to take turns reading through example sentences (a) and (b) and then (c)–(e).
- Discuss the use of the negative form, as explained in the notes.

- Review the example sentences containing modifiers in (f) and (g).

   Expansion: Discuss the examples in the chart. Then, for reinforcement, ask the students to cover the chart and tell you about the four people in the pictures. Or use the ages of three students in your class and a child (possibly yours or a student's) to elicit the same structure as in the examples.

❏ EXERCISE 5. Game. Page 232
Time: 10–20 minutes

> These comparisons are included mostly for fun and for vocabulary development. The native speaker may find these expressions old-fashioned or trite, but second language learners often find them entertaining. If the students learn a few of these phrases, it does not mean that their writing will become trite and hackneyed. Rather, they may enjoy knowing these phrases that are so common that almost any native speaker can supply the traditional completion to the comparison. The ones in this exercise are only a few out of many such phrases. Some others that students may enjoy: *proud as a peacock, easy as pie, quiet as a mouse, happy as a clam, dead as a doornail, good as gold, sly as a fox, wise as an owl, busy as a bee.*

- Separate students into teams, ideally with equal representation from different language and national backgrounds (if you have a mixed nationality class).
- Give a time limit for each team to work through and complete the items.
- When time is up, review as a class, keeping score of which team wins.
- Ask students to stay in their teams and share any such similar phrases that are unique to their background.
- Ask volunteers from each team to write additional such phrases on the board. Have students guess which country the phrase originates from.

❏ EXERCISE 6. Warm-up. Page 233
Time: 5 minutes

- Encourage students to complete each of these items independently.
- Ask students to share their completions and see whether all class members agree.
- If there is any disagreement about the pictures and who looks the youngest (and oldest) of all, discuss what features informed students' decisions.

   Expansion: Ask students a few discussion questions about age, aging, and whether it is okay to discuss age within their cultures. Students may be surprised that it is considered somewhat taboo to ask a woman who is older than 35 how old she is, and that some people even lie about their age.

   Sample questions include:
   1) Is it okay to ask someone his or her age in your country?
   2) Is it okay to ask a man his age, but not a woman, or vice versa?
   3) At what age (if any) is it impolite to ask someone his or her age?
   4) In the United States, we receive many messages, from all media forms, that it is important to be young, look young, and be perceived as younger than a person is. How have you seen this message communicated?
   5) Are older or even elderly people in your country treated with a higher degree of respect than they are in the United States? What evidence do you have of this?
   6) If you could have plastic surgery to look younger, would you?
   7) What do you think is the ideal age in a person's life? Why? What is the most difficult age? Why?

CHART 9-2. Comparative and Superlative.
Page 233
Time: 10–15 minutes

> This chart introduces the concepts and terminology of comparisons with *more/-er* and *most/-est*. A presentation of forms follows in Chapter 9-3.
>
> Be sure that the students understand and use the definite article with every superlative. *The* must be part of a superlative.
>
> Be aware that many of the students will be at least somewhat familiar with this structure and may be ready to practice using it with minimal presentation.

- Ask students to look around the classroom and find a point of comparison with one other student.
- Write the basic structure for both comparative and superlative structures on the board to serve as a visual support for students. For example:

   COMPARISON:
   Compares two people, places, or things.
   X is -er/more <u>adjective</u> than Y.
   SUPERLATIVE:
   One that is the best, most, -est among three or more people, places or things.
   X is the -est/most <u>adjective</u> of all in the group.

- Ask students to come up with sentences that compare themselves to other students in the group and / or make a superlative statement about themselves among the whole class.
- Remind students to be gentle with one another: the point is to practice the target grammar in a real classroom setting, not to embarrass anyone else.
- Write the students' statements on the board and highlight the target elements. For example:

   Joao: I am <u>older than</u> Frances.
   Biki: I look <u>more tired than</u> Alonzo.
   Vilson: I am <u>the tallest</u> in the class.
   Luisa: I am <u>the hungriest</u> in the class.

- Ask students to take turns reading example sentences (a)–(c) aloud.
- Remind students that *than* is required to make a grammatical comparison.

- Now ask other students to read example sentences (d)–(f) aloud.
- Emphasize that with any superlative, the group must be more than two in number, and the definite article *the* has to be used.

❑ EXERCISE 7. Game. Page 233
Time: 10–15 minutes

- Divide students into new teams, taking care to have as equal national representation as possible (if you have a mixed nationality group).
- Give students 5–10 minutes to complete the game in teams.
- Compare the answers of the teams and discuss the content while correcting the pronunciation of the target elements.
- Remind students to be sure to pronounce *than*, with an *n*. (Sometimes students say *that* simply because they are familiar with the word.)

CHART 9-3. Comparative and Superlative Forms of Adjectives and Adverbs. Page 235
Time: 10–15 minutes

Discuss the chart to help the students understand how comparative and superlative forms relate to the number of syllables in the adjective or adverb.

The text concentrates almost solely on adjectives in comparisons. You might want to give a quick overview of the basic uses of adjectives (to modify nouns) and adverbs (to modify verbs).

Examples:

*Adjectives: Ms. Bender is a **wise** woman.*

*Adverbs: Ms. Bender acts and speaks **wisely**.*

Students might note that the comparative and superlative forms for *good* (adjective) and *well* (adverb) are the same: *better* and *the best*. For example: In the sentence, *Anna speaks good English, good* is an adjective modifying the noun "English." In the sentence *Anna speaks English well, well* is an adverb modifying the verb *speaks*. The comparative form of the two is the same:

Adjective: Anna speaks better English than I do.

Adverb: Anna speaks English better than I do.

The basic distinction between *good* and *well* is that *good* is an adjective and *well* is an adverb. However, confusion sometimes occurs because *well* can also be an adjective meaning "healthy," "not sick." In the sentence, *Anna is well, well* is an adjective describing the noun *Anna*. It means that Anna is not sick; she is a well person.

As a further side note on a question that often arises, the expressions "feel well" and "feel good" are both correct. *Feel* is a linking verb and, therefore, can be followed by an adjective; either adjective, *well* or *good*, is correct. In the sentence *I don't feel well, well* limits the meaning to physical health, whereas the statement *I don't feel good* could refer to one's emotional state and / or to one's physical health.

- Explain to students that though the list may look long and daunting, they will readily become used to learning how to manipulate the adjectives and adverbs depending on how many syllables they have.
- Discuss each category of adjectives and adverbs in the order presented in the chart.
- Remind students that as important as the comparative and superlative forms themselves are, the additional necessary words (*than* for comparisons and *the* to precede any superlative) are equally important.
- Ask students to reconsider each category of adjective and adverb. Identify any terms they are not already familiar with.
- Using comparative adjectives from each category, ask students to make their own sample sentences. Write these on the board. For example:

  The weather in Italy is <u>more pleasant than</u> the weather in Antarctica.

  My sister is <u>more clever than</u> I am.

  Health and happiness are <u>more important than</u> wealth and fame.

- Ask students to then create superlative sentences and write these on the board:

  My daughter's wedding was <u>the best</u> day of my whole life.

  Wei-Ling's mother is <u>the gentlest</u> person in her family.

  "July" is <u>the most fascinating</u> movie at the theater.

- Review the irregular adjectives and irregular adverbs with students and address any further questions students may have.

❑ EXERCISE 10. Looking at grammar.
Page 236
Time: 5–10 minutes

Expansion: Ask students to each construct five sentences including these comparative and superlative forms. Ask for volunteers to put one of their sentences on the board. Review these sentences as a class.

❑ EXERCISE 11. Looking at grammar.
Page 236
Time: 10 minutes

Expansion: Divide the class into two to four teams, depending on the size of the class. Each team will try to score points according to the following system. (It is a good idea to write this scoring system on the board.)

SCORING:

1) One point for the correct <u>meaning</u> of the adjective

2) One point for the correct <u>comparative</u> form of that adjective

3) One point for a clear <u>sentence</u> with the comparative form

Example: dependable

Teacher: *What does dependable mean?*

Team: *"Dependable" means "responsible or reliable." People who do their jobs well every day are dependable.*

Teacher: *Good. One point. And what is the comparative form?*

Team: *More dependable than.*

Teacher: *Great. One point. And can you give me a sentence with that form?*

Team: *Vegetables are <u>more dependable than</u> fruit.*

Teacher: *No, that doesn't make sense.*

Team: *Adults are <u>more dependable than</u> children.*

The teams should prepare for the competition by discussing the words in the list below, looking them up in the dictionary if necessary, and making up possible sentences.

List of adjectives to choose from:

absent-minded	confusing	fresh	pleasant
active	cute	friendly	polite
attractive	dangerous	heavy	soft
bright	delightful	hectic	sour
calm	dim	high	straight
clever	easy	humid	wild
common	flexible	intelligent	wonderful

❏ **EXERCISE 14.** Let's talk: pairwork.
Page 238
Time: 15–20 minutes

> This practice could be used for written homework or for small group, collaborative work. Some of the comparisons may not be readily obvious, and students may need additional time to think through each item.

- Assign students partners or put them in small groups.
- Inform students that there may be a number of comparative forms that can be used meaningfully.
- Encourage pairs and groups to take time thinking and creating the most meaningful sentences using as many comparative forms as make sense.
- Invite members of each pair or group to write one or more of their sentences on the board until there is one sentence for each item on the board.
- Compare content and review structure. Ask students to read their sentences aloud and correct non-target pronunciation and intonation as a group.

❏ **EXERCISE 15.** Listening. Page 238
Time: 5–10 minutes

- Remind students that the task here is to choose the statement that has a similar meaning, not to choose a statement that sounds the most similar.
- After students have completed the exercise, review each item by having students read their choices aloud.

CHART 9-4. Completing a Comparative.
Page 239
Time: 10–15 minutes

> The use of object pronouns (for example: *me* and *him*) after *than* is common and today, becoming increasingly acceptable. In the sentence, *Tom is older than me,*

some grammatical analyses consider that *than* functions as a preposition that is correctly followed by the objective case. Some older prescriptive grammars didactically state that *than* is a conjunction that must be followed by the subjective case even when the verb is not expressed: *Tom is older than I (am).*

This text skirts the issue by calling the use of object pronouns "informal." Guide your students according to their best interests.

If native speakers use a subject pronoun after *than*, they often also include the auxiliary verb. In other words, it's typical for many native speakers to say *I'm older than he is* rather than *I'm older than he.* The text does not state this observation, but through example, it encourages the use of auxiliary verbs with subject pronouns following *than.* You might want to make special mention of this pattern to your students.

- Write the beginning of a comparative sentence on the board, stopping after *than . . .*
- Use your students' lives as the context of this sentence so that students can easily complete it. For example:

  Ming Jie and Olivier are <u>more energetic than</u>
  _____.

- Ask students to complete this sentence in any way that works.
- Write both formal (*subject pronoun* or *subject pronoun + auxiliary*) and informal (*object pronoun*) options on the board.
- Explain to students that it is helpful for them to become familiar with the formal version first and depart from its use later, as they gain more confidence with the structures.
- Ask students to take turns reading example sentences (a)–(c) aloud. Review all the notes on the right-hand side of the chart.
- Now explain that students can use a similar structure when comparing adverbs.
- With your students help, create a sample sentence on the board, completing a comparative adverb. (An easy choice of topic, and one which students can agree on, is a comparison of when students arrive to class.) For example:

  Beatrix and Layla arrived to class <u>earlier than</u>
  _____.

- Write students' completion of this on the board, and if students can't agree on who arrives later than the others, encourage an active discussion using the target forms. For example:

  Beatrix and Layla arrived in class <u>earlier than Miguel and Omar</u>.

  Student: *No, I think we should say: Beatrix and Layla arrived in class <u>later than Saul and Ciara</u>.*

- Put many example sentences on the board utilizing both formal and informal completions.
- Ask students to read example sentences (d) and (e). Discuss the accompanying notes.
- Introduce the last section of the chart by asking students to compare physical attributes or possessions.

- Ask students to give you sample sentences. Write these on the board with the target structures underlined. For example:

  Georgi's hair is <u>shorter than</u> Vincent's.

  Shia's backpack is <u>bigger than</u> mine.

- Call on students to read the example sentences (f) and (g) aloud. Answer any questions about the chart.

❑ EXERCISE 18. Warm-up. Page 240
Time: 5 minutes

> You may want to give students an opportunity to discuss weather in general, and its variations depending on region. These questions elicit the most helpful responses if students are living in a region where the weather does vary from day to day.

CHART 9-5. Modifying Comparatives.
Page 240
Time: 15–20 minutes

> A fairly common error is the use of *very* with a comparative.
>
> INCORRECT: *My brother Raul is very older than me.*
>
> The use of *far* as an intensifier with comparatives may seem odd to some learners. Emphasize that in this usage, *far, much,* and *a lot* (but <u>not</u> *a lot of*) have the same meaning and function.

- Distribute index cards or name tags to all your students.
- Ask students to pick just one adjective to describe their current mood, feeling, condition, or state, and to write their chosen adjective on their index card or name tag. It is not important for each student to have his / her own, unique adjective. In fact, the presentation works best if several students have the same adjective. (If the class is in the morning, you may get several responses of "tired.")
- You can choose to participate in this yourself by writing an adjective for yourself on your index card / name tag.
- Instruct students to display their adjective prominently and walk around the room conversing with one another.
- Tell students to converse with one another about why they have chosen the adjective they have selected.
- After 5–10 minutes, ask students to return to their seats.
- Read the adjective of a student and, with help from the class, create an example sentence on the board. Leave the adjective modifier blank in the sample sentence. For example:

  Akiko is _____ tired today.

- Write two basic adjective modifiers on the board: *very* and *a little.*

- Based on other students' interactions with the student featured in the sentence, ask students to pick one of the modifiers and insert it in the sentence, accordingly. For example:

  Akiko is <u>very tired</u> today.

- Now select another student, preferably one who chose an adjective similar in meaning, and write a comparative sentence comparing the two students. For example:

  Solange is <u>much more tired than</u> Akiko.

- Repeat this presentation using other students and enlist students to create new comparative sentences featuring modifiers. For example:

  Yoo Bae is <u>a little bit more excited than</u> Stephane.

  Dani is <u>far happier than</u> Jae Woon.

  Ivan seems <u>a lot hungrier than</u> anyone else here.

- Ask students to take turns reading example sentences (a)–(f) aloud. Discuss each point as much as needed.

❑ EXERCISE 20. Warm-up. Page 240
Time: 5 minutes

> Students' impressions of relative expense may be quite different depending on where they are from and their level of experience as an independent adult. Encourage students to disagree with one another and justify their perspectives. Doing so gives them a chance to use the target structures in a very natural way and also highlights how important being able to make such comparisons is.

- Encourage students to answer the Warm-up questions as accurately as they can.
- Welcome any disagreements that may arise (particularly with item 4) and use any differences of opinion as springboards for natural conversation.
- Correct students' basic mistakes in target structures right away and feel free to challenge any statements about the topic you know to be inaccurate.

CHART 9-6. Comparisons with *Less ... Than* and *Not As ... As.* Page 241
Time: 10–15 minutes

> In the use of *less,* the text fails to state one exception. The explanation should state that *less* is not used with <u>two-syllable adjectives that end in -y,</u> such as *easy, happy,* and *hungry.*
>
> INCORRECT: *less easy than, less happy than, less hungry than*
>
> CORRECT: *not as easy as, not as happy as, not as hungry as*
>
> Exceptions to this practice are *friendly* and *angry,* which <u>can</u> be used with either *less* or *not as ... as.*

Sometimes the text may err on the side of simplification in an attempt to present basic patterns without too many exceptions.

- Ask your students to think of characteristics that describe them and that have increased with age and maturity.
- Direct students to come up with an accurate sentence about this character trait (in adjective form).
- In order to get the ball rolling, come up with a sentence about yourself and write it on the board, with a modifier if you like. For example:

  I am <u>very opinionated.</u>

- Explain to students that this trait, being "opinionated," has increased with age, and that, therefore, you can use it to create a comparative sentence about yourself at a younger age.
- Write your sentence on the board, underlining the new target structure. For example:

  When I was a child, I was <u>less opinionated than</u> I am now.

- With this template on the board, invite other students to make up sentences comparing their current characteristics with their younger traits.
- Write a few such sentences on the board. For example:

  When Carlos was a little boy, he was <u>not as calm as</u> he is now.

  When Natasha was a child, she was <u>less studious than</u> she is now.

- Explain to students that only adjectives with just one syllable must be preceded by *not as . . . as.*
- Have students take turns reading through example sentences (a)–(c) aloud.
- Review the notes and encourage any additional questions.

❑ EXERCISE 22. Game. Page 241
Time: 15–20 minutes

Tell students that this game is a free association exercise. Students may spontaneously produce sentences in which *more* is used with nouns to make comparisons. For example: *The sun produces more energy than the moon does.*

- Divide the class into teams and have teams elect one person to record all the comparisons.
- Instruct the class that they should simply say whatever comparisons come to mind and speak spontaneously while the team "writer" records these sentences.
- At the end of 15 minutes, have students read their sentences to the class.
- Lead the other students in correcting the sentences offered.
- Compare final scores and announce the winner.

CHART 9-7. Using *More* with Nouns.
Page 242
Time: 10–15 minutes

More is frequently used with nouns, functioning as the comparative form of the adjectives *many* and *much.* Sometimes, as in (d), it functions as a noun substitute.

More is used with plural (not singular) count nouns and with noncount nouns.

In comparatives with nouns, the opposite of *more* is either *less* or *fewer.* In formal or, one might say, educated English of the past, *fewer* is said to be used with count nouns and *less* with noncount nouns.

Examples:

*There are **fewer students** (count noun) in this class than in that class.*

*Mr. Black assigns **less homework** (noncount noun) than Mr. Green.*

In actual usage, *less* seems to be used with nearly every noun. In common usage, many native speakers would say, *There are less students in this class than that class.* The use of fewer is becoming somewhat rarer in everyday language, but there are many people who maintain that the use of *less* with count nouns does not "sound right." You may or may not choose to discuss the use of *less* vs. *fewer* with nouns; it depends upon the level and interests of your students.

- Write the following question on the board.

  What do you want <u>more</u> of?

- Tell students to write down one noun that reflects what they want *more* of in their lives.
- Inform your students that this "thing" can be concrete or abstract, but that they should be prepared to explain why they want *more* of this thing.
- Ask students to share what they want more of.
- Use this information to create sentences using *more,* and write these on the board, comparing content. For example:

  Mari wants <u>more</u> free time.

  Kyung Jin would like <u>more</u> money and <u>more</u> financial security in his life.

  Diego wants <u>more</u> friends and <u>more</u> opportunities to travel.

- Ask students to take turns reading example sentences (a) and (b) aloud. Compare this use to the one above.
- Review the notes on the right-hand side of the chart.
- Introduce example sentence (c) and discuss this comparative use of *more,* reminding students that this use also includes *than.*
- Review the final point and ask students if they have any further questions.

❏ EXERCISE 26. Looking at grammar.
Page 243
Time: 10 minutes

Optional Vocabulary

available	mature
miserable	behave
respect differences	health care
trustworthy	rural

❏ EXERCISE 27. Warm-up. Page 244
Time: 5 minutes

- Discuss students' responses to each item.
- Ask students how repeating a comparative changes the "feeling" of a sentence.

CHART 9-8. Repeating a Comparative.
Page 244
Time: 10 minutes

> You might mention that repeating the comparative once is generally sufficient, but in oral storytelling traditions, a speaker might repeat a comparative several times for effect. For example:
>
> *The wolf stopped abruptly when she saw the rabbit. Slowly, the wolf crept **closer and closer and closer and closer** toward the rabbit. Alas, the rabbit sensed the wolf's presence too late. The wolf pounced, and that was the end of the rabbit.*

- Explain that the repetition of a comparative gives the impression that a certain condition is intensifying or getting stronger over time.
- Create example situations that clearly illustrate the rhetorical use of repeating a comparative. Make sure that the situations give enough context to show how the repeated comparative shows increasing intensity.
- Write these situations on the board and highlight the repeated comparison. For example:

  When I was a little girl, my teacher asked me to answer some questions when I hadn't done my homework. I was terrified but followed her instructions when she told me to stand up. I was so embarrassed, standing in front of the whole class. I could feel my face becoming <u>redder and redder</u>.

  Once, on vacation in Spain, my husband and I got desperately lost. We had rented a car but somehow misread the map. My husband wouldn't ask for directions. In the meantime, we were getting <u>more and more lost</u>.

- Ask students to take turns reading the example sentences on the board. Discuss the notes on the right-hand side of the chart.

CHART 9-9. Using Double Comparatives.
Page 245
Time: 10–15 minutes

> It is important to discuss the meaning of this structure, and explain that it expresses a cause-and-effect relationship.
>
> The idioms in (d) and (e) are included for fun and to enrich students' knowledge of common expressions that they are likely to hear at some stage in their studies. The vocabulary *merry-merrier* will need to be explained, as *merry* is not commonly used. The one in (e) is very common and should be useful in the students' creative production.
>
> This is an infrequent pattern. It is included more in the interest of assisting reading comprehension than in expectation that the students will adopt the pattern in their own production.

- Explain that double comparatives are special devices used infrequently in written English and less often in speech.
- Explain the term *common expression* to students and discuss how these set phrases fit this definition.
- Write a template for double comparatives on the board and highlight the important elements. For example:

  the + comparative form, the + comparative form
  The _____, the _____.

- Looking at the template on the board, begin some common double comparative phrases and invite students to complete them by leaving the second part blank.

  The bigger, _____.
  The sooner, _____.
  The more, _____.
  The more things change, _____.
  The harder they come, _____.

- Complete each double comparative by writing the missing words in the blank space on the board. For example:

  The bigger, <u>the better</u>.
  The sooner, <u>the better</u>.
  The more, <u>the merrier</u>.
  The more things change, <u>the more they stay the same</u>.
  The harder they come, <u>the harder they fall</u>.

- Discuss the meaning of the above phrases.
- Ask students to read example sentences (a)–(e) aloud, taking turns.
- Review all the notes and answer any remaining questions students may have.

CHART 9-10. Using Superlatives. Page 246
Time: 10–15 minutes

A useful way to explain the superlative is to say that it compares one part of a group to all other things or people in that group. In example sentence (a), a city, Tokyo is being compared to all other large cities in the world. In (b), David is being compared to all other people the speaker knows and has ever known. In (c), the group consists of three books, with one book being compared to the other two.

The emphasis in the text is on how superlatives are completed.

- Ask students to think of the most and least attractive places they have ever visited.
- Using students' responses to this prompt, make sentences illustrating the correct use of the superlative.
- Write these superlatives on the board in complete sentence form. For example:

    Florence is <u>*the most attractive city*</u> *Joon has ever visited.*

    Trenton is <u>*the least attractive city*</u> *Juan has ever visited.*

- Ask students to take turns reading (a)–(c) aloud. Review the accompanying notes.
- Reiterate that *least* is the opposite of *most*, and that the superlative structure is the same (though the meaning is opposite).
- Ask students to take turns reading through (d)–(h). Go over the notes, answering any additional questions.
- Draw students' attention to **one of** + *superlative* + *noun* and remind students that *one* is always singular, no matter what phrase follows it.

❏ EXERCISE 33. Looking at grammar.
Page 247
Time: 10 minutes

Expansion: Put students in pairs. Prepare pairs of index cards with five names of "superlative" places or things. Students then use superlatives to describe places or things to each other. Students should prompt their partners to say the names of the items on the card.

Sample Card Set:

Card 1	Card 2
blue whale	Mount Everest
giraffe	UAE's Burj Khalifa
Nile River	Great Canyon of Yarlung
Sahara Desert	Tsangpo River
Pacific Ocean	Victoria Falls
	Mauna Loa volcano

❏ EXERCISE 35. Let's talk: pairwork.
Page 248
Time: 10–15 minutes

Patterns with **one of** + *superlative* are common and useful but can also be a source of grammatical errors. Typical mistakes:

INCORRECT: One of the most beautiful **country** *in the world is Switzerland.*

INCORRECT: One of the most beautiful countries in the world **are** *Switzerland.*

❏ EXERCISE 36. Grammar and listening.
Page 248
Time: 10–15 minutes

Remind students that **never** + *comparative* = *superlative*, as illustrated in (g) and (h) in the previous chart.

If students find Part I challenging, lead the class through each item, pointing out what the sentence means, element by element.

Be prepared to play the audio multiple times to give students an opportunity to comprehend.

❏ EXERCISE 39. Looking at grammar.
Page 250
Time: 10 minutes

- Explain that this exercise is a review of the charts students have studied thus far in Chapter 9.
- Ask students to first complete the items individually.
- Review the completed items as a class and ask students to explain the rationale behind their completions.

Optional Vocabulary
heavy metal
nag
snout
jaw
requires
structure
volcanic explosion
event
rate

CHART 9-11. Using *The Same, Similar, Different, Like, Alike.* Page 252
Time: 15–20 minutes

Typical errors in the use of *the same as:*

—omission of *the* with *same:*

INCORRECT: *All of the students in our class use same book.*

—the use of *a* instead of *the:*

INCORRECT: *Tom and Anna have a same book.*

—the use of *like, from,* or *than* instead of *as*

INCORRECT: *Tom's book is the same like Anna's.*

INCORRECT: *Tom's book is the same from Anna's.*

INCORRECT: *Tom's book is the same than Anna's.*

Typical errors in the use of *similar to:*

INCORRECT: *My book is similar with Anna's.*

INCORRECT: *My book is similar from Anna's.*

Some grammars claim that only *from* should follow *different.* Students at this level don't need to be concerned with this debate over *than* vs. *from.* In almost all situations in which they will use *different* in their own production, *from* will also be correct. It should also be noted that in British English, *to* may also follow *different: Although they are brothers, Bob is different to Tom in many ways.*

- Explain to students that there are many ways to express similarity.
- Illustrate use of *the same* by asking students whether they all have *the same book.*
- Write their response on the board and highlight the important elements of this structure. For example:

  All the students in the class have <u>the same book</u>.

- Explain that a definite article is required because one noun is known and named **the** *same book* = *one known, shared book.*
- Tell students that **similar** and **different** can also be used as adjectives, but these do not require the use of a definite article.
- Review example sentences (a)–(f) and write additional examples on the board.
- Introduce the next section of the chart by stating that by adding prepositions after the adjectives, one noun can be compared to another.
- Review example sentences (g)–(j) and write additional examples to ensure student understanding.
- Explain *like* vs. *alike* by illustrating the main difference on the board. For example:

  <u>Like</u> *can precede a noun.*

  She is <u>like</u> *her mother.*

  <u>Alike</u> *cannot precede a noun; it must follow the verb* <u>be</u> *or similar verbs.*

  She and her mother look <u>alike</u>.

- Review example sentences (k)–(n) from the chart and go over the additional notes.
- Keep students focused on the main difference between *like* and *alike* for now and remind students that as they gain practice, they will be able to expand their understanding.

❑ EXERCISE 45. Reading. Page 255
Time: 15–20 minutes

You may want to ask students these pre-reading discussion questions to tap into their existing knowledge of the topic.

Do you have siblings?

What is your birth order position in your family?

Do you think birth order influenced how you developed as a child and person?

What are some typical traits of oldest, middle, and youngest children?

What are some typical traits of only children?

- Discuss the above questions or others like it briefly and put students' opinions on the board, prior to their reading.
- Give students ample time to read the passage on their own.
- Then work through the reading together by having students take turns reading various sections aloud.
- Correct pronunciation, cadence, and intonation.
- Ask students to paraphrase various pieces of information as they read the passage.
- Discuss the question that follows the last paragraph: *Do you see any similarities to your family?*
- Encourage students to respond to the above question using the target structures from Chart 9-11.
- Lead students through answering the true / false questions at the end.

Optional Vocabulary

influence	weaker
personality	helpless
controlling	self-centered
peacekeeper	

❑ EXERCISE 46. Writing. Page 256
Time: 15–20 minutes

Part I
- Put students into groups to discuss the vocabulary included in the shaded box.
- Review as a class and give examples of unknown vocabulary words used in sentences.

Part II
- Give students time to complete items 1–4 using their own family members as subjects.
- Ask students to compare their completed sentences with their classmates and discuss who they most resemble in their families.

Part III
- Have students begin writing their paragraph while you walk around and discuss the topic and structure with them.
- Assign the paragraph as homework and ask students to hand in their completed paragraph at the next class meeting.

Chapter 10
The Passive

CHAPTER SUMMARY

OBJECTIVE: Because the passive is frequently used in English, it is essential that second language learners be able to understand and use it on a frequent basis. This chapter highlights this important structure and offers plenty of controlled and less controlled practice to promote autonomous mastery of it.

APPROACH: The chapter begins by showing the relationship between active and passive sentences. After a brief explanation of transitive and intransitive sentences, the focus shifts to the omission of the *by*-phrase. Next, the passive is used with progressive verbs and modal auxiliaries. A section of the chapter then deals with other uses of past and present participles, concluding with some idiomatic expressions containing participles.

TERMINOLOGY: The term "passive" is used here most commonly without the additional term "voice." The term used for explicit identification of the agent in a passive structure is "the *by*-phrase" because the preposition *by* is its first element.

❏ **EXERCISE 1.** Warm-up. Page 258
Time: 5–10 minutes

> It might help to ask students to consider the action from the perspective of both the worm and the bird. You can also ask students to identify who is doing the action in each sentence.

CHART 10-1. Active Sentences and Passive Sentences. Page 258
Time: 5–10 minutes

> The emphasis in this introductory chart is on the form of the passive as well as the meaning in equivalent active sentences.
>
> The passive is most commonly used without a *by*-phrase. All the example sentences in the initial charts and exercises, however, include a *by*-phrase as an aid to understanding the form and meaning of the passive. The omission of the *by*-phrase is discussed in Chart 10-4.

The text concentrates on the form of the passive and its basic use. The passive expresses the accomplishment of an action when the doer of the action is not known, or it is not important to know this. For example, in the sentence *Corn is grown in Iowa*, who grew the corn is not important or is not known. The passive forms a legitimate and necessary function in English rhetoric, especially in scientific and technical writing. For example in the sentence, *Energy can be changed from one form to another, but it cannot be destroyed*, the passive describes a situation in which there simply is no particular actor or doer of the action, nor any need to identify an actor. In such situations, the passive is a common and useful structure.

Languages differ on passiveness. English is rather flexible in attributing actions and volition to inanimate objects. For example, it accepts as grammatical, *My shoe fell off.* Other languages insist that sentences must always be in a passive form; a shoe could never will or cause itself to fall off. Students from such language backgrounds may attempt to "stretch" the grammar of English to conform to the "logic" of their grammars.

- Ask students to take turns reading sentence (a) and sentence (b) aloud.
- With help from the class, create a new pair of sentences that illustrate the subject's role in an active sentence vs. the subject's role in a passive one. Try to draw the first example from class dynamics, for example:

     S   **V**   **O**
  Nikita took Milo's grammar book.

- Label the parts of the sentence by asking:

  What's the action?
  Who's doing it?
  What's being acted on?

- Write the label *ACTIVE* above this sentence.

         ACTIVE
     S   **V**   **O**
  Nikita took Milo's grammar book.

- Explain that in English there's another way to write this same sentence. Write it on the board.

  Milo's grammar book was taken by Nikita.

- Then ask the same three questions (students may have difficulty here), and label the sentence.

    S   **V**

    Milo's grammar book was taken by Nikita.

- Explain that this is a called a passive sentence, and label it on the board.
- Then draw arrows on the board (or ask a student to do so) to show the following:

    the subject initiating the action = an active sentence

    the subject receiving the action = a passive sentence

    ACTIVE

    S   V   O

    Nikita took Milo's grammar book.

    Nikita ⇒ *Milo's grammar book.*
        took

    PASSIVE

    S   V

    Milo's grammar book was taken by Nikita.

    Milo's grammar book ⇒ *by Nikita.*
            was taken

- Review example sentences (c) and (d) by asking students to read these aloud and reiterate the differences between the two.

CHART 10-2. Form of the Passive. Page 259
Time: 10–15 minutes

> Though the chart is very clear, it may help students for you to rewrite its basic elements on the board for fresh presentation and then discuss these as a group. You can then read through the elements of the chart.

- Emphasize that when switching from active to passive (and back to active), the tense is not changed but the form of the verbs do change.
- Simply rewrite the example sentences from the chart or create new sentences of your own. Start with the present tense. Show that the passive version is in the same tense by underlining the simple present of the verb *to be*.
- Make sure students notice your underlining each verb tense (as conjugated) in the active sentence and matching it with the tense of the verb *be* in the passive version. For example:

Tense	Active ⇒	Passive
Simple Present	Authors *write* books.	Books *are* written (by authors).
Simple Past	Jose *angered* Marco.	Marco *was* angered by Jose.
Present Prog.	Ava *is cleaning* the table.	The table *is being* cleaned by Ava.
Past Prog.	Lara *was teaching* the class.	The class *was being* taught by Lara.
Present Perfect	Wu-Hei *has taken* the picture.	The picture *has been* taken by Wu-Hei.
Future	Yao *will* bring the food.	The food *will be* brought by Yao.

- Ask students to take turns reading the example sentences from Chart 10-2 aloud. Review the notes.

❏ EXERCISE 2. Looking at grammar.
Page 259
Time: 5–10 minutes

> In this exercise, students are asked to transform not only the verb form but also the subject pronouns. In addition, they need to pay attention to subject-verb agreement. Be sure to tell students to pay attention to the three changes they need to make in each transformation.
>
> 1) active to passive form
> 2) subject pronoun
> 3) agreement of subject-verb
>
> You may want to write the above on the board.

❏ EXERCISE 3. Listening. Page 260
Time: 10 minutes

> This listening and grammar exercise emphasizes that every passive verb has a form of *be*, and it is *be* that expresses tense and number. The main verb is always in the past participle form.

Optional Vocabulary

janitors	discovered
security guard	announce

❏ EXERCISE 4. Looking at grammar.
Page 261
Time: 5–10 minutes

- Inform students that there are auxiliaries in many of the sentences, and, therefore, they need to look for the verb *be* + past participle.
- Tell students to check for the *by*-phrase, which is often included with passive voice.
- When reviewing as a class, ask students to discuss what activities the dentist or dental assistant does and to compare past experiences.
- For example, you can ask students what the dentist or dental assistant is checking <u>for</u>.

Optional Vocabulary

cavity	schedule
filling	appointment

❏ EXERCISE 5. Looking at grammar.
Page 261
Time: 5–10 minutes

> The emphasis here is still on the basic form and meaning of the passive. The text teaches the meaning of the passive by showing its relationship to the active in each item. Many of the situations presented are very typical of passive sentences, where the action is more important than the doer of that action.

Optional Vocabulary
employs   fax
hired   examining

❏ EXERCISE 6. Looking at grammar.
Page 262
Time: 10 minutes

> It may help to write the examples on the board and draw arrows showing the action. You can point to them to reiterate the relationship between them as you work through the exercise.

- Give students ample time to attempt these alone.
- Then ask various students to read each item after you have modeled the example.

Expansion: Ask a few students to leave the classroom and stand outside in the corridor, where they cannot see what is going on in the classroom. Instruct the students still remaining in the classroom to move items around and change the appearance of the classroom in a noticeable way. For example, students can remove a clock from the wall, move desks, overturn chairs (carefully), move books from students' desks to the floor or other unexpected places, and / or empty the contents of a bag or backpack (with permission) onto a desk. Instruct students to do these things quietly and carefully and then return to their seats.

Invite the student(s) waiting in the hall to return to the classroom. Explain to everyone that some actions in the class were done during the students' absence. Instruct the student(s) who were in the hall to ask questions using the passive voice in order to determine what actions took place and who did them. The remainder of the class should answer these questions. Encourage the student(s) to ask more specific questions using passive to discover all the actions that were done in their absence.

If you like, you can have one student act as the secretary and record the questions asked on the board. Take the time to correct questions asked in the incorrect form.

Sample questions may include:

Were desks moved? Was that desk moved by Hsin-Hao?

Was the clock removed? Was the clock removed by Juan?

Were backpacks placed on the desk? Were backpacks placed on the desk by Lola and Esme?

Was the board erased? Was the board erased by our teacher?

❏ EXERCISE 8. Warm-up. Page 263
Time: 5 minutes

> Before students begin the Warm-up, you can ask a student to describe the role of an object in a sentence. Assist students in defining an object and write students' definitions on the board. (It is fine if these definitions are descriptive and very general rather than definitive and precise.) For example:
>
> *Object*
>
> *The noun that the action happens to*
>
> *The word that comes after the verb*
>
> *Not the subject*

CHART 10-3. Transitive and Intransitive
Verbs. Page 263
Time: 10–20 minutes

> Not infrequently, learners try to use intransitive verbs in a passive form. Examples of some of the most common learner errors are:
>
> *I am agreed with you.*
>
> *He was died five years ago.*
>
> *An interesting event was happened to me when I was a child.*
>
> The intention of this chart is to demonstrate and explain why some verbs can never be used in the passive.
>
> Point out that information about whether a verb is transitive or intransitive can be found in a dictionary. Some common abbreviations are *v.t, v.i.,* or *T* and *I,* or *V* and *V + O.* Perhaps you can help students find this information about various verbs in their dictionaries.
>
> To help the students understand the grammar terminology, relate the word *transitive* to other words that begin with the prefix *trans.* For example, ask students what they know about the words *transportation, translate, transfer,* and *transform.* Explain that *trans-* means "across" or "carrying over to the other side."
>
> A transitive verb "connects or bridges" the subject and object. It carries the meaning or transfers the meaning of the verb "across" from the subject to the object. You can easily draw this process with an arrow on the board.

By contrast, an intransitive verb does not connect to an object. An adverbial usually completes a clause with an intransitive verb by giving information about place, time, and manner. Point out that the prefix *in-* is negative (*intransitive = not transitive*) as in words such as *inactive, inexpensive,* and *incapable.*

Some verbs have both transitive and intransitive uses. Examples of these are:

*Everyone **eats** (intransitive verb) and **sleeps** (intransitive verb) every day.*

vs.

*I **eat** (transitive verb) breakfast every day.*

*Flowers **grow** (intransitive verb) best in a sunny environment.*

vs.

*My mother **grows** (transitive verb) flowers in her garden.*

- Write a simple transitive sentence on the board, using one or more of your students as the "stars" of the sentence.
- Draw an arrow showing that the action goes from the subject to the object. For example:

$$S \Rightarrow\Rightarrow\Rightarrow\Rightarrow\Rightarrow\Rightarrow\Rightarrow O$$
$$V$$

Marta hugged her mother.

- Now choose an intransitive verb and show that the action is not transferred to a object. Show this by simply making the arrow wrap around the verb itself.

For example:

$$\Downarrow S \Uparrow \quad V$$

Jin-Hyuk fell down.

- Stress the fact that when an intransitive verb is used, there is no recipient of the action and the action revolves around the subject.
- Explain that because there must be an object of the active verb to make a new sentence in passive, intransitive verbs cannot be made passive.
- Write (c) on the board and ask students if it is active or passive.
- Then ask the class to make it passive and write that sentence on the board.
- Do the same process with item (f).
- Reiterate that because intransitive verbs are not followed by an object they cannot be used in the passive.
- Ask students to take turns reading (a)–(c) aloud and to compare these with sentences (d)–(f).
- Go through the list of common intransitive verbs with students and remind them that they will already instinctively know that many of these verbs can't have objects (and, therefore, can't have passive versions).
- Review sentences (g) and (h) vs. (i)–(k) by asking students to read these aloud and compare them.

□ **EXERCISE 9.** Looking at grammar.
Page 264
Time: 5–10 minutes

- As a way of aiding identification of transitive vs. intransitive verbs, ask students first to look for objects of the verbs in the sentences.
- Remind students that if there is no object, the verb is intransitive.
- Ask students to read the sentences aloud, identifying each one as either "no change" or giving a new, passive version of the active sentence.

Optional Vocabulary

felt	cure
existed	invent
agree	

CHART 10-4. Using the *by*-Phrase. Page 265
Time: 10–15 minutes

Very often, it is not necessary or even possible to identify who the exact performer, actor, or doer of an action is. In this situation, the passive is a very useful structure. Students should understand that usually the passive occurs <u>without</u> a *by*-phrase.

It is beyond the scope of this text to deal with all the various rhetorical or stylistic reasons for using the passive <u>with</u> a *by*-phrase. The focus remains on a basic introduction to the form and meaning of the passive, with the goal being the ability to use the passive in typical situations (for example: *Spanish is spoken in Mexico.* or *Tom and Ann are married.*) and comprehend its meaning in written passages.

- Ask your students if they have ever made or created something that they were very proud of. Suggest that, in this case, the *by*-phrase is important because the "maker" can be identified.
- If a student has created something, write an example sentence on the board using his / her name. For example:

Those earrings were made <u>by Atsuko</u>.

- Explain that when the "who" is important or interesting, we use the *by*-phrase.
- Ask a student to read example sentence (a). Review the notes.
- Next, explain that <u>usually</u> when we use passive voice, we are not interested in or simply don't know who actually did the action.
- Emphasize that it is often because the actor is unimportant in the first place that we use passive, and, therefore, it only makes sense that most of the time, we don't need the *by*-phrase.
- Ask students to take turns reading example sentences (b)–(e) aloud. After each sentence ask, *Is it important to know who?* The answer should be *no*.
- Then ask students to suggest more situations / sentences in which the passive is used without the *by*-phrase.
- Finally, have students read (f) and (g) aloud. Discuss the accompanying notes.

❏ EXERCISE 12. Looking at grammar.
Page 265
Time: 5–10 minutes

> The point of the exercise is to readily demonstrate that a *by*-phrase is usually unnecessary.

Optional Vocabulary

hammers	published
hypnotized	

❏ EXERCISE 14. Looking at grammar.
Page 266
Time: 5–10 minutes

- Give students a few minutes to make passive sentences from the cues.
- Ask students to then take turns reading the sentences aloud.
- Ask students if this sequence of events is similar to what would happen in such a situation in their country.

❏ EXERCISE 15. Listening. Page 267
Time: 10 minutes

- Play the audio through completely once and see if students have been able to complete each blank. If not, play it again without stopping.
- Ask students to take turns reading their completed items aloud.
- Discuss any unfamiliar vocabulary.
- Play individual items again as needed for final correction and clarification.

Optional Vocabulary

dorm entrance	treated
ambulance	bruises
emergency room	reckless

❏ EXERCISE 16. Looking at grammar.
Page 267
Time: 10–15 minutes

> Some students may have difficulty accepting some of the correct answers because their native languages allow more verbs to be changed into the passive. Discuss any problem items as a class.

Optional Vocabulary

interrupt	violent
breaking news	power company
composition	

❏ EXERCISE 17. Listening. Page 268
Time: 10 minutes

- Ask students to close their books before you play through the audio the first time.
- Before playing the audio a second time, ask students to open their books and see if they can complete any of the blanks without a second listening.
- Play the audio a second time.
- Correct and review by having students read their completed items aloud.

❏ EXERCISE 18. Warm-up. Page 269
Time: 5–10 minutes

- Ask students to read and complete the true / false items independently first.
- Have students take turns reading the items aloud and supplying the "T" or "F."
- Ask students to refer to the passage in order to locate specific pieces of information.

CHART 10-5. Passive Modal Auxiliaries.
Page 269
Time: 10–15 minutes

> Emphasize again that every single passive has a form of the verb *be* as the auxiliary to the main verb.
>
> The text does not present the past forms of modals, so past forms in the passive are not found here either (for example: *should have been mailed*). If need be, see *Understanding and Using English Grammar* for presentation of past modal auxiliaries.

- Ask a student to give you a simple sentence containing a modal.
- Write this sentence on the board. For example:

    Alexei <u>can</u> make tasty Russian food.

- Ask students to label the subject, verb, and object.

    S   **V   O**

    Alexei <u>can</u> make tasty Russian food.

- Explain to students that each passive form, including passive modals, has a form of the verb *be*.
- As a class, create a new passive sentence, first asking what the new subject will be.
- Begin writing the new sentence on the board. For example

    S

    Our dinner . . .

- Continue writing the new sentence, with the help of students. For example:

    S   V

    Our dinner <u>might be made</u> by Hiroko.

- Work through the chart by asking individual students to read the example sentences aloud.
- Discuss the changes required for the transformation from active to passive.

A focus of this passage is on analyzing when the passive is or is not used and why. In general, the passive is used when there is no need or way to identify the actual performers of an action. In English rhetoric, the passive is used in preference to active sentences with indeterminate subjects such as *someone, people,* and *you* (used as an impersonal pronoun meaning anyone in that situation).

The passage switches back and forth between passive and active verbs. When there is a subject that students know by name (and *Levi Strauss* is a well-known name), the verbs are in active. When the process of developing the jeans we know today as Levis is described, the passive is used. Ideally, you can facilitate students' "discovering" this distinction on their own.

Part I
- Give students time to read through the passage once on their own. Then have them go back and underline the passive verbs.
- As a class, consider why those particular verbs are in the passive.
- Discuss why passive is used for some verbs but not for those following *Levi Strauss*.

Part II
- Ask students to take turns reading sentences or paragraphs of the passage aloud.
- Ask students about optional vocabulary items as they read, giving them a chance to use their English to discuss vocabulary and take a break from reading aloud.
- Give students time to answer the questions alone. Then review as a class.

Optional Vocabulary

created	miner
invented	designed
immigrant	overall
canvas	tab
wagon	identified

CHART 10-6. Using Past Participles as Adjectives (Non-Progressive Passive). Page 271
Time: 10–15 minutes

The non-progressive passive is common in English. The text intends for the listed expressions to become familiar enough that the students begin to use them comfortably and correctly. Time needs to be spent discussing vocabulary and creating examples.

The use of incorrect forms is a common problem with this structure. Typical mistakes include wrong forms of the past participle and omission of *be*.

INCORRECT: We were very frighten.

INCORRECT: My briefcase made of leather.

Another common problem is misuse of prepositions.

INCORRECT: Tom is married with Alice.

See Chart 10-7 for a discussion of the problem of confusing present and past participles used as adjectives, for example: *interesting* vs. *interested.*

The non-progressive passive is also sometimes called "stative passive." The term "stative" has historically been used to describe a state or status of existence. (This form of the passive has also been termed the "finished-result passive.") However, it will be most useful for your students to simply refer to it as "the non-progressive passive" as stative verbs have already been referred to as "non-progressive" in this text.

In the non-progressive passive, usually any action took place earlier than the situation that is being described. For example, *I am acquainted with Tom* means we became acquainted at an earlier time. *My watch is broken* means something happened to my watch earlier.

- Write the following questions on the board:

  Are you tired?

  Are you married?

- Ask students if they understand these questions (they will) and point out that they are already familiar with this adjective form.
- Instruct students to give you complete sentence answers. Write these on the board, with their names as introductions.
- Because answers will be in the first person, involve other students in changing each one to third person.
- Underline the forms of the verb *be* and the *-ed* ending in each student-generated sentence. For example:

  Victor: I <u>am</u> not marri<u>ed</u>.

  Victor <u>is</u> not marri<u>ed</u>.

  Selena: I <u>am</u> tir<u>ed</u>.

  Selena <u>is</u> tir<u>ed</u>.

- Explain that when *be* is followed by a past participle, the participle acts like an adjective.
- Ask students to take turns reading aloud and comparing example sentences (a)–(c) with (d)–(f).
- Review the notes on the right-hand side of the chart with students.
- Next, explain that very often these past participles are combined with prepositions in order to link them to objects.
- Review example sentences (g)–(i) and discuss the expressions below.
- Ask students to look through the list of expressions. Discuss the meanings of any that are unfamiliar to them.

❏ **EXERCISE 22.** Looking at grammar.
Page 272
Time: 10 minutes

Explain to students that this exercise will help them recognize common expressions that are composed of *past participles + prepositions + objects*.

Ask students to describe the meaning of the past participle expressions as you correct the exercise with the whole class.

❏ **EXERCISE 24.** Looking at grammar.
Page 273
Time: 5–10 minutes

Optional Vocabulary

ecology   digital
fiancé   pixels

❏ **EXERCISE 25.** Looking at grammar.
Page 273
Time: 5–10 minutes

Encourage students to complete this exercise on sight, and without looking at Chart 10-6, if they can. Assist with the meanings of some of the less familiar participial adjectives and discuss the meanings of the sentences.

CHART 10-7. Participial Adjectives: *-ed* vs. *-ing*. Page 276
Time: 10–15 minutes

The present participle conveys an active meaning. The past participle conveys a passive meaning. The text seeks to make the distinction clear by saying that the past participle describes a feeling that was caused by something and that the present participle describes the cause of that feeling. The author has not yet found an easy way to explain the difference in meaning between the two forms. It is hoped that the exercises serve to clarify this grammar. (It may help to refer to the explanation of transitive–transfer of action–given for Chart 10-3.)

In (b) and (d), the form may look like a progressive verb tense, but it is not. Perhaps you could explain that these sentences consist of the main verb *be* followed by an adjective (that happens to be a present participle). In other words, *is interesting* and *was surprising* are not the present and past progressive tenses respectively; they are **be** + *adjective*, just like *is good* or *was happy*.

Some grammars analyze some *-ing* adjectives as gerunds rather than present participles:

(a) *a chair that is rocking = a rocking chair*, in which *rocking* is a present participle

(b) *a chair that is designed for rocking = a rocking chair*, in which *rocking* is a gerund, used as a noun adjunct.

This text designates all *-ing* adjectives as participial.

- Explain the following difference between *-ing* and *-ed* adjectives to students and write it on the board:

  -ing = cause of *-ed*

- Write the following two sentences on the board:

  I am boring.
  I am bored.

- Ask your students which of these sentences they would rather use to describe themselves and why.

- Remind students that both *-ing* and *-ed* participial adjectives are adjectives, like any other descriptive adjective.

- Tell students that they can follow the verb *be* and other non-progressive verbs such as *seem, look,* and *appear.*

- Tell students that participial adjectives can also precede nouns.

- Ask students to take turns reading the example sentences (a)–(d). Review the notes included on the right-hand side of the chart.

- Have students read the final example sentences.

❏ **EXERCISE 31.** Listening. Page 276
Time: 5–10 minutes

These forms can be hard for students to hear, so be prepared to play the audio multiple times.

❏ **EXERCISE 32.** Looking at grammar.
Page 277
Time: 5–10 minutes

These contrasting participles are always more difficult for learners to understand and control. Take time to discuss any misunderstood items in this exercise.

Optional Vocabulary

subject   exploration
marine biology

Expansion: Prepare index cards by writing a mix of both *-ing* and *-ed* adjectives (eight in total) on each card. Put students into pairs and decide who will "go" first. The game is modeled on the TV game show Password. In this game show, one person gives clues about a word (without ever saying the word or any part of it) until the person "receiving" guesses the exact word.

The "giver" should talk about an adjective until his / her partner guesses the exact adjective. Importantly, "receivers" must guess the correct form, whether -ing or -ed, in order for the giver to move to the next adjective.

It may be helpful for you to first model the activity so that students can see that, for the most part, -ing clues will be both simple nouns and situations described by full sentences. The -ed clues are likely to be just situations (When you are sitting in class, and the teacher is not interesting, you feel _____.).

To make the expansion easier for students, do not put two forms of one participial on the same card. Sample cards may look like the following:

fascinating	tiring
bored	thrilled
frightening	embarrassed
excited	shocking

CHART 10-8. Get + Adjective; Get + Past Participle. Page 278
Time: 10–15 minutes

> Get expresses the idea of become when it is followed by an adjective or past participle.
>
> The passive with get is common, especially in spoken English. It is a somewhat informal structure, although it is also sometimes found in formal writing.
>
> The text intends for the students to become familiar enough with the listed expressions to use them easily in creative production. These expressions can be quite useful.

• Ask students to think about a situation in which they became angry.
• Ask a student to describe every step in the process of becoming angry, and write these steps on the board, using third person. For example:

  Ji-Hye and her husband were driving to the mountains.
  Ji-Hye's husband, Alain, took the wrong turn.
  Ji-Hye and Alain were driving in the wrong direction.
  Ji-Hye realized that they were lost.
  Ji-Hye told Alain that they were lost.
  Ji-Hye suggested that they stop and ask for directions.
  Alain didn't want to stop and ask for directions.
  Alain continued driving.
  They argued, and, finally, they turned around.
  They had wasted a lot of time going in the wrong direction.
  They didn't arrive at their destination until late at night.
  They were both hungry and tired.
  Ji-Hye was very angry.

• The story you write on the board doesn't have to be as lengthy as the one above, but it should have at least five to six separate sentences.
• Ask another student, not the "star" of the sentence, to describe when Ji-Hye became angry.

• Ask the student to mark the point at which Ji-Hye started to become angry.
• Draw an arrow from that point to the point at which Ji-Hye was very angry. For example:

  Ji-Hye and her husband were driving to the mountains.
  Ji-Hye's husband, Alain, took the wrong turn.
  Ji-Hye and Alain were driving in the wrong direction.
  Ji-Hye realized that they were lost.
  Ji-Hye told Alain that they were lost.   ⇓ a bit angry
  Ji-Hye suggested that they stop and ask   ⇓ a bit angry
  for directions.
  Alain didn't want to stop and ask for   ⇓ angrier
  directions.
  Alain continued driving.   ⇓ angrier
  They argued, and, finally, they turned
  around.
  They had wasted a lot of time going in   ⇓ angrier
  the wrong direction.
  They didn't arrive at their destination   ⇓ angrier
  until late at night.
  They were both hungry and tired.
  Ji-Hye was very angry.   ANGRY!!!

• Tell your students that Ji-Hye's story illustrates the get + adjective structure.
• Explain that because it usually takes some time to move from one mood or state to another, get + adjective and get + past participle are extremely useful structures.
• Ask students to take turns reading (a) and (b) and then (c) and (d) aloud. Review the additional chart notes as you go.
• Review the list of get + adjective and get + past participle combinations at the bottom of the chart with students and discuss any unknown vocabulary.

❑ EXERCISE 39. Reading. Page 281
Time: 10 minutes

• Ask students what they think the term "blended family" means and put their ideas about it on the board.
• As a class, build a working definition of "blended family" and put it on the board, next to the term itself. For example:

  blended family = family made up of blood and non-blood relatives

• Ask students if this model of family is common in their country of origin and lead a mini-discussion on the topic.
• Give students time to read the passage.
• Ask a student to read the first true / false question aloud and to locate the information within the text to answer it.
• Proceed as above with the other two questions.
• If students want to discuss the topic more, give them time to do so.

CHART 10-9. Using *Be Used/Accustomed To* and *Get Used/Accustomed To.* Page 282
Time: 10–15 minutes

> The structures in this chart are common and useful, but learners frequently have some difficulty with them. Common errors: *I'm use to living here. I'm used to live here.* Also, *accustomed* is often misspelled as *acustomed, accustommed,* or *acustommed.*
>
> In British English, *to* may be considered part of an infinitive phrase in the expression *be accustomed to,* allowing the simple form of a verb to follow: *I'm accustomed to **live** in a warm climate.* In American English, *to* is considered a preposition, requiring that a gerund follow as the object of the preposition.
>
> For example: *I'm accustomed to **living** in a warm climate.*

- Ask your students what situations and living conditions they are currently used / accustomed to.
- Write descriptions about students' responses on the board and highlight the important elements of the structure. For example:

  Violetta is used to eating pasta for dinner.

  Rolf is accustomed to getting up before 6:00 A.M. each day.

  Takehiro is used to working 12 hours, six days a week.

- Ask students to take turns reading example sentences (a)–(d) aloud. Review the notes on the right-hand side of the chart with them.
- Read example sentence (e) aloud and remind students that they have previously learned the structure *get + adjective / past participle.*
- Write the structure *get + past participle* on the board.
- Write the structure *get + used / accustomed to + gerund* on the board.
- Underline the *-ed* in *used / accustomed to* and remind students that *used / accustomed* are past participles. For example:

  *get + past participle (-ed ending) ⇒ get + us**ed** / accustom**ed** to + gerund*

- Ask students if there is anything they are *getting accustomed to* and them create sentences.

❏ EXERCISE 41. Looking at grammar.
Page 282
Time: 10 minutes

Optional Vocabulary

raised	recently
hometown	rarely
exercises	multiple-choice

❏ EXERCISE 42. Listening and speaking.
Page 282
Time: 10–20 minutes

Part I
- Play the audio.
- Correct students' completions and ensure students have accurate questions with which to interview one another.

Part II
- Ask students to move around the room, interviewing one another.
- Invite each student to tell the class one piece of information he / she learned during the interview process.

❏ EXERCISE 44. Let's talk. Page 283
Time: 10–15 minutes

> Encourage students to contrast their own former habits or first experiences with later experiences in their lives, according to the topic they are working on. Students should not think *I am used to* is the same as *I usually.*

- Put students into small groups of three or four, if possible.
- Ask students to select one or more of the topics provided.
- Circulate around the room, helping students activate passive vocabulary and facilitating and refining ideas that you hear as you interact with each group.
- After ample time, invite students to share some of their groups' responses. Put some on the board.

CHART 10-10. *Used To* vs. *Be Used To.*
Page 284
Time: 10 minutes

> *Used to* and *be used to* can be confusing for students. This chart seeks to clarify their differences in form and meaning.

- Tell students that *used to* is very different from *be used to.*
- Explain that *used to* is <u>only</u> used to express past habits.
- Write the formula for *used to* on the board. For example:

  used to + simple form = habitual past

- Ask your students what they *used to* do when they were children and write their responses on the board, using third person. For example:

  Antonio <u>used to</u> go to sleep at 7:30 P.M.

  Lei-Hsao <u>used to</u> practice the piano every day, for two hours.

  Vianna <u>used to</u> walk two miles to school, twice a day.

- Explain that *be used to* is followed by the *-ing* form of the verb to express a situation that the subject is currently accustomed to.
- Write the formula for *be used to* + *-ing* on the board.
- Write a sample sentence for *be used to* + *-ing* on the board and discuss the contrast with *used to*. For example:

  I *am used to* teaching English to foreign students.

- Ask students to read the example sentences aloud and to review the notes.

❏ EXERCISE 47. Looking at grammar.
Page 284
Time: 10 minutes

> To help students understand when *be* + *used to* + *gerund* is needed, advise them to look for either present tense or present perfect tense. Often, the use of the present perfect in an existing sentence indicates that *be* + *used to* + *gerund* is required.

CHART 10-11. Using *Be Supposed To*.
Page 285
Time: 10 minutes

> *Be supposed to* is included in this chapter because its form is passive. In meaning, it is related to the modals *should / ought to*. (See Chapter 9 in *Understanding and Using English Grammar* for a comparison of the meanings of *should* and *be supposed to*.) This text emphasizes that the idea of expectation is included in the meaning of *be supposed to:* it communicates the idea that somebody expects something.

- Ask students what they *are supposed to do* before traveling to another country. Ask them, specifically what documents they *are supposed to have*.
- Write the formula for *be supposed to* + *simple form* on the board.

  be supposed to + simple form = event that is expected
                                 to or should happen

- Below the formula, write the responses to your travel and documents questions.
- You can write these answers both as exact quotes from the students who responded as well as in third person. For example:

  We *are supposed to* have our passports with us when we travel.

  Because Hector is from Brazil, he *is supposed to* have a travel visa to enter the United States.

  Travelers *are supposed to* follow all the rules of the United States while they are traveling within the country.

- Ask students to take turns reading example sentences (a) and (b) aloud.

- Review the chart notes with students.
- Read the example sentence for (c) aloud and discuss its particular meaning with students.

❏ EXERCISE 52. Reading, grammar, and listening. Page 286
Time: 20–30 minutes

Part I
- Ask students to read the pre-reading questions. Then lead a mini-discussion about them.
- If students come from different language backgrounds, this general topic (zoos) could be a good point of comparison.
- Give students ample time to read the passage.

Part I Optional Vocabulary

common	encourage
established	settings
institutions	breeding
research	programs

Part II
- Lead students through this segment.
- Have students take turns reading the items in each set aloud.
- Ask students which of the statements are grammatically correct. Ask students to explain why they are correct and what is missing or wrong in those they think are incorrect.

Part III
- Give different students the opportunity to read the final comprehension questions aloud, answer them, and then locate the specific and supporting information in the original text.

❏ EXERCISE 54. Reading and writing.
Page 289
Time: 10–15 minutes

Part I
- Ask students to read through the passage independently and to underline the passive structures.
- Review these passive structures as a class and discuss why passive was the best way to express these thoughts.

Part II
- Describe the writing assignment to students.
- Ask them to consider which sentences should be passive.
- Give students in-class time to begin writing either individually or in groups.
- Collect the written work as homework during the next class meeting.

Chapter 11
Count/Noncount Nouns and Articles

CHAPTER SUMMARY

OBJECTIVE: The chapter seeks to lay a firm understanding of the difference between count and noncount nouns, which some students can find illogical and confusing. However, just as students need to gain understanding and mastery of the tense system of English, they need to understand and be able to use count/noncount nouns and the articles that introduce them. Though meaning is not always compromised when count/noncount and article usage isn't clear, students themselves feel much more confident when they have control of this grammatical area.

APPROACH: Because article usage cannot make sense without an understanding of the distinction between count and noncount nouns, this distinction is the first order of business. The first half of the chapter lays the groundwork for the basics of article use as presented in Chart 11-8.

TERMINOLOGY: "Count" and "noncount" may also appear in some texts as "countable" and "noncountable."

❏ EXERCISE 1. Warm-up. Page 290
Time: 5 minutes

Students at this level will have already encountered correct article usage and both count and noncount nouns although they may not be able to articulate the grammar. Encourage students to rely on what sounds right and remind them that they have been absorbing much more grammar (since they first encountered English) than they even know.

CHART 11-1. A vs. An. Page 290
Time: 5–10 minutes

Let students tell you what they already know about the use of these articles and encourage them to explain their understanding of article usage.

Discuss the pronunciation of **a** and **an**. When unstressed, they are pronounced as weak vowels: /ə/ and /ə + n/. Only when they are emphasized are they pronounced /ey/ and /æn/.

- Ask students what they already know and/or notice about the use of **a** and **an**.
- Before looking at the chart, write students' own explanations of the difference between the two articles on the board. For example:

  A always comes before consonants.

  An comes in front of vowels.

- Ask a student to read sentences (a)–(d) aloud. Follow with reading the accompanying notes.
- Ask students to compare the sounds of words that begin with **u** and then have a student read (e)–(h) and the related notes aloud.
- Finish by asking a student to read example sentences (i) and (j) aloud and examining the related notes.

❏ EXERCISE 2. Looking at grammar.
Page 291
Time: 5–10 minutes

- Remind students (and perhaps ask students to reiterate) the different pronunciations of **u** and **h**.
- Give students a few minutes to go through and decide which article should be used with each singular noun.
- Ask students to give brief and impromptu definitions of the words and phrases after they have given the correct article for each item.

Optional Vocabulary

abbreviation	urgent message
uniform	universal problem

❏ EXERCISE 4. Warm-up. Page 291
Time: 5 minutes

- Ask students what they think of when they hear the term "noncount."
- Invite students to take turns reading through each item and ask which noun might be noncount.

CHART 11-2. Count and Noncount Nouns.
Page 292
Time: 10 minutes

To make the initial distinction between count and noncount, concentrate on the examples in Chart 11-2 (*chair* vs. *furniture*) and in Exercise 7 (*banana* vs. *fruit*, *letter* vs. *mail*, *question* vs. *information*). Point out which ones can take a final -*s* and which "count or amount words" (for example: quantifiers or expressions of quantity) can be used. Try to get across the concept that noncount nouns represent "masses" or "whole categories." (See Chart 11-3).

Typical mistakes involve using final -*s* at the end of noncount nouns and using improper expressions of quantity (for example: *too many homeworks*).

Most nouns are used as count nouns. Some nouns are used only as noncount nouns. Many nouns also have both count and noncount uses (see Chart 11-6), *Fruit* is an example of a noun that can be used as either, but for pedagogical purposes it is presented as a noncount noun throughout this chapter. (When some nouns that are used predominantly or typically as noncount are used as count nouns, they may refer to "different kinds of." For example, *apples, bananas,* and *pears* are <u>fruits</u> not vegetables. Other examples would be different kinds of *breads, foods, teas, soups,* and *world Englishes*.) It is the text's view that students at this level of language study would find these subtleties confusing and disruptive rather than beneficial.

- Ask students if they can think of some nouns of physical substances or items that are hard, if not impossible, to count.
- Write the question, *Can you count it?* and *Yes / No* on the board and ask students to offer nouns that you can examine as a class.
- If students don't suggest mass nouns, help them get started by demonstrating <u>why</u> noncount nouns are very helpful. For example:

<u>Noun</u>	<u>Can you count it?</u> <u>Yes / No</u>
horse	Yes, can say "three horses"
sugar	No, not possible to count such tiny grains
water	No, can only talk about quantity of substance
stars	Yes, not possible for average human to do so / each one is a separate thing
furniture	No, it describes a bunch of nouns in the same furniture category

- Emphasize that noncount nouns make sense because they tend to be nouns that it would be physically hard if not impossible to separate and count.
- Ask students to take turns reading the Count Noun and Noncount Noun sections of Chart 11-2 aloud and to review the accompanying notes.

CHART 11-3. Noncount nouns. Page 293
Time: 10 minutes

It is important for students to understand the <u>concept</u> of a noncount noun. That is the purpose of this chart. Discuss the concept in relation to some of the words listed at the bottom of the chart, all of which are "wholes."

In addition to understanding the concept of a noncount noun, it helps if students simply become aware of some of the common nouns that are usually noncount. Making students familiar with these is the purpose of the lists at the bottom of this chart and in the subsequent chart (11-4).

It is strongly suggested that you wait until Chart 11-5 to discuss the possible count usages of any of the words in this chart (for example, **works** of art, **literatures** of France and England, green **peppers**, the **sands** of time). Chart 11-5 deals briefly with that type of usage in a way appropriate to the students' level.

- Ask students to describe furniture. Encourage them to tell you any nouns they know. Write their examples on the board. For example:

  couch
  bed
  table
  chair
  dresser
  desk

- Now ask students to tell you what each of the above examples has in common with one another. Write their suggestions on the board. For example:

  They are big things in your house that you use every day.
  They are not small objects like plates or glasses.
  You can sit at or on many of them.
  You can put smaller items in or on them.

- Explain that because all of the above nouns have the same characteristics, as described by the students, they belong to the same category, furniture.
- Tell students that many such categories in English are noncount nouns.
- Explain that the category can be viewed as a whole, and the individual examples or things in this category are its parts.
- Ask a student or students to read the individual parts and wholes presented in examples (a), (b), and (c) in the chart aloud.
- Ask another student to read the notes to the right aloud.
- Encourage students to become familiar with the groups in the list in the chart. In order to help students begin to do so, ask them to give you a couple of examples of each group (spontaneously, just calling out nouns that fit each category).

❏ **EXERCISE 7.** Looking at grammar.
Page 293
Time: 10 minutes

The purpose of this exercise is to clarify the use of indefinite articles, final -s/-es, and expressions of quantity used with two different kinds of nouns.

Remind students that their experience of English to date can help them greatly here. Trying to use noncount nouns with actual numbers will often sound strange to students though they may not be able to articulate why.

Explain that a/an or some will be looked at more closely later, but that they are indefinite articles that can be thought of as any one (a/an) or any amount (some).

❏ **EXERCISE 8.** Grammar and speaking.
Page 294
Time: 10 minutes

The troublesome -s/-es is revisited here. You might want to use this practice in class discussion to review pronunciation of final -s/-es. (See Chapter 6, Chart 6-1, for information about pronunciation.) Omission of final -s/-es in speech and writing, even when the students understand the grammar thoroughly, may often be due to the fact that the learners don't hear it clearly. Extra work on production of -s/-es can help reinforce habits of correct usage.

You can lead this exercise by asking students to read each sentence aloud, on sight, and decide whether a final -s/-es is appropriate. Because students will often be able to "hear" what is correct, encourage their ability to do so in deciding whether final -s/-es can be added.

Optional Vocabulary

similar	memorize
reliable	karaoke

CHART 11-4. More Noncount Nouns.
Page 295
Time: 10 minutes

This chart provides information for the students to use if and as they can; this information will have varying degrees of usefulness. The students do not need to memorize those noncount nouns, but the information can be quite useful for learners who already know and use many of these words. Students to whom much of the vocabulary is new may not benefit a great deal immediately in terms of appropriate use of noncount nouns in their own speech and writing. For them, it can serve principally as a reference when they attempt these exercises and the Workbook practices.

• Ask students to define liquids, solids, and gases, and write their ideas on the board. For example:

   Liquids, solids, and gases are different states of matter.
   Liquids are anything watery.
   You can pour and often drink liquids.
   Solids are dry things that you can touch.
   Solids are matter or material that is real and concrete.
   Gases are in the air.
   You can wave your hand through gases without getting messy.

• Ask students if there are any nouns in section (a) of the chart that they do not know.
• Discuss section (b) of the chart by asking students to describe the weather events listed there.
• Ask students about the distinction between the material world (things you can touch) and the world of abstractions (things you can't touch, but that you feel or experience) as they begin to look at section (c) of the chart.
• Ask students if they make this same distinction in their native language.
• Discuss any vocabulary items from section (c) that students are not already familiar with.

❏ **EXERCISE 12.** Let's talk. Page 296
Time: 10–15 minutes

This exercise presents a few common sayings in English that the students might find interesting. These sayings illustrate the use of abstractions as noncount nouns. There is no reason to expect the students to know these sayings already, but they may have encountered loose translations in their own languages. Use this exercise as an opportunity to foster a lively discussion of cross-cultural differences in regard to these sayings. Encourage students to talk about their interpretations and reactions to them as they try to define them for their classmates.

• Ask students what a "common saying" is and write the following expression on the board:

   When the cat is away, the mice will play.

• Ask students what they think this expression means and if they have any similar expressions in their language.
• Explain to students that they will be looking at common sayings in English and describing / defining their meanings.
• Ask students to remind the class what "abstract" means and put notes on the board. For example:

   Not concrete
   An idea
   A concept

• Put students into small groups and ask them to analyze two sayings to explain as fully as they can.

- Circulate, helping students activate needed vocabulary in their definitions.
- Review as a class by having groups provide explanations of the phrases.

Expansion: Write student-generated explanations of the common sayings from Exercise 12 on the board. Ask students to vote on the clearest and most descriptive definition. After doing so, ask students to think of real situations where these phrases would readily apply. Ask students whether they have an expression to say the same idea in their language and discuss these and the differences between these foreign expressions and their American English counterparts.

❏ EXERCISE 13. Let's talk. Page 296
Time: 10–15 minutes

> The purpose here is for students to reach for nouns that are abstractions. Most of the noncount nouns students will attempt to use can also be found in Chart 11-4. Suggest that students consult this chart and use you as a walking dictionary if they can't locate the abstract noun they need to complete the items meaningfully.

- Give students time to complete each item. Walk around the room offering help and suggestions of vocabulary as they do.
- Put students into pairs and have them compare completed items. Encourage lively discussion of their respective answers.
- Discuss the completed items as a class, comparing opinions and correcting all target material.
- Help students frame examples of personal priorities with regard to personal qualities and characteristics.

❏ EXERCISE 14. Game. Page 296
Time: 10 minutes

- Divide the class into teams.
- Distribute blank paper to each of the teams.
- Instruct students to list everything they would normally see in this imagined setting and to write it on their list using the correct quantifiers.
- Encourage students to draw pictures as needed in order to better imagine the setting and include more nouns.

Expansion: If you need more settings than are included in the game instructions, choose among the following. You may also choose to give one setting to each student, who then lists everything he / she can "see" on an index card. Then, by exchanging index cards, other students must guess the original place simply by reading the nouns that would be visible in this place.

a doctor's office
a hospital
a train station
a gym
a swimming pool
a ski lodge
a kindergarten classroom
a public library
a sports stadium
a farm
a mechanic's workshop
a beauty salon
a movie theater
an ocean liner/a cruise ship
a factory

❏ EXERCISE 15. Warm-up. Page 297
Time: 5 minutes

- Remind students that the final *-s* on *apples* indicates a plural count noun.
- Ask students to complete the Warm-up and then read each completed item aloud, taking turns.
- Ask students to identify amount words and determine which ones go with plural count nouns.

CHART 11-5. Using *Several, A Lot Of, Many / Much,* and *A Few / A Little.* Page 297
Time: 10–15 minutes

> To introduce this concept, you may want to use the classroom as your context and ask the students how many desks is *several desks* and how many desks is *a lot of desks*?
>
> You might mention that *a lot of* occurs principally in informal English. You might also mention that *lots of* is the even more informal equivalent of *a lot of*.
>
> Students may want an absolute numerical definition of *a few* and / or *several*. Most people conceive of *a few* as three to four and *several* as more than three and significantly less than *many,* but you should stress that there is no absolute number to equate to these terms.
>
> Explore students' preconceptions of *several* and *a few* by asking one student to make a pile of *several* books on his / her desk while asking another to make a pile of *a few* books.

- Ask students to take turns reading the examples (a)–(d) aloud. Discuss the notes included at the right.
- After you have gone through the chart, ask students to close their books.
- Write the following headings on the board:

    Count / Noncount   *Noncount Only*   *Count Only*

- Read the quantity phrases from the chart aloud and have students write these phrases beneath the appropriate heading.

Expansion: Write the following nouns (or student-generated nouns) on the board:

friends

problems

money

interests

boyfriends / girlfriends

parties

memories

peace

time

courage

Write the following statement on the board and read it to your students:

It is better to have	*a few / a little* _____.
	several
	a lot of
	many / much

For example: friends

Ask students to make complete sentences using the expression of quantity above that they choose. Example sentence (generated by students):

It is better to have <u>a lot of</u> friends.

You can then ask the rest of the students if they agree, and hopefully some will oppose the statement with something along the lines of:

It is better to have <u>a few good</u> friends.

Continue having students make sentences using the nouns above or other nouns and discuss both the grammar and the relative truth of the statements they create. Put sentences on the board and facilitate opposing points of view whenever possible, to foster a lively discussion.

❏ EXERCISE 16. Looking at grammar.
Page 297
Time: 5–10 minutes

> The sentence with the spelling error is item 10. Spelling "a lot" as one word is a common error. You may want to remind students to look at the endings of nouns to make sure that count nouns agree with count phrases of quantity, and noncount with noncount.

❏ EXERCISE 18. Let's talk: interview.
Page 298
Time: 10 minutes

- Instruct students to get up and move around the room so that they can discuss the questions with many different classmates.
- Remind students to look for *-s* to ensure they are using *How many_____?* with count nouns.
- Review the questions as a class by having individual students read the questions aloud and others report on the habits of their classmates.

- Put students' answers in sentence form on the board, and encourage further discussion of any topics that could arise by asking follow-up questions.

❏ EXERCISE 19. Looking at grammar.
Page 299
Time: 10 minutes

> This text does not deal with the differences between *a few* vs. *few*, *a little* vs. *little*. See Chapter 7 in *Understanding and Using English Grammar* for this distinction.

- Lead students through this exercise on sight, calling on different students out of order.
- Correct both the answers and the pronunciation of non-target words.
- Put any challenging items on the board and illustrate / circle which part of the noun indicates count or noncount and link this to the correct expression of quantity.

CHART 11-6. Nouns That Can Be Count or Noncount. Page 300
Time: 10–15 minutes

> The nouns presented here are just a few of those that have dual count-noncount usages. The intention here is simply to introduce the students to the idea that such a possibility exists in English. Again, the purpose in this text is to get across the <u>concept</u> of a noncount noun, for it is this concept that will serve the students well as they gain experience with English and expand their usage ability. The ultimate goal is for learners to use nouns as count or noncount as naturally as a native speaker does. In the meantime, it helps students to pay a little special attention to this phenomenon in English. In this chart, discuss how the noncount usages deal with "wholes" and the count usages deal with individual items.

- Explain to students that though the distinction between count and noncount is clear, there are many nouns that can have both usages. Stress that when the same noun seems to have both a noncount and a count usage, the meaning of the word is, in fact, very different.
- Stress that the noncount usage always sees the noun as a material, a whole, a substance that may have parts, elements, or pieces.
- Emphasize that the count version distinguishes the actual pieces, parts, or elements themselves.
- Write notes to this effect on the board. For example:

Noncount Version: whole, substance, material

Count Version: elements, pieces, particles

- Ask students to take turns reading aloud the nouns on the left-hand side of the chart and then the sample sentences illustrating both noncount and count uses.
- Answer any questions students may have, be prepared to show *hair* vs. *a hair*, and illustrate the nouns as best as you can.

Optional Vocabulary

meal	raised
stuffed	belong

Expansion: Explain to students that it is common to have one word for the animal itself and a different word for the meat taken from that animal. Write the following examples on the board:

Animal	_Meat from Animal_
pig	pork
cow	beef
sheep	mutton
deer	venison

In every case (even _sheep_ and _deer_, which are irregular count nouns), the animal itself is countable but the meat is a noncount substance. Ask your students questions about this distinction and the effect it has on our relationship with animals whose meat we eat.

Questions:

Why do animals and the meat from them have different names?

What effect does this distinction have on society's perception of the animal world?

In your native language, is there a similar distinction?

Do you think there would be fewer meat eaters in the world if the meat eaten shared the exact name of the animal it came from?

You can tell your students that the real reason that these terms differ has to do with the class system and England's relationship with France during the Middle Ages. The peasants working in the fields spoke Old English but the lords in their castles and their chefs spoke French. So, in the field, an animal had an English name, but once it got to the kitchen and became food, the French name was used. Over time, the expertise of the French-speaking chefs was passed on to regular people and the words for the ingredients (including the terms used for meat dishes) came with this knowledge. The words changed somewhat, but if you know French, you can still see their relationship to their original counterparts in French.

CHART 11-7. Using Units of Measure
with Noncount Nouns. Page 302
Time: 10 minutes

These units of measure are also called "partitives," but most students will not have occasion to see this term.

Some other units of measure not introduced in the text are _carton, dozen, head_ (of lettuce or cabbage), _pack, package, roll_ (of film or paper towels), _tablespoon,_ and _tub_ (or butter or margarine). Additional non-metric terms not in the text are _ounce, pint, inch, foot,_ and _yard._

The United States is one of the only leading industrial countries that does not use the metric system. Non-metric terms continue to have little meaning to most students and little use unless the students are living in the United States and have to do their own food or gas shopping.

Non-metric terms originated in England in the 1200s and are called "English" or "British" units. The metric system was created by French scientists late in the 18th century. At that time, each country had its own system of measurements that had developed from local traditions. By late in the 19th century, most major countries had recognized the need for an international system of measurements and had adopted the metric system. The United States government is still wrestling with the problem of if and how to convert to metric measurement, like the rest of the world.

The spellings "metre" and "litre" are chiefly British. The spellings "meter" and "liter" are used in American English.

- Explain to students that when referring to a noncount noun in general, the indefinite quantity _some_ or even no quantity is used.
- Write the following sentences on the board. For example:

    I like tea.
    I would like some tea.

- Ask students what form of matter tea is: solid, liquid, or gas.
- Ask students what would happen if they just held or took the liquid tea in their hand. Get them to envision and articulate that it would spill everywhere, go through their fingers, etc., and they wouldn't be able to drink it.
- Ask them if they have ever ordered tea and what container it comes in, eliciting _cup._
- Ask what other containers tea may be in: pot, bottle (for iced tea), etc.
- Explain that specific quantities of a noncount noun are often named by the amount and / or the container filled by the liquid and / or the shape of the substance.
- Write the following examples on the board:

    cup of tea
    bottle / pint / glass of beer, water, wine, other liquids
    can / bottle of soda
    piece / slice of bread, pizza, toast
    tube of toothpaste
    bar of soap
    sheet / piece of paper

- Ask a student (or students taking turns) to read example sentences (a)–(d).
- Discuss the notes as a class.

❏ **EXERCISE 24.** Looking at grammar.
Page 303
Time: 10–15 minutes

There may easily be more than one possible completion. Often only one is idiomatically apt or culturally appropriate and the expression a native speaker would use. Highlight this by asking students how these noun uses compare to similar nouns in their country. For example, it is grammatically correct to say *a bag of olives*, but *can* and *jar* are the words idiomatically and culturally appropriate in the U.S. for quantifying olives.

Remember that though these quantity nouns and their correct uses may seem insignificant to a native speaker, this vocabulary and its usage is interesting to students as it allows them to function much more independently when negotiating shopping and other daily transactions.

Expansion: For fun, weave questions into the exercise review. You can ask students which of these containers / quantities students have in their homes right now. You can also ask how long it takes them to consume an item in its purchasable quantity or simply ask questions that allow them to compare the norms in their country with those here.

Sample questions:

In the United States, grocery stores are very big and often far from people's homes. It is common for people to buy items in large quantities.

How many boxes of cereal (crackers, etc. / bottles of juice or soda) do you buy and / or consume in a month?

Is it common to purchase cans of soup in your country, or do people usually make their own?

It has become more popular for people in the U.S. to carry and drink from bottles of water, and some people worry this is causing a lot of pollution. Is this a problem in your country too?

Is it polite to keep a jar of jam or jelly on the table during a meal in your country?

Some people prefer to drink soda from a bottle, and some people prefer to do so from a glass. What is common in your country? Is it considered rude to drink from a bottle?

Do you keep baking ingredients in your home? Do you have a bag of flour or sugar in your cupboard?

❏ **EXERCISE 26.** Warm-up. Page 305
Time: 5–10 minutes

The key point students need to understand from this exercise is that article usage often depends upon what the speaker assumes the listener is familiar with and is thinking about. If they have shared knowledge and are thinking about the very same object or person (or, in the case of this Warm-up, dogs), the speakers use *the*.

CHART 11-8. Guidelines for Article Usage.
Page 306
Time: 15–25 minutes

This chart presents the basics of article usage. It by no means covers the myriad uses of articles in English. Almost all students find article usage somewhat difficult to learn, and many teachers and textbook authors find articles difficult to teach. There are many idiomatic uses, complex patterns, intricate variations, and subtleties. Proficient use of articles can only come with experience over time, but this chart does provide a clear basis for reference. Reassure your students that they will master article usage and remind them that articles are just one small part of English. Encourage students not to get frustrated.

Most students need help with this chart because it contains too much information to be grasped independently.

For more information about articles, see Chapter 7 in *Understanding and Using English Grammar*.

- Write the heading *Article Usage* on the board.
- After you have written this, and while still holding the chalk or marker you wrote the heading with, ask a student to come to the front of the class and take *the* marker. For example, say and write:

  Juan, could you please come to the front and take the marker back to your desk?

- The student invited to do so should come to the front of the class and take *the* marker you have been writing with from your hand and return to his / her seat.
- If the student attempts to take a different marker, remind him / her to take *the* marker, redirecting him / her to the one in your hand.
- Now directing the students to look at all the pieces of chalk or markers near the board, ask another student to come to the front of the class and take *a* marker. For example, say and write:

  Amy, could you please come to the front and take a marker back to your desk?

- The student should come to the board and take any marker or piece of chalk.
- Ask students to again articulate the difference between *a* and *the*.
- Explain to students that the *a* is an *indefinite article* and the *the* is a *definite article*.
- Write the following notes on the board and emphasize that the most important point to remember is:

  indefinite articles = any item, not a specific one that is commonly referenced

  vs.

  definite articles = one known noun or set of nouns, a common reference

- Turn to the chart itself and ask students to take turns reading the example sentences, section by section, and reviewing notes.

- If students become fatigued of the topic, focus just on the difference between indefinite and definite articles for the time being and focus on the remainder of the chart at another time.

❏ EXERCISE 28. Looking at grammar.
Page 310
Time: 10–15 minutes

> Again, the key point here is what the speaker assumes the listener is familiar with and thinking about. Reiterate the same point: *the* requires that the noun in question is known and familiar and not simply *any* of many.

❏ EXERCISE 31. Reading. Page 312
Time: 10–20 minutes

- Ask students to read the passage twice before covering it to answer the comprehension questions.
- After students have completed these questions, review the comprehension questions and ask students to locate their responses in the original text.

❏ EXERCISE 32. Looking at grammar.
Page 312
Time: 10 minutes

- Lead students through this exercise on sight.
- After students have completed each item, ask each student to state key words that illustrate that either *the* or *no article* is needed.

Optional Vocabulary
dairy product   reduce
humid   yard

❏ EXERCISE 34. Listening. Page 313
Time: 10 minutes

- Ask students if they have ever had a headache after eating ice cream or other very cold substances.
- Play the audio.
- Give students time to complete the passage after they have listened a second time.
- Review by having students read their completed items aloud. Correct and discuss content.

Optional Vocabulary
suddenly
occur
roof of mouth
nerves
blood vessels
swell up

❏ EXERCISE 36. Warm-up. Page 315
Time: 5 minutes

- Ask students what they notice about the names that are preceded by *the*.
- Students should notice that when *the* precedes a name, a geographical feature also follows that name. (For example: *the Amazon **River**, the Mississippi **River**, the Ural **Mountains**, the Indian **Ocean**,* and *the Red **Sea**.*)
- Students should notice that when no *the* is used, there is only a unique name and not a common geographical word following the name. (For example: *Mount Fuji,* and *Australia. Mexico City* is unusual as "city" is part of its actual name.)

CHART 11-9. Using *The* or Ø with Names.
Page 315
Time: 10–15 minutes

> Using a world map, point to places and ask the students to identify them:
> *That is **the** Nile. That is Ø Brazil. That is Ø Beijing. Those are **the** Alps. Etc.*
>
> American English uses a period (.) at the end of abbreviated titles:
> *Mr. Wang, Mrs. Doe, Ms. Jackson, Dr. Singh*
>
> British English does not use a period (.):
> *Mr Wang, Mrs Doe, Ms Jackson, Dr Singh*

- With students' involvement, read through the example sentences aloud and discuss the notes on the right-hand side of the chart.
- To simplify the notes given in the chart, explain to students that *the* is included before a name that also precedes a geographical feature, such as mountains and rivers, seas, oceans, and with mountain ranges (though the word *mountain* may not follow.)
- Write the following on the board:

  The Amazon River
  The Mississippi River
  The Himalayan Mountains
  The Rocky Mountains (The Rockies)
  The Indian Ocean

- Again, if students find the chart contains too much information to readily absorb, have them focus on the relatively few cases in which *the* is included.

CHART 11-10. Capitalization. Page 317
Time: 10 minutes

> One of the principal ideas for the students to understand from this chart is that nouns are capitalized when they are part of a name or title, or what is called a "proper noun." The text doesn't use the term "proper noun," and you can decide whether it will help or hinder your class's understanding.

Correct capitalization can be a problem in student writing, as can correct pronunciation. Some language groups, such as Spanish and German speakers, have very different rules for capitalizing words. For example, words related to nationality are not capitalized in Spanish but are in English. In German, nouns are capitalized. Some students think that capitalization is not important, and they don't realize that it is important in achieving grammatical accuracy in English. It may be necessary to emphasize that proper capitalization is a value in English rhetoric because it signals the user / writer's competent, educated use of the language.

This is a reference chart. You might want to proceed directly to the exercises, and then refer to the chart as questions arise.

❏ EXERCISE 41. Grammar, reading, and writing. Page 319
Time: 20–30 minutes

This exercise includes review of the entire chapter. Give students time to edit the reading first and then review this as a class, before examining content. You may want to put students in pairs.

Part I
- Give students ample time to read and add capital letters as necessary.
- Ask students to take turns reading the passage aloud.

Part II
- Ask students to read each true / false item aloud. Discuss the answers.
- Students should be able to refer back to the passage to cite where their answer originated.

Part III
- Present the writing assignment in class and ask students to think about an organization they could write about.
- Discuss the use of articles in "Roots and Shoots."
- Give students time to begin their own work in class.
- During this time, go around to students and give them support and ideas, and help them narrow the topic so that they can continue the writing exercise at home, as homework.

Optional Vocabulary
fascinated
fictional
lifelong
arranged
guidance
trust
observations
formed
observing
service projects
community project
marketplace

Chapter 12
Adjective Clauses

CHAPTER SUMMARY

OBJECTIVE: This chapter focuses on helping students understand the function of adjective clauses, comprehend them when encountered, and produce them naturally. By learning to use adjective clauses, students will greatly expand their ability to communicate and comprehend complex descriptions, definitions, contrasts, etc.

APPROACH: To keep the focus on main patterns, the text presents only restrictive (identifying) adjective clauses. These include fundamental structures with subject and object relative pronouns, omission of the object pronoun from an adjective clause, the placement of prepositions within a clause, and the use of *whose*. The text is designed so that the students first gain control of the basic patterns; they can wrestle with the punctuation of nonrestrictive and restrictive clauses at a later stage of their study of English in *Understanding and Using English Grammar*. The most important task is to foster recognition that by comprehending and using adjective clauses, students can describe their world very effectively.

TERMINOLOGY: Minimal terminology to describe dependent (subordinate) clauses is introduced in the extensive footnote to Chart 12-1. Some books use the term "relative clause" instead of "adjective clause," and "relative pronoun" instead of "adjective clause pronoun." Some students may find the terminology helpful; others will understand and gain control of the structures in this chapter without paying much attention to the terminology of grammar descriptions.

The extent to which you emphasize terminology in your teaching is your decision and, in large part, depends on the predominant learning styles of your students. Academically oriented students often like and need descriptive labels for grammar structures. Students interested in conversational English often concentrate more on understanding the examples than on trying to grasp the grammar explanations. There is no "right" way to incorporate terminology in the teaching of grammar. The intention of the text is to offer just enough so that teacher and students can communicate about the structures.

CHART 12-1. Adjective Clauses: Introduction. Page 321
Time: 10–15 minutes

There are three principal kinds of dependent clauses in English: (1) an adverb clause, (2) an adjective clause, and (3) a noun clause. The text presents the fundamentals of all three kinds.

The concept of a dependent clause (for example, a "time clause" or an *"if*-clause") is presented first in Chapters 2 and 3 in conjunction with the study of verb tenses. The terminology "adverb clause" is first used in Chapter 8 with the use of *because* and *even though*. This chapter presents adjective clauses. The third type of dependent clause, the noun clause, is introduced in Chapter 14.

The approach in this chart is to connect the function of adjectives to the function of adjective clauses. One problem in examples (a)–(d) in this chart is that some students may think an adjective clause needs to have an adjective in it. That is not true. Point out to students that example (e) contains no adjective; the information in the clause itself serves to describe the noun; for example, the function of the clause is the same as the function of an adjective, and that's why these clauses are called adjective clauses. The real point here is that adjectives in a noun phrase precede the noun, whereas adjective clauses <u>follow</u> the noun.

The approach of the text is to connect the use of personal pronouns and relative pronouns. In a simple sentence or main clause, *he, she it, they, him, her, them, his,* and *their* are used. Their counterparts in an adjective clause are *who, whom, that, which,* and *whose.* The object of this chapter is to show how these relative pronouns are used.

- Discuss with students how they describe nouns and what kinds of words they use to do so.
- From the above discussion, pick a few *adjective + noun* phrases and write some of these on the board. For example:

  a mysterious letter
  boring books
  lively music

- To expand on these ideas, ask students questions such as:

  What kind of a letter is a mysterious letter?

  Which books are boring to you?

  What kind of music is lively music?

- Students will naturally give you approximations of actual adjective clauses.

- Write their descriptions on the board. For example:

  A <u>mysterious</u> letter:

  > <u>I want to read</u> it
  > It is not boring
  > With a secret in it

- With help from the class, create a new sentence on the board, drawing from the ideas about the phrase and containing an adjective clause.

- Tell students that adjective clauses provide ways for people to identify nouns with clauses. Explain that this is very useful because often the way we want to describe something does not have its own adjective. For example:

  A <u>mysterious letter</u> is something <u>that I want to read</u>.

- Explain that by using the clause *that I want to read*, students can identify nouns on exactly their own terms.

- Ask students to read the example sentences (a) and (b) aloud. Discuss each one in contrast with (c)–(e).

- Read through the grammar notes with students and answer any questions students may have.

- Rather than having students simply read the notes on clauses, ask them to define these terms and to put the definitions on the board.

❏ **EXERCISE 3.** Warm-up. Page 322
Time: 5–10 minutes

Expansion: Ask students what other specialist names they know and define them in the same way as in the Warm-up.

Other specialist titles include:

a podiatrist

an endocrinologist (a doctor that treats hormonal disorders)

a gerontologist (a doctor that treats elderly people)

a psychiatrist (a doctor that treats mental illness)

an obstetrician (a doctor that treats pregnant women)

an ophthalmologist (a doctor that treats eye disorders)

an oncologist (a doctor that treats cancer)

a neurologist (a doctor that treats diseases of the nervous system)

You can further expand this by asking students to distinguish the names of specializations and see if they can distinguish two types of specialty names. Students should be able to identify that some specialties are named for the person that the doctor treats (children, elderly people, pregnant women) and some specialists are named for the disease that they treat.

CHART 12-2. Using *Who* and *That* in Adjective Clauses to Describe People.
Page 322
Time: 10 minutes

The text presents a little information at a time about the patterns of adjective clauses. This chart presents the subject pronoun *who*. Importantly, the chart also illustrates that the *who* in an adjective clause describing a person can also be replaced with the general subject pronoun *that*.

Review the terms "subject" and "object" with your students and ask them to define "subject," while introducing the topic.

> INCORRECT: *The man who **he** lives next to me is friendly.*

> INCORRECT: *The woman that **she** works in our pediatrician's office is helpful.*

Typical mistakes are including (or repeating) the personal pronoun in addition to the personal pronoun. Learners need to understand that *who* and *that* are used <u>instead of</u> personal pronouns but never <u>in addition to</u> personal pronouns.

This text does not present nonrestrictive adjective clauses. All the adjectives presented here define and identify the nouns they modify. For a discussion of nonrestrictive adjective clauses, please see *Understanding and Using English Grammar,* Chapter 13.

At this stage in language study, learners generally still do not use adjective clauses idiomatically. Because they are not completely comfortable using them, students may avoid these altogether. Assure students that their idiomatic usage ability will grow as they gain more experience with the language. Conversely, they will not be able to grow their language and develop confident usage ability without using these challenging target structures. Remind students that mastering adjective clauses allows them limitless new opportunities for description of nouns and thereby, overall expression. They can simply say so much more when they are not limited to a list of adjectives already in existence. As the English saying goes, from a small acorn, the great oak grows. It is counterproductive for the grammar teacher or text to present the whole oak tree right at the beginning.

- Emphasize to students that adjective clauses allow English users to describe any person, place, or thing much more specifically and accurately.

- Tell students adjective clauses free them to describe people in many more ways.

- Ask for a student volunteer. Explain that the class is going to describe this student nicely. (You can encourage the students by saying that demonstration gives students a chance to know what their classmates think of them. If no one offers, use yourself in this role.)

- Write the following simple sentences on the board (if you are using yourself as the subject). If not, create a new simple sentence to introduce the student others will describe.

  <u>The woman is patient</u>. She teaches our grammar class.

- Now show students how to combine these sentences into one sentence. Show every step you take in doing so by crossing out, moving, and adding words. Explain each step you take:

  The woman is patient. ⇒ *She teaches our grammar class.*

  The woman who teaches our grammar class is patient.

- Now ask students to offer other sentences as alternatives to the first sentence in the original pair of sentences. For example:

  The woman is strange but funny.
  The woman loves grammar.
  The woman bikes to work.
  The woman eats ice cream frequently.

- Ask students to make new combinations from the clauses above and write these on the board. For example:

  The woman who teaches our grammar class is strange but funny.
  The woman who teaches our grammar class loves grammar.
  The woman who teaches our grammar class bikes to work.
  The woman who teaches our grammar class eats ice cream frequently.

- Explain that *that* is also a subject pronoun and can replace *who* in the above sentences.
- Ask a student or students to replace the *who* with *that* and read the resulting sentences aloud.
- Ask a student to read through example sentences (a) and (b). Review the chart notes on the right.
- Ask a different student to read example sentences (c) and (d) aloud. Answer any questions that remain.

❑ **EXERCISE 5.** Looking at grammar.
Page 323
Time: 5–10 minutes

- Allow students a few minutes to complete each item.
- Ask a few students to write the sentences on the board, underline the adjective clause, and draw an arrow to the noun modified.
- Leave the sentences on the board and correct any mistakes that students may have made.

❑ **EXERCISE 8.** Let's talk. Page 324
Time: 10–15 minutes

- Put students into pairs or small groups.
- Ask students to see how many sentences they can readily make from each item given.
- Walk around the room, encouraging students to try out new vocabulary, and correct and support them as they do so.
- Take notes on errors that you hear. The errors can range from target structures to any other words or phrases, or simple pronunciation mistakes.
- If one group or pair finishes earlier than others, have them use *that* in each item and create new sentences just by changing the noun being modified.

- Call students' attention to the board as you bring the exercise to a close and write some of the errors on the board, as you heard them made.
- Have students offer corrections for the mistakes written on the board and review them.

❑ **EXERCISE 9.** Warm-up. Page 324
Time: 5 minutes

- You can introduce this exercise by discussing teachers and what makes a good teacher.
- Create a sentence regarding a teacher you had when you were in school, and then ask students to complete each item.
- Review and discuss their completed items along with the qualities they describe.

CHART 12-3. Using Object Pronouns in Adjective Clauses to Describe People.
Page 324
Time: 10–15 minutes

Help students focus on the fact that adjective clauses can be used to describe both subject and object pronouns. Reiterate that students can use the adjective clause pronoun *that*.

A few notes on the use of *whom*: It is used infrequently in adjective clauses (and questions and noun clauses as well). It is presented here as a device to help students distinguish between subject and object relative pronouns in adjective clause patterns. However, though *whom* is used for object pronouns in adjective clauses, *that* is much more commonly used.

In actual usage:

who is preferred to *that* as a <u>subject</u> pronoun

that is preferred to *who* and *whom* as an <u>object</u> pronoun

in everyday use, omission of the object pronoun is usually preferred to either *that* or *whom*.

The text does not give the students this information. Rather it aims to help students gain control of a few basic patterns.

Explain to students that the only time you can omit a pronoun with an adjective clause is when you are modifying the object; this is not possible with a subject.

- Present this chart with the same approach you used in Chart 12-2. Have students make up sentences describing a classmate with a view to combining these step-by-step with an adjective clause. For example:

  The student is from Colombia. I met her in this class.
  The student is from Colombia. ⇒ *I met ~~her~~ in this class.*
  that
  The student that I met in this class is from Colombia.

- Ask students to take turns reading the example sentences (a)–(c). Review the notes to the right of those.

- Ask other students to take turns reading the example sentences (d)–(f) aloud. Review the second set of notes.

❏ EXERCISE 15. Warm-up. Page 326
Time: 5–10 minutes

> You can begin this Warm-up by discussing pets in general.
>
> Possible discussion questions:
>
> *How common are pets in your country?*
>
> *What pets are popular?*
>
> *What reasons do people have pets?*
>
> *What is your impression of U.S. pet ownership and / or the role of pets within a U.S. family?*

CHART 12-4. Using Pronouns in Adjective Clauses to Describe Things. Page 327
Time: 10–15 minutes

> *Which* is also used in questions to ask for a choice between known items (for example: *Which book is yours?*) Students are learning a different use of *which* in this chart.
>
> A fairly common error is the use of *what* in place of *which*:
>
> INCORRECT: *The book **what** I read was very interesting.*
>
> *What* is never used as an adjective clause pronoun.

- Because students have now been walked through two presentations of adjective clauses step-by-step, you can invite students to help lead the presentation as much as possible.
- Start by putting two sample sentences on the board and asking a student to come to the board and combine them using *that*. For example:

  English is a language. Many people study it.

- Instruct students at their seats to remind the student combining the sentences at the board of all the steps that must be taken. These include:

  removing the first period

  removing / crossing out the final pronoun <u>it</u>

  adding <u>that</u> between the two clauses

- Review the new combined sentence:

  English is a language that many people study.

- Invite students to create new combinations based on alternatives to *Many people study it.*
- Write these on the board. For example:

  <u>English is a language</u> + *It is easy to learn.*
  It is not very melodic.
  It has simple grammar.
  It is used in international business.

- Ask students to make new combinations.

  English is a language that is not very melodic.

  English is a language that is easy to learn.

  English is a language that has simple grammar.

  English is a language that is used in international business.

- Ask students to read the example sentences (a)–(c) aloud. Review the notes.
- Turn to example sentences (d)–(g) and discuss the use of object pronouns.
- Review the explanations on the right-hand side of the chart.
- Explain to students that the only time you can omit a pronoun with an adjective clause is when you are modifying the object; this is not possible with a subject.

❏ EXERCISE 16. Looking at grammar. Page 327
Time: 5–10 minutes

- Give students time to complete this item as seatwork.
- Review the completed exercise.
- Have students either put the sentences on the board to underline each adjective clause and show which noun is modified, or simply explain aloud.

❏ EXERCISE 17. Looking at grammar. Page 328
Time: 5 minutes

> Two or three students can respond to each item, each student giving a different form of the answer. Or, the sentences can be written on the board by various students.

❏ EXERCISE 22. Game. Page 330
Time: 10–20 minutes

Expansion: Prepare index cards with lists of random items, places, and people. Distribute these, one to each student. Have students sit in pairs. Instruct students that they need to use adjective clauses correctly and effectively in order to get their partner to say the names of the nouns listed on the index card. Partner A must describe the items on the card until Partner B says the item, person, or place described. Move around the room and assist students with the vocabulary. Make sure students can describe each item, person, or place using adjective clauses.

> *a toothbrush*
> *Tiger Woods*
> *a doctor's office*
> *a parakeet*

```
yellow stickies
fish sticks
a flashlight
Barack Obama
apple juice
a shoe horn
an electric guitar
a crossword puzzle
Tom Cruise
an ocean reef
a helicopter
```

```
robots
Paris, France
Jennifer Aniston
Skype
chocolate chip cookies
```

```
a DVD
Swiss cheese
makeup
a disco
laundry detergent
```

CHART 12-5. Singular and Plural Verbs in Adjective Clauses. Page 331
Time: 10 minutes

Relative pronouns in English have the same forms in singular as in plural, but they carry the same number as their antecedents; verbs must agree with that number.

Special attention is paid to subject-verb agreement in adjective clauses because it is a common source of errors. (Indeed, subject-verb agreement even in simple sentences remains a problem at this level and beyond.)

INCORRECT: *My brother knows several people who **is** from Lebanon.*

INCORRECT: *I know a woman who **live** in the Courtyard Apartments.*

• Explain to students that it is critical that they can identify the noun that the adjective clauses describe.
• Demonstrate the importance of identifying the noun that is referred to by creating a very long phrase before the noun and the relative pronoun.
• For example, write the following example (or one of your own creation) on the board.

   The student who now takes classes at two universities is friendly with Jin.

• Ask students to come to the board and label the subjects and verbs using capital letters for the subject

and verb of the main clauses and lowercase for the subject and verb of the adjective clause. For example:

S   s   v   V
The student who now takes classes at two universities is friendly with Jin.

• With your students' direction, draw arrows from the subjects to their respective verbs and from the adjective clause pronoun to the noun it refers to.
• Discuss the importance of subject-verb agreement with students and show students how to locate the relative pronoun and locate its antecedent, to ensure agreement.
• Ask students to take turns reading the example sentences (a) and (b) aloud. Discuss the accompanying notes.

❑ EXERCISE 25. Warm-up. Page 332
Time: 5 minutes

• Ask students to complete the items and then have them read and discuss the items aloud briefly, comparing responses.
• Then, have students underline the adjective clause in each sentence.
• Review their answers as a class.

CHART 12-6. Using Prepositions in Adjective Clauses. Page 332
Time: 10 minutes

Discuss the concept of formal vs. informal English. Formal English is found, for example, in academic journals, a school or business report, official correspondence, or nonfiction books. Informal English occurs in everyday conversation, a letter to a friend or family member, a relaxed classroom, an email, etc.

The pattern in example (d) is uncommon and very formal ("careful English"). A native speaker might use *who* instead of *whom* but would be more likely to use the patterns in (b) and (c). The pattern in (e) is only used in very formal English.

• Continuing from the Warm-up above, ask students to give you examples of verbs that are followed by prepositions, and write some of these on the board. For example:

   listen to
   look forward to
   talk about
   care about
   think about

• Ask students questions that use each of the above *verb + preposition* combinations. For example:

listen to	What kinds of music do you like to listen to?
look forward to	What kinds of events do you look forward to?
talk about	What kinds of topics do you enjoy talking about?

- Ask students to use adjective clauses when responding to the questions above.
- Help students to form answers using adjective clauses.
- Give explicit instructions about the placement of the prepositions and tell students that prepositions can come at the end of the adjective clause.
- Explain that omitting the relative pronoun (*that, whom, which*) is helpful in keeping sentences brief and clear. Students can omit the relative pronoun more readily as they gain mastery of this grammar.
- Have students write some of their responses to the earlier questions on the board:

   The music *I like to listen to* is slow and lyrical.

   The events *that I always look forward to* are usually big family gatherings.

   The topics *which I enjoy talking about* are sports and international news. The topics *I don't enjoy talking about* are Hollywood gossip and fashion news.

- Ask students to take turns reading the example sentences (a)–(e) aloud.
- Elaborate on the notes to the right and ask for any further questions.
- Have students read (f)–(j) aloud. Summarize the final notes and examples, using the board as needed.

❏ **EXERCISE 26.** Looking at grammar.
Page 332
Time: 5–10 minutes

> Students could write their combinations and then exchange papers, or they could write the completed combinations on the board.

❏ **EXERCISE 27.** Looking at grammar.
Page 333
Time: 10–15 minutes

> Students sometimes ask how they are supposed to know which preposition they need to use. This exercise consists of preposition combinations with verbs, as listed in Appendix Unit C. Preposition combinations can be memorized, but principally in most teachers' teaching experience, these combinations need to be practiced until they "sound right." Appendix Unit C contains preposition exercises, as does the Appendix section in the *Workbook*. The intention of the text is for the teacher to intersperse work on prepositions throughout the teaching term, using the material in the Appendix as it best fits in with his / her syllabus.

❏ **EXERCISE 29.** Reading and grammar.
Page 334
Time: 10–20 minutes

Part I
- Discuss the pre-reading questions with the class and write as many of students' thoughts and responses on the board.
- Ask students to take turns reading through the passage aloud.
- Correct pronunciation and clarify any adjective clauses.
- Ask students to tell you which nouns are antecedents for the adjective clauses identified.

Part II
- Ask students to complete the sentences by paraphrasing what was read in the passage.
- If needed, refer back to the passage and have students read key sentences aloud.

CHART 12-7. Using *Whose* in Adjective Clauses. Page 336
Time: 10 minutes

> The use of *whose* in adjective clauses is difficult for most learners. It occurs relatively infrequently. The text presents only a brief introduction and does not anticipate any degree of usage mastery by the learners.
>
> Pronounce *whose* and *who's* for the students, pointing out that they sound identical. One can discern the meaning (as a possessive or as a contraction of *who* and *is*) from the structure and context.
>
> Point out that *whose* always accompanies a noun in an adjective clause; it does not stand alone as a pronoun as do *who, which,* and *that. Whose* functions as a possessive adjective; grammatically it is equivalent to the personal possessive adjectives *their, his,* and *her.* (*Whose* can also be the equivalent to the possessive *its,* but the text does not introduce the use of *whose* to modify "things" as well as "people"; for example, *an organization **whose** membership exceeds a thousand people.* See *Understanding and Using English Grammar.*)

- Explain that *whose* shows possession or, in a more general sense, belonging.
- Write two observations in two sentences about a student, on the board. For example:

   There is a woman in our class.

   Her sense of humor amuses us.

- Explain to students that by using *whose,* the possessive adjective can be omitted and the second clause used to describe the first. For example:

   There is a woman in our class whose sense of humor amuses us.

- With your students, create another example for the board, by starting with two related sentences. For example:

  I like the young man.

  His face is kind.

  I like the young man whose face is kind.

- Ask students to take turns reading (a) and (b) aloud. Then review the notes on the right.
- Repeat these instructions with (c)–(f), respectively.

❏ EXERCISE 31. Looking at grammar.
Page 336
Time: 10 minutes

> In explaining the direction line, make sure students understand the rationale behind steps 1–4. The purpose is to make sure students don't miss a step and that they fully understand which noun *whose* refers to.

- Ask students to work through this exercise independently while you circulate, offering help and support.
- Invite students to write the correct combined sentences on the board for analysis and correction.
- Provide clear and immediate correction and give students multiple examples of the correct use of *whose.*

Optional Vocabulary
resigning
burglarized

❏ EXERCISE 32. Let's talk: pairwork.
Page 337
Time: 10–15 minutes

> First ask the students to find the possessive adjective for each item in the given sentences. For example, in item 1, the possessive adjective is *his.* Then have them change *his* to *whose.* Ask students to identify to whom *his* and *whose* refer. (Point out that *his* and *whose* have an identical meaning.) They refer to *the man.* *His = the man's* and *whose = the man's.* The man in sentence (a) lost his car to thieves. Tell students to keep *whose* with the noun that immediately follows (*car*), and move the phrase *whose car* immediately after the noun it modifies. That is how an adjective clause with *whose* is formed.
>
> Some students find these clauses confusing, especially in a case such as item 4, in which the word order changes from simple sentence to adjective clause, with the object (in this case *sister*) preceding the subject and verb.

❏ EXERCISE 33. Listening. Page 337
Time: 5 minutes

- Write *who's* (*who* + *is*) and *whose* on the board for students to refer to while listening.
- Remind students that *who's* already has a verb (*to be*) included in it.
- As you review the correct items, point to the corresponding word on the board.
- Review any particularly challenging items.

❏ EXERCISE 35. Looking at grammar.
Page 338
Time: 5–10 minutes

- Give students time to complete this review on their own, as seatwork.
- Then ask students to take turns reading their completed items aloud.
- Discuss all possible answers in the cases where more than one completion works.
- Put any particularly challenging items on the board for analysis.

Optional Vocabulary
audition
collapsed
heat exhaustion
budget
dented

❏ EXERCISE 38. Let's talk: interview.
Page 340
Time: 10–15 minutes

> This exercise can also work well when teacher-led. However, if you can get students to interview each other in-depth, they will have more opportunities to rephrase questions just as they would need to do in real conversations with native speakers.
>
> This exercise presents a typical pattern in which adjective clauses are used. It also draws attention to problems of number when *one of* and *some of* are part of the subject of a sentence.
>
> The pattern with *one of* seems to be a particular source of errors. It is a useful pattern, and it would work well to follow this interview with more oral exercises like the Expansion.

Expansion: Give students a noun and the pronoun, *I,* and write the topic and form on the board. Have the students complete this pattern in referring back to the topic.

One of the + plural noun + adjective clause + singular verb + rest of sentence.

For example:

Teacher: *Cities, I.*

Student: *One of the cities I like best is Bangkok.*

Teacher: *Books, I.*

Student: *One of the books I use in my English classes is (name of a book).*

Topics for this expansion and oral practice:

books	numbers
places	movies
people	cuisines
women	holidays
men	restaurants
problems	students
buildings	teachers
classes	animals
countries	

☐ **EXERCISE 41.** Reading and writing.
Page 341
Time: 10–20 minutes

Expansion: Ask students the following related discussion questions before moving on to the writing element.

Do you know many people who are vegans?

Have you ever considered becoming one?

What are some of the challenges to maintaining such a diet?

Is the cuisine of your country suited to being a vegan?

Would people find it particularly difficult to follow a vegan diet while living in your country? Why or why not?

Do you know many people who are vegetarians? What do you think of this type of diet?

Have you ever followed any kind of strict diet? Do you think there is any advantage to human beings to eating meat-based protein products?

What is something you eat every day or every other day?

What do you almost never eat?

Most people prefer the food of their home country to any other. Why is the cuisine of your home country so good? What complaints do people have about it?

Part II

- Give students time to start writing their paragraph in class.
- Walk around the room checking in with students, encouraging them, and providing additional assistance to help them feel motivated to write.
- Ask students to complete the paragraph at home and bring it to the next class for review and correction.

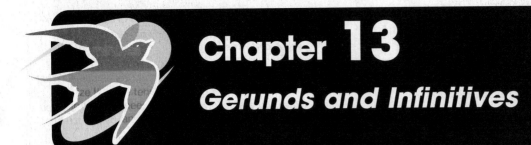

Chapter 13
Gerunds and Infinitives

CHAPTER SUMMARY

OBJECTIVE: To this point in the text, the learners have focused on the forms of the verbs used as the main verb of a sentence or clause. In this chapter, students will learn other forms and uses of verbs, specifically, gerunds and infinitives. The ability to use these verbals and their associated verbs is indispensable; they are exceedingly common and very useful for students in expressing their wants, needs, dislikes, hopes, plans, attitudes, and activities.

APPROACH: Gerunds and infinitives are often a source of errors for English language learners. Because which verbs take gerunds and which take infinitives is not a matter of logic, per se, students should be encouraged to increase their familiarity with the material. To that end, the text first presents a chart of *verb + gerund* combinations, in order to provide students a manageable starting point. The text goes on to present additional charts that reflect other common uses of gerunds, including those verbs that can be followed by both gerunds and infinitives. Infinitive combinations are also presented, along with special expressions such as infinitives used with *too* and *enough*.

TERMINOLOGY: A **gerund** is sometimes called a "verbal noun." Calling it merely "the *-ing* form of a verb" invites confusion with the present participle, which has different grammatical functions.

In this text, an **infinitive** is defined as **to** + *the simple form of a verb*. The text does not use the term "*to*-less infinitive" or "base infinitive" or "the infinitive form without *to*" to describe the verb form that follows, for example, modal auxiliaries (as in *must go*) or *let's* (as in *let's go*). Rather, the text simply calls those the "simple form" of a verb. For students' purposes, the simple form of the verb is defined as the form found in a dictionary listing (Chapter 2).

❑ EXERCISE 1. Warm-up. Page 342
Time: 5 minutes

- Ask students to both check those completions that they enjoy and to add other gerund activities that they also enjoy.
- Ask those students who say they don't enjoy certain activities to explain their preferences.

CHART 13-1. Verb + Gerund. Page 342
Time: 10–15 minutes

The *verb + gerund phrase* is a source of errors for many students. Although relatively few verbs are followed by gerunds, those phrases occur with some frequency in both spoken and written English. It is easy for learners to confuse *verb + gerund phrases* with *verb + infinitive phrases*. For example, *I want to watch TV. I enjoy watching TV.* Learners commonly mix these elements and make errors such as the following:

INCORRECT: *I enjoy to watch TV.*

The text presents a few common verbs and verb phrases followed by gerunds that students might find useful. As their vocabularies grow, students will encounter other verbs followed by gerunds, such as *risk, deny,* and *delay*. (See *Understanding and Using English Grammar,* Chapter 14, for a longer list of verbs followed by gerunds.) Here, however, the focus is on only a few phrases as a starting point.

You might want to note that not all *-ing* verbs are gerunds; some are present participles.

*I enjoy **working*** = gerund, used as a noun, in this case as the object of the verb.
(*I* = subject; *enjoy* = verb; *working* = object)

*I am **working*** = present participle
(*I* = subject; *am working* = verb)

Note on some of the verbs listed in this chapter:

- **Stop** can also be followed by an infinitive of purpose:

  *Jane was walking home. When she saw a coin on the sidewalk, she **stopped (in order) to pick** it **up**.*

- **Keep** and **keep on** have the same meaning when followed by a gerund.

- **Consider** is followed by a gerund when it means "think about," as in the example in the text; it is followed by a (pro)noun object + infinitive when it means "believe" (*We **consider** him to be our closest friend*).

- Write a couple of sentences using *enjoy* on the board. Follow the verb with simple nouns as objects. Label the subjects, verbs, and objects. For example:

  S   V   O

  Martha enjoys ice cream.

          S   V   O

Javier enjoys movies.

- Ask students to tell you additional activities that they enjoy or don't enjoy. Write a few of their preferences on the board.
- In order to involve students maximally, use students' names and specific likes. For example:

    Mieko doesn't enjoy spending money stupidly.
    Francisco enjoys watching American football on TV.
    Wang enjoys hearing techno music.

- Ask students to come to the board to label the subjects and verbs respectively. For example:

        S   V

    Mieko doesn't enjoy spending money stupidly.

        S   V

    Francisco enjoys watching American football on TV.

    S   V

    Wang enjoys hearing techno music.

- Explain that in the above sentences regarding activities, the *-ing* gerund form is the object of the verb *enjoy*.
- Ask students to label the gerunds as objects. For example:

        S   V   O

    Mieko doesn't enjoy spending money stupidly.

        S   V   O

    Francisco enjoys watching American football on TV.

    S   V   O

    Wang enjoys hearing techno music.

- Ask students to take turns reading example sentences (a)–(m). Discuss the notes included on the right-hand side of the chart.

❑ EXERCISE 3. Looking at grammar.
Page 343
Time: 10 minutes

> This exercise can be done without the students preparing it. Just ask students to call out possible completions. The intention of the exercise is to get across the idea that one verb can immediately follow another verb.
>
> You might also note for students that gerunds, as verb forms, can be followed by objects. In *We postponed visiting the zoo*, *zoo* is the object of the gerund *visiting*.

❑ EXERCISE 5. Warm-up. Page 344
Time: 5 minutes

- Put students into pairs to discuss the illustrations, asking if they do / don't like to *go _____-ing* when they are on vacation.
- Ask students to contribute other activities they know that are expressed with *go + _____-ing*.

CHART 13-2. *Go + -ing.* Page 344
Time: 10 minutes

> Definitions of some vocabulary items in the chart:
>
> *bowling* = a game in which a heavy ball is rolled down a wooden alley
> *camping* = vacationing outdoors in a tent or trailer
> *hiking* = walking a great distance through rural areas, up mountains and along trails
> *sailing* = traveling on water in a boat with sails
> *window shopping* = looking at articles in store windows without making a purchase
> *sightseeing* = looking at the sights and visiting local places of interest when traveling
> *ice skating* = gliding (moving or sliding smoothly) on ice, wearing special shoes with blades to slide on ice
> *skiing* = the sport of gliding on skis (Note: Double "i" is rare in English spelling.)
> *water-skiing* = gliding on water on special skis while pulled by a motorboat
> *skydiving* = jumping from an airplane and opening a parachute
>
> A typical error in using this structure is the addition of *to* after *go*:
>
> INCORRECT: *Did you go <u>to</u> shopping?*
> CORRECT: *Did you go shopping?*
>
> Make the following distinctions for students:
>
> *go* = travel to a place
> *go + _____-ing* = take part in an activity or sport
>
> The list in the chart presents only some of the more common expressions with *go + -ing*. See *Understanding and Using English Grammar*, Chapter 14, for additional items.

- Ask students what kind of outdoor activities are popular in their countries.
- Write a selection of the following questions on the board and encourage discussion among students. For example:

    Do people from _____
    go dancing?
    go bowling
    go clubbing?
    How often / When do people from _____
    go hiking?
    go camping?
    Where / Why / How do people from _____
    go skiing or snowboarding?
    go hunting or fishing?
    go skating?

- Ask students what they want to try and have them form sentences using the targeted structure.
- Write student-generated sentences on the board. For example:

    Juan and Anita want to go bungee jumping, but they are afraid to try it.

    Miguel wants to go clubbing and dancing, but he is too young to enter nightclubs in the U.S.

If Meiko had more money, she would go shopping.
These days, she just wants to go window shopping.

- Ask students to take turns reading the example sentences (a)–(c).
- Discuss common expressions with students.

❏ **EXERCISE 6.** Let's talk: pairwork.
Page 345
Time: 10–15 minutes

> The purpose here is to discuss the meaning of the *go* + *-ing* expressions listed in Chart 13-2.

- Put students into pairs.
- Ask students to read the cues aloud and discuss which of the activities from Chart 13-2 the description refers to.
- Encourage students to discuss if more than one expression is possible.

❏ **EXERCISE 7.** Let's talk: interview.
Page 345
Time: 10 minutes

> You may want to write the following questions on the board to give students additional questions to ask:
> *When did you go* + *-ing?*
> *How often did you go* + *-ing?*
> *Where did you go* + *-ing?*
> *Was it expensive to go* + *-ing?*
> *I know you haven't been* + *-ing, but do you want to go* + *-ing?*
> *Why do or don't you want to go* + *-ing?*

❏ **EXERCISE 8.** Warm-up. Page 346
Time: 5 minutes

- First, ask students to check the sentences that are true for them.
- Then ask students to expand on the four sentences by providing an additional plan, intention, desire, etc., using the grammar presented.

CHART 13-3. Verb + Infinitive. Page 346
Time: 10–15 minutes

> In this text, an infinitive is defined as a verb form that consists of **to** + *the simple form*; "**to**-less infinitives" such as those used following modal auxiliaries (*must go*) are simply called "the simple form" in this text.
>
> *To* is simply a marker; it has no meaning in and of itself in the infinitive structure.

The *to* in an infinitive is normally unstressed in speech. It is usually pronounced /tə/ instead of /tu/.

The text presents just a few of the common verbs followed by infinitives. See *Understanding and Using English Grammar*, Chapter 14, for a more complete reference list.

Forget and *try* are listed in this text as being followed by infinitives because that is how they are most commonly used. They can, however, be followed by gerunds but with a change of meaning. (See *Understanding and Using English Grammar*, Chapter 14.) As mentioned in an earlier chapter in this Teacher's Guide, the text is planting acorns from which the tree will grow. The text does not present the entire tree— this means that teachers may be asked questions about branches this text does not cover. It is for this reason that there are notes and references to a higher-level textbook.

- Using the student-generated sentences from the Warm-up, ask students to tell you about plans, hopes, and desires they have for the future. Put these on the board, in sentence form.
- Underline the infinitive structure in the sentences. For example:

  Min plans <u>to attend</u> at least one concert while he is studying in the United States.
  Rebekkah intends <u>to return</u> to work after she has her baby.
  Lucas and Jana hope <u>to travel</u> to California for the school break.

- Ask students to read the example sentences (a)–(c) aloud from Chart 13-3.
- Review the verbs followed by infinitives that are included in Chart 13-3 and answer any questions students may have about them.
- Stress that the verbs included in the chart are <u>followed by</u> infinitives and the verbs listed in the next exercise (Exercise 9) <u>follow</u> infinitives.

CHART 13-4. Verb + Gerund or Infinitive.
Page 347
Time: 10–15 minutes

> In using the main verbs listed in this chart, native speakers may have a preference for either a gerund of an infinitive in certain instances, or there may be a difference in preferences in American English and British English. However, the learners will be grammatically correct if they use either form following the common verbs listed here.
>
> There is usually no substantial difference in meaning between one form or the other following these verbs, but there may be some subtle differences that learners at this stage would have trouble discerning. (One common example used to illustrate this is *I hate singing* vs. *I hate to sing*. *I hate singing* can mean the speaker hates it when other people sing or hates it when he / she sings. *I hate to sing* means the speaker hates it

when the speaker sings. In other instances, however, there is only a very small and very subtle difference between a gerund or an infinitive following *hate*: *I hate being late for appointments.* This is generally too much information for students at this level.)

This might be a good opportunity to discuss the difference between *like* and *would like*: *Do you like to dance?* (Do you enjoy this?) vs. *Would you like to dance?* (an invitation).

Can't stand (meaning "hate") may be new for your students. It is used principally in informal spoken English. It isn't quite as strong as the word *hate*, but it is stronger than *do not like*.

- Distribute index cards or have students take a half-sheet of paper to write on.
- Explain to students that you want them to write two words or phrases on the paper.
- Write the requirements for these words or phrases on the board:

  Write the name of:

  one activity that you love to do / doing

  one activity that you hate to do / doing

- Tell students to choose specific activities. Explain that their preferences for or against these activities should help identify them among their classmates.
- Collect the papers and either keep them to read aloud yourself or redistribute them so that each student has someone else's paper.
- As a class, read the activities and discuss whose likes and dislikes each paper describes.
- Create sentences using this target structure to put on the board.
- Alternate between *love / hate to do* and *love / hate doing*. For example:

  Ming-Hsu loves to clean her house, even if it is very dirty.

  Emiliano hates cooking. He even hates putting frozen food in the microwave!

- Ask students to read the example sentences from the chart. Discuss the notes.
- If students raise questions regarding this use with other verbs such as *stop*, where there is a difference, answer them briefly. However, if possible, avoid discussion of the few cases in which there is a difference in meaning.

❏ **EXERCISE 12.** Let's talk: pairwork.
Page 348
Time: 10–15 minutes

This practice encourages students to discuss their likes and dislikes. The class can work in small groups. The goal is meaningful communication that employs the target structure.

Point out that *enjoy*, which is included in the list, is always used with a gerund.

- Put students into pairs.
- Instruct them to combine the words in the list above with each numbered item and to take turns, ensuring that both partners have equal talk time.
- Walk around the room, asking and answering students' questions and facilitating their discussions.
- Model questions that students can ask one another to further the conversation and find out more about one another's preferences.
- For example, you may want to write the following questions on the board.

  Why do you love cooking? I like to eat, but I hate cooking!

  I'm surprised. Most people can't stand washing dishes. Why do you enjoy doing it?

  Really? I also don't mind flying, but I know lots of people who don't like to do it.

❏ **EXERCISE 13.** Grammar and speaking.
Page 348
Time: 10 minutes

This exercise should be of real interest to your students. Take ample time to discuss and compare the content of their answers, and talk about the pros and cons of some of these strategies.

- Give students time to complete each item and then determine whether they engage in it, personally.
- After students have completed the items, have them take turns reading each one aloud and explaining whether they do or do not do it.
- Encourage lively discussion and if appropriate, ask for a show of hands to determine which among these coping strategies is most commonly used.
- Compare the merits and problems of each one.

Expansion: Using this exercise, have students come up with other, alternative behaviors that they may or may not engage in when they don't understand a native speaker's English. Have students recreate the list of items from the exercise above and add additional items to it, also in interview or question form. Instruct students to take an informal poll of others in the school or program, and report back with their findings on which strategies are employed most frequently and which are most successful in increasing non-native speaker comfort. If there is time, the class can create a report describing their findings in terms of percentages to share with the other learners they polled.

□ **EXERCISE 14.** Looking at grammar.
Page 349
Time: 10 minutes

> Some students want to try to memorize the lists in the charts, but the intention of the text is to supply plenty of practice to help the students become comfortable and familiar with common verbs followed by gerunds and infinitives. Remind students that it is more useful for them to simply continue practicing with gerunds and infinitives, and develop an ear for what sounds right, than it is for them to memorize entire lists. To that end, you may want to lead students through this exercise and give them only minimal time to complete each item. This will help them develop their sense of what sounds correct.

□ **EXERCISE 15.** Let's talk: pairwork.
Page 350
Time: 10–15 minutes

> Encourage students to use a variety of place names by telling them they can use one place name only one time.
>
> Student A needs to monitor Student B's responses for correct usage of gerunds and infinitives. Student A can look at the charts, if necessary, to ascertain whether B's response is correct.

- Ask students to stand up and move into pairs.
- Encourage students to work with partners they have not yet been assigned.
- Walk around the room, correcting and encouraging students as necessary, and gathering information.
- When most students have gotten through the majority of the items, ask students to return to their seats and do a rapid-fire review as a class.
- While going through the exercise, ask each partner to repeat one sentence his / her partner said.

□ **EXERCISE 16.** Looking at grammar.
Page 350
Time: 10 minutes

> The purpose of this exercise is to illustrate parallel usage of gerunds and infinitives. Lack of parallelism is a common problem. For example:
> INCORRECT: *I enjoy getting up early and watch the sunrise.*
> Note: Without *and*, the sentence *I enjoy getting up early (in order) to watch the sunrise* is also possible.

- Explain that when you are using two phrases, both must either be gerunds or infinitives.
- Put the following <u>incorrect</u> examples on the board:

I love dancing and to sing.
I hate cleaning and to do the laundry.

- Ask students to read the incorrect sentences aloud and discuss whether they sound correct.
- Some students will say they don't sound correct, while others may not be able to hear that the above combinations are wrong. Tell students that with time, they will be able to hear when verbal forms are not parallel and don't "match" as they should.
- Ask students to correct the above sentences. Leave the corrections on the board while they complete Exercise 16 as seatwork. For example:

INCORRECT: *I love dancing and to sing.*
CORRECT: *I love dancing and ~~to~~ singing.*
INCORRECT: *I hate to clean and doing the laundry.*
CORRECT: *I hate to clean and ~~doing~~ do the laundry.*

- Explain to students that when infinitives are connected by *and*, it is not necessary to repeat the *to*.
- Review all the completions with students by having them take turns reading items aloud.

CHART 13-5. Preposition + Gerund.
Page 352
Time: 10–15 minutes

> A gerund, <u>not</u> an infinitive, immediately follows a preposition. (In the idiomatic expression *to be **about to do** something, about* functions as an adjective [meaning "ready"], not a preposition. The whole phrase means "just ready, just prepared.")
>
> The text does not introduce gerunds that have their own "subjects" that can occur between a preposition and the gerund: *Kate insisted on Jake ('s) coming with us.* (See *Understanding and Using English Grammar,* Chapter 15.)

- Clearly explain that a gerund follows a preposition and that an infinitive does <u>not</u>.
- Ask students if they can imagine why this is the case and elicit responses.
- Students may have no idea; if this is the case, ask if they know the meaning of *look forward to* and ask them to try to use it with an infinitive.
- They will try to say something along the lines of:

I look forward to to go away for the weekend.

- Write the above <u>incorrect</u> sentence on the board and invite students to try to say it fast.
- Students will stumble in attempting this awkward and incorrect sentence. This will show them that using a gerund with a preposition works far better.
- Ask students to take turns reading the example sentences from Chart 13-5 aloud (a)–(c).
- Review the notes with students before reading through the list of common expressions with prepositions followed by gerunds.
- Go through the list of common expressions and be ready to explain phrases that are new to students by coming up with examples.

❑ EXERCISE 19. Looking at grammar.
Page 352
Time: 10 minutes

> Students can refer to the chart to find the correct prepositions. They can also test themselves by trying not to look at the chart, and relying on what sounds right. Let students know that *verb + preposition* combinations and idiomatic phrasal verbs are challenging even for very advanced students and that there are simply too many such combinations to commit to memory. Reassure them that they will acquire familiarity with and mastery of these over time and through use.

Optional Vocabulary

appointment	insisted
veterinarian	responsible

❑ EXERCISE 20. Let's talk: pairwork.
Page 352
Time: 10 minutes

> Item 9 might cause some confusion. *Plan* can be followed immediately by an infinitive, or by a preposition and a gerund (*I'm planning **to go to** a movie tonight.* OR *I'm planning **on going to** a movie tonight.*)

- Assign students to pairs.
- Encourage students to come up with more than one sentence for each phrase listed.
- Walk around the room, interacting with, correcting, and encouraging students.
- Review by asking each student to tell you one piece of information he / she learned about his / her partner, using correct *gerund + preposition* structure.

❑ EXERCISE 21. Looking at grammar.
Page 353
Time: 10 minutes

> You could make up a quick oral exercise to help the students learn the preposition combinations in this exercise: start a sentence and have the students call out the correct preposition.
>
> For example:
> Teacher: *I don't like big dogs. I'm afraid . . .*
> Class: ***Of!***
> Teacher: *Right! Afraid **of** them.*

- Lead students through this exercise, on sight.
- Encourage students to call out prepositions and complete the items.
- Provide immediate and clear correction.

❑ EXERCISE 22. Listening. Page 354
Time: 5–10 minutes

> This listening includes a number of gerunds and infinitives, and illustrates how useful and common these verbals are.

CHART 13-6. Using *By* and *With* to Express How Something is Done. Page 355
Time: 10–15 minutes

> In general, *by* is used with means of transportation or communication, and *with* is used with tools and parts of the body. Note that *by hand* is an exception to this.

- Tell students that ***by*** + *gerund* is used to show how something is done or achieved.
- Ask students how they make themselves feel better if they are down or feeling sad. Encourage a variety of answers and write these answers on the board. For example:

  I make myself feel better   *by calling a friend.*
  by eating something sweet.
  by taking a nap.
  by watching a funny movie.

- Discuss the relative merits of these approaches and include as much student information as possible.
- Ask a student to read sentence (a) aloud.
- Now explain that ***by* and *with*** are used with nouns to express how something is done (by what means, with what object, etc.).
- Ask students to take turns reading example sentences (b) and (c) aloud.
- Review the remainder of the chart beneath and answer any questions regarding certain phrases.

❑ EXERCISE 26. Looking at grammar.
Page 356
Time: 10 minutes

- Lead this exercise on sight.
- Correct students on their choice of *by* or *with*.
- Correct students' pronunciation and ask follow-up questions to engage students in spontaneous conversation. For example:

  How else could you travel from Frankfurt to Vienna?
  If you don't have a ruler handy, how can you draw a straight line?

❏ EXERCISE 27. Warm-up. Page 357
Time: 10 minutes

- Ask one student to read the passage aloud.
- Then give students time to read it silently.
- When discussing the questions, ask students what kind of subjects people from their cultural / language background are likely to lie about and compare these with similar topics in the U.S.

CHART 13-7. Using Gerunds as Subjects; Using *It* + Infinitive. Page 357
Time: 10–15 minutes

Point out that a gerund phrase as subject is singular and takes a singular verb, even if the gerund is followed by a plural noun: ***Reading*** books **is** *fun.* In this sentence, *reading,* not *books,* determines the verb.

Confusion may arise in cases where the *-ing* word is used as an adjective to modify a noun: *Reading **books** (i.e., books that teach reading skills)* **are** *usually collections of essays and stories.* (Some grammars analyze this use of *reading* as a gerund used as a noun adjunct; others view it as a present participle used as an adjective.)

Other examples:

Washing (gerund) *dishes isn't much fun.* vs.
Washing (adjectival) ***machines*** *are expensive.*
Helping (gerund) *other people is important.* vs.
Helping (adjectival) ***verbs*** *are also called "auxiliaries."*

The text does not address these grammar points, but questions may arise.

Keep the students' focus on the two patterns presented in examples (a) and (b). Infinitives can, of course, be used as the subject of a sentence: *To ride horses is fun.* The text chooses to emphasize the more common pattern that uses a gerund as the subject. It is also possible for a gerund to follow *it: It is fun riding horses.* Again, the text chooses to emphasize the more common pattern of *it* + *infinitive.*

- Ask students to give you a sentence with a simple subject. Write this on the board. For example:

    Pizza is enjoyable.

- Ask students to label the parts of speech. Then ask how they could add a gerund without changing the essential meaning of the sentence.

    S   V
    Pizza is enjoyable.
    Eating pizza is enjoyable.

- Again, have students label the parts of speech and discuss with them the meaning.

    S   V
    Eating pizza is enjoyable.

- Now explain to students that an infinitive can be used in the same way and write the following example:

    S V
    It is enjoyable to eat pizza.

- Ask students to read aloud the example sentences from the chart. Discuss the notes for each one.

❏ EXERCISE 30. Warm-up. Page 358
Time: 5–10 minutes

- Give students time to decide for themselves about each item.
- Ask students to share their opinions on each item. Offer other cultural norms for further discussion.

CHART 13-8. *It* + Infinitive: Using *For (Someone).* Page 358
Time: 10 minutes

This chart expands the *it* + *infinitive* pattern by adding *for (someone).* This is a frequent and productive sentence type, especially in spoken English.

- Remind students of the *it* + *infinitive* pattern that they already know. Ask students to give you spontaneous examples of the pattern. Write these on the board. For example:

    It is fun to get gifts.

- Explain to students that by adding **for** + *someone,* this pattern can be made more specific and is very common and useful in English.
- Make the above sentence more specific by asking students, *Who particularly likes to get gifts?* (Children come to mind.)
- Write a new sentence incorporating **for** + *this specific someone.* For example:

    It is fun for children to get gifts.

- Ask students to take turns reading each pair of sentences aloud. Reiterate that the meaning between each item in the pair is very similar.

❏ EXERCISE 33. Reading and grammar.
Page 360
Time: 10–15 minutes

This reading passage provides many topics for discussion and many ways for students to express themselves. Give them clear models to do so by writing patterns on the board that they can readily use when discussing body language in their countries.

Part I

- Give students time to read the passage silently.
- Then ask students to take turns reading the passage aloud.
- Stop their reading frequently to ask students to paraphrase and to check on their comprehension.

Expansion: Use the following additional questions to expand the topic. Encourage students to use target grammar in their responses.

How do you greet someone you know well in your country? Do you shake hands (wave, bow, hug, kiss, etc.)?

How do you greet someone you don't know well?

What gestures do you use when leaving someone?

Do you usually make eye contact with strangers? Is it okay to smile at or say a friendly word in passing to strangers?

How far do you stand from someone you are speaking to?

How do you show excitement (disappointment, anger, skepticism, displeasure, nervousness) with your face and body?

How do you indicate that someone should move closer? How do you indicate that you would like to join or even interrupt the flow of conversation?

What percentage of social cues do you think we receive from gestures? Try having a conversation in English with someone and only utilizing your voice (no facial expressions or bodily gestures). Comment on this experience.

What does it mean if you:

-clear your throat?

-raise your eyebrow?

-wave?

-sigh?

-shrug your shoulders?

-put your hand to your ear?

❑ EXERCISE 34. Warm-up. Page 360
Time: 5 minutes

- Ask students to check the items. Then discuss whether all students are in agreement about which are grammatically correct.
- Ask students which item sounds most like what they would say if they needed to go to the store to buy groceries.

CHART 13-9. Expressing Purpose with *In Order To* and *For*. Page 361
Time: 10–20 minutes

Common mistakes are:

INCORRECT: *She came here for studying English.*

INCORRECT: *She came here for to study English.*

INCORRECT: *She came here for study English.*

There is an exception in which *for* is followed by a gerund to express purpose. The phrase *be used for*

expresses the typical or general purpose of a thing. In this case, the preposition *for* is followed by a gerund: *A saw is used for cutting wood.* Also possible: *A saw is used (in order) to cut wood.*

- Ask students what they are going to do this coming weekend and put various student responses on the board. For example:

    Juana is going to sleep late.

    Michele is going to travel to New Jersey.

    Viola is meeting her sister downtown.

- Now ask those same students, *Why?, For what purpose?,* and *In order to do what?* with regard to those questions.
- Write their responses on the board and underline the part of the sentence that explains purpose. For example:

    Juana is going to sleep late <u>because she has been out until 2 A.M. every night this week.</u>

    Michele is going to travel to New York <u>in order to meet his family.</u>

    Viola is meeting her sister downtown <u>for dinner.</u>

- Remind students that there are several different ways of expressing purpose and that expressing purpose is similar to using a *because*–clause.
- Ask students to take turns reading (a)–(c) aloud and review the notes with them.
- Ask other students to read (d) and (e) aloud. Review the accompanying notes.

❑ EXERCISE 38. Reading and grammar.
Page 362
Time: 10–15 minutes

Part I

- Ask students to read the passage silently.
- Then ask students to, in their own words, paraphrase each paragraph.

Part II

- Call on different students to read each item aloud, completing the sentence accordingly.
- Provide correction and ask students to refer back to the text to locate particular pieces of information.

Optional Vocabulary

owning	maintenance
sharing	variety
organizations	benefits
reservations	reducing
rate	effective
insurance	alternative

Expansion: Expand on the discussion questions by asking the following.

In the United States, most people prefer to own their own cars. In addition, many people trade their cars in to get new cars whether the old ones are worn out or not. Is this true in your country as well? Do you often see old or outdated cars, or are most models new?

Many American families have as many cars as there are family members. Comment on the number of cars owned in an average family of your cultural background. How many cars are in most families' driveways? How long do people keep the same car before trading it in?

In various countries, cars serve as very visible "status symbols." What is a "status symbol"? Is this also true in your country? What other possessions do people use to show their social status?

What kind of cars do people want to own? Is it important for the car to be high quality? flashy? expensive? environmentally sound?

Why do people prefer to "own" their own cars, homes, etc., rather than sharing them, renting them, or using them temporarily? What advantages does ownership have over renting, and what advantages does renting have over owning?

Would you classify your country as very materialistic? Do you think that the United States is materialistic? What examples can you give?

CHART 13-10. Using Infinitives with *Too* and *Enough*. Page 364
Time: 10–15 minutes

Review the meanings and spellings of *to*, *too*, and *two*, all of which have the same pronunciation.

to = a preposition or part of an infinitive

too = 1) an adverb meaning "also" that comes at the end of a sentence; or

2) as in this chart, a modifier that means "excessive"

two = the number 2

Note that *too* is not used before adjectives immediately followed by nouns:

CORRECT: *We didn't go swimming because the water was **too cold**.*

INCORRECT: *We didn't go swimming because of the **too cold water**.*

There is another possible but infrequent pattern with *too* and a singular count noun: ***too** + adjective + **a** + noun* Example:

*It was **too hot a day** for hard work in the sun.*

A common problem results from learners attempting to use *too* as an intensifier meaning "very, very."

INCORRECT: *We all enjoyed the scenery a lot. It was too beautiful!!!*

Explain that the use of *too* implies a negative result, brought about by an excess. It indicates that something *can't* happen as in *This ring is too expensive. I can't buy it.* It does <u>not</u> mean "very, very." In a negative sentence, of course, the opposite is true

and *too* implies a positive result: *The ring wasn't too expensive. I could afford to buy it.*

Enough means "sufficient" or "sufficiently." It conveys the presence of the necessary extent, amount, or degree of something to produce a certain result. The result is expressed in the infinitive phrase: *I'm tall enough to touch the ceiling. = My being able to touch the ceiling is the result of the fact that I have the necessary height.*

Explaining the meaning of *enough* by using synonyms or definitions is not easy. Usually students can understand its meaning simply from the examples in the charts and exercises.

Perhaps you can think of a way to illustrate *too* and *enough* in the classroom. One idea would be to pick a high spot, maybe the top of a window. Ask, *Who is tall enough to touch it? Who isn't tall enough? Who is too short? Is anyone too short to touch the top of the window?*

- Ask students the following questions.

  At what age are you considered an "adult" in your country?

  How do you know you are considered an "adult"?

  What do you know about being considered an "adult" in the United States?

- These questions will be used to introduce *too young to _____* and *old enough to_____*.

- Write students' thoughts on the board. For example:

  In my country, you are an adult when you are 18 years old. You can vote in the election then.

  The United States is strange. You are <u>too young to drink</u> at age 18 but <u>old enough to vote</u>.

- Expand on this topic by asking more questions about age and abilities or appropriateness of certain actions / situations. Possible questions include:

  Is 16 too young to marry?

  Is 18 too young to live on your own?

  Is 21 old enough to decide what kind of career you want to have?

  Is 25 old enough to become a parent?

- Write students' responses on the board.

- Highlight the target grammar and discuss the differences among students' responses.

  Miki: Sixteen is <u>too young to marry</u> because you don't really know yourself.

  Hye-Won: Eighteen is <u>not too young to live alone</u>. At 18, you are <u>old enough to take care</u> of yourself.

  Phillippe: For some people, 21 is <u>old enough to decide</u> what career you want to have, but for me, it was <u>too young to decide</u>.

  Lilla: I think 25 is <u>too young to become</u> a parent, but my mother had three children at age 23!

- After you have practiced the structure with student-generated examples, ask students to read the example sentences (a)–(c), (d) and (e), and (f) and (g) aloud.

- Discuss the notes and answer any questions students have.

❑ EXERCISE 45. Reading and grammar.
Page 366
Time: 15–20 minutes

Part I
- Give students time to read the passage themselves.
- If time permits, ask students to take turns reading paragraphs aloud and paraphrasing the story.
- Ask students questions to check on their comprehension of the passage.
- Invite students to share similar embarrassing travel stories as this will prepare them for the following writing exercise.

Optional Vocabulary
manufactures
equipment
products
deep breath
broadly
ground floor
helplessly
figure out
incident

❑ EXERCISE 46. Let's write. Page 368
Time: 15–25 minutes

- Discuss some embarrassing travel anecdotes with students and invite students to share theirs.
- Discuss with students how adding certain details will make their writing more interesting. Encourage them to help the reader "feel" their embarrassment by choosing descriptive adjectives.

- Walk around the class as students get started on the writing.
- Remind students to include gerunds and infinitives
- Assign a final or finished draft for homework and collect them when students are next in class.

❑ EXERCISE 47. Check your knowledge.
Page 368
Time: 10–15 minutes

As in other error-analysis exercises, almost all entries are adapted from actual student writing. Students might like to know that students before them made the same errors they make but have gone on to successful second-language acquisition. Making errors is just part of the process—you could compare it to learning a musical instrument. No one can sit down and play perfectly from the beginning or just from studying a manual. It takes practice, practice, practice (mistakes and all)—as does language learning.

Optional Vocabulary
cash(ing) a check
campfire
settle down

Chapter 14
Noun Clauses

CHAPTER SUMMARY

OBJECTIVE: The objective of this chapter is to enable students to easily comprehend and use noun clauses. The successful use of noun clauses allows students to engage in natural conversation, in which they can discuss how to get and give information. In addition, they will gain a working knowledge of reported speech, which they can use to relate past conversations and share information gained indirectly.

APPROACH: The first part of the chapter is organized around the three types of noun clauses: those introduced by (1) question words, (2) *if / whether,* and (3) *that.* In the first few sections, noun clauses are presented as transformations of information questions and yes / no questions.

In the second part of the chapter, students also learn to report the words of another person. This is useful in situations ranging from informal conversation to formal academic writing.

TERMINOLOGY: Other terms for some types of noun clauses are "nominal clause," "*wh*-clause," "*that*-clause," and "included, embedded, or indirect questions." In this text, subordinating conjunctions (e.g., *who, what, if, that*) are simply called "words that introduce noun clauses." Quoted speech is also called "direct speech" or "direct discourse." Reported speech is also called "indirect speech" or "indirect discourse."

❑ **EXERCISE 1.** Warm-up. Page 370
Time: 5 minutes

> After students have marked their answers, you might want to have them find the subject, verb, and object in each item.

CHART 14-1. Noun Clauses: Introduction.
Page 370
Time: 10–15 minutes

> The principal problem learners have with noun clauses is correct word order. Students may use question word order (i.e., inverted subject and verb) in noun clauses introduced by a question word.

> INCORRECT: *I wanted to know why did Ann leave early.*

Similarly, students may use noun clause word order in questions:

> INCORRECT: *Why you left early?*

Another difficulty stems from tense changes in noun clauses. For example, the spoken question, *Why is Tom absent?* sometimes changes tense if the reporting verb is past: *The teacher wanted to know why Tom was absent.*

The formal sequence of tenses in noun clauses is presented in Chart 14-10. Until that point in the chapter (i.e., until all three forms of noun clauses have been introduced and practiced), no introductory verbs are past tense if the student is required to supply the noun clause verb. In this way, students can avoid the complicated problem of changing noun clause verbs to past forms. You should remember to use only present introductory verbs such as *I don't know* when making up your own examples or quizzes.

- Start by putting a simple sentence on the board featuring an object noun that can easily be replaced by a noun clause. For example:

  I love <u>my home</u>.

- Explain that *my home* can be replaced with a noun clause.
- Ask students to tell you what the elements of any clause are, and put these on the board. For example:

  a <u>clause</u> has a <u>subject</u> and a <u>verb</u>

- Ask students to come up with a way to replace *my home* with a noun clause. For example:

  my home = where I live

- Ask students to label the parts of the above clause. For example:

  question word + subject + verb
  my home =   where   I   live

- Tell students that just as nouns can be subjects or objects, noun clauses, which take the place of nouns, can replace either a subject or an object.
- Ask students to take turns reading aloud the example sentences (a)–(f) from the chart.
- Go through the notes that accompany each example sentence and discuss these with students.

❏ **EXERCISE 2.** Looking at grammar.
Page 370
Time: 5 minutes

- Explain to students that if a sentence also has a noun clause, it will have more than one subject and more than one verb.
- Give students time to underline the noun clauses they see and ask them to also identify the subjects and verbs in each item.
- Ask students to read each sentence aloud and then state the noun clause.

CHART 14-2. Noun Clauses That Begin with a Question Word. Page 371
Time: 10–15 minutes

The focus in this chart and the accompanying exercises is on word order in noun clauses that begin with question words. A quick review of question forms at this point is helpful for students.

This is an ideal time to remind students that they often "ask" questions merely by adding an inflected question mark at the end of statement word order. Reiterate that though most native speakers understand what they mean, their English suffers by not using proper question syntax.

- Ask students to explain what changes are needed when making a statement into a question.
- Put students' explanations on the board. For example:

  To make a question, you have to change the order of the subject and verb, so the verb comes first.
  You have to use an auxiliary with simple present.
  I want to go to the movies.
  <u>*Do you want*</u> *to go to the movies?*

- Remind students of the common *wh*-question words and what pieces of information they elicit. Write these on the board. For example:

Where	*a place*
When	*a time*
What	*a piece of information*
How	*in what way, or what manner*
Why	*a reason*
Who	*a person*
Whose	*a person's*

- Remind students that these question words precede the question itself in a regular question and write an example of this on the board. For example:

  Where does she work?

- Then write a noun clause next to the question that uses the same information. For example:

  Where does she work?
  I don't know where she works.

- Explain that with noun clauses, question word order is not used and instead, the *wh*-word precedes normal *subject* + *verb* word order.

- Explain that question word order is not used in a noun clause because a question is not actually being asked, though we understand that a question is implied.
- Ask students to take turns reading the example sentences (a)–(j) aloud. Answer any questions.

❏ **EXERCISE 4.** Looking at grammar.
Page 372
Time: 5–10 minutes

The difference between an actual question and a noun clause with an embedded question lies in word order. This distinction is what students are being asked to distinguish in this exercise.

- Remind students that if there is a noun clause (and thus if *I don't know* can sensibly start the sentence), there is no inverted subject and verb order.
- Give students time to work through the items on their own.
- Review by having students read both (a) and (b) items aloud and correct each one accordingly.

❏ **EXERCISE 5.** Looking at grammar.
Page 372
Time: 10 minutes

This exercise attempts to give students an idea of how noun clauses are typically used in conversation. Speaker B could, of course, simply stop after saying, "I don't know," but often a speaker will repeat what has been asked, often repeating nouns and proper names instead of substituting pronouns.

- Remind students to take the time to first identify the parts of speech in Speaker A's part.
- Explain that part of the task of turning the <u>subject</u> and <u>verb</u> in Speaker A's line into the completion of Speaker B's line is choosing the correct tense.
- After students have had time to complete the items, review as a class.
- Be prepared to put Speaker B completions on the board so that students can see all the changes that were required, particularly in terms of tense.

❏ **EXERCISE 6.** Let's talk: pairwork.
Page 373
Time: 10–15 minutes

- Put students into pairs.
- Begin the exercise by asking students how to change the word order of a question to a noun clause and writing an example on the board. For example:

  Question Auxiliary S   V
  How   do   we make noun clauses?
     Question   S   V
  Diego, can you tell me how we make noun clauses?

- In the example, make it clear that students realize that question mark is related to the *can you tell me*.
- Give students plenty of time to work with their partners while you circulate, answer questions, and facilitate discussion.
- Review by inviting students to change each item into a noun clause and writing these new questions with *can you tell me* on the board.

□ **EXERCISE 10.** Warm-up. Page 376
Time: 5 minutes

- Encourage students to read each item aloud in order to hear those items where something is incorrect.
- Ask students what they think *whether* means.

CHART 14-3. Noun Clauses That Begin with *If* or *Whether*. Page 376
Time: 10–15 minutes

> In everyday usage, native speakers generally prefer *if* to *whether* to introduce noun clauses. The text emphasizes the use of *if* while acquainting the students with the use of *whether*.
>
> Point out that *weather* and *whether* have the same pronunciation but very different meanings and spellings (they are homophones).
>
> All possible patterns with *whether* and *if* are not presented here. See *Understanding and Using English Grammar*, Chapter 12, for an expanded discussion of these patterns.

- Explain that there are a number of ways to rephrase a yes / no question as a noun clause.
- Tell students the most common way is to introduce the yes / no noun clause with *if*.
- With the involvement of students, create a new sentence including a noun clause about a yes / no question regarding a student in the class.
- Write this example on the board and underline the *if*. For example:

  We don't know <u>if</u> Marco has a girlfriend.

- Explain that there are a couple of other ways to indicate the same yes / no question as a noun clause.
- Tell students that one way to show this yes / no aspect of the noun clause is to use the phrase *or not*. This phrase indicates that the question presented is equally likely and equally unlikely.
- Write a sentence featuring *if . . . . or not*. For example:

  We don't know <u>if</u> Marco has a girlfriend <u>or not</u>.

- Make sure that students realize that this *or not* phrase can only come at the end of the sentence.
- Next, explain that *whether* can also be used to introduce such a yes / no clause or embedded question.
- Change the example accordingly and write the new version, featuring *whether*.

- Explain that *whether* can also be followed by *or not*, but that *whether* can be followed immediately by *or not*. The *or not* can also be located at the end of the sentence, the way it occurs with *if*.
- Make it clear that there are two options for the location of *or not* with the *whether*. For example

  We don't know <u>whether (or not)</u> Marco has a girlfriend <u>(or not)</u>.

- Ask students to read aloud example sentences (a)–(c) from the chart. Discuss the notes.
- Instruct students to read (d) and (e) aloud. Review the rest of the notes in the chart.

CHART 14-4. Noun Clauses That Begin with *That*. Page 379
Time: 10–15 minutes

> Students should find this task exceedingly simple because they are already using this grammar point everyday. Now you are asking them to expand their usage ability by learning more words that introduce these clauses, such as *assume* and *realize*.
>
> Discuss the meaning of the verbs followed by *that*-clauses in this chart by eliciting examples from the class.
>
> The word *that* has no semantic meaning in this structure. It marks or signals the beginning of a clause. Its omission does not affect the meaning of a sentence. In everyday English, especially in spoken English, *that* is usually omitted. If it is not omitted, it is almost always unstressed and pronounced /thət/.

- Write *I think that* on the board and have students complete the sentence with noun clauses. For example:

  I think that <u>English grammar is easy to learn.</u>
  I think that <u>American food is not very good.</u>
  I think that <u>L.A. is an expensive city.</u>

- Ask students to label subjects and verbs in the examples. For example:

            S   **V**
  I think that <u>English grammar is easy to learn.</u>
            S   **V**
  I think that <u>American food is not very good.</u>
           S **V**
  I think that <u>L.A. is an expensive city.</u>

- Explain that the *that*-noun clauses presented in this chart are noun clause objects of verbs that express thinking, opinions, etc.
- Tell students that it is also possible to have a *that*-clause be the subject of a sentence, but that this is far less common. For example:

      S   **V**
      S **V**
  <u>That L.A. is an expensive city</u> is common knowledge.

- Ask students to read through the example sentences (a)–(d) aloud. Review the notes.
- Have students read (e) and (f). Review the list of verbs followed by *that*-clauses.

☐ EXERCISE 17. Let's talk: pairwork.
Page 379
Time: 10 minutes

- Assign students pairs.
- Remind students of the variety of verbs they can use to express their opinions and combine with *that*.
- Ask pairs to share answers with the class. Use these answers to promote a discussion of items 4, 5, and 6.

Expansion: Because the *that*-clause structure lends itself so well to discussions of beliefs and personal philosophies, foster a discussion of item 4 in the exercise above. Additional questions that will allow students to share personal and worldviews include the following:

What do you think the most important invention of the 20th century was?

Who do you think was the most important historical figure to date?

Do you think that the world is getting better or worse?

Do you think that technological advances are always beneficial?

Do you think that people are basically good, bad, or neutral?

What do you think is the most important lesson you have ever learned?

Do you think that it is better to be realistic, optimistic, or pessimistic?

Do you believe that you can fall in love at first sight?

Be sure to ask students to give examples to support their opinions and to use *that*-clauses.

CHART 14-5. Other Uses of *That*-Clauses.
Page 380
Time: 10–15 minutes

This chart seeks to acquaint learners with common expressions in which *that*-clauses are used.

Discuss the meaning of the expressions in this chart followed by *that*-clauses by eliciting examples from the class.

- Put some of the phrases that can precede *that*-clauses on the board with the names of your students and ask those students featured to complete them. For example:

Svetlana is certain that _____.

Magnus is happy that _____.

Wei-Wang is lucky that _____.

Felipe and Mara are surprised that _____.

We are all sorry that _____.

- Stress that these phrases use the verb *be* with adjectives describing feeling, certainty, knowledge, etc.
- Remind students that because there is not an action verb in these phrases, the subject is equated with the adjective in the phrase.
- Ask students to read example sentences (a)–(d) aloud. Read the accompanying notes.
- Have students read (e) and (f) aloud. Finish by reviewing the notes and the additional expressions followed by *that*-clauses.

☐ EXERCISE 19. Looking at grammar.
Page 380
Time: 10 minutes

The ability to recognize when the clause marker *that* has been omitted can be important in reading comprehension. Whenever a reader (native or non-native speaker) is trying to figure out what a particularly confusing sentence means, an understanding of the underlying structure of the sentence is helpful if not essential. It's important for language users to know that optional parts of a structure (such as introductory *that*) might be omitted.

☐ EXERCISE 20. Let's talk. Page 381
Time: 10–20 minutes

Part I
- Explain to students that these words all describe ways to support one's health.
- Tell students that in many Western countries, these practices are considered alternative to typical medical approaches.
- Ask students if they can provide working definitions of each word.

Part II
- Ask students to complete the three items independently.
- As a class, discuss the completed items and compare students' opinions.

☐ EXERCISE 22. Warm-up. Page 382
Time: 5 minutes

- First ask students to read aloud the three items that follow each exchange.
- Ask students to identify which items do not match the meaning of the dialogue.
- Ask students what they notice, if anything, about the use of *so* and *not*.

CHART 14-6. Substituting *So* for a *That-Clause* in Conversational Responses. Page 382
Time: 10–15 minutes

> This structure allows speakers to answer yes / no questions without committing themselves to a definite, black-and-white, *yes-or-no* answer. It allows for "gray areas" in speakers' knowledge.
>
> Focus students' attention on the meaning of *so* in expressions such as *I think so.* In this structure, *so* functions as a substitute for a noun clause introduced by *that.*
>
> The word *so* has various uses. A dictionary will label it an adverb, adjective, pronoun, conjunction, and interjection. To the second language learner, *so* is probably one of the most confusing and unpredictable words in English. You could explain to your students that English has more than one *so*, each with a different function and meaning.

- Write the following two questions on the board:

  Is the sun going to rise tomorrow?

  Do you think it is going to rain tomorrow?

- The first question should elicit *Yes* answers. The second question should elicit, *Maybe, I don't know,* or *I think so* answers.
- Explain to students that *so* softens an answer and indicates that the speaker is <u>not</u> 100% certain.
- Ask students to take turns reading the example sentences (a)–(c) aloud. Review the accompanying notes.
- Ask students to read (d)–(f) aloud. Review the notes.

❑ EXERCISE 24. Let's talk: pairwork.
Page 383
Time: 10–15 minutes

> These short dialogues are typical of everyday conversations. Remind students that their conversations can develop in any direction that seems natural. You may want to have different pairs perform a few of the dialogues.

❑ EXERCISE 25. Warm-up. Page 383
Time: 5–10 minutes

- After students circle punctuation and discuss differences, ask them to describe what is happening in the "scene" represented by the quotes.

❑ EXERCISE 14-7. Quoted Speech.
Page 384
Time: 10–15 minutes

> Using examples on the board, go through punctuation and capitalization of quotations step-by-step. This information will probably be new to at least a few of the students.
>
> Learning how to use quotations in writing will help the students improve their narrative-descriptive writing as well as prepare them for academic writing in which they must cite sources (i.e., use the words of another writer or author). Students who are not interested in the conventions of written English could skip this unit, but most will surely benefit from understanding how to read quotes they find in newspapers and other everyday writings.
>
> Information not included in the chart: When reporting words are not at the beginning of a quotation, the reporting phrase is sometimes inverted. For example, *"Cats are fun to watch,"* **said Jane**. This inversion is used in writing rather than in speaking, and students don't need to concern themselves with this form.
>
> Also, reporting words can come in the middle of a quoted sentence. *"Cats," said Jane / Jane said, "are fun to watch."* Give your students as much information as will be useful to them without overloading them. Most students at this level don't require a survey of all the variations possible in writing quotations.

- Explain to students that quotations are meant to represent what was actually said, word for word, the <u>exact</u> wording.
- Ask a student to tell you a saying or quote that he / she is familiar with. Use this to teach the steps for punctuating quotations. For example:

  Taka: When the cat is away, the mice will play.

- Explain that the first step is to choose a verb to show who spoke. Write this first step on the board. For example:

  Taka said

- Tell students that after *said*, they need to place a comma and then add quotation marks and the word *said.* For example:

  Taka said, "When the cat is away, the mice will play

- Tell students that if the quote is a statement, they should add the period and then closing quotation marks.

  Taka said, "When the cat is away, the mice will play."

- Ask students to take turns reading the example sections / sentences (a)–(c) aloud from the chart.
- Have students continue to read example sentences (d)–(g) aloud and help them inflect the actual quote correctly, to distinguish it from the *said*-phrase.
- Review all the notes with your students and answer any questions.
- Remind students that it is useful for them to be able to recognize and read quoted speech, and, therefore, this level of familiarity is helpful for them.

❏ EXERCISE 27. Looking at grammar.
Page 385
Time: 10 minutes

- Lead students through this exercise, asking them to call out the required punctuation marks while you take direction and write the correct items on the board.
- Discuss how to indicate through inflection the parts of the quoted speech and explain that with the *said*–phrase, the voice usually drops its inflection.

Optional Vocabulary
sign language
replied
deaf

Expansion: Cut comic strips from a newspaper or other source. Use white-out to block the actual words "said" by each character. Ask students to work in groups and write new conversations for the comic characters, using correct quotation punctuation.

You can pick either the same comic strip for the whole class or different ones for each group. Then compare dialogues.

Another expansion for quotes can be done with film clips. Take a very short film clip with a lot of overt action. Prepare it for the class so you can play the entire clip without sound. Play it frame by frame, pausing after each action or obvious character speech and give students time to write down what they think must have just been said. Instruct students to use appropriate quotation punctuation. Finally, compare the different quotations students create.

❏ EXERCISE 28. Reading and writing.
Page 385
Time: 20–30 minutes

Part I
- Give students time to read through the entire passage and to underline all the quoted speech.
- Ask students if they are already familiar with this story. Then ask them to take turns paraphrasing the parts of the story.

Optional Vocabulary
nest	wandered
ducklings	reeds
hatch	reflection
ugly	beamed
clumsy	

Part II
- Discuss the story and the lessons learned through reading it.
- Discuss how similar stories inform the shared culture of children (fairy tales, fables, universal stories).
- Ask students if they know who Aesop is and what his fables are.

CHART 14-8. Quoted Speech vs. Reported Speech. Page 387
Time: 10–15 minutes

> The purpose of this chart is to introduce the concept of "reported speech."
>
> Point out that *I* in reported speech (a) becomes *she* in (c) because the *I* in the quotation refers to Ann, the original speaker. You could illustrate this by using names of students and having them read short sentences from the board for other students to report.
>
> Be ready to remind students of all necessary changes including tenses, pronouns, and adverbs of time and place.
>
> Example:
>
> Sentence on board: *I'm sleepy.*
> Speaker A: *I'm sleepy.*
> Speaker B: *Natasha said that **she was** sleepy.*
> Speaker C: *I'm also sleepy.*
> Speaker B: *Po said that **he was** also sleepy.*

- Ask students to tell you how they are feeling at the moment. Put their responses on the board. For example:

  Kiyoko: I am a little confused about reported speech.
  Bo-Sung: I am not confused, but I am really hungry.
  Juan: I am really nervous because I am waiting for an important phone call.

- Tell your students that several changes take place when reporting direct or quoted speech.
- Explain that one change is the tense. If the speaker originally speaks in present, a short amount of time lapses and thus, a change in tense happens to put the verb in the past.
- Tell students that another change is in pronoun use. Though above, Kiyoko uses *I* about herself, others describing what she said have to use *she* to refer back to her original statement.
- After you have explained these necessary changes to students, ask them to help you very carefully make the changes in the sentences on the board. For example:

  Kiyoko: I am a little confused about reported speech.
  Kiyoko said (that) <u>she was</u> a little confused about reported speech.
  Bo-Sung: I am not confused, but I am really hungry.
  Bo-Sung said (that) <u>he was</u> not confused but (that) <u>he was</u> really hungry.
  Juan: I am really nervous because I am waiting for an important phone call.
  Juan said (that) <u>he was</u> really nervous because <u>he was waiting</u> for an important phone call.

- Point out that these transformations to reported speech are new sentences containing noun clauses as the object of the verb *say*.
- Explain that the clause marker *that* is optional but can be useful when first writing reported speech.
- Ask students to take turns reading example sentences (a) and (b) aloud. Then discuss the notes.

- Emphasize the changes made in order to transform the direct speech to reported speech and ask students to read (c) and (d) aloud.

❏ **EXERCISE 31.** Warm-up. Page 387
Time: 5–10 minutes

- Ask students to read each of the four items, (a)–(d), aloud.
- Ask students to explain the changes they have noticed in tenses. Then ask them to imagine what these changes relate to.

CHART 14-9. Verb Forms in Reported Speech. Page 388
Time: 10–15 minutes

> Students probably will not have control of these patterns, but the exercises that follow the chart gives students lots of opportunities for practice.
>
> Some students might benefit from a quick reminder of names and meanings of the verb forms in Chapters 1, 2, 3, 4, and 7. Perhaps focus on the fact that auxiliaries carry most of the information about tense and number.
>
> The following are the sequence of verb forms in the examples in the text:
>
> simple present ⇒ simple past
> present progressive ⇒ past progressive
> present perfect ⇒ past perfect
> simple past ⇒ past perfect
> am, is, are going to ⇒ was, were going to
> will ⇒ would
> can ⇒ could
>
> Other changes not introduced in this text (but covered in *Understanding and Using English Grammar*, Chapter 12): *may* ⇒ *might*; *have to* ⇒ *had to*; *must* (meaning "necessity") ⇒ *had to*; *should* ⇒ *should* (no change); *ought to* ⇒ *ought to* (no change).
>
> In actual usage, there is no consistent rule for changing verb forms in noun clauses. The chart provides guidelines, but that is all they are.
>
> After discussing the verb changes in the chart, use a different verb and ask the class to change it appropriately. For example, conduct an oral exercise using the verb *watch*.
>
> Teacher: *I watch TV a lot.*
> Student: *You said you watched TV a lot.*
> Teacher: *I am not watching TV right now.*
> Student: *You said you weren't watching TV right now.*

- Ask students to give you a simple present sentence. Show both immediate and later reporting by writing both versions on the board. For example:

  Ahmed: *I am very thirsty.*
  Immediate reporting: *Ahmed said he is thirsty.*
  Later reporting: *Ahmed said he was thirsty.*

- Lead your students through the changes in tenses by asking students to report your sentences after you. Write the sequences on the board and highlight changes in both tenses and pronouns or adverbs.

  You: *I run a few miles every night.*
  Students: *You said you run a few miles every night.*
  You: *I ran a few miles last night.*
  Students: *You said you ran a few miles last night.*

- Ask students to take turns reading example sentences (a)–(d) aloud.
- Review the notes.
- Highlight the difference between immediate reporting and later reporting and then ask students to read the example sentences (e)–(f) aloud. Review the notes.
- Ask students to read (g) aloud. Then have students take turns reading aloud the transformed sentences immediately below.

❏ **EXERCISE 32.** Looking at grammar. Page 388
Time: 10 minutes

- Give students time to work through these items as seatwork.
- When students have completed the items, ask them to first read the quoted or direct speech (and remind students to inflect the speech meaningfully).
- After one student has read the direct speech, invite another student to read the reported speech completion.
- Provide immediate correction and go through necessary changes step-by-step as needed.

❏ **EXERCISE 33.** Looking at grammar. Page 389
Time: 10–15 minutes

> The focus here is on the tenses used to report a statement that was made in the past. Anticipate the exercise to proceed quite slowly and require a lot of discussion, repetition, and boardwork.

CHART 14-10. Common Reporting Verbs: *Tell, Ask, Answer / Reply.* Page 389
Time: 10 minutes

> The main point the students need to understand from this chart is simply that *tell* is always followed by a (pro)noun object when used to report speech.
>
> Another pattern with *say* that is not mentioned in the chart is the use of *to* + a (pro)noun object: *Ann said **to me** that she was hungry.* Native speakers generally prefer *told me* to *said to me*, but both are correct.

As a side note, the pattern *said . . . to me* is used idiomatically to report greetings and goodbyes: *Tom said good morning to me. I said hello to him. We said goodbye to each other.*

> INCORRECT: *Tom **said me** good morning. I said him hello. We said each other good-bye.*

❑ EXERCISE 37. Looking at grammar.
Page 391
Time: 10 minutes

Make sure that students understand the format of the cartoons. For example, remind them that the story should be read from top left to top right to bottom left to bottom right.

❑ EXERCISE 40. Reading. Page 392
Time: 10-15 minutes

Part I
- Give students time to read through the passage on their own first.

- Ask students to then retell the story included in the passage in their own words.

Optional Vocabulary

lecture	survive
series	tend
wisdom	appropriately
uplifting	

Part II
- Ask students to work in groups, discussing the advice they read in Randy Pausch's lecture.
- Ask them to support their agreement or disagreement with examples from their own lives and observations of the world.
- Walk around the room, facilitating lively discussing, joining groups, and asking provocative questions.
- End the discussion by coming together again as a class and writing students' thoughts on the board, using the target noun clause and reported speech forms.

Index

Student Book Answer Key

Exercise 5, p. 4.
1. happening right now
2. happening right now
3. happening right now
4. happening right now
5. usual activity
6. happening right now
7. happening right now
8. happening right now
9. usual activity
10. usual activity
11. usual activity

Exercise 6, p. 5.
1. usual activity
2. happening right now
3. happening right now
4. usual activity
5. happening right now

Exercise 7, p. 5.
2. am sitting . . . sit
3. speaks . . . is speaking
4. A: Does it rain
   B: is
5. A: Is it raining?
   B: is starting
6. is walking
7. A: walks . . . Do you walk
   B: Does Oscar walk

Exercise 9, p. 6.
1. Does it
2. Does it
3. Are you
4. Do you
5. Do we
6. is it

Exercise 10, p. 7.
1. runs   T
2. run   T
3. live F [According to a 1993 study: the death rate for right-handed people = 32.2 percent; for left-handed people = 33.8 percent, so the death rate is about the same.]
4. cover   T
5. has   F [The official Eiffel Tower Web site says 1665.]

6. spoils F [Honey never spoils.]
7. is   T
8. takes   T
9. beats   T
10. die   T

Exercise 12, p. 9.
1. It grows one-half inch per month or 15 centimeters a year.
2. They don't hurt because the hair on our scalp is dead.
3. About 100,000.
4. (*Any country near the equator.*)

Exercise 16, p. 11.
1. c. Kazu frequently doesn't shave . . .
   d. Kazu occasionally doesn't shave . . .
   e. Kazu sometimes doesn't shave . . .
   f. Kazu always shaves . . .
   g. Kazu doesn't ever shave . . .
   h. Kazu never shaves . . .
   i. Kazu hardly ever shaves . . .
   j. Kazu rarely shaves . . .
   k. Kazu seldom shaves . . .

2. a. I usually don't eat breakfast.
   b. I don't always eat breakfast.
   c. I seldom eat breakfast.
   d. I don't ever eat breakfast.

3. a. My roommate generally isn't home . . .
   b. My roommate sometimes isn't home . . .
   c. My roommate isn't always home . . .
   d. My roommate is hardly ever home . . .

Exercise 17, p. 12.
2. sometimes makes
3. frequently / often goes
4. is frequently / often late
5. always cooks
6. almost always reads
7. seldom does
8. never goes

Exercise 19, p. 13.
1. A dolphin swims.
2. Dolphins swim.

Exercise 20, p. 13.
3. verb, singular
4. noun, plural
5. verb, singular
6. noun, plural
7. noun, plural
8. verb, singular

Exercise 21, p. 14.
2. create Ø, floods
3. flood Ø, causes
4. towns, floods, buildings, homes, roads
5. flood Ø, town Ø, needs, repairs

Exercise 22, p. 14.

add -s only	*add -es*	*add -ies*
stays	wishes	studies
takes	mixes	tries
speaks		

Exercise 23, p. 15.
3. A boat <u>floats</u> on water. (*no change*)
4. Rivers <u>flow</u> toward the sea. (*no change*)
5. My mother <u>worries</u> about me.
6. A student <u>buys</u> a lot of books at the beginning of each term.
7. Airplanes <u>fly</u> all around the world. (*no change*)
8. The teacher <u>asks</u> us a lot of questions in class every day.
9. Mr. Cook <u>watches</u> game shows on TV every evening.
10. Water <u>freezes</u> at 32°F (0°C) and <u>boils</u> at 212°F (100°C).
11. Mrs. Taylor never <u>crosses</u> the street in the middle of a block. She always <u>walks</u> to the corner and <u>uses</u> the crosswalk.

Exercise 24, p. 15.
3. hopes
4. teaches
5. moves
6. kisses
7. pushes
8. waits
9. mixes
10. bows
11. studies
12. buys
13. enjoys
14. tries
15. carries

Exercise 26, p. 16.
(*Order of sentences may vary.*)
1. A car causes air pollution.
2. A rubber band stretches when you pull on it.
3. A hotel supplies its guests with clean towels.
4. Oceans support a huge variety of marine life.
5. A bee collects nectar from flowers.
6. Does exercise improve your health?
7. A hurricane causes great destruction when it reaches land.
8. A river flows downhill.
9. An elephant uses its long trunk like a hand to pick things up.
10. Brazil produces one-fourth of the world's coffee.

Exercise 27, p. 16.
Charlie: a, a
Dad: a, a

Exercise 28, p. 17.
2. a
3. a
4. A: a
   B: a
5. B: b
   A: b

Exercise 29, p. 18.
2. think
3. am thinking
4. are having
5. have

Exercise 30, p. 18.
2. Do you need . . . Do you want
3. A: think . . . know . . . forget
   B: remember
4. A: Do you believe
   B: exist
5. are . . . are having . . . have . . . are building . . . like . . . are lying . . . (are) listening . . . aren't listening . . . hear

Exercise 31, p. 19.
1. a
2. a
3. b

Exercise 32, p. 20.
2. A: Is it raining
   B: it isn't . . . don't think
3. A: Do your friends write
   B: they do . . . get
4. A: Does the weather affect
   B: it does . . . get
5. A: Is Jean studying
   B: she isn't . . . is . . . is playing
   A: Does Jean play
   B: No, she doesn't . . . studies
   A: Is she
   B: she is . . . plays
   A: Do you play
   B: I do . . . am not

Exercise 33, p. 21.
1. Do you
2. Does it
3. Does she
4. Does he
5. Does she
6. Am I
7. Is it
8. Does he
9. Do they
10. Do we

Exercise 34, p. 22.
1. Is the earth revolving around the sun right now? [Yes.]
2. Does the moon revolve around the earth every 28 days? [Yes.]

3. Are the sun and moon planets? [No.]
4. Is Toronto in western Canada? [No.]
5. Do whales lay eggs? [No.]
6. Does your country have gorillas in the wild?
7. Are gorillas intelligent? [Yes.]
8. Do mosquitoes carry malaria? [Yes, some do.]
9. Do you like vegetarian food?
10. Is our teacher from Australia?
11. Is it raining outside now?
12. Are you tired of this interview?

Exercise 35, p. 22.

1. b	3. a	5. b
2. a	4. a	6. a

Exercise 36, p. 22.

2. A: Are they watching
   B: aren't . . . are playing

3. A: Are you listening
   B: want

4. A: are
   B: am
   A: are you doing
   B: am trying

5. A: do you think
   B: think . . . don't think . . . do you think
   A: don't think . . . count

6. A: are you thinking
   B: am thinking . . . am not thinking
   A: don't believe . . . are thinking

7. A: Do you know
   B: do
   A: is
   B: doesn't make
   A: know

Exercise 37, p. 24.

Part I.

2. prefer	6. are doing
3. makes	7. Do you exercise
4. need	8. Are you exercising
5. work	

Part II.

1. believe	11. are listening
2. go	12. are doing
3. like	13. are exercising
4. is	14. Do
5. increases	15. like
6. are	16. Do
7. beats	17. get
8. brings	18. Do
9. work	19. do
10. have	

Exercise 38, p. 25.

Omar's Visit

(1) My friend Omar **owns** his own car now. It's brand new. Today he **is** driving to a small town north of the city to visit his aunt. He **loves** to listen to music, so the CD player is **playing** one of his favorite CDs — loudly. Omar is very happy: he is **driving** his own car and **listening** to loud music. He's **looking** forward to his visit with his aunt.

(2) Omar **visits** his aunt once a week. She's elderly and **lives** alone. She **thinks** Omar **is** a wonderful nephew. She **loves** his visits. He **tries** to be helpful and considerate in every way. His aunt **doesn't hear** well, so Omar **speaks** loudly and clearly when he's with her.

(3) When he's there, he **fixes** things for her around her apartment and **helps** her with her shopping. He **doesn't stay** with her overnight. He usually **stays** for a few hours and then **heads** back to the city. He **kisses** his aunt good-bye and **gives** her a hug before he **leaves**. Omar is a very good nephew.

Chapter 2: Past Time

Exercise 2, p. 27.

2. She didn't drink . . . Did she drink
3. They didn't play . . . Did they play
4. I didn't leave . . . Did I / you leave
5. They didn't wear . . . Did they wear
6. We didn't have . . . Did we / you have
7. It wasn't . . . Was it
8. You weren't . . . Were you / Was I

Exercise 3, p. 27.

(Answers may vary.)

2. I didn't come . . . I came . . . .
3. The students in this class didn't swim . . . They walked . . . .
4. (_____) isn't . . . He/She is a teacher.
5. I didn't sleep . . . I slept in a bed.
6. The Internet didn't become . . . It became popular in the 1990s.

Exercise 4, p. 27.

1. French, together, last week
2. yesterday, last summer
3. in the evening, behind the mountains
4. our class, yesterday
5. two weeks ago

Exercise 5, p. 28.

1. wasn't		6. wasn't
2. was		7. was
3. weren't		8. was
4. were		9. were
5. was		10. weren't

Exercise 6, p. 28.

Part I.

giving   hitting   dying   trying

Part II.

stopped   studied   enjoyed   tied

Exercise 7, p. 29.

1. waiting . . . waited
2. cleaning . . . cleaned
3. planting . . . planted
4. planning . . . planned
5. hoping . . . hoped
6. hopping . . . hopped
7. playing . . . played
8. studying . . . studied
9. trying . . . tried
10. dying . . . died
11. sleeping
12. running

Exercise 8, p. 30.

2. opening
3. opened
4. listening . . . listened
5. lying
6. enjoyed
7. enjoying
8. happened

Exercise 9, p. 30.

2. stayed . . . stayed . . . staying
4. gave . . . given . . . giving
5. was / were . . . been . . . being

Exercise 10, p. 33.

Sample answers:

1. rode . . . took
2. froze
3. chose
4. hung
5. rang . . . woke
6. rose . . . set
7. sent
8. taught
9. stole
10. caught
11. shook
12. flew
13. dug
14. spent
15. wore

Exercise 11, p. 34.

2. We left . . . We didn't leave . . . Did we leave
3. She does . . . She didn't do . . . Did she do
4. He was . . . He wasn't . . . Was he
5. We drove . . . We didn't drive . . . Did we (you) drive
6. You were . . . You weren't . . . Were you (Was I)
7. I planned . . . I didn't plan . . . Did I (you) plan

Exercise 12, p. 34.

2. Yes, I fell down.
3. Yes, I hurt myself when I fell down.
4. Yes, I broke my arm.
5. Yes, I went to the emergency room.
6. Yes, I saw a doctor.
7. Yes, I sat in the waiting room for a long time.
8. Yes, the doctor put a cast on my arm.
9. Yes, I paid a lot of money.
10. Yes, I came home exhausted.

Exercise 13, p. 34.

2. A: Did Ella's plane arrive
   B: it did . . . got
3. A: Did you go
   B: I didn't . . . stayed . . . didn't feel
4. A: Did you eat
   B: I didn't . . . didn't have . . . didn't ring
5. A: Did da Vinci paint
   B: he did . . . painted

Exercise 14, p. 35.

Part I.

3. didn't ride
4. got
5. didn't watch
6. made
7. brought
8. didn't read
9. didn't fix

Part II.

3. took
4. didn't go
5. fell
6. came
7. didn't lie
8. thought
9. didn't begin
10. finished

Exercise 16, p. 37.

2. did . . . spent
3. did . . . met
4. did . . . sold
5. did . . . broke
6. did . . . kept
7. did . . . read
8. did . . . lost
9. did . . . found
10. did . . . upset

Exercise 17, p. 37.

2. had
3. ate
4. drank
5. met
6. shook
7. danced
8. sat . . . talked

Exercise 18, p. 38.

The Daily News

Yesterday morning, Jake read the newspaper online. He wanted to know the latest news. He enjoyed the business section most. His wife, Eva, didn't read any newspapers on her computer. She downloaded them on her ebook reader. She looked at the front pages first. She didn't have a lot of time. She finished the articles later in the day. Both Jake and Eva were very knowledgeable about the day's events.

Exercise 19, p. 38.

Part II.

1. T
2. F
3. F

Part III.

1. kills
2. killed
3. began
4. lasted
5. spread
6. died
7. kill
8. were
9. was
10. made

Exercise 20, p. 39.
Part I.
1. different   3. different
2. same   4. same

Part II.
1. /t/   3. /t/
2. /d/   4. /əd/

Exercise 21, p. 39.
1. agree   5. ended
2. agreed   6. stopped
3. arrived   7. touched
4. explains

Exercise 22, p. 40.
1. every day.   4. last weekend.
2. last week.   5. every day.
3. six days a week. 6. yesterday.

Exercise 23, p. 40.
2. /d/   6. /t/   10. /t/
3. /əd/   7. /d/   11. /d/
4. /t/   8. /t/   12. /əd/
5. /əd/   9. /əd/

Exercise 24, p. 40.
Sample answers:
1. He went to a water-slide park and loved the fast slides.
2. She visited her aunt.

Exercise 25, p. 41.
1. b
2. a

Exercise 26, p. 43.
2. was eating . . . came
3. came . . . was eating
4. was sleeping
5. was sleeping . . . rang
6. rang . . . was sleeping
7. began
8. was walking . . . saw
9. saw . . . was standing . . . was holding
10. waved . . . saw

Exercise 27, p. 44.
3. spilled . . . was sitting
4. was standing . . . sent
5. ran into . . . was standing
6. dropped . . . was standing
7. avoided . . . was swimming
8. was swimming . . . saw
9. was swimming . . . found

Exercise 29, p. 45.
1. Julia
2. James
3. Paul

Exercise 30, p. 46.
1. F   4. F
2. T   5. F
3. F

Exercise 31, p. 46.
1. B: Did you find . . . was looking . . . didn't see
   A: It's
2. A: looks . . . Did you
   B: thought . . . had . . . guess
3. A: Did you have
   B: had
   A: were
   B: was . . . was

Exercise 32, p. 47.
Underlined verbs:
2. were traveling
3. A: was . . . talking
   B: were describing
4. A: 's (is) . . . talking
   B: 's (is) describing

Exercise 33, p. 47.
2. is doing   11. looks
3. isn't studying   13. was doing
4. is staring   14. wasn't studying
5. wants   15. was staring
6. is looking   16. wanted
7. are you looking   17. was looking
8. am watching   18. pointed
9. is turning   19. said
10. is   20. offered

Exercise 34, p. 48.
Checked sentences: 1, 2, 3

Exercise 35, p. 49.
Clauses: 2, 3, 4, 5, 6, 7

Exercise 36, p. 49.
1. b. <u>I remembered my coat in the backseat</u> (2) <u>after the taxi dropped me off</u> (1).

2. a. <u>Before I got out of the taxi</u> (2), <u>I double-checked the address</u> (1).

   b. <u>Before I double-checked the address</u> (2), <u>I got out of the taxi</u> (1).

3. a. <u>As soon as I tipped the driver,</u> ² <u>he helped me with</u>
        <u>my luggage.</u>

    b. ¹ <u>As soon as the driver helped me with my luggage,</u>
        ² <u>I tipped him.</u>

Exercise 37, p. 49.

2. Before I left my apartment this morning, I
   unplugged the coffee pot.
   I unplugged the coffee pot before I left my
   apartment this morning.
3. Until I was seven years old, I lived on a farm.
   I lived on a farm until I was seven years old.
4. As soon as I heard the doorbell, I opened the door.
   I opened the door as soon as I heard the doorbell.
5. When it began to rain, I stood under my umbrella.
   I stood under my umbrella when it began to rain.
6. While I was lying in bed with the flu, my friends
   were swimming at the beach.
   My friends were swimming at the beach while I was
   lying in bed with the flu.
   While my friends were swimming at the beach, I was
   lying in bed with the flu.
   I was lying in bed with the flu while my friends were
   swimming at the beach.

Exercise 38, p. 50.

2. bought . . . went
   [before I went to the hospital to visit my friend]
3. went . . . got . . . was . . . was planting . . . was . . .
   was changing . . . were playing . . . was changing . . .
   were throwing
   [When I got there]
   [while Mr. Lopez was changing the oil in the car]
4. hit . . . was using . . . hurt
   [while I was using the hammer]
5. heard . . . began
   [As soon as we heard about the hurricane]
6. got . . . stopped . . . rested . . . felt
   [until he felt strong enough to continue]

Exercise 39, p. 51.

2. need	11. was reaching
3. call	12. lost
4. is sitting	13. ran
5. came	14. stopped
6. was	15. is
7. had	16. isn't
8. was driving	17. needs
9. rang	18. feels
10. reached	19. made

Exercise 41, p. 52.

2. used to think
3. did you use/used to live
4. Did you use/used to work

5. didn't use to wake up / didn't used to wake up . . .
   used to sleep
6. used to watch . . . didn't use to watch / didn't used
   to watch . . . did you use to watch / did you used to
   watch

Exercise 43, p. 53.

2. did you used to go/did you use to go
3. used to play
4. used to skip
5. didn't used to like/didn't use to like

Exercise 44, p. 53.

2. Junko used to **work** for an investment company.
3. **Margo used** to teach English, but now she works at
   a publishing company.
4. Where **did** you used to live?
5. I **didn't used/use** to get up early, but now I do.
6. **Did** you used to live in Singapore?
7. My family used to **go** to the beach every weekend,
   but now we don't.

Exercise 45, p. 54.

1. F	4. T
2. T	5. F
3. F	

Chapter **3**: Future Time

Exercise 1, p. 55.

Sentences: 1, 3

Exercise 2, p. 56.

1. yes	5. no
2. yes	6. no
3. no	7. yes
4. yes	8. yes

Exercise 4, p. 57.

1. am going to pick
2. A: is Alex going to go
   B: is going to stop
3. A: Are you going to finish
   B: I am going to finish
4. A: is Dr. Ahmad going to talk
   B: is going to discuss
5. A: are you going to call
   B: am not going to call . . . am going to text

Exercise 5, p. 57.

Questions:
1. Where are you going to go . . .
2. What time are you going to wake up . . .
3. What are you going to have . . .
4. Are you going to be . . .

5. Where are you going to be . . .
6. Are you going to become . . .
7. Are you going to take . . .
8. Are you going to do . . .

Exercise 6, p. 58.

2. are going to
3. are going to
4. are you going to
5. are going to
6. Are
7. going to
8. is
9. going to
10. is
11. going to
12. are going to

Exercise 7, p. 58.

1. What did you do yesterday? (*also possible:* were you doing)
2. What are you going to do tomorrow? [*Note:* The present progressive (*are you doing*) can replace *going to.*]
3. What are you doing right now?
4. What do you do every day?
5. What are you going to do a week from now?
6. What did you do the day before yesterday? (were you doing)
What were you doing the day before yesterday?
7. What are you going to do the day after tomorrow?
8. What did you do last week? (were you doing)
9. What do you do every week?
10. What are you going to do this weekend?

Exercise 10, p. 60.

2. You'll
3. We'll
4. He'll
5. it'll
6. They'll
7. She'll

Exercise 11, p. 61.

2. will make
3. will call
4. will help
5. will be
6. will cost
7. will explain

Exercise 12, p. 61.

1. 50%
2. 50%
3. 100%
4. 90%
5. 100%
6. 100%

Exercise 13, p. 62.

1. 100%
2. 90%
3. 50%
4. 90%
5. 100%
6. 50%

Exercise 14, p. 63.

2. She probably won't go / She probably isn't going to go to work tomorrow.
She'll probably stay / She is probably going to stay home and rest.
3. He'll probably go / He is probably going to go to bed early tonight.
He probably won't stay / He probably isn't going to stay up all night again tonight.

4. She probably won't run / isn't going to run in the marathon race this week.
She'll probably skip / She is probably going to skip the race.

Exercise 15, p. 63.

2. Maybe Lisa won't get here.
3. You may win the contest.
4. Maybe the plane will land early.
5. Sergio may not pass the class.

Exercise 18, p. 64.

2. will
3. will
4. will
5. won't
6. will
7. will
8. won't
9. will

Exercise 19, p. 65.

Conversation 1

Exercise 20, p. 66.

1. no
2. yes
3. no
4. yes
5. no
6. yes
7. A: yes
   B: no

Exercise 21, p. 66.

1. I'm going to be away for three weeks.
2. My husband and I are going to stay in small towns and camp on the beach.
3. We're going to bring a tent.
4. We're going to celebrate our wedding anniversary there.
5. My father, who was born in Thailand, is going to join us, but he's going to stay in a hotel.

Exercise 22, p. 66.

3. am going to
4. will (I'll)
5. am going to
6. will (I'll)
7. are going to
8. will (I'll)
9. will (I'll)

Exercise 23, p. 67.

1. a
2. b
3. b
4. a

Exercise 25, p. 68.

2. returns
3. lands
4. find
5. are
6. find out
7. isn't . . . is

Exercise 26, p. 69.

2. is going to call . . . returns
3. go . . . am going to make
4. are going to take . . . visits
5. am going to keep . . . calls
6. misses . . . isn't going to understand
7. gets . . . are going to eat

Exercise 28, p. 70.

2. Before Sue picks up groceries, she is going to go to the dentist.
3. Before Sue has lunch with Hiro, she is going to pick up groceries.
4. After Sue picks up groceries, she is going to have lunch with Hiro.
5. Before Sue takes her father to his doctor's appointment, she is going to have lunch with Hiro.

Exercise 29, p. 70.

Sample answers:
1. will see changing scenery
2. will turn on the lights
3. the lights will be on
4. will remember the temperature a person likes
5. he/she can lock the doors with a remote control
6. will move
7. will deliver warm clothes
8. will be inexpensive

Exercise 30, p. 71.

2. goes . . . will email / is going to email
3. went . . . took
4. was taking . . . rang
5. rang . . . jumped
6. gets . . . will brush
7. brushes . . . gets

Exercise 31, p. 71.

All three sentences express future time.

Exercise 32, p. 72.

1. B: are you doing
   A: am going . . . are going
   B: am meeting
2. A: are you majoring
   B: am majoring
   A: are you taking
   B: am taking
3. A: are you doing
   B: am cutting

Exercise 33, p. 73.

A: am going
B: are . . . going
B: Are . . . flying . . . driving
A: 'm flying
A: 'm taking
B: 'm staying

Exercise 36, p. 74.

1. a, b
2. a, b, c
3. b, c
4. a, c

Exercise 37, p. 74.

1. a, b, c
2. b, c
3. b, c
4. a, b, c
5. b, c
6. a, b, c
7. a, b, c
8. b, c
9. b, c
10. a, b, c

Exercise 38, p. 75.

Picture B

Exercise 39, p. 76.

(Answers may vary.)
1. The chimpanzee is about to eat a banana.
2. The man is about to pour coffee.
3. The plane is about to land.
4. The man is about to answer/pick up the phone.
5. The dog is about to go to sleep.
6. The man is about to start a fire.
7. The woman is about to hit a fly.
8. The man is about to leave.
9. The astronauts are about to meet creatures from outer space.

Exercise 41, p. 77.

1. a, b
2. f

Exercise 42, p. 77.

1. was reading . . . listening
2. will move . . . look . . . graduates
3. calls . . . complains
4. is crying . . . laughing
5. get . . . am going to take . . . go
6. was carrying . . . climbing . . . landed . . . stung . . . dropped . . . spilled

Exercise 43, p. 78.

1. was raining . . . took . . . got . . . found
2. opens . . . leave
3. A: cut . . . is bleeding
   B: 'll / will get
4. A: is ringing
   B: know
   A: Do you want
   B: don't answer
5. A: is . . . are flashing
   B: know . . . know . . . see
   A: is going . . . Are you speeding
   B: am driving
   A: is passing (*also possible:* is going to pass)

Exercise 44, p. 79.

B: does . . . say
A: will receive
B: will be . . . want
C: solves . . . don't understand . . . I'll . . . smile
D: work . . . will be
A: looks . . . will have

Exercise 45, p. 79.

My Cousin Pablo

I want to tell you about Pablo. He **is** my cousin. He **came** here four years ago. Before he came here, he **studied** statistics in Chile. He **left** Chile and **moved** here. Then he went to New York and **stayed** there for three years. He graduated from New York University. Now he **is studying** at this school. After he **finishes** his master's degree, he **will/is going to** return to Chile.

Chapter 4: Present Perfect and Past Perfect

Exercise 1, p. 81.
3. helped
4. visited
7. written
8. seen

Exercise 2, p. 82.
1. called
2. spoken
3. done
4. known
5. met
6. come
7. eaten
8. cut
9. read
10. been

Exercise 3, p. 82.
2. had
3. thought
4. taught
5. lived
6. heard
7. studied
8. died
9. bought
10. started

Exercise 4, p. 82.
1. a
2. b

Exercise 5, p. 84.
3. since
4. since
5. for
6. for
7. for
8. since
9. for
10. for
11. since
12. since
13. since
14. for
15. since
16. for
17. for
18. since
19. since
20. since

Exercise 7, p. 85.
2. has interviewed
3. has met
4. has found
5. has made
6. has become
7. has signed
8. has shaken
9. has written
10. has thought

Exercise 9, p. 86.
2. has changed . . . started
3. was . . . have been
4. haven't slept . . . left

5. met . . . has not thought
6. has had . . . bought
7. A: have you eaten . . . got
   B: have eaten

Exercise 11, p. 87.
2. A: Have you ever stayed
   B: have . . . have stayed
3. A: Have you ever met
   B: haven't . . . have never met
4. A: Has Ted ever traveled
   B: has . . . has traveled
5. A: Has Lara ever been
   B: hasn't . . . has never been

Exercise 12, p. 88.
1. seen
2. flown
3. ridden
4. done
5. torn
6. had
7. fallen
8. felt
9. spoken
10. wanted

Exercise 13, p. 88.
Questions: Have you ever . . .
1. cut your own hair?
2. caught a big fish?
3. taken care of an injured animal?
4. lost something very important?
5. sat on a bee?
6. flown in a private plane?
7. broken your arm or your leg?
8. found something very valuable?
9. swum near a shark?
10. thrown a ball and broken a window?

Exercise 14, p. 89.
Questions: How long have you . . .
1. lived in (_____)?
2. studied English?
3. been in this class/at this school?
4. had long hair/short hair?
5. had a beard/a mustache?
6. worn glasses/contact lenses?
7. had a roommate/a pet?
8. been interested in (_____)?
9. been married?

Exercise 15, p. 89.
1. b
2. a
3. b
4. a

Exercise 16, p. 91.
1. a, b
2. b, d
3. a, b, c

Exercise 17, p. 91.
2. given
3. changed
4. taken
5. woken
6. done
7. been

Exercise 18, p. 92.
2. No, he hasn't picked up his kids at school yet.
3. Yes, he has already taken his car for an oil change.
4. No, he hasn't finished his errands yet.
5. Yes, he has already shopped for groceries.
6. No, he hasn't had lunch with Michael yet.

Exercise 19, p. 92.
1. is
2. has
3. is
4. is
5. has
6. has

Exercise 20, p. 93.
1. you've done
2. I've worked
3. I've worked
4. I've worked
5. I've done
6. have you changed
7. have you applied
8. I've been
9. I've heard

Exercise 21, p. 94.
Pamela

Exercise 23, p. 95.
3. present perfect . . . unspecified
4. simple past . . . specified
5. simple past . . . specified
6. present perfect . . . unspecified
7. present perfect . . . unspecified
8. simple past . . . specified
9. present perfect . . . unspecified
10. simple past . . . specified

Exercise 24, p. 95.
3. have . . . have eaten . . . ate
4. have already seen . . . saw
5. have already written . . . wrote
6. A: Has Antonio ever had
   B: has . . . has had . . . had
7. have already read . . . read
8. A: have you visited
   B: have visited . . . visited . . . was

Exercise 26, p. 97.
1. spent
2. made
3. sent
4. left
5. slept
6. driven
7. sung

Exercise 29, p. 99.
2. is waiting . . . has been waiting
3. are talking . . . have been talking
4. are doing . . . have been doing

5. A: are you doing
   B: am working
   A: have you been working
   B: have been working

Exercise 31, p. 100.
2. month has
3. parents have
4. cousins have
5. friend has
6. friends have
7. work has
8. roommate has

Exercise 32, p. 100
a. 1
b. 3
c. 1

Exercise 33, p. 102.
4. have been reading
5. have read
6. have stayed
7. has been crying
8. has been teaching / has taught
9. A: has been playing / has played
   B: have been playing / have played
10. B: has been working / has worked
    B: has worked

Exercise 34, p. 103.
1. has
2. been changing
3. We've
4. had
5. have
6. seen
7. have been building
8. We've been saying
9. We've
10. seen

Exercise 35, p. 103.
Checked sentences:
1. a, b
2. a
3. b
4. a, c
5. d, e

Exercise 36, p. 104.
1. b
2. b
3. a
4. a

Exercise 38, p. 105.
1. b
2. c
3. b, c
4. b
5. b, c

Exercise 39, p. 106.
1. F
2. T
3. T
4. F
5. F

Exercise 40, p. 107.

2. am
3. am studying
4. have been
5. arrived
6. began
7. came
8. have done
9. have met
10. went
11. met
12. spoke
13. didn't practice
14. were
15. came
16. have met
17. know
18. have become

Exercise 41, p. 108.
Answer b.

Exercise 42, p. 109.

3. a. 1st
   b. 2nd
4. a. 2nd
   b. 1st
5. a. 1st
   b. 2nd
6. a. 2nd
   b. 1st
7. a. 1st
   b. 2nd

Exercise 43, p. 110.

1. has
2. had
3. had
4. have

Exercise 44, p. 110.

2. I started English classes at this school four weeks ago and I **have been learning / have learned** a lot of English since then.
3. I **have wanted** to learn English since I **was** a child.
4. I have been thinking about how to improve my English skills quickly since I came here, but I **haven't** found a good way.
5. Our teacher likes to give tests. We **have had** six tests since the beginning of the term.
6. I like learning English. When I was young, my father found an Australian girl to teach my brothers and me English, but when I **moved** to another city, my father didn't find anyone to teach us.
7. I **have met** many friends in this class. I **met** Abdul in the cafeteria on the first day. He was friendly and kind. We **have been** friends since that day.
8. Abdul **has** been **studying** English **for** three months. His English is better than mine.

Chapter 5: Asking Questions

Exercise 1, p. 111.

1. b
2. d

Exercise 2, p. 111.

1. Is . . . is
2. Do . . . do
3. Did . . . did
4. Was . . . wasn't
5. Is . . . is
6. Are . . . am
7. Was . . . was
8. Have . . . haven't
9. Will . . . will

Exercise 3, p. 112.

2. A: Do snakes have legs?
   B: they don't
3. A: Is Mexico in North America
   B: it is
4. A: Will you be at home tonight?
   B: I won't.
5. A: Do you have a bike?
   B: I do
6. A: Has Simon left?
   B: Yes, he has.
7. A: Did Simon leave with Kate?
   B: Yes, he did.
8. A: Does acupuncture relieve pain?
   B: Yes, it does.

Exercise 4, p. 113.

1. b
2. a
3. b
4. c
5. b

Exercise 5, p. 113.
Questions:

1. Do you like animals?
2. Have you ever had a pet snake?
3. Is it cold in this room?
4. Is it raining right now?
5. Did you sleep well last night?
6. Are you tired right now?
7. Will you be here next year?

Exercise 6, p. 113.

1. Is she
2. Is he
3. Is that
4. Is there
5. Did it
6. Has it
7. Does it

Exercise 7, p. 114.

1. a, c
2. a, d
3. b, c

Exercise 8, p. 115.

2. Do they live a simple life?   b
3. What do they pick from the trees?   a
4. Do they have electricity?   a
5. Do they enjoy their life?   a
7. Are they happy?   b

Exercise 9, p. 116.

1. Do you know
2. I do
3. Have you seen
4. I haven't.
5. Did they go
6. they did
7. Are you going to see
8. I am
9. Will they be
10. they won't

Exercise 10, p. 116.
1. Where . . . b
2. Why . . . c
3. When . . . a

Exercise 11, p. 117.
2. are your kids transferring to
   are your kids transferring to Lakeview Elementary
   School
3. will you meet Taka at the mall
   will you meet Taka at 10:00
4. does class begin
   does class begin
5. did you stay home from work
   did you stay home from work

Exercise 12, p. 118.
1. How come you are going?
   What are you going for?
2. How come they came?
   What did they come for?
3. How come he needs more money?
   What does he need more money for?
4. How come they are going to leave?
   What are they going to leave for?

Exercise 13, p. 118.
1. When did Tom get home?
2. Where was his wife?
3. What did Tom buy?
4. Why was Tom late?
5. What present did Nina get?

Exercise 14, p. 118.
1. c   4. b
2. b   5. a
3. a

Exercise 15, p. 118.
1. b   3. c
2. d   4. a

Exercise 16, p. 119.
3. Who knocked on the door?
4. Who(m) did Talya meet?
5. What did Mike learn?
6. What changed Gina's mind?
7. Who(m) is Gina talking about?
8. What is Gina talking about?

Exercise 17, p. 120.
1. Who   4. What
2. What   5. Who
3. Who   6. Who

Exercise 18, p. 120.
Questions:
1. What   5. What
2. What   6. What
3. Who   7. Who
4. What

Exercise 19, p. 120.
1. What did he   4. What did he
2. Did he tell   5. Why . . . you tell
3. Who did he

Exercise 22, p. 121.
2. What did you do
3. What are you going to do
4. What do you want to do
5. What would you like to do
6. What are you doing
7. What do you do
8. A: What do you do . . . A: What does . . . do

Exercise 25, p. 123.
3. Which pen / Which one / Which would you like?
4. What did Hassan borrow from you?
5. What do you have in your hand?
   Which piece / Which one / Which would you like?
6. What did Tony buy?
7. What / Which countries did you visit?
   Which country did you enjoy the most?

Exercise 27, p. 125.
1. b
2. a

Exercise 29, p. 126.
1. Who's   4. Who's
2. Whose   5. Whose
3. Whose   6. Who's

Exercise 30, p. 126.
1. Whose   4. Whose
2. Who's   5. Who's
3. Who's   6. Whose

Exercise 31, p. 126.
1. e   4. b
2. d   5. c
3. a

Exercise 32, p. 127.
(*Answers may vary.*)
1. He's very tall. He's six foot, six inches (2 meters).
2. He's fourteen years old.
3. He doesn't sleep well.
4. He's very uncomfortable.
5. He likes / prefers to travel by train.

Exercise 33, p. 128.
2. How important is education?
3. How did you get to school?
4. How deep is the ocean?
5. How are you going to get to Buenos Aires?
6. How difficult was the test?
7. How high is Mt. Everest?
8. How did you get here?

Exercise 34, p. 128.
1. How fresh
2. How cheap
3. How hard
4. How clean
5. How hot
6. How noisy
7. How serious

Exercise 35, p. 129.
1. c
2. d
3. b
4. a
5. e

Exercise 37, p. 130.
1. How old are
2. How tall are
3. How much do
4. how well do
5. How quickly do
6. How often do
7. How tired are
8. How many times a week do
9. How are
10. How soon can

Exercise 38, p. 131.
1. 774 miles / 1,250 kilometers
2. 227 miles
3. 1,030 kilometers

Exercise 39, p. 131.
2. How far is it from Montreal to Quebec?
3. How far is it from here to the post office?
4. How far do you live from work?

Exercise 43, p. 133.
2. How long will Mr. McNally be in the hospital?
3. How long does it take to learn a second language?
4. How long have you been living here?
5. How long did you live in Oman?
6. How long have you known Mr. Pham?
7. How long has he been living in Canada?

Exercise 44, p. 134.
1. is
2. will
3. did
4. are

Exercise 46, p. 135.
1. Who are
2. How are
3. What did
4. Why did
5. Why is
6. Why are
7. When will
8. Who will
9. When is
10. How will

Exercise 47, p. 135.
1. Where are you
2. Who are you
3. Who is
4. How long have you
5. Where did you
6. Where does he
7. Is he
8. What time will you
9. Why are you
10. Why are you
11. Why am I

Exercise 48, p. 136.
1. What do you
2. What are you
3. What are you
4. What are you
5. What do you
6. What are you
7. What do you
8. What do you

Exercise 49, p. 136.
1. a
2. a
3. 1, 2

Exercise 52, p. 138.
A: <u>Let's invite the Thompsons over for dinner.</u>
B: Good idea! <u>How about next Sunday?</u>
A: <u>Let's do it sooner.</u> <u>What about this Saturday?</u>

Exercise 53, p. 138.
1. a
2. c
3. b
4. a

Exercise 55, p. 139.
1. yes
2. no

Exercise 56, p. 140.
1. a
2. a
3. a

Exercise 57, p. 141.
1. b. doesn't
   c. don't
   d. doesn't
   e. isn't
   f. aren't
   g. does
   h. is
   i. aren't

2. a. didn't c. were
   b. did d. wasn't

3. a. aren't d. weren't
   b. is e. was
   c. is

4. a. hasn't d. hasn't
   b. haven't e. has
   c. have f. hasn't

Exercise 59, p. 142.
Expected answers:
1. Yes. 6. Yes.
2. Yes. 7. Yes.
3. Yes. 8. No.
4. No. 9. Yes.
5. No. 10. No.

Exercise 60, p. 142.
2. Where **do I** buy subway tickets?
3. Whose **backpack is that**?
4. What kind of tea **do you** like best?
5. It's freezing out and you're not wearing gloves, **are** you?
6. Who **did you study** with at school?
7. She is going to work this weekend, **isn't** she?
8. How long **does it** take to get to the airport from here?
9. How **tall is your father**?
10. It's midnight. Why **are** you so late? Why **did** you forget to call?

Exercise 61, p. 143.
1. b 6. b
2. a 7. c
3. a 8. a
4. c 9. b
5. b 10. b

Exercise 63, p. 144.
(Answers may vary.)
1. He wanted husbands for them.
2. A frog claimed Trina because he found the diamond.
3. She ran away from the castle and went to live in the woods.
4. She met him in a lake.
5. She felt great affection for him.
6. The evil wizard changed a man from a prince into a frog.
7. They had unhappy lives.
8. They lived happily ever after.

Chapter 6: Nouns and Pronouns

Exercise 1, p. 146.
5. pronoun 9. adjective
6. noun 10. pronoun
7. adjective 11. noun
8. preposition 12. preposition

Exercise 2, p. 146.
1. two 3. two 5. two
2. one 4. one 6. two

Exercise 3, p. 147.
1. chairs 8. leaves
2. window 9. half
3. wishes 10. beliefs
4. dish 11. wolves
5. taxes 12. radios
6. boys 13. sheep
7. hobbies 14. foot

Exercise 4, p. 148.
People
babies	heroes
boys	thieves
children	women
girls	

Food
fish	sandwiches
potatoes	tomatoes

Things people catch
fish	mosquitoes
mice	thieves

Places people visit
cities	zoos
libraries	

Exercise 5, p. 149.
supplies	dresses
shirts	outfits
jeans	shoes
pants	babies

Exercise 6, p. 149.
1. no 4. no
2. yes 5. yes
3. yes 6. no

Exercise 7, p. 150.
1. /s/ 4. /z/
2. /z/ 5. /əz/
3. /əz/ 6. /s/

14 Student Book Answer Key

Chapter 6

Exercise 8, p. 150.
1. different
2. same
3. same
4. different
5. same
6. same
7. different
8. different

Exercise 9, p. 150.
3. /z/
4. /s/
5. /əz/
6. /z/
7. /s/
8. /əz/
9. /z/

Exercise 10, p. 150.
1. sizes
2. fax
3. faxes
4. price
5. glasses
6. prize

Exercise 12, p. 151.

3. | Cows | eat | grass |
   | subject | verb | object of verb |

4. | The actor | sang | *(none)* |
   | subject | verb | object of verb |

5. | The actor | sang | a song |
   | subject | verb | object of verb |

6. | Accidents | happen | *(none)* |
   | subject | verb | object of verb |

7. | The accident | injured | a woman |
   | subject | verb | object |

Exercise 13, p. 152.
3. noun
4. verb
5. verb
6. noun
7. verb
8. noun
9. noun
10. verb

Exercise 15, p. 153.
Checked sentences:
2. in a <u>minute</u>
4. down the <u>hill</u>
5. next to the <u>phone</u>
7. in a few <u>hours</u>
8. from my <u>parents</u>

Exercise 16, p. 153.

         P   Obj. of P
2. a. Kimiko saw a picture on the wall.

            P   Obj. of P
   c. Kimiko looked at the picture closely.

          P   Obj. of P
3. b. Annika lost her ring in the sand.

          P Obj. of P P Obj. of P
   c. Annika lost her ring in the sand   at the beach.

           P   Obj. of P
4. a. A talkative woman sat with her husband.

       P   Obj. of P
   b. We were at a meeting.

         P   Obj. of P
   c. She talked to her husband the entire time.

Exercise 19, p. 155.
1. Birds and insects.
2. The understory is above the ground and under leaves.
3. In the understory.
4. The emergent layer is the top layer. It gets sun. The understory is lower. It is dark and cool, etc.

Exercise 21, p. 156.
1. in
2. in
3. in
4. at
5. on
6. on
7. on
8. at
9. at
10. on
11. on
12. in
13. in
14. in
15. in
16. at
17. at
18. in

Exercise 22, p. 157.
Completed questions:
1. in
2. at
3. on
4. on
5. on
6. in
7. in

Exercise 23, p. 157.
1. a, c
2. a, b

Exercise 24, p. 157.
1. to Paris next month
2. through Turkey last week
3. Alexi works at his uncle's bakery on Saturday mornings
4. My plane arrived at the airport in the early morning

Exercise 25, p. 158.
1. Ø
2. s
3. Ø
4. s
5. Ø
6. Ø

Exercise 26, p. 159.
1. barks
2. bark
3. roar
4. roar
5. hisses
6. chirps
7. meow
8. bark
9. hisses
10. chirp

Exercise 27, p. 159.

         S   V
3. <u>Every student</u> in my class speaks English well.

        S   V
  <u>All students</u> in my class speak . . .

              V   S
4. (There) are <u>five students</u> from Korea in Mr. Ahmad's class.

             V   S
5. (There)'s <u>a vacant apartment</u> in my building.
   (no changes)

6. Do (aux verb) <u>people</u>^S in your neighborhood know^V
each other?

7. <u>The neighbors</u>^S in the apartment next to mine are^V
very friendly and helpful.

Exercise 28, p. 159.
1. s	8. s	15. s
2. s	9. Ø	16. Ø
3. s	10. s	17. s
4. s	11. s	18. s
5. s	12. Ø	19. s
6. Ø	13. s	20. Ø
7. Ø	14. s	

Exercise 30, p. 160.
Checked phrases:
3. <u>famous</u>
4. <u>small</u>, <u>dark</u>, <u>smelly</u>
6. <u>long</u>, <u>short</u>

Exercise 31, p. 160.
1. Red roses are beautiful flowers.
2. The waiter poured hot coffee into my empty cup.
3. Mrs. Fields gave the hungry children a fresh snack.
4. After our delicious dinner, Frank helped me with
the dirty dishes.

Exercise 33, p. 161.
3. hot chicken
4. chicken recipe
5. chicken soup

Exercise 34, p. 162.
2. vegetable garden
3. bean soup
4. magazine articles
5. toy factory
6. mountain villages
7. art lesson
8. flag poles

Exercise 35, p. 162.
1. (*no change*)
2. computers
3. (*no change*)
4. Airplanes
5. Bicycles
6. (*no change*)
7. (*no change*)
8. vegetables

Exercise 37, p. 163.
1. subject
2. subject
3. object
4. object
5. object

Exercise 38, p. 164.
1. a. apples
   b. children
2. a. bees
   b. bees
   c. bees
3. a. table tennis
   b. table tennis
   c. my brother
   d. my brother

Exercise 39, p. 165.
1. me
2. me
3. I
4. me . . . us
5. them . . . They are

Exercise 40, p. 165.
2. He . . . them
3. They . . . her
4. it
5. They . . . them

Exercise 41, p. 166.
1. B
2. A

Exercise 42, p. 166.
2. more than one
3. more than one
4. one
5. more than one
6. one

Exercise 43, p. 167.
2. Lisa's
3. Lisa's
4. Monica's
5. William's
6. William's
7. Ned's
8. William's

Exercise 44, p. 167.
1. earth's   T
2. elephant's F [gray and wrinkled]
3. man's   T
4. woman's   T
5. women's   T
6. Men's   T [about 11% to 12% bigger]
7. person's   T
8. People's   F [Men's voices have a higher pitch.]

Exercise 45, p. 167.
Checked responses: 1, 2, 4, 5, 7, 8

Exercise 46, p. 168.
2. his
3. It's . . . its
4. its . . . its
5. Hers
6. her
7. mine
8. yours
9. A: my . . . yours
   B: mine . . . Yours . . . your
10. a. They
    b. Their
    c. Our . . . theirs
    d. They're . . . there . . . they're . . . their

Exercise 48, p. 170.
2. himself
3. yourself . . . themselves
4. itself
   (*also possible:* himself, herself)
5. ourselves
6. herself
7. yourself
8. myself

Exercise 49, p. 170.
1. yourself
2. ourselves
3. herself
4. themselves
5. himself
6. myself

Exercise 51, p. 171.
Picture B

Exercise 52, p. 172.
2. a. another
   b. The other
3. a. Another
   b. Another
   c. Another
   d. Another
4. another
5. The other
6. another

Exercise 53, p. 172.
1. Picture A
2. Picture B

Exercise 55, p. 174.
2. other
3. The others
4. The other
5. Others
6. Other . . . others
7. The other
8. The others

Exercise 56, p. 175.
(Answers may vary.)
1. One is by imagining a peaceful place. Another is deep breathing. Another is exercise.
2. It makes them tired.

Exercise 57, p. 176.
2. the other
3. Others
4. Other
5. Others . . . other
6. another
7. The other
8. another
9. The others
10. Other

Exercise 58, p. 176.
1. a
2. b
3. b
4. b
5. a

Exercise 59, p. 177.
B: other . . . others
A: the other . . . other

Exercise 60, p. 177.
2. I had some black **bean** soup for lunch.
3. The windows in our classroom **are** dirty.
4. People in Brazil **speak** Portuguese.
5. **There** are around 8,600 types of birds in the world.

6. My mother and father work in Milan. **They're teachers**.
7. Today many **women** are carpenters, pilots, and doctors.
8. **There** is a new student in our class. Have you met her?
9. There are two pools at the park. The smaller one is for **children**. The **other** (**one**) is for adults.
10. The highways in my country are **excellent**.
11. I don't like my apartment. **It's** in a bad neighborhood. **There is** a lot of crime. I'm going to move to **another** neighborhood.

Chapter 7: Modal Auxiliaries

Exercise 1, p. 178.
Correct sentences: 1, 4

Exercise 2, p. 179.
1. may come
2. should come
3. ought to come
4. will not (won't) come
5. could not (couldn't) come
6. might come
7. had better come
8. has to come
9. has got to come
10. is not (isn't) able to come

Exercise 3, p. 179.
3. Ø
4. Ø
5. to
6. Ø
7. to
8. Ø
9. to
10. Ø

Exercise 4, p. 179.
(Answers will vary.)

Exercise 5, p. 180.
1. can . . . can't
2. can . . . can't
3. can't . . . can
4. can . . . can't

1. A dog is able to swim, but it isn't able to fly.
2. A frog is able to live on land and in water, but a cat isn't (able to).
3. A bilingual person isn't able to speak three languages, but a trilingual person is (able to).
4. People with a Ph.D. degree are able to use "Dr." in front of their name, but people with a master's degree aren't (able to).

Exercise 7, p. 181.
1. can't understand
2. can help
3. Can you explain
4. can't figure
5. can do
6. Can you meet
7. can't meet

Exercise 9, p. 182.
Checked sentences:
Group A: 1, 2, 3
Group B: 4, 5
Group C: The sentences have different meanings; no checkmarks.

Exercise 10, p. 183.
2. may/might . . . may/might . . . possibility
3. may/can . . . permission
4. may/might . . . may/might . . . possibility

Exercise 11, p. 183.
1. It might snow tonight.
   Maybe it will snow tonight.
2. You may need to wear your boots.
   Maybe you will need to wear your boots.
3. There may be a blizzard.
   There might be a blizzard.

Exercise 13, p. 184.
1. ability
2. possibility
3. permission
4. possibility
5. permission

Exercise 14, p. 184.
1. a future possibility
2. a present possibility
3. a past ability

Exercise 15, p. 185.
2. Past, Ability
3. Present, Possibility
4. Past, Ability
5. Future, Possibility
6. Present, Possibility

Exercise 17, p. 186.
1. could be
2. might be
3. could ask
4. may be
5. can

Exercise 18, p. 186.
Checked sentences: 1, 2, 3

Exercise 19, p. 187.
1. B: Can / May I / Could I speak/talk
2. B: May I / Could I speak / talk
   (*possibly too informal:* Can I)
   A: May I / Could I ask
3. B: Can I talk (*more formal:* Could I)
4. B: May / Could / Can I help
5. B: Could / Can I speak / talk
   Can / Could I take
6. B: May / Could / Can I speak / talk
   B: May / Could / Can I leave

Exercise 21, p. 188.
Checked sentences: 1, 2, 4, 5
More polite sentences: 2, 5

Exercise 22, p. 189.
(*Answers may vary.*)
2. Formal: Could you please talk in another room?
   Informal: Can you be quiet?
3. Formal: Could you please check the bill? I think there's a mistake.
   Informal: Will you fix the bill? It has a mistake.

Exercise 26, p. 191.
(*Answers may vary.*)
More serious or urgent sentences: 1, 3

Exercise 28, p. 192.
2. Anna shouldn't **wear** shorts to work.
3. **I should go** to the post office today.
4. I ought **to pay** my bills today.
5. **You'd better call** the doctor today.
6. You **shouldn't** stay up too late tonight.
7. **You'd better** not **leave** your key in the door.
8. Mr. Lim is having a surprise party for his wife. He ought **to tell** people soon.

Exercise 30, p. 193.
Sentence 1 is more common in writing.
Sentences 2 and 3 are more common in speaking.

Exercise 32, p. 194.
1. has to
2. You don't have to . . . has to
3. You've got to
4. You've got to
5. You have to
6. You don't . . . have to
7. You don't have to
8. has to

Exercise 34, p. 195.
Sentence b.

Exercise 35, p. 196.
3. doesn't have to
4. doesn't have to
5. must not
6. don't have to
7. must not

Exercise 37, p. 197.
3. must
4. must not
5. must not
6. must
7. must
8. must

Exercise 38, p. 198.
(Answers may vary.)
2. She must be happy.
3. She must be cold.
4. She must love movies.
5. He must be hot.
6. He must be strong.

Exercise 40, p. 198.
1. must be
2. had to stay
3. have to work
4. must be

Exercise 41, p. 199.
3. can't
2. will
3. wouldn't
4. do

Exercise 42, p. 199.
1. can't
2. will
3. wouldn't
4. do
5. should
6. can't
7. wouldn't
8. doesn't
9. shouldn't
10. won't
11. could
12. don't

Exercise 43, p. 200.
Group 1 speaker: a police officer
Possible situation: a person speeding
Group 2 speaker: a doctor
Possible situation: a doctor examining a patient's throat

Exercise 44, p. 201.
(Sentence order may vary.) 3, 1, 4, 5, 7, 2, 8, 9, 6

Exercise 45, p. 201.
1. Write . . . Write . . . Write
2. Double
3. Add
4. Multiply
5. Add
6. Subtract

Exercise 47, p. 203.
Checked items: 2, 3

Exercise 50, p. 204.
Correct order:
1. go dancing
2. go to a movie
3. go to a restaurant

Exercise 52, p. 204.
4. to
5. than
6. than
7. to
8. than
9. than
10. than
11. to
12. than

Exercise 55, p. 206.
1. c
2. a
3. a
4. b
5. c
6. b
7. c
8. b
9. a
10. c
11. b
12. b
13. a
14. b
15. b
16. a
17. c
18. a

Chapter 8: Connecting Ideas

Exercise 1, p. 208.
Checked sentences: 2, 3, 5

Exercise 2, p. 209.
adjective + adjective
3. <u>wide</u> and <u>deep</u>

adjective + adjective + adjective
4. <u>wide</u>, <u>deep</u>, and <u>dangerous</u>

verb + verb + verb
5. <u>played</u> music, <u>ate</u> pizza, and <u>told</u> ghost stories

verb + verb
6. <u>played</u> music and <u>ate</u> pizza

noun + noun + noun + noun + noun
7. My <u>mom</u>, <u>dad</u>, <u>sister</u>, and <u>grandfather</u> . . . my <u>son</u> + noun
and <u>daughter</u>

verb + verb + verb
8. <u>mooed</u> like a cow, <u>roared</u> like a lion, and <u>barked</u> like a dog

Exercise 4, p. 210.
3. I talked. He listened.
4. I talked to Ryan about his school grades, and he listened to me carefully.
5. The five most common words in English are *the*, *and*, *of*, *to*, and *a*.
6. The man asked a question. The woman answered it.
7. The man asked a question, and the woman answered it.
8. Rome is an Italian city. It has a mild climate and many interesting attractions.
9. You should visit Rome. Its climate is mild, and there are many interesting attractions.

Exercise 6, p. 211.
4. , but
5. but
6. , and
7. and
8. , but
9. or
10. , or

Exercise 7, p. 211.
1. Laptops are electronic devices. Cell phones are electronic devices.
2. Laptops and portable DVD players are electronic devices, but flashlights aren't.
3. Passengers can't use these electronic devices during takeoffs and landings. They can use them the rest of the flight.
4. During takeoffs and landings, airlines don't allow passengers to use laptops, DVD players, electronic readers, or PDAs.
5. The devices may cause problems with the navigation system, and they may cause problems with the communication system.

Exercise 8, p. 211.

1. b
2. a

Exercise 9, p. 212.

3. so
4. but
5. but
6. so
7. so
8. but
9. but
10. so

Exercise 10, p. 212.

1. Some tarantulas can go two and a half years without food. When they eat, they like grasshoppers, beetles, small spiders, and sometimes small lizards.
2. A female elephant is pregnant for approximately twenty months and almost always has only one baby. A young elephant stays close to its mother for the first ten years of its life.
3. Dolphins sleep with one eye open. They need to be conscious or awake in order to breathe. If they fall asleep when they are breathing, they will drown, so they sleep with half their brain awake and one eye open.

Exercise 11, p. 213.

Paying It Forward

A few days ago, a friend and I were driving from Benton Harbor to Chicago. We didn't have any delays for the first hour, but we ran into some highway construction near Chicago. The traffic wasn't moving. My friend and I sat and waited. We talked about our jobs, our families, and the terrible traffic. Slowly it started to move.

We noticed a black sports car on the shoulder. Its right blinker was blinking. The driver obviously wanted to get back into traffic. Car after car passed without letting him in. I decided to do a good deed, so I motioned for him to get in line ahead of me. He waved thanks, and I waved back at him.

All the cars had to stop at a toll booth a short way down the road. I held out my money to pay my toll, but the tolltaker just smiled and waved me on. She told me that the man in the black sports car had already paid my toll. Wasn't that a nice way of saying thank you?

Exercise 13, p. 214.

Part I.

3. isn't
4. aren't
5. didn't
6. hasn't
7. haven't
8. isn't
9. aren't
10. won't

Part II.

3. is
4. are
5. did
6. has
7. have
8. is
9. are
10. will

Exercise 15, p. 215.

1. didn't
2. wasn't
3. did
4. didn't
5. could
6. can't
7. don't
8. won't

Exercise 16, p. 216.

1. B
2. B
3. C
4. C

Exercise 17, p. 217.

1. b. so does James.
2. a. Ivan doesn't either.
   b. neither does Ivan.
3. a. Omar is too.
   b. so is Omar.
4. a. James isn't either.
   b. neither is James.

Exercise 18, p. 217.

Part I.

2. do
3. is
4. are
5. did
6. has
7. have
8. is
9. are
10. will

Part II.

2. don't
3. isn't
4. aren't
5. didn't
6. has
7. have
8. is
9. are
10. will

Exercise 20, p. 219.

1. So did I.
2. So do I.
3. So would I.
4. Neither am I.
5. Neither have I.
6. So is . . .
7. Neither do . . .
8. So does . . .
9. So did I.
10. Neither do I.
11. So is . . .
12. Neither does . . .
13. Neither have I.
14. So do . . .
15. So can . . .
16. So would I.

Exercise 23, p. 220.

Logical completions: a, c

Exercise 24, p. 221.

2. The children were hungry because there was no food in the house. OR
   Because there was no food in the house, the children were hungry.
3. We can't get across the river because the bridge is closed. OR
   Because the bridge is closed, we can't get across the river.
4. My car didn't start because the battery was dead. OR
   Because the battery was dead, my car didn't start.

5. Tayla and Patti laughed hard because the joke was very funny. OR
Because the joke was very funny, Tayla and Patti laughed hard.

Exercise 25, p. 221.
2. Mr. El-Sayed had a bad cold. **B**ecause he was not feeling well, he stayed home from the office.
3. Judy went to bed early because she was tired. **S**he likes to get at least eight hours of sleep a night.
4. Frank put his head in his hands. **H**e was angry and upset because he had lost a lot of work on his computer.

Exercise 26, p. 222.
2. The room was hot, so I opened the window.
3. It was raining, so I stayed indoors.
5. Because the water in the river is polluted, we shouldn't go swimming there.
6. Because my alarm clock didn't go off, I was late for my job interview.

Exercise 27, p. 222.
2. Jim was hot and tired, so he sat in the shade.
3. Jim was hot, tired, and thirsty.
4. Because he was hot, Jim sat in the shade.
5. Because they were hot and thirsty, Jim and Susan sat in the shade and drank iced-tea.
6. (*no change*)
7. Jim sat in the shade, drank iced-tea, and fanned himself with his cap because he was hot, tired, and thirsty.
8. Because Jim was hot, he stayed under the shade of the tree, but Susan went back to work.

Exercise 28, p. 223.
Understanding the Scientific Term "Matter"

   The word *matter* is a chemical term. **M**atter is anything that has weight. **T**his book, your finger, water, a rock, air, and the moon are all examples of matter. **H**eat and radio waves are not matter because they do not have weight. **H**appiness, dreams, and fears have no weight and are not matter.

Exercise 29, p. 223.
Sentences: 1, 3

Exercise 30, p. 223.
1. a. isn't
   b. is
   c. is
2. a. didn't go
   b. didn't go
   c. went

Exercise 31, p. 224.
3. Even though
4. Because
5. Even though
6. Because
7. because
8. Because . . . even though
9. even though

Exercise 32, p. 224.
2. b
3. c
4. a
5. c
6. b

Exercise 33, p. 225.
1. c
2. b
3. a
4. b
5. c

Exercise 35, p. 226.
1. Because
2. Even though / Although
3. Even though / Although
4. so
5. Because
6. so

Exercise 36, p. 227.
2. Gold, silver, and **copper are** metals.
3. The children crowded around the **teacher because** he was doing a magic trick.
4. I had a cup of coffee, and so **did** my friend.
5. My roommate didn't go **and neither did I**. OR My roommate didn't go **and I didn't either**.
6. Even **though** I was exhausted, I didn't stop working until after midnight.
7. Although I like **chocolate, I** can't eat it because I'm allergic to it.
8. I like to eat raw eggs for breakfast, and everybody else in my family **does** too. OR . . . , and **so does** everybody else in my family.
9. A hardware store sells **tools, nails, plumbing supplies,** and **paint**.
10. Most insects have wings. **S**piders do not. OR Most insects have wings, but spiders do not.

Chapter 9: Comparisons

Exercise 1, p. 229.
1. E
2. B
3. C

Exercise 2, p. 230.
2. not nearly as
3. just as
4. almost as / not quite as
5. not nearly as
6. just as
7. almost as / not quite as

Exercise 3, p. 230.
(*Answers will vary.*)

Exercise 4, p. 231.
1. is as old as
2. isn't as old as
3. aren't as old as
4. isn't quite as old as
5. is almost as old as

Exercise 5, p. 232.
2. an ox
3. a bird
4. a mule
5. a rock
6. the hills
7. a cat
8. a feather
9. a kite
10. a hornet

Exercise 6, p. 233.
1. David
2. David/Paolo
3. Matt

Exercise 7, p. 233.
1. T
2. T
3. T
4. F [The Arctic Ocean is the coldest.]
5. F [The South China Sea is the biggest.]
6. T
7. F [Asia is the largest continent in the world.]
8. T
9. F [It's South America.]
10. T

Exercise 9, p. 234.
Sample answers:
2. A . . . C
3. B . . . A
4. C . . . A
5. C
6. A
7. C . . . A

Exercise 10, p. 236.
2. better, the best
3. lazier, the laziest
4. hotter, the hottest
5. neater, the neatest
6. later, the latest
7. happier, the happiest
8. more dangerous, the most dangerous
9. more slowly, the most slowly
10. more common, the most common
11. friendlier, the friendliest
12. more careful, the most careful
13. worse, the worst
14. farther / further, the farthest / the furthest

Exercise 11, p. 236.
2. funnier
3. more dangerous
4. more confusing
5. darker
6. cleaner
7. prettier
8. wetter

Exercise 12, p. 237.
1. younger
2. tallest
3. happy
4. happier
5. older
6. funniest
7. hard
8. hard

Exercise 13, p. 237.
2. b
3. b
4. a, b
5. a, b
6. b
7. a, b

Exercise 15, p. 238.
1. a
2. a
3. b
4. b
5. b
6. b
7. b
8. a
9. a

Exercise 17, p. 239.
2. she is / her
3. they are / them
4. he can / him
5. he did / him
6. she can / her
7. mine . . . hers
8. theirs . . . ours

Exercise 19, p. 240.
3. An airplane is **very** fast.
4. Taking an airplane is **much / a lot / far** faster than driving.
5. Learning a second language is **very** difficult for many people.
6. Learning a second language is **much / a lot / far** more difficult than learning chemistry formulas.
7. You can live **much / a lot / far** more inexpensively in student housing than in a rented apartment.
8. You can live **very** inexpensively in student housing.

Exercise 21, p. 241.
1. b
2. a, b
3. b
4. a, b
5. a, b
6. b

Exercise 23, p. 242.
1. a. F
   b. T
2. a. T
   b. F
3. a. F
   b. T
4. a. F
   b. F
   c. T
5. a. T
   b. T
   c. F
   d. T

Exercise 24, p. 242.
Seattle and Singapore have more rain than Manila in December.
(Manila: 58 mm. or 2.3 in.; Seattle: 161 mm. or 6.3 in.; Singapore: 306 mm. or 12 in.)

Exercise 25, p. 243.
2. Indonesia has more volcanoes than Japan.
3. Saturn has more moons than Venus.
4. Sao Paulo, Brazil, has more people than New York City.
5. Finland has more islands than Greece.
6. Nepal has more mountains than Switzerland.
7. A banana has more sugar than an apple.
8. The dark meat of a chicken has more fat than the white meat of a chicken.

Exercise 26, p. 243.

Underlined nouns: doctors, happiness, information, mistakes, responsibilities
2. more information
3. happier
4. more happily
5. more happiness
6. more mistakes
7. more responsibly
8. more responsibilities
9. more responsible
10. more doctors

Exercise 28, p. 244.
2. bigger and bigger
3. better and better
4. louder and louder
5. longer and longer
6. warmer and warmer
7. more and more discouraged
8. harder and harder . . . wetter and wetter
9. more and more tired

Exercise 30, p. 245.
2. The closer . . . the warmer
3. The sharper . . . the easier
4. The noisier (The more noisy) . . . the angrier (the more angry)
5. more shrimp . . . the pinker
7. The more he thought about his family, the more homesick he became.
8. The darker the sky grew, the faster we ran to reach the house.

Exercise 32, p. 246.
3. the most beautiful . . . in
4. the worst . . . in
5. the farthest / furthest . . . in
6. the best . . . of
7. the oldest . . . in
8. the most comfortable . . . in
9. the most exhausted of

Exercise 33, p. 247.
2. The highest mountains on earth
3. the biggest bird
4. The two greatest natural dangers
5. the most popular forms of entertainment
6. The three most common street names
7. The longest river in South America

Exercise 34, p. 248.
1. the best experiences
2. the nicest times
3. the most difficult courses
4. the worst mistakes
5. the most beautiful buildings
6. the easiest exams

Exercise 36, p. 248.
1. a   5. b
2. b   6. a
3. a   7. b
4. a   8. a

Exercise 37, p. 249.
Questions:
2. What is the most interesting sport to watch on TV?
3. What is the most crowded city you have ever visited?
4. Where is the best restaurant to eat around here?
5. What is the most fun place to visit in this area?
6. Who is the kindest person you know?
7. What is the most important thing in life?
8. What is the most serious problem in the world?
9. Who is the most interesting person in the news right now?

Exercise 39, p. 250.
2. easier . . . than
3. two more wheels *than*
4. longer . . . narrower (more narrow) . . . wider
5. more education
6. the longest
7. the friendliest . . . most delightful
8. the most famous . . . in
9. the loudest . . . in
10. The harder . . . the more impossible
11. the biggest . . . in . . . more people than
12. shorter
13. the highest . . . of
14. The longer . . . the more difficult
15. faster than / as fast as . . . the fastest
16. The greatest . . . in

Exercise 40, p. 251.
(Answers for items 3 and 6 may vary.)
1. C . . . E   6. A . . . B
2. A . . . D   7. C . . . E
3. A . . . B   8. A . . . D
4. C . . . E   9. A . . . D
5. A . . . D

Exercise 41, p. 252.
2. as   6. as
3. from   7. from
4. Ø . . . Ø   8. Ø . . . Ø
5. to

Exercise 42, p. 253.
1. to   8. like
2. the   9. the
3. the   10. as
4. as   11. alike
5. from   12. to
6. more   13. from
7. than

Exercise 43, p. 254.
(Answers may vary.)
2. similar to
3. similar
4. the same
5. different from
6. the same as
7. the same as

Exercise 44, p. 254.
(Answers may vary.)
3. different from / not the same as
4. the same
5. the same . . . as
6. like
7. the same
8. the same . . . as
9. alike . . . alike
10. like / the same as / similar to

Exercise 45, p. 255.
1. T   4. T
2. F   5. F
3. F

Exercise 47, p. 257.
2. Alaska is **the** largest state in the United States.
3. A pillow is **softer** than a rock.
4. Who is **the** most generous person in your family?
5. **The harder** you work, **the more successful** you will be.
6. One of **the** biggest disappointments in my life was when my soccer team lost the championship.
7. My sister is **much taller** than me.
8. A firm mattress is **more comfortable** for many people than a soft mattress.
9. One of the most talkative students in the class is Frederick.
10. Professor Bennett's lectures were the **most** confusing I have ever heard.

Chapter 10: The Passive

Exercise 1, p. 258.
1. b
2. a, b
3. a, b

Exercise 2, p. 259.
1. c. We are
2. a. He was
   b. They were
3. a. We are being
   b. She is being
4. a. I was being
   b. He was being

5. a. She has been
   b. He has been
6. a. I will be
   b. We are going to be

Exercise 3, p. 260.
2. are . . . ed
3. is being . . . ed
4. have been . . . ed
5. was . . . ed
6. was
7. will be . . . ed
8. are going to be . . . ed

Exercise 4, p. 261.
Checked sentences: 2, 4, 7

Exercise 5, p. 261.
2. are employed
3. has been hired
4. are going to be faxed
5. was bought
6. will be done
7. was being examined

Exercise 6, p. 262.
2. a. Erin is surprised
   b. Are you surprised
3. a. Greta will be shocked
   b. Will Pat be shocked
4. a. The birthday card is being signed
   b. Is it being signed
5. a. The card was signed
   b. Was it signed
6. a. It was being signed
   b. Was it being signed
7. a. It has been signed
   b. Has it been signed
8. a. It is going to be signed
   b. Is it going to be signed

Exercise 7, p. 262.
2. Are hair dryers provided by the hotel?
3. Were extra towels brought by housekeeping?
4. Has our meal been brought by room service?
5. Is our luggage being brought to our room by the bellhop?
6. Is the air-conditioning going to be fixed by maintenance?
7. Will our room be upgraded by the front desk?

Exercise 8, p. 263.
Checked sentences:
2. the truck
5. the driver

Exercise 9, p. 264.
Underlined verbs:
3. fell, v.i.
4. slept, v.i.
5. felt, v.t. *Passive:* An earthquake was felt by many people yesterday.
6. existed, v.i.
7. agree, v.i.
8. die, v.i.
9. discover, v.t. *Passive:* A cure for cancer will be discovered by scientists someday.
10. invent, v.t. *Passive:* Was spaghetti invented by the Italians?

Exercise 10, p. 264.
3. a. Princess Diana was killed in a car crash in 1997.
4. j. Marie and Pierre Curie discovered radium.
5. f. Oil was discovered in Saudi Arabia in 1938.
6. g. Mahatma Ghandhi and Martin Luther King Jr. were arrested several times for peaceful protests.
7. b. Michael Jackson died in 2009.
8. d. Leonardo da Vinci painted the Mona Lisa.
9. e. John F. Kennedy was elected president of the United States in 1960.
10. i. Nelson Mandela was released from prison in 1990.

Exercise 11, p. 265.
1. Pearson Longman
2. Betty Azar . . . Stacy Hagen
3. Don Martinetti . . . Chris Pavely

Exercise 12, p. 265.
2. This house was built in 1904.
3. Rice is grown in India.
4. Is Spanish spoken in Peru?
5. The telephone was invented by Alexander Graham Bell.
6. When was the first computer invented?
7. Hammers are sold at a hardware store.
8. Have you ever been hypnotized?
9. *The Origin of Species* was published in 1859.
10. *The Origin of Species* was written by Charles Darwin.

Exercise 13, p. 266.
2. b. = was built; no, b
3. a., b., c. = was designed; the *by*-phrases tells who designed the building. The important information is in c.
4. was ruled; It means that Thailand has never had a ruler.

Exercise 14, p. 266.
2. The driver was told to get out of the car by the police.
3. The driver took out his license.
4. The driver gave his license to the police officer.
5. The license was checked.
6. The driver was given a ticket.
7. The driver was told to drive more carefully.

Exercise 15, p. 267.
1. happened
2. was hit
3. Was
4. injured
5. called
6. was taken
7. treated
8. happened
9. was arrested
10. wasn't killed

Exercise 16, p. 267.
2. was interrupted
3. belongs
4. is delivered
5. is not pronounced
6. happened
7. arrived . . . was met
8. heard . . . was not surprised . . . was shocked
9. will be built / is going to be built
10. wrote . . . was written
11. was kicked . . . attended
12. agree . . . prefer
13. was your bike stolen
14. A: Have you paid
    B: will be shut off / is going to be shut off

Exercise 17, p. 268.
2. were
3. built
4. Was
5. built
6. swam
7. was designed
8. did not become
9. built
10. began
11. were
12. became
13. are found

Exercise 18, p. 269.
1. F
2. T
3. T
4. T
5. T

Exercise 19, p. 269.
2. should be planted
3. cannot be controlled
4. had to be fixed
5. can be reached
6. ought to be washed
7. may cooked . . . (may be) eaten
8. could be destroyed
9. must be kept

Exercise 20, p. 270.
Possible answers:
1. He was an immigrant from Germany. He invented Levi jeans.
2. He went to California because his brother wanted him to open a store.
3. They were created for miners.
4. Denim is a cotton fabric.

5. Rivets were put in pants, and a red tab was added to the rear pocket.
6. Rivets made the pants stronger.
7. A red tab was added so the jeans could be more easily identified.
8. They are known as Levis.

Exercise 21, p. 271.
1. sand
2. whales
3. China . . . Mongolia
4. small spaces

Exercise 22, p. 272.
2. a, c
3. b, c
4. a, c
5. b
6. a, b, c
7. a, c

Exercise 23, p. 272.
1. about
2. of
3. of
4. of
5. from
6. about
7. with
8. in
9. in
10. with

Exercise 24, p. 273.
2. is interested
3. am . . . finished
4. am satisfied
5. is married to
6. are opposed
7. Are . . . prepared
8. is composed

Exercise 25, p. 273.
1. with
2. for
3. to
4. to
5. with
6. to
7. with
8. about

Exercise 26, p. 274.
1. with
2. of
3. about
4. for
5. in
6. with
7. to
8. of

Exercise 27, p. 274.
2. is made of
3. is crowded
4. is located in
5. am exhausted
6. are disappointed
7. is spoiled
8. is composed of
9. am . . . qualified for
10. am . . . acquainted with

Exercise 28, p. 275.
1. is spoiled
2. was closed
3. is located in

4. scared of
5. Are . . . hurt
6. am lost
7. Are . . . related to
8. gone
9. are broken
10. Are . . . shut

Exercise 29, p. 275.
1. A
2. B
3. No picture matches.
4. A

Exercise 30, p. 276.
1. man
2. roller coaster
3. girl
4. roller coaster
5. roller coaster
6. girl

Exercise 31, p. 276.
1. boring
2. shocked
3. confusing
4. embarrassed
5. surprise
6. scary

Exercise 32, p. 277.
2. a. excited
   b. exciting
3. a. fascinating
   b. fascinated
4. a. depressed
   b. depressing
5. a. interested
   b. interesting

Exercise 33, p. 277.
1. embarrassed
2. embarrassing
3. shocked
4. shocking
5. surprised
6. surprised
7. upsetting
8. depressed
9. interesting
10. interested

Exercise 35, p. 279.
2. busy
3. lost
4. dirty
5. nervous
6. late
7. rich
8. serious
9. bald
10. hurt

Exercise 37, p. 280.
Sample answers:
1. cold
2. hot
3. tired
4. bald
5. thirsty
6. sick

Exercise 38, p. 280.
2. get well
3. get married
4. gets hungry
5. gets dark
6. get dry
7. getting tired
8. getting worried
9. got killed
10. getting cold
11. got lost
12. get crowded
13. get . . . angry
14. get involved
15. got dressed

Exercise 39, p. 281.
1. T
2. F
3. T

Exercise 41, p. 282.
2. is used to
3. am not used . . . am used to
4. are used to
6. am accustomed to . . . am not accustomed to
7. are accustomed to
8. are not accustomed to

Exercise 42, p. 282.
1. are you accustomed to
2. are you used to
3. are you accustomed to
4. Are you accustomed to
5. Are you used to
6. Are you used to
7. are you accustomed to
8. Are you used to

Exercise 46, p. 284.
3. am
4. Ø
5. Ø
6. are
7. is
8. Ø

Exercise 47, p. 284.
3. used to eat
4. is used to growing
5. is used to eating
6. used to have
7. am used to taking
8. used to go

Exercise 49, p. 285.
2. The weather is supposed to be cold tomorrow.
3. The plane is supposed to arrive at 6:00.
4. I am supposed to work late tonight.
5. The mail was supposed to come an hour ago, but it didn't.

Exercise 50, p. 286.
2. Ann is supposed to call Lena at nine.
3. Johnny is supposed to make his bed before he goes to school.
4. The students are supposed to read the test directions carefully and raise their hands if they have any questions.
5. The patient is supposed to take one pill every eight hours and drink plenty of fluids.

Exercise 51, p. 286.
1. T
2. F
3. T
4. F
5. T
6. F
7. T
8. T

Exercise 52, p. 286.
Part I.
1. a, c
2. b
3. b, c
4. a, b, c
5. a, b

Part II.
2. established
3. were established
4. were supposed to
5. became
6. were given
7. were
8. were studied
9. kept
10. are put
11. are fed
12. are watched
13. have
14. are treated
15. have saved

(*Answers to questions may vary.*)
1. It was established for an Egyptian queen for her enjoyment.
2. They were dark holes or dirty cages.
3. The purpose was to study animals.
4. They keep animals in large, natural settings, feed them a healthy diet, and watch them for signs of disease.
5. They want to encourage breeding to save different types of animals.

Exercise 53, p. 288.
2. Something **happened**.
3. This pen **belongs** to me.
4. I'm **interested** in that subject.
5. He is **married to** my cousin.
6. Mary's dog **died** last week.
7. Were you **surprised** when you heard the news?
8. When I went downtown, **I got** lost.
9. The **bus arrived** ten minutes late.
10. We're not suppose**d** to have pets in our apartment.

Exercise 54, p. 289.
My Favorite Holiday

(1) New Year's is the most important holiday of the year in my country. New Year's <u>is celebrated</u> for fifteen days, but my favorite day is the first day.

(2) The celebration actually begins at midnight. Fireworks <u>are set off</u>, and the streets <u>are filled</u> with people. Neighbors and friends greet each other and wish one another good luck for the year. The next morning, gifts <u>are exchanged</u>. Children <u>are given</u> money. It <u>is wrapped</u> in red envelopes because red is the color for good luck. When I was younger, this was always my favorite part of the holiday.

(3) On New Year's Day, everyone wears new clothes. These clothes <u>are bought</u> especially for the holiday. People are very polite to each other. It <u>is considered</u> wrong to yell, lie, or use bad language on the first day of the year. It is a custom for younger generations to visit their elders. They wish them good health and a long life.

Chapter 11: Count/Nouncount Nouns and Articles

Exercise 2, p. 291.
2. an	8. an	14. a
3. a	9. an	15. a
4. an	10. an	16. a
5. an	11. a	17. an
6. a	12. an	18. an
7. a	13. an	

Exercise 3, p. 291.
1. a	6. Ø
2. Ø	7. a
3. an	8. an
4. Ø	9. a
5. an	10. Ø

Exercise 4, p. 291.
1. a	3. a, b
2. a	4. a, b

Exercise 5, p. 292.
3. Correct.
4. some furniture OR four chairs
5. Correct.
6. some furniture OR a chair
7. some chairs
8. some furniture

Exercise 6, p. 292.
advice: ideas, suggestions
mail: letters, postcards
jewelry: bracelets, rings

Exercise 7, p. 293.
3. a, count	7. some, noncount
4. some, noncount	8. an, count
5. a, count	9. some, noncount
6. some, noncount	10. a, count

Exercise 8, p. 294.
3. Ø	10. Ø
4. s . . . s	11. Ø
5. Ø	12. s
6. s	13. es
7. s	14. Ø
8. Ø	15. s
9. s	16. Ø

Exercise 10, p. 295.
3. Ø	8. s . . . s
4. es	9. Ø
5. Ø	10. s
6. Ø is . . . s are	11. Ø
7. Ø	12. Ø

Exercise 11, p. 296.
1. Ø	6. s
2. Ø	7. Ø
3. s	8. Ø
4. Ø	9. Ø
5. Ø	10. Ø

Exercise 15, p. 297.
1. apples	4. fruit
2. apples/fruit	5. apples
3. apples	6. fruit

Exercise 16, p. 297.
3. Correct.
4. Correct.
5. Correct.
6. too **many** new words
7. a few **words** / **a little** vocabulary
8. Correct.
9. several new **words**
10. **are a lot** of new words / **is a lot** of new **vocabulary**
12. are a lot of new **words** / **is** a lot of new vocabulary

Exercise 17, p. 298.
1. d. many cars
   e. much stuff
   f. much experience
2. a. much fruit
   b. many vegetables
   c. many bananas
   d. many tomatoes
   e. many oranges
   f. much food
3. a. much fun
   b. much help
   c. much time
   d. much information
   e. many facts
   f. much money

Exercise 18, p. 298.
6. [Canada has ten provinces.]
7. [There are 47 countries on the continent of Africa and six island nations.]

Exercise 19, p. 299.
3. a little help
4. a little pepper
5. a few things
6. a few apples
7. a little fruit

8. a little advice
9. a little . . . money
10. A few friends
11. a little rain
12. a little French
13. a few . . . hours

Exercise 20, p. 299.
1. C
2. A
3. B

Exercise 21, p. 300.
1. E   4. C
2. B   5. A
3. F   6. D

Exercise 22, p. 301.
3. papers
4. paper
5. a . . . paper
6. works
7. work
8. hair . . . hair
9. hairs
10. glasses
11. glasses
12. glass
13. Iron is
14. Irons are
15. experiences
16. experience
17. some . . . chicken
18. chickens
19. are . . . lights
20. A: light . . . isn't
    B: It ⁄

Exercise 24, p. 303.
(Other completions are possible.)

Part I.
3. bottle   8. bottle
4. jar   9. can/bottle
5. can   10. bag
6. can   11. can
7. bag/box   12. box

Part II.
15. piece   22. bowl/cup
16. slice/piece   23. glass
17. slice/piece   24. bowl
18. glass/cup   25. slice/piece
19. bowl/cup   26. bowl/cup
20. slice/piece   27. bowl/cup
21. glass   28. slice/piece

Exercise 27, p. 308.
1. 1   3. 2   5. 4
2. 3   4. 5   6. 6

Exercise 28, p. 310.
3. A: a
   B: a
4. A: the . . . the
5. B: the . . . the
6. the
7. A: a
   B: a
8. the
9. a
10. the
11. a
12. A: the . . . the . . . the . . . the . . . the . . . the

Exercise 29, p. 311.
2. singular, general   6. singular, specific
3. plural, general   7. plural, specific
4. singular, general   8. noncount, specific
5. noncount, general

Exercise 30, p. 311.
2. a. Mountains
   b. The mountains
3. a. The water
   b. Water
4. a. The information
   b. information
5. a. Health
   b. the health
6. a. Men . . . women
   b. the men . . . the women
7. a. problems
   b. the problems
8. a. The vegetables
   b. Vegetables

Exercise 31, p. 312.
Sample answers:
1. salt and shells (*also possible:* beads)
2. coins
3. money
4. credit . . . debit cards (*also possible:* paper money)
5. plastic (credit or debit cards) . . . paper money

Exercise 32, p. 312.
2. the   5. Ø . . . Ø
3. Ø The   6. Ø Trees . . . Ø
4. the   7. Ø The

Exercise 33, p. 313.
2. some . . . some . . . the . . . the
3. a . . . some . . . the . . . the
4. B: a . . . a . . . The . . . the
5. a . . . some . . . some . . . The . . . the . . . some
   . . . the . . . a . . . The

Exercise 34, p. 313.

2. an
3. Ø
4. Ø
5. The
6. Ø

7. Ø
8. a
9. Ø
10. The
11. the

Exercise 35, p. 314.

2. Ø
3. the . . . The
4. a . . . the
5. the
6. Ø . . . the . . . The
7. Ø . . . Ø . . . Ø
8. the . . . the
9. a
10. The . . . the . . . the . . . the
11. A: the
    B: the

Exercise 36, p. 315.

3. Ø
4. the
5. the
6. Ø

7. the
8. the
9. Ø
10. Ø

Exercise 37, p. 316.

1. Ø . . . Ø   T
2. The . . . Ø   T
3. Ø . . . Ø   F [Austria]
4. The . . . Ø   T
5. The . . . the   F
6. The . . . Ø . . . the   T
7. Ø   F [psychology / psychiatry]
8. Ø . . . Ø   T
9. Ø . . . the   T
10. The   F [The Himalayas]

Exercise 40, p. 318.

2. Do you know **R**ichard **S**mith? **H**e is a professor at this university.
3. I know that **P**rofessor **S**mith teaches at the **U**niversity of **A**rizona.
4. (*no change*)
5. John is a **C**atholic. **A**li is a **M**oslem.
6. Anna speaks **F**rench. **S**he studied in **F**rance for two years.
7. (*no change*)
8. I'm taking **M**odern **E**uropean **H**istory 101 this semester.
9. We went to **V**ancouver, **B**ritish **C**olumbia, for our vacation last summer.
10. Venezuela is a **S**panish-speaking country.
11. Canada is in **N**orth **A**merica.
12. Canada is north of the **U**nited **S**tates.
13. (*no change*)
14. The **M**ississippi **R**iver flows south.
15. The **A**mazon is a river in **S**outh **A**merica.
16. We went to a zoo. We went to **B**rookfield **Z**oo in **C**hicago.
17. The title of this book is *Fundamentals of English Grammar.*
18. I enjoy studying **E**nglish grammar.
19. On **V**alentine's **D**ay (February 14th), sweethearts give each other presents.
20. I read a book called *The Cat and the Mouse in My Aunt's House.*

Exercise 41, p. 319.

Part I.

Jane Goodall

(1) Do you recognize the name **J**ane **G**oodall? Perhaps you know her for her studies of chimpanzees. She became very famous from her work in **T**anzania.

(2) Jane Goodall was born in England, and as a child, was fascinated by animals. Her favorite books were *The Jungle Book,* by **R**udyard **K**ipling, and books about Tarzan, a fictional character who was raised by apes.

(3) Her childhood dream was to go to **A**frica. After high school, she worked as a secretary and a waitress to earn enough money to go there. During that time, she took evening courses in journalism and **E**nglish literature. She saved every penny until she had enough money for a trip to Africa.

(4) In the spring of 1957, she sailed through the **R**ed **S**ea and southward down the African coast to **M**ombasa in **K**enya. Her uncle had arranged a job for her in **N**airobi with a **B**ritish company. When she was there, she met **D**r. Louis Leakey, a famous anthropologist. Under his guidance, she began her lifelong study of chimpanzees on the eastern shore of **L**ake Tanganyika.

(5) Jane Goodall lived alone in a tent near the lake. Through months and years of patience, she won the trust of the chimps and was able to watch them closely. Her observations changed forever how we view chimpanzees—and all other animals we share the world with.

Part II.

1. T
2. F

3. F
4. T

5. F
6. F

Chapter 12: Adjective Clauses

Exercise 2, p. 322.
Checked sentences: 1, 2, 5

Exercise 3, p. 322.

1. An orthopedist
2. A dermatologist
3. A surgeon
4. A pediatrician

Exercise 4, p. 323.
1. a, d
2. c, d

Exercise 5, p. 323.
2. The manager <u>that hired me</u> has less experience than I do.
3. I like the manager <u>that works in the office next to mine</u>.
4. My mother is a person <u>who wakes up every morning with a positive attitude</u>.
5. A person <u>who wakes up with a positive attitude every day</u> is lucky.

Exercise 6, p. 323.
1. The police officer who/that gave me directions was friendly.
2. The waiter who/that served us dinner was slow.
3. I talked to the women who/that walked into my office.
4. The man who/that sat next to me on the plane talked a lot.
5. The people who/that live next to me have three cars.

Exercise 7, p. 323.
2. The man who/that answered the phone was polite.
3. People who/that paint houses for a living are called house painters.
4. I'm uncomfortable around married couples who/that argue all the time.
5. While I was waiting at the bus stop, I stood next to an elderly man who/that started a conversation with me about my school.

Exercise 10, p. 325.
Checked sentences: 2, 3, 5, 8

Exercise 11, p. 325.
1. a, b, c, d   3. a, b, c, d
2. a, c   4. a, c

Exercise 12, p. 325.
2. b. them; The couple that/who/whom I invited for dinner was two hours late.
3. b. him; The man that/who/whom I sat next to on the plane snored the entire flight.
4. b. him; The man that/who/whom police arrested tried to shoplift some groceries.
5. b. her; The chef that/who/whom the company hired is very experienced.

Exercise 13, p. 326.
2. The man who/that answered my question . . .
3. The man who/that/Ø/whom I called . . .

4. The man who/that/Ø/whom you recommended . . .
5. The man who/that is the owner . . .
6. The man who/that you invited . . .
7. The man who/that was walking with his kids . . .
8. The man who/that/Ø/whom I saw in the waiting room . . .
9. The man who/that sold us our museum tickets . . .
10. The man who/that gave us a discount . . .

Exercise 14, p. 326.
1. who, that
2. that, Ø, who, whom
3. who, that
4. that, Ø, who, whom
5. that, Ø, who, whom
6. who, that

Exercise 16, p. 327.
2. The food <u>we ate at the sidewalk café</u> was delicious.
3. The bus <u>that I take to school every morning</u> is usually very crowded.
4. Pizza <u>which is sold by the slice</u> is a popular lunch in many cities throughout the world.
5. Piranhas are dangerous fish <u>that can tear the flesh off an animal as large as a horse in a few minutes</u>.

Exercise 17, p. 328.
2. The soup that/Ø/which I had for lunch was too salty.
3. I have a class that/which begins at 8:00 A.M.
4. The information that/Ø/which I found on the Internet helped me a lot.
5. My daughter asked me a question that/Ø/which I couldn't answer.
6. Where can I catch the bus that/which goes downtown?

Exercise 18, p. 328.
2. . . . you wore ~~it~~ to class yesterday
3. . . . you to meet ~~her~~
4. . . . to rent ~~it~~ had two bedrooms
5. . . . we bought ~~it~~ for our anniversary
6. . . . you met ~~her~~ at
7. . . . cat that ~~it~~ likes
8. . . . cat catches ~~them~~ live

Exercise 19, p. 328.
1. that, Ø, which
2. who, that
3. that, which
4. that, Ø, which
5. that, Ø, who, whom
6. that, which

Exercise 20, p. 329.

1. who
2. Ø
3. that
4. which
5. that
6. Ø
7. that
8. whom

Exercise 21, p. 329.

2. **The** student who/that raised her hand in class asked the teacher a question.
   The student who/that sat quietly in his seat didn't.
3. **The** girl who/that won the bike race is happy.
   The girl who/that lost the bike race isn't happy.
4. **The** food that/which/Ø we ate from our garden was inexpensive.
   The food that/which/Ø we ate at the restaurant was expensive.
5. **The** man who/that was listening to the radio heard the special report about the earthquake in China.
   The man who/that was sleeping didn't hear it.
6. **The** person who/that bought a large car probably spent more money (than the person who bought a small car).

Exercise 22, p. 330.

2. b. who/that tells jokes.
3. f. who/that delivers babies.
4. h. who/that can be shaped . . .
5. e. who designs buildings.
6. i. that can be difficult to solve.
7. j. that eats meat.
8. c. that forms when water boils.
9. k. that has a hard shell . . .
10. a. who leaves society . . .
11. d. that is square . . .

Exercise 23, p. 330.

The verb in the adjective clause agrees with the noun that precedes it.

Exercise 24, p. 331.

2. tools . . . are
3. woman . . . lives
4. people . . . live
5. cousin . . . works
6. miners . . . work
7. athlete . . . plays
8. athletes . . . play
9. books . . . tell
10. book . . . tells
11. men . . . were
12. woman . . . was

Exercise 26, p. 332.

2. The man that/Ø/who/whom I told you **about** is over there.
   The man **about** whom I told you is over there.

3. The woman that/Ø/who/whom I work **for** pays me a fair salary.
   The woman **for** whom I work pays me a fair salary.
4. Alicia likes the family that/Ø/who/whom she is living **with**.
   Alicia likes the family **with** whom she is living.
5. The picture that/Ø/which Tom is looking **at** is beautiful.
   The picture **at** which Tom is looking is beautiful.
6. I enjoyed the music that/Ø/which we listened **to** after dinner
   I enjoyed the music **to** which we listened after dinner.

Exercise 27, p. 333.

2. to . . . [we went **to**]
3. in/at . . . [we stayed **in/at**]
4. to . . . [we listened **to**]
5. for . . . [Sally was waiting **for**]
6. to . . . [**to** whom I talked]
7. [that I was looking **for**]
8. [I had graduated **from**]
9. [**with** whom he is living]
10. [who is staring **at** us]
11. [**with** whom I almost always agree]
12. [you introduced me **to** at the restaurant last night]
13. [I've always been able to depend **on**]
14. [you waved **at**]
15. [**to** whom you should complain]

Exercise 28, p. 334.

1. b, c
2. c
3. a, b, c
4. b
5. c

Exercise 29, p. 334.

Part II.

1. family
2. activities
3. people
4. way (of life)
5. things
6. customs and habits
7. things

Part III.
Sample answers:

1. was their eating customs
2. who were similar to him in their customs and habits
3. the way of life that his host family had
4. he had in common with them

Exercise 30, p. 335.

Checked sentences: 2, 4

Exercise 31, p. 336.

1. The C.E.O. whose company lost money is resigning.
2. Let me introduce you to the woman whose company is hiring right now.
3. I talked to the couple whose house was burglarized.
4. The child whose foot you stepped on is fine.
5. The man whose cell phone you found is on the phone.

Exercise 32, p. 337.

2. There is the woman **whose husband** writes movie scripts.
3. Over there is the man **whose daughter** is in my English class.
4. Over there is the woman **whose sister** you met yesterday.
5. There is the professor **whose course** I'm taking.
6. That is the man **whose daughter** is a newscaster.
7. That is the girl **whose brother** I taught.
8. There is the boy **whose mother** is a famous musician.

Exercise 33, p. 337.

1. whose	3. who's	5. who's
2. whose	4. whose	6. who's

Exercise 34, p. 338.

Sample answers:

1. b. who invited us to his party
   c. whose son broke our car window
   d. whose dog barks all night
   e. who is standing out in the rain
   f. whose wife is an actress

2. a. whose picture was in the paper
   b. whose father climbed Mt. Everest
   c. who helped me when I cut myself
   d. that works for Dr. Lang
   e. whose purse I found
   f. whose father I worked with

3. a. whose pages are torn
   b. that is on the table
   c. that Sam lost
   d. whose cover is missing
   e. that I gave to you
   f. which I found

Exercise 35, p. 338.

3. who, that	9. who, that
4. whose	10. who*m that*
5. who, that, Ø, whom	11. whose
6. whom	12. ~~that, which~~ *whom*
7. whose	13. that, Ø, which
8. that, Ø, which	

Exercise 36, p. 339.

1. that	4. that
2. Ø	5. whose
3. which	

Exercise 37, p. 339.

2. whose son was in an accident
3. I slept on in a hotel last night
4. that/which erupted in Indonesia
5. whose specialty is heart surgery
6. that/which lived in the jungles of Southeast Asia
7. whose mouth was big enough to swallow a whole cow in one gulp

Exercise 40, p. 340.

2. The woman **that I met yesterday was nice**.
4. I met a woman **whose husband** is a famous lawyer.
5. Do you know the people who **live** in that house?
6. The professor **who/that** teaches Chemistry 101 is very good.
7. The people **whose house I painted** want me to do other work for them.
8. The people who I **met at** the party last night were interesting.
9. I enjoyed the music that we listened **to**.
10. The apple tree **that we planted last** year is producing fruit.
11. Before I came here, I didn't have the opportunity to speak to people **whose native** tongue is English.
12. One thing I need to get **is** a new alarm clock.
13. The people who **were** waiting to buy tickets for the **game were** happy because their team had made it to the championship.

Exercise 41, p. 341.

My Friend's Vegan Diet

I have a friend <u>who is a vegan</u>. As you may know, a vegan is a person <u>who eats no animal products</u>. When I first met him, I didn't understand the vegan diet. I thought *vegan* was another name for *vegetarian*, except that vegans didn't eat eggs. I soon found out I was wrong. The first time I cooked dinner for him, I made a vegetable dish <u>which had a lot of cheese</u>. Since cheese comes from cows, it's not vegan, so he had to scrape it off. I also served him bread <u>that had milk in it</u> and a dessert <u>that was made with ice cream</u>. Unfortunately, there wasn't much <u>that he could eat that night</u>. In the beginning, I had trouble thinking of meals <u>which we could both enjoy</u>. But he is a wonderful cook and showed me how to create delicious vegan meals. I don't know if I'll ever become a complete vegan, but I've learned a lot about the vegan diet and the delicious possibilities <u>it has</u>.

Chapter 13: Gerunds and Infinitives

Exercise 2, p. 342.

1. a. working
   b. closing
   c. hiring

2. a. smoking
   b. eating
   c. sleeping

3. a. paying
   b. handing in
   c. cleaning

Exercise 3, p. 343.
Sample answers:
2. buying
3. sweeping
4. getting
5. talking
6. working
7. opening

Exercise 4, p. 343.
1. finish doing
2. talked about seeing
3. Would you mind explaining
4. thinking about not attending
5. Keep trying

Exercise 6, p. 345.
2. Nancy and Frank like to go fishing.
3. Adam went camping.
4. Tim likes to go shopping.
5. Laura goes jogging/running.
6. Fred and Jean like to go skiing.
7. Joe likes to go hiking.
8. Sara often goes bowling.
9. Liz and Greg probably go dancing a lot.
10. The Taylors are going to go (ice) skating.
11. Alex and Barbara like to go sailing/boating.
12. Tourists go sightseeing on buses.
13. Colette and Ben like to go skydiving
14. (*Answers will vary.*)

Exercise 7, p. 345.
Questions:
2. Do you like to go water skiing?
3. Do you like to go bowling?
4. Do you go dancing on weekends?
5. Do you go jogging for exercise?
6. Do you go fishing in the winter?
7. Do you go camping in the summer?
8. Do you like to go snow skiing?

Exercise 9, p. 346.
Sample answers:
2. to be
3. to visit
4. to get to
5. to be
6. to be
7. to be . . . to hear
8. to buy
9. to lend
10. to eat
11. to watch . . . to go to
12. to get to
13. to see
14. to hurt
15. to tell

Exercise 10, p. 347.
Checked sentences: 1, 2

Exercise 11, p. 347.
1. b, c
2. b, c
3. b, c
4. c
5. b, c
6. c
7. b, c
8. b, c

Exercise 13, p. 348.
1. to understand
2. listening
3. to get . . . to stop
4. repeating
5. to nod / nodding
6. to look / looking
7. speaking

Exercise 14, p. 349.
1. eating
2. to help
3. moving
4. to go / going
5. to be
6. living
7. to give
8. to say
9. to sleep / sleeping
10. trying
11. to want to leave . . . talking

Exercise 15, p. 350.
1. to go / going
2. to go / going
3. to go
4. to go
5. to go
6. to go
7. to go / going
8. to go
9. going
10. going
11. to go
12. going
13. to go
14. to go / going
15. going
16. going
17. to go
18. going
19. going
20. to go

Exercise 16, p. 350.
1. to relax
2. to stay . . . relax
3. to stay . . . relax . . . go
4. getting . . . watching
5. getting . . . watching . . . listening
6. selling . . . buying
7. to move . . . find . . . start
8. going . . . letting
9. quitting . . . going
10. unplugging . . . turning off . . . locking

Exercise 17, p. 351.
Verbs:
1. plan to go
2. consider going
3. offer to help
4. like to visit / visiting
5. enjoy reading
6. intend to get
7. can't afford to buy
8. seems to be
9. put off writing
10. would like to go swimming

11. postpone going
12. finish studying
13. would mind helping
14. begin to study / studying
15. think about going
16. quit trying
17. continue to walk / walking
18. learn to speak
19. talk about going
20. keep trying

Exercise 19, p. 352.
2. for holding
3. about being
4. in going
5. for being
6. of flying
7. about taking
8. about seeing
9. on paying
10. about / of becoming
11. like eating
12. for not writing
13. of living
14. in being
15. on meeting
16. for cleaning
17. from entering
18. at cutting

Exercise 21, p. 353.
2. in telling
3. of drowning
4. to taking
5. like telling
6. on paying
7. for causing
8. at remembering
9. from doing
10. for taking
11. of not having
12. to having
13. A: about / of quitting
    B: of quitting

Exercise 22, p. 354.
1. wanted to stay
2. traveling
3. packing
4. unpacking
5. to travel
6. wanted to take
7. decided to stay
8. be
9. to do
10. would like to take
11. began talking
12. excited about seeing

Exercise 24, p. 355.
2. by washing
3. by watching
4. by smiling
5. by eating
6. by drinking
7. by guessing
8. by waving
9. by wagging
10. by staying . . . taking

Exercise 25, p. 356.
2. with a needle and thread
3. with a saw
4. with a thermometer
5. with a spoon
6. with a shovel
7. with a hammer
8. with a pair of scissors

Exercise 26, p. 356.
3. with
4. by
5. with
6. with
7. by
8. by
9. with
10. by

Exercise 28, p. 357.
2. Making friends here takes time.
3. Getting around town is easy.
4. Is living here expensive?
6. It's dangerous to walk alone at night.
7. It's fun to explore this town.
8. Is it difficult to find affordable housing?

Exercise 31, p. 359.
2. for teachers to speak clearly.
3. for us to hurry.
4. for a fish to live out of water for more than a few minutes.
5. for working parents to budget their time carefully.
6. for a young child to sit still for a long time.
7. for my family to spend birthdays together.
8. for my brother to travel.
9. for you to understand Mr. Alvarez.

Exercise 33, p. 360.
Sample answers:
1. to offer a strong handshake when people meet one another
2. shaking hands firmly
3 and 4. (*Answers will vary.*)

Exercise 34, p. 360.
Checked sentences: 1, 2, 3, 4

Exercise 35, p. 361.
2. c.   (in order) to listen
3. i.   (in order) to see
4. a.   (in order) to keep
5. d.   (in order) to find
6. b.   (in order) to reach

7. j. (in order) to look
8. f. (in order) to chase
9. h. (in order) to get
10. g. (in order) to help

Exercise 36, p. 361.
3. Sam went to the hospital **in order** to visit a friend.
4. (*no change*)
5. I need to go to the bank today **in order** to deposit my paycheck.
6. On my way home, I stopped at the store **in order** to buy some shampoo.
7. Masako went to the cafeteria **in order** to eat lunch.
8. (*no change*)
9. Pedro watches TV **in order** to improve his English.
10. (*no change*)
11. (*no change*)
12. Jerry needs to go to the bookstore **in order** to buy school supplies.

Exercise 37, p. 362.
3. to
4. for
5. for
6. to
7. to
8. to
9. for
10. for

Exercise 38, p. 362.
1. Car sharing
2. join
3. driving
4. move . . . take
5. owning

Exercise 39, p. 363.
1. heavy
2. strong
3. strength

Exercise 40, p. 364.
3. too busy to answer
4. early enough to get
5. too full to hold
6. large enough to hold
7. too big to get
8. big enough to hold

Exercise 41, p. 365.
2. I was too sleepy to finish my homework last night.
3. Mike was too busy to go to his aunt's housewarming party.
4. This jacket is too small for me to wear.
5. I live too far from school to walk there.
7. I'm not strong enough to move this furniture.
8. It's not warm enough for you to go outside without a coat.
9. I wasn't sick enough to stay home and miss work.

Exercise 43, p. 365.
3. to invite
4. going
5. listening
6. to earn . . . to take
7. to get . . . sleep
8. forgetting
9. using

Exercise 44, p. 366.
1. to follow . . . to slow . . . give
2. Asking . . . getting . . . keep . . . to be
3. to make . . . to see

Exercise 45, p. 366.
1. a, b
2. b, c
3. b
4. a, c
5. c

Exercise 47, p. 368.
2. I went to the bank **to cash** a check.
3. Did you **go shopping** yesterday?
4. I cut the rope **with** a knife.
5. I thanked my friend for **driving** me to the airport.
6. **It is** difficult to learn another language.
7. Timmy isn't **old enough** to get married.
8. **This exercise is easy** to do. OR **It's easy to do this exercise.**
9. Last night **I was** too tired **to do** my homework.
10. I've never **gone sailing**, but I would like to.
11. **Reading is** one of my hobbies.
12. The teenagers began to **build** a campfire to keep themselves warm.
13. Instead of **settling** down in one place, I'd like to travel around the world.
14. I **enjoy traveling** because you learn so much about other countries and cultures.
15. My grandmother likes to **fish/go fishing/likes fishing**.
16. Martina would like to **have** a big family.

Chapter 14: Noun Clauses

Exercise 1, p. 370.
Checked sentences: 1, 2, 4

Exercise 2, p. 370.
1. Where are the Smiths living?
2. I don't know <u>where the Smiths are living</u>.
3. We don't know <u>what city they moved to</u>.
4. We know <u>that they moved a month ago</u>.
5. Are they coming back?
6. I don't know <u>if they are coming back</u>.

Exercise 4, p. 372.

2. a. I don't know where she is living.   NC
   b. Where is she living?   IQ
3. a. Where did Nick go?   IQ
   b. I don't know where Nick went.   NC
4. a. I don't know what time the movie begins.   NC
   b. What time does the movie begin?   IQ
5. a. Why is Yoko angry?   IQ
   b. I don't know why Yoko is angry.   NC

Exercise 5, p. 372.

2. where Frank goes
3. where Natasha went
4. why Maria is laughing
5. how much an electric car costs
6. how long elephants live
7. when the first wheel was invented
8. how many hours a light bulb burns
9. where Emily bought her first computer
10. who lives
11. who Julie talked
12. why Mike is always

Exercise 6, p. 373.

Can you tell me . . .
2. what this means?
3. when I will get my grades.
4. what our next assignment is.
5. how soon the next assignment is due.
6. why this is incorrect.
7. when a good time to meet is.
8. what day the term ends.
9. why I failed.
10. who will teach this class next time.

Exercise 7, p. 374.

3. what a lizard is
4. what is in the bag
5. whose car that is
6. whose car is in the driveway
7. whose Bob's doctor is
8. whose ladder this is . . . whose ladder this is
9. what is at the end of a rainbow

Exercise 8, p. 374.

Do you know . . .
1. where the phone is?
2. why the front door is open?
3. who just called?
4. whose socks are on the floor?
5. why all the lights are on?
6. what happened?
7. what the plumber said about the broken pipe?
8. what the repair is going to cost?

Exercise 9, p. 375.

2. Jason works
   does he work
3. did you see
   I saw
4. does that camera cost
   this camera costs
5. can you run
   I can run
6. did she get
   she got
7. is it
   it is
8. are some people
   some people are

Exercise 10, p. 376.

Checked sentences: 1, 3, 4

Exercise 11, p. 376.

2. if Mr. Piper will be at the meeting
3. if Niko went to work yesterday.
4. if there is going to be a windstorm tonight.
5. if I have Yung Soo's email address.

Exercise 12, p. 377.

2. if you are going to be
3. if Tim borrowed
4. if he can watch
5. if your car keys are
6. if your car has a CD player

Exercise 13, p. 378.

Questions:
2. when this building was built?
3. how far it is from Vancouver, Canada, to Riyadh, Saudi Arabia? [Around 7,774 mi. / 12,511 km.]
4. if Australia is the smallest continent? [Yes.]
5. how many eyes a bat has? [Two.]
6. what the longest word in English is? (*Answers will vary.*)
7. if a chimpanzee has a good memory? [Yes.]
8. how old the Great Wall of China is? [About 2,300 years old.]
9. if all birds fly? [No. For example, penguins don't fly.]
10. if birds **came** from dinosaurs? [Most dinosaur researchers think so.]

Exercise 15, p. 378.

Checked sentences: 1, 2, 3

Exercise 16, p. 379.

2. dreamed that
3. believe that
4. notice that . . . hope that
5. believe that she told the truth

Exercise 19, p. 380.
2. B: pleased that
3. B: surprised that . . . think that
4. A: aware that
   B: certain that
5. surprised that
6. true that

Exercise 21, p. 381.
Sample answers:
1. a. her English teacher is really good.
   b. she is enjoying her class.
2. a. her son has the flu.
   b. he doesn't have the flu.
3. a. the woman failed her chemistry course.
   b. she won't be able to graduate on time.
4. a. Rachel is there.
   b. she is there / she was invited.
5. a. Carol won't come back.
   b. she will be back.

Exercise 22, p. 382.
1. a, c
2. b, c

Exercise 23, p. 382.
Sample answers:
2. I don't believe that we are going to have a grammar test tomorrow.
3. I hope that Margo will be at the conference in March.
4. I believe that horses can swim.
5. I don't think that gorillas have tails
6. I don't think that Janet will be at Omar's wedding.
7. I hope my flight won't be cancelled because of the storms.

Exercise 26, p. 384.
2. Ann **asked,** "Is your brother a student?" OR
   "Is your brother a student?" Ann **asked.**
3. Rita **said,** "We're hungry." OR
   "We're hungry," Rita **said.**
4. Rita **asked,** "Are you hungry too?" OR
   "Are you hungry too?" Rita **asked.**
5. Rita **said,** "Let's eat. The food's ready." OR
   "Let's eat," Rita **said.** "The food is ready." OR
   "Let's eat. The food's ready," Rita **said.**
6. John F. Kennedy **said,** "Ask not . . . do for you. Ask what . . . for your country." OR
   "Ask not . . . do for you," John F. Kennedy **said.**
   "Ask what . . . for your country." OR
   "Ask not . . . do for you. Ask what . . . for your country," John F. Kennedy **said.**

Exercise 27, p. 385.
"You know sign language, don't you?" I asked Roberto.

"Yes, I do," he replied. "Both my grandparents are deaf."

"I'm looking for someone who knows sign language. A deaf student is going to visit our class next Monday," I said. "Could you interpret for her?" I asked.

"I'd be happy to," he answered. "Is she going to be a new student?"

"Possibly," I said. "She's interested in seeing what we do in our English classes."

Exercise 29, p. 386.
they . . . their

Exercise 30, p. 387.
1. she . . . her
2. he . . . me
3. he . . . us . . . our . . . he . . . his . . . his

Exercise 32, p. 388.
2. was meeting
3. had studied
4. had forgotten
5. was going
6. would carry
7. could teach

Exercise 33, p. 389.
2. Kristina said (that) she didn't like chocolate.
3. Carla said (that) she was planning . . . her family.
4. Tom said (that) he had already eaten lunch.
5. Kate said (that) she had called her doctor.
6. Mr. Rice said (that) he was going to go to Chicago.
7. Eric said (that) he would be at my house at ten.
8. Emma said (that) she couldn't afford to buy a new car.
9. Olivia said (that) she couldn't afford to buy a new car.
10. Ms. Todd said (that) she wanted to see me in her office after my meeting with my supervisor.

Exercise 34, p. 389.
1. a, c
2. a, c

Exercise 35, p. 390.
4. said
5. told
6. asked
7. told . . . said . . . asked . . . told . . . said
8. said . . . asked . . . told . . . asked . . . said

Exercise 37, p. 391.
(that) he wasn't going to have . . . wasn't hungry . . . had eaten . . . he had come . . . he needed to talk to her about a problem he was having at work.

Exercise 38, p. 391.

1. In the middle of class yesterday, my friend tapped me on the shoulder and asked me, **"What are you doing after class?"**

   "I will tell you later," I answered.

3. When I was putting on my hat and coat, Robert asked me, **"Where are you going?"**

   "I have a date with Anna," I told him.

   "What are you going to do?" he wanted to know.

   "We're going to a movie," I answered.

Exercise 39, p. 392.

1. asked
2. was
3. told
4. was
5. asked
6. would be
7. said
8. would be
9. asked
10. could do
11. said
12. needed
13. could help
14. told
15. would leave

Exercise 41, p. 393.

2. I don't know **what your email address is.**
3. I **think that** Mr. Lee is out of town.
4. Can you tell **me where** Victor is living now?
5. I asked my uncle what kind of movies **he likes.**
6. I **think that** my English has improved a lot.
7. **It is** true that people are basically the same everywhere in the world.
8. A man came to my door last week. I **didn't** know who **he was.**
9. I want to know **if Pedro has** a laptop computer.
10. Sam and I talked about his classes. He told **me** that he **didn't** like his algebra class.
    (*also possible:* doesn't like)
11. A woman came into the room and **asked** me **where my brother was. / asked me, "Where is your brother?"**
12. I felt very relieved when the doctor said, **"You** will be fine. It's nothing serious.**"**
13. My mother asked **me,** "When **will you** be home?"